THE FINANCIAL SECTOR OF THE AMERICAN ECONOMY

EDITED BY
STUART BRUCHEY

A GARLAND SERIES

Reform of the Federal Reserve System in the Early 1930s

The Politics of Money and Banking

SUE C. PATRICK

GARLAND PUBLISHING, INC.
NEW YORK & LONDON
1993

Library of Congress Cataloging-in-Publication Data

Patrick, Sue Carol, 1954 –
Reform of the Federal Reserve System in the early 1930s : the politics of money and banking / Sue C. Patrick.
p. cm. — (Financial sector of the American economy)
Revision of the author's thesis (1988).
Includes bibliographical references and index.
ISBN 0-8153-0970-8 (alk. paper)
1. Board of Governors of the Federal Reserve System (U.S.)—History. 2. Banks and banking—United States—History. 3. Banking law—United States—History. 4. Monetary policy—United States—History. I. Title. II. Series.
HG2563.P38 1993
332.1'1'0973—dc20 92-35097
CIP

Printed on acid-free, 250-year-life paper
Manufactured in the United States of America

CONTENTS

NEW PREFACE

This work is a revised version of my dissertation, which was completed in 1988. There are only a few differences in the texts of the two studies except in the final chapter, where I discuss developments since the 1930s. However, throughout the work I have revised the notes to reflect scholarship since 1987 that is relevant to my exposition.

I wish to thank Dean Mary H. Somers of the University of Wisconsin Center–Barron County for providing institutional support for my revision of the dissertation. I also extend my thanks to Sharon Rubin, a gem among secretaries, whose care and patience made this project infinitely easier. Finally, I want to extend my gratitude to my husband, Oscar B. Chamberlain, for everything he has done to make my life easier, not only while I was amending my dissertation but always. To you, my love, I dedicate this book.

July 16, 1992

Sue C. Patrick

ORIGINAL PREFACE

When I began this project in 1981, I had little idea of the overwhelming amount of research material available. A simple listing of manuscript collections, such as those in my bibliography, gives few hints about the hundreds of boxes in the Records of the Federal Reserve System at the National Archives or the hundreds of pages in the Diary of Charles S. Hamlin at the Library of Congress. Perhaps the magnitude of the task explains why no one before me had attempted to examine in detail the bureaucratic and political maneuvering surrounding the enactment of banking and monetary reforms in the 1930s.

Although banking reform influenced the politics of both the Hoover and Roosevelt presidencies, most surveys devote only a few pages to monetary disturbances and the reforms passed as a result. Economic historians who have entire chapters devoted to the 1930s pay more attention to monetary policy than to reform legislation. Susan Kennedy's *The Banking Crisis of 1933* (1973) is an excellent study but narrower than my essay. The only other published work related directly to legislative change, *The American Banking Community and the New Deal Banking Reforms, 1933–1935* (1974) by Helen M. Burns, focuses on the influence of American bankers and their professional organizations, neglecting somewhat the influence of other lobbyists, economists, legislators, and reserve and Treasury officials.[1] Burns overlooked such relevant manuscript sources as the papers of Eugene Meyer (governor of the reserve board from September 1930 to May 1933), Marriner S. Eccles (governor of the reserve board from 1934 to 1948), Senator William G. McAdoo (D–CAL), Senator Arthur H. Vandenberg (R–MICH), the Treasury Department, and the Federal Reserve Board.

As I began writing, I realized that I should consult the literature on bureaucratic and congressional politics and the economic literature about regulation. I discovered that most such research was not applicable to my topic. Study of bureaucratic politics began only in the

1970s, concentrating initially on discussions about how complex organizations make decisions. Most researchers have used case studies, which relied on interviews to establish the motivations and thoughts of bureaucrats, to describe the process of decision making in a particular bureaucracy. No case study has examined a government bureaucracy prior to World War II, and none that I read seemed appropriate for the Treasury Department or the reserve system in the 1930s. Students of Congress have examined interest groups, committees, partisanship, and other factors in the behavior of legislators but have developed no theory capable of predicting congressional actions.[2]

Most economists researching regulation have chosen to concentrate on incentives influencing politicians or regulators. Those focusing on politicians have argued that regulation serves to transfer income to certain groups in exchange for their voting support and monetary contributions during electoral campaigns. Economists with this view have predicted that groups with more political power will receive income transfers from those with less influence as a result of the regulatory process. Unfortunately, these theorists have not explained why politicians desiring to distribute favors to organized groups sometimes chose regulation and at times relied on other instruments of public policy. Nor have they explained the passage of legislation benefiting unorganized consumers, such as laws establishing the FDIC and the Securities Exchange Commission. Most who have concentrated on regulatory agencies and their personnel also predicted an outcome favorable to the best-organized interest groups. Such economists have built their theories upon comparisons of the resources, organizational structures, and economic stakes of each group in the decision-making process, but all of these variables are difficult to measure empirically.[3] Only one case study, *Regulation: Politics, Bureaucracy, and Economics* (1985) by Kenneth J. Meier, had relevant information about regulation in the 1930s. Meier viewed financial regulation as "extremely salient" during the decade, and he concluded that policy decisions were made in a "macropolitical system with Congress and the president playing major roles."[4] I agree.

I wish to thank many people. I appreciate the depositories that permitted me to use their manuscript collections, and I want to recognize the courtesy and dedication of archivists across the country. Particularly helpful to me were the librarians at the Herbert Hoover Presidential Library in West Branch, Iowa, the Manuscript Division of the Library of Congress in Washington, D.C., and the Franklin Delano Roosevelt Library in Hyde Park, N.Y. I owe thanks to the members of my committee, who helped me sharpen my presentation. Finally, I wish to acknowledge the contribution of my husband, Oscar B. Chamberlain. He helped with research, read rough drafts of chapters, listened to my complaints, and offered valuable advice. For all this and more, I thank him.

Sue C. Patrick
May 1, 1988

NOTES

1. Examples of historians giving only a few pages to banking reform include William E. Leuchtenburg, *Franklin D. Roosevelt and the New Deal, 1932–1940* (New York: Harper and Row, 1963); Harris Gaylord Warren, *Herbert Hoover and the Great Depression* (New York: W.W. Norton, 1967 [1959]). Examples of economic historians who used several chapters to discuss the 1930s include Elmus R. Wicker, *Federal Reserve Monetary Policy, 1917–1933* (New York: Random House, 1966); Lester V. Chandler, *American Monetary Policy, 1928–1941* (New York: Harper and Row, 1971). Susan Estabrook Kennedy, *The Banking Crisis of 1933* (Lexington: University of Kentucky, 1973); Helen M. Burns, *The American Banking Community and New Deal Banking Reforms, 1933–1935* (Westport, Conn.: Greenwood, 1974).

2. Examples of research on bureaucratic politics include Robert C. Fried, *Performance in American Bureaucracy* (Boston: Little, Brown, 1976); Francis E. Rourke, *Bureaucracy, Politics, and Public Policy*, 3d ed. (Boston: Little, Brown, 1984). Examples of case studies include Martha Derthick, *Uncontrollable Spending for Social Services Grants* (Washington, D.C.: Brookings Institution, 1975); Richard G. Hewlett and Francis Duncan, *Nuclear Navy, 1946–1962* (Chicago: University of Chicago, 1974); Morton H. Halperin, *Bureaucratic Politics and Foreign Policy* (Washington, D.C.: Brookings Institution, 1974). For examples of theories explaining congressional decision making, see Randall B. Ripley, *Congress: Process and Policy*, 3d ed. (New York: W.W. Norton, 1983); William L. Morrow, *Congressional Committees* (New York: Charles Scribner's Sons, 1969); Michael T. Hayes, *Lobbyists and Legislators: A Theory of Political Markets* (New Brunswick, N.J.: Rutgers University, 1981).

3. For an excellent summary of the research on economic regulation and its problems, see Paul L. Joskow and Roger G. Noll, *Regulation in Theory and Practice: An Overview* (Cambridge, Mass.: MIT, Department of Economics, 1978).

4. Kenneth J. Meier, *Regulation: Politics, Bureaucracy, and Economics* (New York: St. Martin's, 1985), 54.

Reform of the Federal Reserve System in the Early 1930s

CHAPTER ONE

INTRODUCTION

Members of Congress and many other Americans made wide-ranging suggestions to reform the Federal Reserve System between the stock market crash of October 1929 and the passage of the Banking Act of 1935. Probably the most radical proposals would have nationalized the banking system through government ownership of reserve banks or individual local banks. Others recommended establishment of a National Monetary Authority that would assume the duties of the reserve system and Treasury Department.[1] Although Congress made many changes in the reserve act between 1930 and August 1935, banks remained privately owned, and the reserve system survived the Great Depression. The system's policy environment changed little, although the reserve board was better equipped after 1935 to counteract swings in the business cycle.

FEDERAL RESERVE SYSTEM BEFORE 1930

Passed in 1913 during the administration of President Woodrow Wilson, the Federal Reserve Act became law only after considerable debate about the future of the country's banks. The national banking system had demonstrated two weaknesses by 1900—an inelastic currency supply and an occasional inability to provide sufficient credit to move crops to market in the autumn. The currency was national bank notes, which had to be backed by equal amounts of government bonds. Whenever yields on such bonds dropped below the return on other investments, bankers bought fewer bonds and issued fewer notes. At best, the government bonds authorized by Congress for use as collateral placed an absolute limit on the issue of national bank notes.[2] Moreover, banks were sometimes unable to provide funds to move crops to market because of the pyramiding of bank reserves. The National Bank Act and most state laws permitted banks to keep part of their reserves in other financial institutions. Bankers in rural areas deposited funds in banks in the nearest large city. City bankers usually kept reserve funds in New York City. This pyramiding made the New York City bankers lenders of last resort in time of stress. Rural and city bankers also deposited excess funds in New York to be lent on call to stock brokers and dealers. Every autumn, small town bankers withdrew funds from other institutions to make agricultural marketing loans. When New York City bankers, in turn, demanded repayment of call loans, the ensuing scramble for liquidity could cause a monetary panic, often accompanied by economic recession. Such a panic occurred in October 1907 with the failure of Knickerbocker Trust Company of New York. Out-of-town bankers tried to withdraw balances from New York banks, and depositors deluged them. These events brought the defects of the banking system into sharp relief.[3]

After the crisis of 1907 eased, Congress moved slowly toward permanent bank reform. The Aldrich–Vreeland Act of 1908 prepared emergency measures useful in event of another panic and established a National Monetary Commission to study banking problems and recommend reform. The commission examined the history of banking in the United States and researched banking laws and customs in Europe. Published in 1912, its report called for a central bank with regional branches that bankers would own and operate. The chairman of the commission, Senator Nelson W. Aldrich (R–RI), then sponsored a bill that had the support of most eastern bankers. It met opposition from the populist element of the Democratic Party and from rural midwestern bankers, for it did not eliminate concentration of economic power in New York. Carter Glass (D–VA), chairman of the House Banking and Currency Committee, rewrote the measure to establish a regional system of reserve banks under the guidance of a politically appointed board. The board would operate as an independent regulatory commission to prevent dominance either by bankers or politicians, and regional banks would exercise independence in meeting needs of member banks. Congress passed the bill, and Wilson signed the Federal Reserve Act in December 1913.[4] According to its title, the system was created to "provide for the establishment of the Federal reserve banks, to furnish an elastic currency, to afford means of rediscounting commercial paper, to establish a more effective supervision of banking in the United States, and for other purposes."[5]

At the time of the stock market crash in the autumn of 1929, the Federal Reserve System was still decentralized, with final authority for policy divided between the Federal Reserve Board and regional banks. The board tried to coordinate activities of twelve reserve banks (in Boston, New York, Philadelphia, Cleveland, Richmond, Atlanta, Chicago, St. Louis, Minneapolis, Kansas City, Dallas, and San Francisco). Each reserve bank, in turn, kept informed about the condition of member banks in its district. All national banks, which were chartered and examined by the comptroller of the currency, and many of the largest state-chartered banks were members of the reserve system. Because most of them did not have the capital required by the reserve act, few small state banks became members.[6]

Local member banks formed the base of the reserve system and influenced its operations and policies. Each member bank purchased stock in its district bank and in exchange received a 6% dividend on paid-in capital stock every year that its reserve bank made a profit. About one-third of all banks in the United States were members of the system in 1930, but members controlled two-thirds of the resources of the nation's banks. Member banks had to maintain reserves at a district bank against savings (time) and checking (demand) deposits.[7]

Management of each regional bank rested with nine directors. The Federal Reserve Board chose three, known as class C directors, and designated one as the federal reserve agent, who also served as chairman of the district bank's board of directors. Member banks chose the remaining six directors. To prevent the largest banks from dominating selections, the reserve act divided member banks in each district into three groups based on capital. Each group chose one class A and one class B director. The reserve act stipulated banking experience for class A directors, while requiring class B directors to be from business, industry, or commerce. The nine directors of each district bank chose a governor to supervise its daily affairs, and the twelve governors became the most powerful reserve bank officials. System control over money and credit rested on the ability of regional banks to alter the level of member bank reserves (and, thus, their lending and investing) through changing the discount (interest) rate for loans to member banks and making purchases and sales of certain classes of securities in the open market. (More about that later.) District banks issued and redeemed federal reserve notes and provided a national system of check collection and clearance.[8]

The Federal Reserve Board in Washington provided a little unifying control for this decentralized system. The board included six presidential appointees, confirmed by the Senate for ten-year terms. The secretary of the Treasury and the comptroller of the currency were ex officio members. When selecting the appointive members, the president had to consider fair representation for the financial, agricultural, industrial, and commercial interests of the country as well as geographical regions. While in office, appointive members could not hold any post in a member bank. Although the secretary of the Treasury was chairman of the board, he did not attend meetings regularly. The governor, whom the president designated annually, was the board's active head. The board had power to "review and determine" rates regional banks charged member banks for discounting, to remove or suspend officers or directors of a district bank, to examine accounts and reports of reserve banks, to rearrange bank districts, to interpret the reserve act, and to issue rulings with regard to collateral (called "paper") eligible for discount and for purchase during open market operations. Most important, the board had responsibility for determining the system's monetary policies.[9]

While board members were accountable for policy formation, two other groups influenced decisions. The reserve act had created a Federal Advisory Council, one member from each district selected by the reserve bank's board of directors. The council could call for information regarding credit and recommend action, but the board did not have to take the council's advice.[10] More important than the advisory council was the Open Market Policy Conference. The reserve board appointed an Open Market Investment Committee in 1923 to coordinate purchases and sales of government securities by the twelve district banks and to bring such operations into line with general monetary policies. Early in 1930, the Open Market Policy Conference replaced the older committee. The OMPC consisted of a representative from each district bank, usually the governor, designated by its directors. Prior to passage of the Banking Act of 1933, the OMPC had to receive reserve board approval before it could undertake any operations. An executive committee of five carried out the OMPC's decisions with the New York Federal Reserve Bank making open market sales and purchases on behalf of district banks choosing to participate.[11]

The system's monetary control rested on the reserve banks' ability to regulate the volume of credit extended by member banks. Officials used two methods to restrain or increase member bank lending—operating in the open market and altering the rate charged by regional banks for discounts to member banks. The reserve act empowered district banks to purchase or sell in the open market bankers' acceptances, bills of exchange, municipal warrants, securities of the United States government, and bonds whose interest the federal government guaranteed to pay. The act explicitly prohibited reserve banks from owning corporate stocks, bonds, or notes. In the early 1930s, the OMPC bought and sold primarily United States government securities of varying maturities. The only other credit instrument purchased by district banks was bankers' acceptances, which were negotiable bills of exchange drawn on banks by merchants and shippers and "accepted" by those banks, which guaranteed payment at a future date. In this way a little-known merchant could buy goods abroad on credit, and his creditor knew that the goods would be paid for at the date and time noted on the acceptance. Since the merchant agreed to pay the bank the funds on or before the maturity date of the acceptance, it provided a low credit risk for the accepting bank. Each reserve bank set a rate at which it would buy acceptances, leaving member banks to initiate sales. Usually reserve banks allowed acceptances to mature rather than reselling them on the open market. After the stock market crash, member banks sold fewer acceptances to district banks because business declines lowered the volume of acceptances. Purchase of government securities or acceptances by reserve banks tended to increase member bank reserves, enhancing banks' ability to lend to customers. Sales of government securities caused a decline in member bank reserves, which would raise interest rates and curb borrowing.[12]

The other tool of reserve policy was the discount window. To avoid panics resulting from insufficient supplies of currency, the reserve act called upon district banks to provide adequate discount facilities for member banks. The act authorized reserve banks to discount notes, drafts, and bills of exchange arising out of commercial transactions of a short-term, self-liquidating nature. The reserve board ruled that to be eligible for discount the loan documents (paper) must result from purchasing, producing, carrying, or marketing goods in agriculture, industry, or commerce and must have a maturity less than nine months for agricultural paper and less than three months for other commercial paper.[13]

After 1916, Congress permitted member banks to borrow reserves from district banks by an advance as well as by discounting. This meant a reserve bank could lend to a member bank on its promissory note backed either by paper eligible for discount or by United States government securities. These advances were for fifteen-day periods. Advances were more common than discounts by the early 1930s because bankers found it easier to use government securities as collateral than to find commercial paper of the correct amount and maturity. The interest rate charged by reserve banks for discounting and advancing was known as the discount rate. According to the reserve act, each district bank was to set this rate so as to accommodate commerce and business, and the reserve board had final "review and determination" of discount rates. Discounts and advances provided funds to member banks for loan operations, and district banks could alter the extent of member bank borrowing by manipulating the discount rate.[14]

The system's influence over economic conditions rested on control of member bank reserves. Each member bank had to maintain deposits with its reserve bank equal to a percentage of its demand and time deposits. The percentage of required reserves in 1930 was 3% on time deposits in all member banks and for demand deposits was 13% in central reserve city banks (banks in New York and Chicago), 10% in reserve city banks (those in other cities with a district bank), and 7% in country banks (all other banks). When member banks made loans or investments, their demand and time deposits rose, which absorbed reserves. Since the system had the ability to alter the volume of member reserves through open market operations and discounting, regional banks could increase or reduce the volume of member bank loans and investments as needed.[15]

Economists relied on two theories to examine monetary policy during the late 1920s and early 1930s—quantity theory and commercial loan theory. Each suggested that officials watch different economic indicators, adopt different goals for policy, and make policy decisions in different ways. Quantity theorists based their work on the equation $MV=PY$, in which M equals volume of money, V is velocity of the circulation of money, P is the price level, and Y is the level of the real gross national product (GNP is a measure of all goods and services produced by a country during a specific period, usually a year). These theorists believed that the reserve system should try to control the total money supply, which they usually defined as currency in circulation, and to keep the price level stable. Price stabilization would lead automatically to economic stabilization, theorists assumed, because the growth rate of real GNP would lead to full employment and because velocity of money would be stable over time. Thus, quantity theorists believed that changes in volume of money would correspond to changes in the level of prices. They urged reserve officials to alter monetary policy on the basis of price levels, changing discount rates and operating in the open market only when the system wished to alter total money in circulation.[16]

The best-known American quantity theorist in the 1920s was Professor Irving Fisher of Yale University. He developed an equation of exchange, $MV + M'V' = PT$, in which M represents quantity of money in circulation, V is velocity of circulation of money, M' is volume of bank deposits subject to checking, V' is velocity of circulation of bank deposits, P is the price level, and T is volume of trade. Fisher improved quantity theory by including bank deposits as money but assumed that normally deposits would have a fixed ratio to money in circulation and that alterations in the quantity of money would not affect velocity. Consequently, he used the equation of exchange to argue that altering currency and bank deposits would lead to proportional changes in prices. His main contribution was to supply a better mathematical basis for later quantity theorists.[17]

Commercial loan theory, also known as the real bills doctrine, was the monetary theory written into the Federal Reserve Act. Provisions relating to the issue of federal reserve notes and to the discount window reflected ideas of a well-known commercial loan theorist, Professor H. Parker Willis of Columbia University, who had worked with Representative Glass in drafting the act. Believers in the real bills doctrine argued that district banks could not overextend or underextend loans to member banks if reserve officials discounted only short-term, self-liquidating commercial paper (also called real bills) that resulted from actual business transactions. If the system prevented use of its discount facilities for speculative and nonproductive loans, volume of "credit" would adjust automatically to trade. As business and commerce increased, the volume of money would rise, and as business and commerce declined or slowed, money would contract. Such theorists believed real bills would provide liquidity for member and district banks and conform the money supply to seasonal and other needs.[18]

Issues of federal reserve notes related to the real bills doctrine because the reserve act required gold and eligible commercial paper as collateral for notes. This tied note issues to availability of short-term commercial paper, as well as to the international gold standard. Most nations settled trade imbalances in gold prior to 1914 and again during the late 1920s. Real bills theorists assumed price inflation would begin whenever too much money entered the economy and that American and foreign consumer and investment dollars would move abroad. The gold outflow would end when the money supply in the United States had declined sufficiently to restore a balance in world prices.[19]

To adjust the volume of "credit" or money to demands of trade, known as passive accommodation, required the system to adopt different policies than those suggested by quantity theory. Commercial loan theorists, among them Willis and Glass, envisioned district banks passively discounting for member banks as long as they presented suitable paper. Stabilization of the money supply or price level was unnecessary for a properly functioning economy as long as reserve banks restricted loans to self-liquidating paper. Such theorists were more concerned with the quality of credit (productive vs. nonproductive, liquid vs. illiquid) than with volume.[20]

Commercial loan theorists deplored anything that broke the connection between short-term paper and reserve bank operations. They disapproved when Congress permitted district banks to make advances to member banks that could be backed by United States government securities, which were ineligible for discount. When the system stumbled onto the use of open market operations to control credit in the early 1920s, a development Glass and Willis had not anticipated, theorists recognized that member banks might obtain funds from district banks without presenting commercial paper.[21]

Today neither of the foregoing hypotheses forms a basis for reserve decisions, although quantity theory is more similar to modern monetary theory. The Great Depression exposed the fallacies of both hypotheses. Generally, wholesale and retail prices had been stable during the 1920s, and onset of the depression demonstrated to quantity economists that price stability alone was inadequate to ensure economic stability. In addition, velocity of money accelerated steeply from 1927 to 1929 and fell even more steeply from 1930 to 1933. The discovery that velocity could fluctuate wildly led quantity theorists to realize that calculations based on stable velocity had been highly inaccurate.[22]

Fallacies of the real bills doctrine were many. The nature of collateral presented for discount at district banks could not indicate how member banks would use the borrowed money. Because a bank offered commercial paper for discount did not mean it would make more short-term, self-liquidating commercial loans with the money. It might use the proceeds of a discount for "speculative" or "nonproductive" investments. Real bills doctrine also failed to recognize that once a loan was made, funds continued to circulate through the economy. Even if first use of the funds could be determined, subsequent uses could not.[23]

The belief of real bills theorists that short-term loans provided liquidity for individual banks and the banking system was also inaccurate. True, in normal times short-term loans for marketing, purchasing, or producing goods were self-liquidating. Once the goods were sold, the loan was repaid. In time of severe economic distress, however, no loans were necessarily self-liquidating. Borrowers were unable to repay, and members banks were reluctant to refuse to renew commercial loans for steady customers.[24]

Passive accommodation of trade needs by the reserve system also tended to accentuate swings in the business cycle. Restrictions on eligible paper did not limit the up side of credit expandability. When business production was rising, accommodation allowed the boom to continue. In the downswing of a cycle, passive accommodation allowed liquidation of loans and investments far greater than desirable. In the early 1930s, district banks found that business had declined so much that scattered member banks did not have commercial paper for discounting in sufficient quantity to meet customers' demands for cash. Thus, responding passively to member banks' demands destabilized the economy. Allowing reserve lending to decline when business contracted also contradicted the idea of the system as lender of last resort. This became increasingly evident in the early 1930s.[25]

Economic theory was in flux in the 1920s and 1930s, when theorists were shifting from classical economics to Keynesian analysis after publication of the *General Theory* in 1936. Throughout Hoover's presidency economists debated the system's policies in financial and economic journals. Unfortunately, theoretical work was slow to influence bankers, industrialists, and others who had learned classical economics in school, and theoretical arguments did not appear in textbooks on money and banking.[26]

Reserve officials had recognized some of the shortcomings of commercial loan theory by 1930, and many adopted elements of quantity theory. Still, there were differences among reserve officials. Some continued to emphasize quality of credit; others urged that system policy be determined by the level of member bank indebtedness. Many of those advocating the latter approach served the New York Federal Reserve Bank. Benjamin Strong, governor of that bank in the 1920s, stated repeatedly that regulating member bank lending through eligibility requirements was impossible because district banks could not control the use to which member banks would put proceeds of discounts. Both W. Randolph Burgess, a staff member, and George L. Harrison, who became governor of the New York bank after Strong's death in 1928, agreed with Strong's position. These men were primarily responsible for the development and use of open market operations, a quantitative control, in the early 1920s. New York reserve officials did not agree with Fisher's claim that price stability should be the only goal. Rather, they attempted to stabilize the economy by restoring and maintaining an international gold standard and by moderating member bank indebtedness in the central reserve cities of New York and Chicago.[27]

In official pronouncements during the 1920s, the reserve board often referred to the need to consider volume of credit and price levels, but such indicators of quantity theory were usually accompanied by pronouncements indicating a need for quality control. In its most complete statement of policy guidelines prior to the stock market crash, *The Tenth Annual Report of the Federal Reserve Board* (1923), the board indicated that the system had a "responsibility to regulate the flow of new and additional credit" to meet needs of commerce and industry. If "business is undergoing a rapid expansion and is in danger of developing an unhealthy or speculative boom," reserve authorities should not passively accommodate member bank credit demands but should restrain growth by increasing the discount rate.[28] The board asserted that credit administration involved a "quantitative as well as a qualitative determination" and that "there will be little danger that credit created and contributed by the Federal Reserve banks will be excessive in volume if restricted to productive uses."[29] Echoing the real bills theory, the report added:

> It is the nonproductive use of credit that breeds unwarranted increase in the volume of credit; it also gives rise to unnecessary

> maladjustment between the volume of production and the volume of consumption, and is followed by price and other economic disturbances. Administratively, therefore, the solution of the economic problem of keeping the volume of credit issuing from the Federal reserve banks from becoming either excessive or deficient is found in maintaining it in due relation to the volume of credit needs as these needs are derived from the operating requirements of agriculture, industry, and trade, and the prevention of the uses of Federal reserve credit for purposes not warranted by the terms or spirit of the Federal reserve act.[30]

The board apparently did not believe the quantity of credit could be controlled simply by regulating the quality of credit granted by reserve banks. Board members may have realized that control of district banks over use of their funds was limited. Nevertheless, qualitative concerns drawn from real bills doctrine and quantitative assumptions appeared together in the 1923 report and in later statements of the board.[31]

Although the system had the tools of monetary management necessary to operate like a central bank, an inadequate understanding of monetary policy constrained the ability of reserve authorities to influence economic activity. Beginning in 1930, officials were confused about what action to take. The decentralized nature of the system accentuated its inability to act. After Strong's death in 1928, the system lacked central leadership. Harrison did not have the stature to influence the OMPC, for most other members had served longer than he. The board tried to determine system policies during the late 1920s and early 1930s, but district banks controlled open market decisions. Independence of reserve banks led to conflict within the OMPC about whether to purchase government securities in 1930 and 1931. Most governors of regional banks and some board members were dubious of the effectiveness of efforts to increase member bank resources through open market purchases. Even Harrison was concerned primarily with reducing member bank indebtedness to district banks in New York and Chicago, not with the level of bank reserves or money supply. Consequently, money supply shrank in 1930 and 1931, the economy fluctuated, currency hoarding began, and many banks failed.[32]

REFORM IN EARLY 1930S

Although an independent regulatory commission, the Federal Reserve Board did not make decisions in a political vacuum. One steady source of pressure came from Congress, specifically from the House and Senate Committees on Banking and Currency, which could alter the reserve act anytime. Another source of influence was the Treasury Department, since both the secretary and the comptroller of the currency sat on the board ex officio. Board members were sensitive to Treasury issues of government securities and their effect on money markets. The comptroller of the currency had always had responsibility for regulating national banks, all of which were members of the system, and he reviewed the reserve board's budget between 1921 and 1933. Both Presidents Herbert Hoover and Franklin D. Roosevelt had close contact with the board. Economists took a large interest in the system, although their principal influence lay with Congress, not reserve officials. Finally, the American Bankers' Association and state banking groups watched the reserve system to detect changes of policy and to study the board's legislative proposals. In addition to internal divisions among reserve officials, cross pressure from such sources created a complex environment for the board.[33]

As the economic situation worsened in 1930 and 1931 and the banking structure weakened, members of Congress held lengthy hearings to investigate conditions and propose legislation. The most extensive hearings in the House of Representatives concerned branch, chain, and group banking. Chain and group banks had developed during the 1920s, and fewer than ten states had regulations to cover them. Because chain and group arrangements permitted ownership of banks in more than one state, the federal government seemed the logical choice as regulator. No consensus emerged about legislation among members of the House Committee on Banking and Currency, however, so they reported no bill. The other significant issue to interest the House committee was deposit insurance. As banks collapsed, depositors began to complain about loss of their money. The House passed a deposit insurance measure in 1932, but it failed to gain Senate approval. In the upper house, Carter Glass had become the dominant figure on the Banking and Currency Committee, and he conducted hearings on a series of bills that he introduced to reform the federal reserve and national banking systems. In particular, he wanted to separate commercial from investment banking, mistakenly believing that integration of such financial services had contributed to the stock market boom and crash. Because his proposals met opposition from bankers and received criticism from reserve officials, no Glass bill passed the Senate until January 1933. The House did not act before the inauguration of Roosevelt, but Congress finally passed a revised version of the bill, the Banking Act of 1933, during the Hundred Days session.[34]

Responding to the depression, Congress did make three changes in banking law during 1932. The first two attempted to extend reserve bank discounting. To aid distressed member banks, the Glass–Steagall Act of February 1932 temporarily broadened eligibility provisions for discounting to allow district bank lending on promissory notes guaranteed by groups of five or more independent member banks and under extreme circumstances to lend on any assets from a member. In addition, this act made United States government bonds eligible as collateral for issues of federal reserve notes, severing reserve operations further from real bills doctrine. Another measure, the Emergency Relief and Construction Act of July 1932, included an amendment to the Federal Reserve Act, providing that with the board's approval district banks could lend to any individual, partnership, or corporation unable to obtain adequate credit for negotiable notes, drafts, or bills of exchange. Prior to this, reserve banks had lent only to other banks. Finally, the Home Loan Bank Act of July 1932 had a section the purpose of which was to expand currency in circulation by making United States bonds bearing interest of 3 3/8% or less eligible as security for national bank notes. Quantity theorists had convinced some members of Congress that prices would rise if currency in circulation increased. These congressmen hoped that enlarging the pool of bonds available as collateral for national bank notes would encourage issue of such notes and, thus, stimulate economic recovery.[35]

After the banking system collapsed in February and March of 1933, the Roosevelt administration sponsored changes in banking law that radically altered the Federal Reserve System. The reforms emerged in an atmosphere of political and economic crisis, and legislation was piecemeal in approach and goals. Only the Emergency Banking Act of 1933 passed without undergoing substantial revision. Although economists and bankers were quite successful in conveying their opinions to Congress, no single economic or banking philosophy guided the legislation, and no single institutional interest dominated.[36]

Still, there was continuity between the financial reforms considered during the Hoover administration and those of the New Deal. In March 1933, Roosevelt approved an emergency bill written largely by Hoover appointees. Parts of the Glass–Steagall Act of 1932 became permanent with the later Banking Act of 1935. Glass's reform bill remained much the same in June 1933 as it had been in January 1932. The act of 1935 continued deposit insurance and increased the power of the Federal Deposit Insurance Corporation over insured banks. Like the provision that expanded issues of national bank notes in 1932, FDR's gold program assumed that an increase in the money supply would generate spending and aid recovery.[37]

Three themes are apparent in the fundamental alterations made in the banking system under Roosevelt. First, power of the reserve system increased over all banks, even private and state banks that were not members of the system. The Banking Act of 1933 gave the reserve board authority to set maximum interest rates payable on time deposits by member banks and to investigate all banks, whether or not members, forming part of a holding company that owned a member bank. The Securities Exchange Act of 1934 allowed the board to prohibit any loan to securities brokers and dealers except when made by member banks or by nonmembers with which the board had specific agreements. The Banking Act of 1935 permitted the board to raise or lower member bank reserve requirements.[38]

Second, power within the reserve system shifted away from district banks to the board, ending the crippling decentralization. The act of 1935 made appointment of the chief officer of each reserve bank subject to board approval. More important, it centralized power over open market operations in the board by reconstituting the Federal Open Market Committee (renamed in 1933) to include five members from reserve banks and seven members from the board. Since 1935 every action by the FOMC has depended upon board approval, and district banks have had to participate in every FOMC purchase and sale.[39]

Third, influence over monetary and economic affairs as a whole shifted from the reserve system to the Treasury and the president. Important to this development was the Gold Reserve Act of 1934, which devalued gold and deprived the reserve system of its gold, substituting gold certificates as collateral for federal reserve notes. After devaluation, an avalanche of gold entered the United States, providing such excess reserves for commercial banks that the system had little control over the monetary situation for the remainder of the decade.[40]

Senator Glass exercised enormous power over banking legislation throughout Roosevelt's administration. He overshadowed the chairman of the Banking and Currency Committee, Duncan U. Fletcher (D–FLA). Ever since Glass had sponsored the reserve act in 1913, he had regarded the system as his personal property. He had served as secretary of the Treasury during World War I and become a United States senator in 1920. In the 1930s, he chaired the subcommittee that investigated proposed banking bills, and few measures to which he objected passed.[41] As one of his subcommittee colleagues remarked,

> Most of us rely upon Senator Glass, of Virginia. He knows that subject better than any of us, better than anyone in the Government, and has had years of experience in dealing with it. If he says a bill on banking is all right it is pretty certain to go through the Senate without much if any opposition. If he says it is wrong, that usually ends the matter.[42]

The senator's influence declined slightly during Roosevelt's first term, when Glass unsuccessfully opposed the administration's gold policies. Still, he was primarily responsible for the terms of the Banking Act of 1933, and his influence led to significant revision of the administration's proposed bill in 1935.[43]

Henry B. Steagall (D–ALA) was chairman of the House Committee on Banking and Currency after 1930. He was a populist and a defender of small independent banks. His greatest contribution to reform legislation was to advocate a federal deposit insurance system. Although both Hoover and Roosevelt opposed this, Steagall received widespread public and political support, and the FDIC became part of the Banking Act of 1933. Otherwise he was a loyal Roosevelt supporter, defending both the Gold Reserve Act and the administration version of the Banking Act of 1935.[44]

While this essay is a detailed examination of the origins of federal banking reform in the 1930s, the discussion also illuminates the current debate about deregulating banks. In the 1960s, bankers and economists began complaining that regulation of interest rates, initiated for member banks by the Banking Act of 1933 and for insured banks by the Banking Act of 1935, inhibited the growth of commercial banks and limited their ability to compete with other types of financial institutions.

Such complaints led to the passage of the Depository Institutions Deregulation and Monetary Control Act in 1980, which ended interest rate regulation in 1987.[45]

More recently, some bankers and economists have advocated changes in the Banking Act of 1933 that would erase the artificial line between commercial banks and other financial intermediaries. Sears, Roebuck and other large corporations have been moving into financial services, and this may soon break down the present distinctions among the businesses of securities underwriting, mortgage banking, personal loan financing, stock brokering, insuring, and deposit banking. Congressional committees have considered further deregulation for several years, but the most recent administration proposals have not passed. Only time will tell whether the limits of the Banking Act of 1933 will be swept away.[46]

NOTES

1. Joseph E. Reeve, *Monetary Reform Movements: A Survey of Recent Plans and Panaceas* (Washington, D.C.: American Council on Public Affairs, 1943), 47, 64–5, 90.

2. Bray Hammond, "Historical Introduction," *Banking Studies*, E.A. Goldenweiser, Elliott Thurston, and Bray Hammond, eds. (Washington, D.C.: Board of Governors of the Federal Reserve System, 1941), 17, 26; Louis A. Rufener, *Money and Banking in the United States* (Boston: Houghton Mifflin, 1934), 427–39; Donald F. Kettl, *Leadership at the Fed* (New Haven, Conn.: Yale University, 1986), 18.

3. Kettl, *Leadership at the Fed*, 18–19; "Fiftieth Anniversary of the Federal Reserve System—Immediate Origins of the System," *Federal Reserve Bank of New York Monthly Review*, 46 (March 1964): 61–2; Edward E. Veazey, "Bicentennial Perspective—Evolution of Money and Banking in the United States," *Federal Reserve Bank of Dallas Monthly Business Review* (December 1975): 6, 8; Luther Harr and W. Carlton Harris, *Banking Theory and Practice*, 2d ed. (New York: McGraw-Hill, 1936), 395–7.

4. Walter Wyatt, "Federal Banking Legislation," *Banking Studies*, Goldenweiser and others, ed., 46–7, Kettl, *Leadership at the Fed*, 19–22; John T. Woolley, *Monetary Politics: The Federal Reserve and the Politics of Monetary Policy* (New York: Cambridge University, 1984), 38–9; "Reforming the Monetary System: Does Economic Change Outmode Some Features of Money and Banking Systems?" *Federal Reserve Bank of Richmond Monthly Review* (June 1961): 4; James T. Lindley, *An Analysis of the Federal Advisory Council of the Federal Reserve System, 1914–1938* (New York: Garland, 1985), 24; Lester V. Chandler, *Benjamin Strong, Central Banker* (Washington, D.C.: Brookings Institution, 1958), 10.

5. William F. Treiber, "Federal Reserve System after Fifty Years," *Federal Reserve Bank of New York Monthly Review*, 46 (June 1964): 98.

6. J.W. Pole and Eugene Meyer, "Extent of Federal Supervision of Banking Today," *Congressional Digest*, 10 (December 1931): 294; Charles C. Chapman, *The Development of American Business and Banking Thought, 1913–1936*, 2d ed. (London: Longmans, Green,

1936), 167; Eugene Nelson White, *The Regulation and Reform of the American Banking System, 1900–1929* (Princeton, N.J.: Princeton University, 1983), 186; Rollin G. Thomas, *Our Modern Banking and Monetary System*, 3d ed. (Englewood Cliffs, N.J.: Prentice–Hall, 1957), 257; A. Jerome Clifford, *The Independence of the Federal Reserve System* (Philadelphia: University of Pennsylvania, 1965), 26; Harold G. Moulton, *The Financial Organization of Society*, 3d ed. (Chicago: University of Chicago, 1930), 535.

7. H. Parker Willis and William H. Steiner, *Federal Reserve Banking Practice* (New York: D. Appleton, 1926), 101; Harold Barger, *The Management of Money: A Survey of American Experience* (Chicago: Rand McNally, 1964), 44–5; Lester V. Chandler, *American Monetary Policy, 1928–1941* (New York: Harper and Row, 1971), 190–1; Chamber of Commerce of the United States, Banking and Currency Committee, *The Federal Reserve System* (Washington, D.C.: Chamber of Commerce of the United States, 1929), 19; John Kenneth Galbraith, *Money, Whence It Came, Where It Went* (Boston: Houghton Mifflin, 1975), 124–7.

8. Edwin Walter Kemmerer, *The ABC of the Federal Reserve System*, 8th ed. (Princeton, N.J.: Princeton University, 1929), 34–5; Rudolph L. Weissman, *The New Federal Reserve System: The Board Assumes Control* (New York: Harper and Brothers, 1936), 28; Clifford, *Federal Reserve*, 27–8; Russell Donald Kilborne, *Principles of Money and Banking* (Chicago: A.W. Shaw, 1927), 411–2; F. Cyril James, *The Economics of Money, Credit and Banking*, 2d ed. (New York: Ronald, 1935), 169; U.S., Congress, Senate, Committee on Banking and Currency, *Operation of the National and Federal Reserve Banking Systems: Hearings before a Subcommittee Pursuant to S.Res. 71*, 71st Congress, 3d session, 19 January–2 March 1931, 124–7; Lawrence S. Ritter and William L. Silber, *Principles of Money, Banking, and Financial Markets*, 3d ed. (New York: Basic Books, 1980), 31, 38; E.A. Goldenweiser, *American Monetary Policy* (New York: McGraw–Hill, 1951), 25, 38–9; Robert E. Weintraub, *Introduction to Monetary Economics: Money, Banking, and Economic Activity* (New York: Roland, 1970), 32.

9. Benjamin Haggott Beckhart, *Federal Reserve System* (New York: American Institute of Banking, 1972), 33; E.A. Goldenweiser, *Federal Reserve System in Operation* (New York: McGraw–Hill, 1925), 15–7, 138–9; Willis and Steiner, *Federal Reserve*, 76–8;

Moulton, *Financial Organization*, 536; Weissman, *New Federal Reserve*, 28–9. At the end of 1929, the board members were Roy A. Young (governor), Edmund Platt (vice-governor), Adolph C. Miller, Charles S. Hamlin, Edward H. Cunningham, George R. James, Andrew W. Mellon (secretary of the Treasury), and John W. Pole (comptroller of the currency).

10. William O. Weyforth, *The Federal Reserve Board: A Study of Federal Reserve Structure and Credit Control* (Baltimore: Johns Hopkins University, 1933), 28; American Institute of Banking, *Money and Banking* (New York: American Institute of Banking, 1940), 442–3; Benjamin Ulysses Ratchford, *The Federal Reserve at Work* (Richmond, Va.: Federal Reserve Bank of Richmond, 1974), 5. At the suggestion of President Wilson, Carter Glass had included the Federal Advisory Council in the Federal Reserve Act to quiet banker opposition to a politically appointed reserve board; Beckhart, *Federal Reserve*, 38.

11. Federal Reserve Board, *Tenth Annual Report Covering Operations for the Year 1923* (Washington, D.C.: U.S. Government Printing Office, 1924), 13–6; Martin Mayer, *The Bankers* (New York: Weybright and Talley, 1974), 400–1; Weyforth, *Reserve Board*, 104–6; E.A. Goldenweiser, "Instruments of Federal Reserve Policy," *Banking Studies*, Goldenweiser and others, eds., 398–400.

12. Mayer, *Bankers*, 401; Howard H. Hackley, *Lending Functions of the Federal Reserve Banks: A History* (Washington, D.C.: Board of Governors of the Federal Reserve System, 1973), 98; Willis and Steiner, *Federal Reserve*, 464–5, 496–500; William J. Shultz and M.R. Caine, *Financial Development of the United States* (New York: Prentice–Hall, 1937), 484; Clay J. Anderson, *Monetary Policy: Decision-Making, Tools, and Objectives* (Philadelphia: Federal Reserve Bank of Philadelphia, 1961), 37; Barger, *Management of Money*, 45; Marcus Nadler, Sipa Heller, and Samuel S. Shipman, *The Money Market and its Institutions* (New York: Ronald, 1955), 98.

13. Weissman, *New Federal Reserve*, 139–40; Beckhart, *Federal Reserve*, 84–5; Hackley, *Lending Functions*, 8–9, 23–4, 29; Harlan M. Smith, *The Essentials of Money and Banking* (New York: Random House, 1968), 43; Thomas D. Simpson, *Money, Banking, and Economic Analysis* (Englewood Cliffs, N.J.: Prentice–Hall, 1976), 220.

14. Harry D. Hutchinson, *Money, Banking, and the United States Economy*, 3d ed. (Englewood Cliffs, N.J.: Prentice–Hall, 1975), 90–1; George W. McKinney, Jr., *The Federal Reserve Discount Window:*

Administration in the Fifth District (New Brunswick, N.J.: Rutgers University, 1960), 12; Simpson, *Money, Banking*, 220–1; New York Clearing House Association, *The Federal Reserve Reexamined* (New York: New York Clearing House Association, 1953), 76–7; Chamber of Commerce, *Federal Reserve*, 35; Goldenweiser, *Federal Reserve*, 23.

15. Goldenweiser, *Federal Reserve*, 84–5; Kemmerer, *ABC of Federal Reserve*, 40; New York Clearing House Association, *Reserve Reexamined*, 99.

16. Thomas F. Cargill, *Money, the Financial System, and Monetary Policy* (Englewood Cliffs, N.J.: Prentice–Hall, 1979), 217–9; Kilborne, *Principles of Money*, 135, 168–9; Chapman, *American Business Thought*, 196–7; John A. Cochran, *Money, Banking and the Economy*, 3d ed. (New York: Macmillan, 1975), 287–8, 295; "The Quantity Theory of Money: Its Historical Evolution and Role in Policy Debates," *Federal Reserve Bank of Richmond Economic Review* (May/June 1974): 1–5. This summary ignores considerable difference in the formulation of theory among economists of the 1920s and 1930s. For more information, see Henry William Spiegel, *The Growth of Economic Thought*, 2d ed. (Durham, N.C.: Duke University, 1981), 590–610, 641–60; Robert B. Ekelund, Jr. and Robert F. Hebert, *A History of Economic Theory and Method* (New York: McGraw–Hill, 1975), 395–403; Thomas M. Humphrey, "Role of Non-Chicago Economists in the Evolution of the Quantity Theory in America 1930–1950," *Southern Economic Journal*, 38 (July 1971): 13–7.

17. Cochran, *Money, Banking*, 289–91; Hugo Hegeland, *The Quantity Theory of Money: A Critical Study of its Historical Development and Interpretation and a Restatement* (Goeteborg: Elanders Boktryckeri Aktiebolag, 1951), 85–95; W.E. Kuhn, *The Evolution of Economic Thought*, 2d ed. (Cincinnati: South–Western, 1970), 304–6; Charles Rist, *History of Monetary and Credit Theory from John Law to the Present Day*, Jane Degras, trans. (New York: Macmillan, 1940), 338–41; Spiegel, *Economic Thought*, 621–7.

18. David R. Kamerschen and Eugene S. Klise, *Money and Banking*, 6th ed. (Cincinnati: South–Western, 1976), 207–8, 283; Allan Sproul, "Policy Norms and Central Banking," *Men, Money, and Policy: Essays in Honor of Karl R. Bopp*, David P. Eastburn, ed. (Philadelphia: Federal Reserve Bank of Philadelphia, 1970), 68–9; Paul B. Trescott, *Financing American Enterprise: The Story of Commercial*

Banking (New York: Harper and Row, 1963), 160; Robert Craig West, "Real Bills, the Gold Standard, and Central Bank Policy," *Business History Review*, 50 (Winter 1976): 504.

19. West, "Real Bills," 511; Jack C. Rothwell, "Who Changed the Rules of the Game? The Evolution and Development of Tools of Federal Reserve Policy," *Federal Reserve Bank of Philadelphia Business Review* (October 1963): 5–6; McKinney, *Discount Window*, 10–1. World War I destroyed the functioning of the international gold standard and temporarily forced reserve officials to use other policy guidelines such as interest rates, the state of business in the United States, changes in the general price level, and economic conditions in Europe. See Elmus R. Wicker, *Federal Reserve Monetary Policy, 1917–1933* (New York: Random House, 1966), 114; Chandler, *American Monetary Policy*, 473; Charles O. Hardy, *Credit Policies of the Federal Reserve System* (Washington, D.C.: Brookings Institution, 1932), 6.

20. White, *Regulation and Reform*, 115–8; J. Marvin Peterson, "The Development of our Monetary Institutions," *American Financial Institutions*, Herbert V. Prochnow, ed. (New York: Prentice–Hall, 1951), 80–1; Chandler, *American Monetary Policy*, 169–70; Woolley, *Monetary Politics*, 40–1.

21. H. Parker Willis, "Later Variations and Amendments," *The Banking Situation: American Post-War Problems and Developments*, H. Parker Willis and John M. Chapman, eds. (New York: Columbia University, 1934), 675–86; McKinney, *Discount Window*, 86; Hardy, *Credit Policies*, 275.

22. Woodlief Thomas, "Monetary Controls," *Banking Studies*, Goldenweiser and others, eds., 331; Thomas Francis McManus, Banking Operations in the United States in Relation to the Great Depression (Ph.D. dissertation, University of Iowa, 1934), 112–3, 177–8; Edwin Walter Kemmerer, *Kemmerer on Money*, 2d ed. (Philadelphia: John C. Winston, 1934), 154; Lawrence Smith, *Money, Credit and Public Policy* (Boston: Houghton Mifflin, 1959), 537.

23. Ray V. Leffler, *Money and Credit* (New York: Harper and Brothers, 1935), 296; Wicker, *Federal Reserve*, 143; Ritter and Silber, *Principles of Money*, 175–6; McKinney, *Discount Window*, 86–7.

24. Ritter and Silber, *Principles of Money*, 131; Lloyd Brewster Thomas, Jr., *Money, Banking, and Economic Activity* (Englewood Cliffs, N.J.: Prentice–Hall, 1979), 251–2; Bruce J. Summers, "Loan

Commitments to Business in United States Banking History," *Federal Reserve Bank of Richmond Economic Review*, 61 (September/October 1975): 18.

25. Chandler, *American Monetary Policy*, 221–2; Thomas, *Money, Banking*, 252–3; Ritter and Silber, *Principles of Money*, 174–5; Weldon Welfling, *Money and Banking in the American Economy*, 2d ed. (Washington, D.C.: American Institute of Banking, 1975), 210.

26. Joseph Dorfman, *The Economic Mind in American Civilization*, 5 v. (New York: Viking, 1946–59), IV: 351–2, V: 773–5; Raymond J. Saulnier, *Contemporary Monetary Theory: Studies of Some Recent Theories of Money, Prices, and Production* (New York: Columbia University, 1938), 391; William J. Barber, *A History of Economic Thought* (New York: Frederick A. Praeger, 1968), 223–6; Kuhn, *Economic Thought*, 290–7; Herman E. Krooss, *Executive Opinion: What Business Leaders Said and Thought on Economic Issues 1920s–1960s* (Garden City, N.Y.: Doubleday, 1970), 125–32; Spiegal, *Economic Thought*, 604–13; Clark Warburton, "Monetary Disequilibrium Theory in the First Half of the Twentieth Century," *History of Political Economy*, 13 (Summer 1981): 288–94.

27. W. Randolph Burgess, ed., *Interpretations of Federal Reserve Policy in the Speeches and Writings of Benjamin Strong* (New York: Harper and Brothers, 1930), 127–9, 182–4; Lester V. Chandler, "Impacts of Theory on Policy: The Early Years of the Federal Reserve," *Men, Money, and Policy*, Eastburn, ed., 44; Elmus R. Wicker, "Federal Reserve Monetary Policy, 1922–33: A Reinterpretation," *Journal of Political Economy*, 73 (August 1965): 329–31, 336, 338, 342–3; Chandler, *Benjamin Strong*, 14–5, 430–1; W. Randolph Burgess, "Guides to Bank of Issue Policy," *Proceedings of the Academy of Political Science*, 13 (January 1930): 512–3; David C. Wheelock, *The Strategy and Consistency of Federal Reserve Monetary Policy, 1924–1933* (Cambridge: Cambridge University, 1991), 45–67.

28. Federal Reserve Board, *Tenth Annual Report, 1923*, 10.

29. Ibid., 34.

30. Ibid., 34–5.

31. Federal Reserve Board, *Fifteenth Annual Report Covering Operations for the Year 1928* (Washington, D.C.: U.S. Government Printing Office, 1929), 9–10; Federal Reserve Board, *Sixteenth Annual Report Covering Operations for the Year 1929* (Washington, D.C.:

U.S. Government Printing Office, 1930), 1–4. These authors have also noted the board's inconsistency: Willis and Steiner, *Federal Reserve*, 83–5; Seymour E. Harris, *Twenty Years of Federal Reserve Policy*, 2 v. (Cambridge, Mass.: Harvard University, 1933), I: 230–1; Lloyd W. Mints, *History of Banking Theory in Great Britain and the United States* (Chicago: University of Chicago, 1945), 265–8; McKinney, *Discount Window*, 17–8; White, *Regulation and Reform*, 121–5.

32. Chandler, *American Monetary Policy*, 47, 516; Karl R. Bopp, "Agencies of Federal Reserve Policy," *University of Missouri Studies*, 10 (October 1935): 78–9; Chandler, *Benjamin Strong*, 465; Wicker, "Reserve Monetary Policy," 327, 329–31, 337–9; Wicker, *Federal Reserve*, 147–63, 169; Wheelock, *Monetary Policy*, 69–74, 96–112.

33. Lindley, *Federal Advisory Council*, 21–4; Woolley, *Monetary Politics*, 20–1; Kettl, *Leadership at the Fed*, 194–6. For more about Hoover's relations with the reserve board, see Wicker, *Federal Reserve*, 159, 189–90; Herbert Clark Hoover, *The Memoirs of Herbert Hoover*, 3 v. (New York: Macmillan, 1951–52), III: 65, 73, 210–2. For more about Roosevelt's influence with the board, see Arthur M. Schlesinger, Jr., *The Age of Roosevelt*, 3 v. (Boston: Houghton Mifflin, 1957–60), III: 292–4, 512–3; Marriner S. Eccles, *Beckoning Frontiers: Public and Personal Recollections* (New York: Alfred A. Knopf, 1951), 175–6, 192, 237–9, 241–7, 262–3, 266–71. The reserve board assessed the district banks to cover its annual expenses, so the board has never relied on Congress to appropriate funds for its operations, unlike most independent regulatory commissions. This removes an important source of congressional restraint on system activities.

34. See Chapter Two for more information about the hearings on branch, chain, and group banking. See Chapters Three, Four, and Five for discussion of the congressional debates over deposit insurance and the Glass bill. The hearings regarding banking reform held prior to March 1933 were U.S., Congress, House Committee on Banking and Currency, *Branch, Chain, and Group Banking: Hearings Pursuant to H.Res. 141*, 71st Congress, 2d session, 25 February–11 June 1930; Senate Committee on Banking and Currency, *Operation of National and Federal Reserve Banking Systems: Subcommittee Hearings*; Senate Committee on Banking and Currency, *Operation of the National and Federal Reserve Banking Systems: Hearings on S. 4115*, 72d Congress, 1st session, 23–30 March 1932; House Committee on Banking and

Currency, *Liberalizing the Credit Facilities of the Federal Reserve System: Hearings on H.R. 9203*, 72d Congress, 1st session, 12 February 1932; House Committee on Banking and Currency, *To Provide Guaranty Fund for Depositors in Banks: Hearings on H.R. (10241) 11362*, 72d Congress, 1st session, 14 March–8 April 1932; Senate Committee on Banking and Currency, *Amendments to Federal Reserve Act Permitting Discounting of Notes of Finance and Credit Companies: Hearings before Subcommittee on S. 4454*, 72d Congress, 2d session, 18 January 1933; Senate Committee on Banking and Currency, *Stock Exchange Practices: Hearings on S.Res. 84 and S.Res. 239*, 72d Congress, 1st and 2d sessions, 11 April–23 June 1932, 11 January–2 March 1933.

35. See Chapter Three for the history of the passage of these laws.

36. Other commentators have noticed the piecemeal nature of the banking legislation passed in the early 1930s. For example, see H.W. Arndt, *The Economic Lessons of the Nineteen-Thirties* (London: Frank Cass, 1963 [1944]), 35; A.S.J. Baster, *The Twilight of American Capitalism: An Economic Interpretation of the New Deal* (London: P.S. King and Son, 1937), 71; James M. Buchanan, "The Economic Constitution and the New Deal: Lessons for Late Learners," *Regulatory Change in an Atmosphere of Crisis: Current Implications of the Roosevelt Years*, Gary M. Walton, ed. (New York: Harcourt, Brace, Jovanovich, 1979), 16; Lester V. Chandler, *America's Greatest Depression 1929–41* (New York: Harper and Row, 1970), 133–4.

37. See Chapter Three for the passage of the Glass–Steagall Act of 1932. Chapters Three, Four, and Five discuss the evolving terms of the Glass bill. See Chapter Seven for the terms and passage of the Banking Act of 1935, and see Chapter Six for more on Roosevelt's gold policies. Chapter Four covers the Banking Crisis of 1933 and the Emergency Banking Act.

38. Chapter Five discusses the passage and terms of the Banking Act of 1933. Chapter Six discusses the Securities Exchange Act of 1934, and Chapter Seven covers the Banking Act of 1935. Few others have noted the reserve board's increasing authority over private and state banks. One exception is Editors of *The Economist*, *The New Deal: An Analysis and Appraisal* (New York: Alfred A. Knopf, 1937), 77.

39. Chapter Seven discusses the passage and terms of the Banking Act of 1935. Those who have noted the centralization of power in the reserve board include Bopp, "Agencies of Policy," 79; Federal Reserve Bank of Philadelphia, *Fifty Years on Chestnut Street* (Philadelphia: Federal Reserve Bank of Philadelphia, [1964]), 22; Mable T. Wallich and Henry C. Wallich, "The Federal Reserve System Since 1940," *The Federal Reserve System*, Herbert v. Prochnow, ed. (New York: Harper and Brothers, 1960), 329–31.

40. Chapter Six discusses President Franklin Roosevelt's gold policies and the passage of the Gold Reserve Act of 1934. Others who have noted the increased influence of the Treasury Department over monetary policy during the New Deal include Chandler, *American Monetary Policy*, 244; Wallich and Wallich, "Federal Reserve," 331; Milton Friedman, "Should There Be An Independent Monetary Authority," *In Search of a Monetary Constitution*, Leland B. Yeager, ed. (Cambridge, Mass.: Harvard University, 1962), 232.

41. Schlesinger, *Age of Roosevelt*, III: 295–6; John Douglas Lyle, The United States Senate Career of Carter Glass of Virginia, 1919–1939 (Ph.D. Dissertation, University of South Carolina, 1974), 13, 17–26; Sidney Hyman, *Marriner S. Eccles: Private Entrepreneur and Public Servant* (Stanford, Cal.: Stanford University, Graduate School of Business, 1976), 162–3.

42. James Couzens (R–MICH), quoted by George E. Anderson, "In the Lifetime of Senator Glass," *Banking*, 31 (August 1938): 22.

43. See Chapter Five for the passage of the Banking Act of 1933. See Chapter Seven for the battle over the Banking Act of 1935. See Chapter Six for Roosevelt's gold policies.

44. Jack Brien Key, "Henry B. Steagall: The Conservative as a Reformer," *Alabama Review*, 17 (July 1964): 198–204. See Chapter Six for the Gold Reserve Act, and see Chapter Seven for the passage of the Banking Act of 1935.

45. For example, see James M. O'Brien, "Interest Ban on Demand Deposits: Victim of the Profit Motive?" *Federal Reserve Bank of Philadelphia Business Review* (August 1972): 13–9; Clifton B. Luttrell, "Interest Rate Controls—Perspective, Purpose, and Problems," *Federal Reserve Bank of St. Louis Monthly Review*, 50 (September 1968): 6–14; Byron Higgins, "Interest Payments on Demand Deposits: Historical Evolution and the Current Controversy," *Federal Reserve Bank of Kansas City Monthly Review* (July/August 1977): 3–11; Scott

Winningham, "The Effects of Removing Regulation Q—A Theoretical Analysis," *Federal Reserve Bank of Kansas City Economic Review* (May 1980): 13–23; Charles R. McNeill, "The Depository Institutions Deregulation and Monetary Control Act of 1980," *Federal Reserve Bulletin*, 66 (June 1980): 444–53; "ABA Goes Public to End Regulation Q," *ABA Banking Journal*, 71 (December 1979): 56–7; "Regulation Q—Shaving the Little Saver," *Citibank Monthly Economic Letter* (April 1979): 3–4.

46. See Chapter Eight for more on the efforts to overturn or amend the Banking Act of 1933.

CHAPTER TWO

ILLUSIONS, CONFUSIONS, AND ECONOMIC DECLINE: BANKING IN 1930–31

The United States had entered an economic recession in August 1929. In the next three years, recession became a full-fledged depression. Both monetary and legislative policies failed to prevent economic decline, largely because officials lacked a consensus about appropriate changes. Federal reserve officials were divided over the wisdom of expanding reserves of member banks before June 1931. The system's united effort to protect the gold dollar in the autumn of 1931 damaged the domestic economy. The 71st Congress (March 1929 to March 1931) did nothing substantial to influence monetary policy or to end massive bank failures, although hearings in 1930 and 1931 set the stage for later legislation. President Herbert Hoover attempted to halt the recession through voluntarism and optimistic statements, an unsuccessful combination. Not until reserve officials, members of Congress, and the president began to work together in 1932 did the government make progress in countering the depression.

RESERVE RESPONSE TO ECONOMIC DECLINE, 1930–JUNE 1931

In the months following the stock market crash of 1929, many economic forecasters hoped that deflation of securities' prices would not destabilize the economy, especially since the crash had not caused a bank panic. These hopes proved too optimistic, as commodity prices, stock and bond values, bank loans and investments, bank deposits, gross national product, and other economic indicators declined dramatically between January 1930 and January 1932.[1] Bank failures increased, with more than 3,600 banks suspending operations in 1930–31 (Table 2A), and few ever reopened.

TABLE 2A
BANK SUSPENSIONS, 1929–31

Month	Number of Banks			Deposits, in Thousands of Dollars		
	1929	1930	1931	1929	1930	1931
Jan.	54	99	202	16,413	28,903	76,553
Feb.	60	85	77	21,746	32,800	34,616
Mar.	51	76	86	9,002	23,769	34,320
Apr.	29	96	64	7,790	33,388	41,683
May	112	55	91	24,090	19,315	43,493
June	48	66	167	19,219	70,566	190,480
July	69	65	93	66,161	32,333	40,745
Aug.	17	67	158	8,532	21,951	180,028
Sep.	39	66	305	10,050	23,666	233,565
Oct.	43	72	522	13,153	24,599	471,380
Nov.	68	254	175	22,646	186,306	67,656
Dec.	52	344	358	15,730	367,119	277,051

Source: *Federal Reserve Bulletin*, 18 (February 1931): 106.

Bank closings during the 1920s and 1930 were concentrated among small undercapitalized state banks in rural areas, many of which did not belong to the reserve system. Federal officials correctly argued that states had chartered too many banks before 1920; areas with high ratios of banks to population had the largest number of failures. During World War I, rural banks had acquired farm mortgages that they could not liquidate in the depressed agricultural markets of the 1920s. When farm commodity prices plummeted in the early 1930s, many mortgages became worthless.[2]

Since not all state banks collapsed, most bankers and government officials cited dishonesty by bank managers or poor loan and investment policies. Such a view was supported by the suspension of the Caldwell chain of banks, encompassing dozens of institutions in Kentucky, Tennessee, and Arkansas, in the autumn of 1930. Investigators later indicted the president of Caldwell and Company (Nashville) for grand larceny and receiving stolen property. Another well-publicized case concerned the failure of Bank of United States in New York City, an institution with more than $200 million in resources. Investigators found that managers and directors had ignored critical comments and helpful suggestions about its portfolio made by state examiners for at least a year before failure in December 1930.[3]

Reserve officials reacted to deepening recession by promoting "easy money" in financial markets. The goals of this policy were to lower interest rates and allow members to repay reserve banks. District banks lowered discount rates throughout 1930 and early 1931. The discount rate in New York was only 1.5% by the end of May 1931, although five districts were still charging 3%. The Open Market Policy Conference bought moderate amounts of government securities, and reserve banks also purchased bankers' acceptances. Aided by importation of $310 million of gold in 1930, reserve policy did result in lower short-term interest rates for borrowers in New York. The volume of reserve credit outstanding declined for much of 1930 (Table 2B), as member banks repaid discounts and money in circulation declined.[4] These policies did not result in economic recovery because bankers were afraid to lend, seeking liquidity to meet possible depositors' demands for cash, and because corporations preferred to rely on the bond market rather than commercial banks. Total loans and investments of banks declined by $1.25 billion between October 1929 and October 1930. Currency in circulation plus bank deposits decreased 3–4% between October 1929 and March 1931.[5]

Officials often disagreed about monetary policy. Many reserve bank governors unenthusiastically purchased government securities because they failed to understand the necessity of using monetary policy to promote recovery. New York reserve officials were the most persistent advocates of such purchases in 1930. They believed that open market purchases would first eliminate member banks' indebtedness to reserve banks and then lead members to pursue more liberal lending and investing policies. As financial institutions found themselves with plentiful reserves, they would lower interest rates to attract borrowers and provide a market for sound investments, especially bonds. New York officials assumed that lack of member bank borrowing and low

TABLE 2B
RESERVE BANK CREDIT OUTSTANDING, 1930–31
(averages of daily figures, in millions of dollars)

Month	Bills Dis-counted	Bills Bought	U.S. Secur-ities	Other	Total
1930					
Jan.	501	314	485	57	1,357
Feb.	378	285	480	38	1,181
Mar.	274	246	540	35	1,095
Apr.	231	266	530	45	1,072
May	247	182	529	38	996
June	251	141	571	37	1,000
July	226	154	583	40	1,003
Aug.	214	153	599	32	998
Sep.	189	197	597	33	1,016
Oct.	196	185	602	37	1,020
Nov.	221	184	599	29	1,033
Dec.	338	257	644	34	1,273
1931					
Jan.	253	206	647	23	1,129
Feb.	216	102	603	15	936
Mar.	176	123	604	18	921
Apr.	155	173	600	24	952
May	163	144	599	20	926
June	188	121	610	26	945
July	169	79	674	32	954
Aug.	222	135	712	38	1,107
Sep.	280	259	736	38	1,313
Oct.	613	692	733	50	2,088
Nov.	695	560	727	53	1,950
Dec.	774	340	777	59	

Source: *Federal Reserve Bulletin*, 17 (January 1931): 10; Ibid., 18 (April 1932): 229.

interest rates proved that money was plentiful. Instead, the level of interest rates reflected the bankers' policy of lending only to safe borrowers for whom money was cheap. Everyone else found bank loans difficult to obtain.[6]

Because stock prices recovered considerably, if temporarily, in the spring of 1930, monetary policy was not aggressively expansive at that time. Reserve officials waited before taking action because interest rates appeared sufficiently low to stimulate recovery. Not until late May did George L. Harrison, governor of the New York Federal Reserve Bank, persuade the Open Market Investment Committee to buy at least $25 million of government securities per week for several weeks. Apparently, he convinced the committee that purchases would not hurt the economy and might help.[7]

The system retreated to passivity during the summer of 1930. Reorganization of the Open Market Investment Committee into the Open Market Policy Conference, which consisted of the twelve reserve bank governors, may have weakened Harrison's influence. In any event, the OMPC's executive committee voted against buying government securities on June 23, believing that easing credit would not improve conditions. Harrison still wanted to buy $25 million per week, but only Eugene R. Black of Atlanta and George Seay of Richmond agreed that further purchases could be helpful. Consequently, the New York bank bought acceptances for its own account, which lowered interest rates and permitted member banks of that district to repay indebtedness. By the beginning of July Harrison concluded that no further open market purchases were necessary.[8] The OMPC noted that bank borrowing and interest rates were falling in September, a time when crop marketing usually required more credit. Several members believed that easy money had failed to stimulate the economy and wished to sell securities to raise interest rates slightly. Harrison and his directors opposed such sales.[9] He persuaded the OMPC to approve a resolution, advising the reserve system to maintain existing money rates.[10]

Economic statistics and reserve policy changed little until a wave of bank failures in November and December of 1930. Many institutions then closing were related to the 40 banks in the Caldwell chain. The closing of Caldwell's Bank of Tennessee (Nashville), National Bank of Kentucky (Louisville), and American Exchange Company (Little Rock) damaged smaller banks, which had deposits in these institutions. As depositors became alarmed, suspensions spread from these banks to others nearby. More than 140 banks closed in those three states alone.[11] The unrelated failure of Bank of United States in December caused uneasiness in New York City and the Northeast in general. Some bankers hesitated to endorse acceptances—normally a safe investment—and sell them to the reserve bank because they feared the accepting bank would close before the acceptance matured and make the endorser liable to the district bank.[12] As a result of bank failures in the closing weeks of 1930, member banks borrowed more, money in circulation rose as people began hoarding, and stock and bond markets became demoralized. Total loans and investments of member banks declined steadily after June 1930 and fell by $700 million

TABLE 2C
MEMBER BANK HOLDINGS OF ELIGIBLE ASSETS, 1930–31
(in millions of dollars)

Date	Holdings of U.S. Securities* & Eligible Paper			
	By Reserve City Banks		By Other Banks	
	U.S. Securities	Paper	U.S. Securities	Paper
1930				
Mar.	2,619	2,542	818	1,662
June	2,640	2,285	772	1,620
Sep.	2,682	2,271	764	1,541
Dec.	2,777	2,100	708	1,438
1931				
Mar.	3,584	2,045	776	1,373
June	3,871	1,870	836	1,328
Sep.	3,942	1,787	994	1,209
Dec.	3,706	1,505	989	1,068

* Exclusive of approximately $650,000 of government securities pledged against national bank note circulation.

Source: *Federal Reserve Bulletin*, 18 (June 1932): 360.

between September 24 and December 31, 1930.[13] Reserve banks met the demand for money by discounting freely without an increase in rates and by purchasing acceptances and government securities. Reserve policy still aimed at low interest rates, which rose slightly in December but declined again in January 1931.[14]

Suspension of Bank of United States led New York reserve officials to discuss, for the first but not the last time, to what extent their supervisory duties made them responsible for preventing failures of member banks. Although the law permitted a reserve bank to examine a member, it could not expel any bank unless the reserve had evidence the bank was violating the Federal Reserve Act. Nor did a reserve bank have the right to refuse to make a loan to a bank simply because the reserve disliked the bank's management. This made it almost impossible for reserve banks to correct poor management.[15]

The system followed a consistent policy in the first six months of 1931, trying to keep interest rates low and members out of debt. The volume of reserve credit outstanding was high at the beginning of the year but fell gradually, sliding to its lowest point in May 1931. A majority of the OMPC remained opposed to efforts to make money easier, and interest rates in New York changed little. Although statistics indicated an economy drifting uncertainly in the first four months of 1931, the downward course resumed in May as the international situation deteriorated. Total loans and investments of member banks declined, and suspensions rose again. Reserve bank credit outstanding increased, as hoarding began again and member banks borrowed currency to pay depositors.[16]

The "easy money" policy generated considerable criticism. Such quantity theorists as James Harvey Rogers, Harry Gunnison Brown, and Irving Fisher proposed extensive purchases of government securities to ease the recession. They believed that continuous open market purchases would cause excess bank reserves, low interest rates, bank purchases of high-grade bonds, and a stronger money market. They assumed that injecting funds into the economy would stimulate production and demand.[17]

Adherents of commercial loan theory thought reserve authorities overreacted to conditions in 1930. They accused district banks of pumping unnecessary credit into the economy. Because the total volume of commercial paper declined steadily in 1930 (Table 2C), commercial loan theorists believed reserve credit outstanding should contract to reflect depressed conditions. Pumping money into the banks would simply allow speculation, as had occurred in 1928–29. Such experts complained that the system was not allowing natural forces of deflation to work and that this interference was to blame for preventing recovery.[18] The conservative *Commercial and Financial Chronicle* declared in January 1931 that "not a dollar" of reserve bank credit was "needed for trade or for trade purposes." The writer believed reserve policy would "encourage ventures which might better be let alone, thereby repeating the unfortunate experiences which culminated in the collapse in the autumn of 1929."[19]

With hindsight it is evident that the Federal Reserve System might have done more to combat recession in 1930 and early 1931, when conditions were disintegrating. Failure of the system to follow an aggressive countercyclical policy may be attributed to differences of opinion and conflicts among reserve officials, which were accentuated by decentralization of power. The consequence was a monetary policy that ignored bank failures, decline of the money supply, and deflation of bank loans and assets.[20]

HOOVER, CONGRESS, AND RECESSION, 1930–JUNE 1931

President Hoover did little to aid banks from the onset of recession to the autumn of 1931. His response to conditions has received much attention in the last two decades. Recent interpretations view Hoover as a transitional president who provided a bridge between the pro-business, elitist attitudes of Calvin Coolidge and the pro-labor, socially concerned attitudes of Franklin Roosevelt's New Deal. Hoover actually did more than any previous president to counter economic problems. His initial efforts focused on voluntarism. He lacked interest in bank reform in 1930, apparently because he believed that financial intermediaries could save themselves through mutual self-help. He proposed no significant banking legislation until the autumn of 1931. Instead, he issued optimistic statements, trying to instill public confidence in the economy and banks, and he promoted public works construction.[21] Addressing the annual convention of the American Bankers' Association in October 1930, he said, "This depression will be shortened largely to the degree that you feel that you can prudently by counsel and specific assistance, instill into your clients from industry, agriculture, and commerce a feeling of assurance."[22] Only after the voluntary approach became clearly and painfully inadequate did he turn to government efforts to stem the depression.

Hoover had a chance to reorganize the Federal Reserve Board in 1930. Apparently dissatisfied with the leadership provided by Governor Roy A. Young during 1929, he wanted to appoint someone in whom he had faith. Young obliged by resigning from the board, accepting a position as governor of the Boston Federal Reserve Bank at a higher salary. Hoover decided to appoint as the new governor Eugene Meyer, Jr., who had served in the War Finance Corporation during and after World War I and led the Federal Farm Loan Board during the 1920s.[23]

Meyer's legal residence was in New York, which presented a problem. According to the reserve act, only one member of the board could be from any reserve district, and the vice governor, Edmund Platt, was from New York. Platt had been a newspaper editor and politician before joining the board in the early 1920s. He had received job offers from private firms, and apparently Mellon informed him that Hoover wished him to accept one, even though eight years remained of his term on the board. Consequently, in September 1930 Platt became vice president of Marine Midland Group, Inc., a bank holding company in New York.[24]

Reorganization did nothing to strengthen the board. Hoover nominated Meyer on September 16 but did not appoint anyone to the other vacancy on the board nor designate a new vice governor. Another member, Edward Cunningham, died on November 28, 1930. Months later Hoover chose Wayland W. Magee of Nebraska to replace Cunningham as the representative of agricultural interests. Meyer's nomination received Senate approval the following February. By then he was one of Hoover's trusted advisers, working closely with the president, Harrison, and Ogden Mills, under secretary of the Treasury, but Meyer often ignored the board.[25]

Hoover was reluctant to rely on Congress to combat the recession because he disliked the group and sectional interests its members represented. He believed politicians were "fools or knaves" who obstructed "constructive" programs. He acknowledged that Congress had statesmen but thought these were few "compared to the demagogues and collectivists."[26] He did not try negotiation with Congress because he believed it would do nothing helpful during the economic crisis. Republican congressional leaders scorned Hoover's naivety about politics, and Democrats had no reason to respect him.[27]

The most controversial issue to emerge in the House of Representatives, when Congress considered banking reform in 1930–31, was the question of branch, chain, and group banking versus unit banking. The unit bank, the entire business of which was conducted from a single building or location, was the traditional organization for banks in the United States, and a majority of depository institutions were unit banks in 1930 (Table 2D).[28]

TABLE 2D
COMMERCIAL BANK OFFICES IN THE UNITED STATES, 1920–35

Year	Unit Banks	Branch Banks	Total Number	
			Of Banks	Of Branches
1920	29,761	530	30,291	1,281
1925	27,722	720	28,442	2,525
1930	22,928	751	23,679	3,522
1935	14,666	822	15,488	3,156

Source: Gerald C. Fischer, *American Banking Structure* (New York: Columbia University Press, 1968), 31.

Only 21 states permitted branch banking in 1930, and several restricted branches to metropolitan areas or single counties (Table 2E). Branch banks were sub-offices of a chartered bank opened for convenience of customers. These smaller offices had no separate legal identity and no separate capital, assets, or liabilities. On the national level, branch banking had been illegal until passage of the McFadden Act in 1927, which permitted national and state member banks to establish branches in their cities or towns if sanctioned by state law. The act required a state bank, wishing to join the reserve system, to relinquish branches outside its home city that were established after February 25, 1927, which restricted the growth of state-wide branch

TABLE 2E
SUMMARY OF STATE LAWS ON BRANCH BANKING,
DEC. 31, 1929

		Total
Permitting State-Wide Branch Banking	Arizona, California, Delaware, Maryland, North Carolina, Rhode Island, South Carolina, Vermont (1), Virginia	9
Permitting Branches In Limited Areas	Georgia (2), Louisiana (3), Maine (4) Massachusetts (5), Mississippi (6), New Jersey (7), New York (8), Ohio (9), Pennsylvania (10), Tennessee (11)	10
Prohibiting Branch Banking	Alabama, Arkansas, Colorado, Connecticut, Florida, Idaho, Illinois, Indiana, Iowa, Kansas, Minnesota, Missouri, Montana, Nebraska, Nevada, New Mexico, Oregon, Texas, Utah, Washington, West Virginia, Wisconsin	22
No Laws On Branch Banking	Kentucky (12), Michigan (13), New Hampshire, North Dakota, Oklahoma, South Dakota, Wyoming	7

(1) Provisions permit state-wide establishment of "agencies." (2) City or municipality. (3) Municipality or parish. (4) County or adjoining county. (5) Same town. (6) Same city. (7) Same city, town, township, borough, or village. (8) City limits. (9) Same city, or city or village contiguous. (10) Corporate limits of same place. (11) County. (12) No provisions on branches, but court decisions permit establishment of additional offices to receive deposits and pay checks. (13) "Industrial banks" may establish branches in city or village of head office, but no provisions on other kinds of banks.

Source: *Federal Reserve Bulletin*, 16 (April 1930): 258.

banking. The McFadden Act was a compromise that satisfied neither supporters nor opponents of branch banking.[29]

Chain banking differed from branch banking in that chains lacked central supervision. Instead, one person or several would acquire control of individually chartered banks through ownership of stock. Chains had no corporate or legal identity; each bank had its own capital and management. No binding relationships existed among members of a chain, but depositors usually assumed that the closing of one institution in a chain indicated problems with the rest. Chain banking had a bad reputation by 1930 because of previous failures. In some cases, investigations had revealed gross mismanagement. Suspensions among the Caldwell chain and indictment of Rogers Caldwell reinforced existing prejudice against chains.[30]

Group banking, unlike chains, used a holding company to purchase control of stock in individual banks. The holding company was incorporated and sold its own stock publicly. Although each bank had a separate charter and capital, every group banker felt a responsibility toward other members of his group, and holding company officers endeavored to enforce standards throughout the group. Otherwise, public distrust of one institution could quickly spread to the rest.[31]

Chain and group banking developed in the 1920s, and these forms of organization presented problems of regulation because they could cross state lines and combine state and national banks into one chain or group. "Creative bookkeeping" within a chain or group could conceal problems from examiners by shifting assets from bank to bank. Since the comptroller of the currency had responsibility for examining national banks, while each state visited its state banks, discovery of mismanagement was difficult. Fewer than ten states in 1930 had regulations to cover chains or groups, and the federal government had not dealt with the issue. Group holding companies were not banks and were not subject to examination. Chains and groups developed rapidly in states prohibiting branch banking, so most bankers believed chains and groups would convert to national charters and branch banking if Congress authorized it. Thus, discussion centered on branch versus unit banking.[32]

In his annual address to Congress in December 1929, Hoover recommended joint congressional and executive investigation of branch, chain, and group banking, but the House of Representatives preferred to rely on its Committee on Banking and Currency, which held hearings beginning on February 25, 1930. By then, three congressmen had introduced bills: one to restrict chain and branch banking (H.R. 8363); one to extend branch banking (H.R. 8005); and one to outlaw chains and groups altogether (H.R. 8367). The diversity indicated lack of agreement, as did the opinions of those testifying.[33] Witnesses divided into two categories: those who adamantly opposed branches, chains, and groups because they believed Congress should sustain and protect unit banks; and those who favored extending branch banking but chose not to wait for governmental action and so supported group banking, regulated by state and federal authorities.

Unit bankers appearing before the House Committee on Banking and Currency argued against substantial change in federal statutes. They feared that their smaller banks would be driven out of business by competition if Congress permitted expansion of groups or branches. They emphasized that both group and branch banking could lead to a "money trust," with ever greater concentration of wealth in the hands of large bankers. While defenders of unit banking recognized that small, rural banks had previously had a higher rate of failure, they believed that country bankers had revised their methods to meet changing economic conditions. The American Bankers' Association and state bankers' associations expressed this view because a majority of their members worked for unit banks.[34]

Many of those testifying at the hearings believed that unit banks were too small and their assets too vulnerable to local and regional economic disturbances, which more efficient and diversified branch banks could survive more easily. Witnesses disagreed on the area within which banks should be able to establish branches. City-wide, county-wide, state-wide, trade area-wide, and nationwide branch banking all had advocates. Most of those favoring expansion of branch banking had no objection to the continuation of group banking as long as regulators could examine the holding company and all its members simultaneously to prevent "creative bookkeeping." A few group bankers would not have converted their institutions into branches but still favored expansion of branch banking. All those favoring branching agreed that unit banking had severe problems and that either groups or branches were necessary and preferable.[35]

The House Committee on Banking and Currency received views of unit bankers most favorably. Even before the hearings, a majority of committee members opposed expansion of branch banking. Several had stock in local banks at home. Some had served as officers or directors of unit banks. Because of the predispositions of committee members and the contradictory nature of the testimony, the committee reached no decision regarding legislation. It issued a report suggesting that investigation continue during the congressional recess, leaving action to an uncertain future.[36]

The Senate investigated branch banking during the 71st Congress in the context of much broader reforms. Senator William H. King (D–UTAH) submitted a resolution (S.Res. 71) in May 1929 to authorize the Banking and Currency Committee or a subcommittee to investigate 21 questions concerning the reserve system or member banks, including the following:

> Whether the banking laws of the United States should be amended so as to restrict the use of general bank credits for speculative purposes or to limit the volume of loans made for the purpose of carrying on marginal transactions in stocks and other transactions of a speculative character . . .;
>
> Whether or not chain banking and branch banking are being developed and the effect and qualities of these types of banking;
>
> . . .
>
> Whether the member banks of the Federal reserve system should be prohibited from forming or being concerned with investment or security trusts.[37]

The Committee on Banking and Currency chose to postpone the resolution during the initial session of the 71st Congress.[38]

During the second session the resolution gained more attention. When the committee met in December 1929, it decided to hold hearings on S.Res. 71 after Christmas recess. Senator Carter Glass (D–VA) prepared a shorter version at the request of Peter Norbeck (R–SD), committee chairman. Because the Smoot–Hawley tariff dominated the Senate calendar, the committee postponed consideration of the resolution until April 1930, when it approved the Glass substitute. After the resolution passed the Senate without debate in May, Norbeck appointed a subcommittee headed by Glass to hold hearings. The Virginian made no effort to start immediately because Congress planned to adjourn in June.[39]

Glass was the Senate's expert on the reserve system and the dominating force on the Banking and Currency Committee. Norbeck, a rural progressive, gave the Virginian a free hand on banking measures. He permitted Glass to chair the subcommittee holding hearings on the resolution, even though he appointed himself a member and had a right to direct the work if he chose. In 1930 Glass was an irascible man of seventy-two, set in his views about money and banking.[40]

Glass had begun work on a reform bill during 1930, aided by H. Parker Willis of Columbia University, who had helped him draft the original reserve act of 1913. The senator wanted to separate member banks from investment banking and speculative markets. Both he and Willis believed that reserve banks had permitted members to speculate in stocks and bonds during the 1920s. Because these men accepted real bills doctrine, they thought commercial banks should confine collateral to short-term, self-liquidating commercial paper and that reserve banks should refuse to discount for member banks making nonproductive and speculative loans. Glass introduced his bill (S. 4723) on June 17, just before the second session of the 71st Congress adjourned. This measure was a tentative proposal that he would use to focus the subcommittee hearings, which would begin in January 1931.[41]

The Glass bill included four paragraphs that he and Willis hoped would forestall speculation with reserve funds. One would restrict national bank loans to brokers, stock market members, finance companies, investment trusts, or similar financial institutions to 10% of a bank's unimpaired surplus funds and paid-in capital. Another would require affiliates of national banks, including securities or investment affiliates, to send the comptroller of the currency regular reports on their condition. A similar proviso would require affiliates of state member banks to provide reports to the Federal Reserve Board. Finally, section 11 would prevent advances by reserve banks to members that were lending money simultaneously to brokers, stock exchange members, or others using securities as collateral.[42]

The bill also had features to strengthen the competitive position of national banks, about 300 of which had converted to less restrictive state charters between 1927 and 1930. One paragraph attempted to give national banks the same general powers allowed to state banks in each state. The controversial section 4 would allow national banks to establish branches in states that permitted branching.[43]

Another way Glass hoped to attract state banks into the reserve system was to increase dividends paid to member banks on reserve earnings. By law regional banks paid an annual 6% dividend on their stock to members. Any district's earnings in excess of these dividends went into surplus until that reserve bank had accumulated an amount equal to capital. Subsequently, the regional bank could add only 10% of earnings per annum to surplus. The remainder of earnings, if any, went to the Treasury as a franchise tax. The Glass bill provided that after a reserve bank paid the 6% dividend, a quarter of remaining earnings would go to the Treasury as a franchise tax, and a quarter would be applied to surplus until surplus equaled capital, after which the second 25%, too, would go to the Treasury. A reserve bank would distribute remaining earnings to members on a pro rata basis. Bankers had long complained about the low rate of return on their mandatory investment in reserve stock, and in several years district banks had had large earnings (Table 2F). Although reserve officials disliked the division Glass proposed, most supported larger dividends to member banks.[44]

No one expected action on the Glass bill during the short session that began in December 1930, since a large number of witnesses waited to be heard. Among those appearing were the comptroller of the currency, four reserve officials, five New York bankers, and the superintendent of banking in New York. Later the committee heard 11 bankers from various parts of the country, professors from Harvard and New York University, and representatives from the American Acceptance Council and the Discount Corporation of New York. Such diversity reflected differences of opinion and led to numerous criticisms of the bill.[45]

John W. Pole, comptroller of the currency, concentrated his testimony on branch, chain, and group banking, recommending branch banking within trade areas. In the course of answering subcommittee questions, he also suggested allowing the comptroller of the currency to remove bank officers who persisted in bad management and to examine affiliates of national banks. He approved a proposal to require segregation of national bank assets purchased with savings deposits from those acquired with demand deposits so that banks could not use money deposited for the short-term to make long-term investments.[46]

The two members of the reserve board to testify were Adolph C. Miller and Charles S. Hamlin, both of whom had been on the board since 1914. Miller, who had been a professor at Harvard, Cornell, Chicago, and California, was the board's only economist. His statement reviewed monetary policy in the 1920s. He was critical of reserve system purchases of government securities in 1924 and 1927, which he

TABLE 2F
DISPOSITION OF FEDERAL RESERVE BANK EARNINGS, 1914–30
(in thousands of dollars)

Year	Gross	Net	Divi-dends Paid	Trans-ferred to Surplus	Fran-chise Tax Paid To U.S. Govt.	Car-ried For-ward
1914-1915	2,173	-142	217			-359
1916	5,218	2,751	1,743			1,008
1917	16,128	9,580	6,802	1,134	1,134	510
1918	67,584	52,716	5,541	48,334		-1,159
1919	102,381	78,368	5,012	70,652	2,704	
1920	181,297	149,295	5,654	82,916	60,725	
1921	122,866	82,087	6,120	15,993	59,974	
1922	50,499	16,498	6,307	-660	10,851	
1923	50,709	12,711	6,553	2,545	3,613	
1924	38,340	3,718	6,682	-3,078	114	
1925	41,801	9,449	6,916	2,474	59	
1926	47,600	16,612	7,329	8,465	818	
1927	43,024	13,048	7,755	5,044	249	
1928	64,053	32,122	8,458	21,079	2,585	
1929	70,955	36,403	9,584	22,536	4,283	
1930	36,424	7,988	10,269	-2,298	17	
Total	941,052	523,204	100,942	275,136	147,126	

Source: *Federal Reserve Bulletin*, 17 (February 1931): 59.

believed had fed stock market speculation. He recommended that five members of the board be required to approve all open market operations, emphasizing that curbs were necessary to avoid inflation. Answering questions, Miller indicated that affiliates of member banks should be examined regularly, that the limit on advances in section 11 of the bill might be undesirable, and that the secretary of the Treasury and comptroller of the currency should be dropped as members of the reserve board, as the bill provided.[47]

Hamlin, a Boston lawyer and politician who had served in the Treasury Department prior to 1914, also focused on events prior to the stock market crash. He responded to questions by recommending that the board be empowered to initiate a discount rate for any regional bank whenever five board members agreed and by suggesting that reserve banks accept government bonds as collateral for advances only in emergencies. He approved of segregating assets purchased with savings deposits from those acquired with commercial deposits.[48]

Harrison presented the view of New York reserve officials and spent days answering questions. He testified that it would be beneficial to unify control over banks by requiring all state institutions to join the reserve system but recognized that many smaller banks had inadequate capital to qualify for membership. He believed trade-area branches could replace those unit banks forced to close because they lacked capital, and he approved examining affiliates. He opposed segregating assets purchased with savings deposits. His testimony centered on what officials could do to prevent members from using reserve funds to make call loans, brokers' loans, and loans with securities as collateral. He maintained that reserve banks could not regulate the use members made of borrowed funds, while Glass kept insisting that the reserve act gave district banks legal authority to do so. Naturally, Harrison opposed section 11 limiting advances, since he believed such loans had not caused speculation.[49]

Bankers agreed on two subjects. First, they recognized the possibility of misuse and bad management that bank affiliates presented but did not want affiliates to be prohibited. Instead, they suggested that affiliates be examined by regulatory authorities. Second, they opposed section 11, which prohibited "speculative" loans by member banks borrowing simultaneously from a district bank on an advance. They had no desire to have advances restricted because such borrowing was far more convenient for members than discounting eligible paper, which was becoming scarcer. They wanted to continue lending with securities as collateral, which Glass wished to restrain.[50]

About half the bankers appearing at the hearings approved of branch banking. One of its strongest advocates was Platt of Marine Midland Group. He believed that for country banks to acquire balanced and diversified portfolios of loans and investments, branch banking had to be extended, and several bankers agreed. As in House hearings, witnesses were far from unanimous about whether to allow an extension of branching and about the extent of a geographic area in which it might be permitted.[51]

The Senate subcommittee's inquiry was wide ranging, but the time the subcommittee spent reviewing events of the 1920s clearly reflected Glass's preoccupation with preventing speculation. In spite of deflation during 1930, Glass focused neither on ending the depression nor on aiding failing banks but on avoiding the recurrence of a speculative boom fueled by reserve funds. He continued to believe that the depression would not have occurred if district banks had not allowed credit to seep into the stock market through call loans and brokers' loans. This assumption would continue to dominate his efforts to reform the Federal Reserve System during the next session of Congress, which would meet starting in December 1931.[52]

Banking legislation that Congress actually enacted in 1930 was less substantive than technical. Either the reserve board or the comptroller of the currency had recommended the bills that became law. One act authorized receivers of failed national banks to compromise shareholders' liability so as to speed liquidation of closed banks. Another law made section 9 of the reserve act, which required a state member bank or trust company to give six months' notice if it wished to withdraw from the system, more flexible by allowing the reserve board to "waive the notice." A third change permitted the board to cancel reserve bank stock held by member banks that had gone out of business but had neither begun voluntary liquidation nor had a receiver appointed, relieving the district bank of paying such banks a dividend. Another act allowed the board to aid state member banks by waiving the assessment against them for examining costs.[53] Altogether, there were eight changes in federal banking law in 1930. Each corrected a technical problem but addressed minor issues on which little debate occurred. None had attempted to deal with the most pressing question, namely, bank failures.[54] When Congress adjourned in the summer of 1930, the reserve system and national banks remained vulnerable to forces of deflation.

No new banking legislation of any kind passed during the final session of the 71st Congress, in spite of the Glass hearings. When the session started in December 1930, the banks were in the grip of the first panic of the depression, begun by failure of the Caldwell chain. Almost 600 banks closed in November and December, and publicity and concern aroused by bank suspensions in the winter of 1930–31 generated new congressional interest in reform. When the failure rate slowed in early 1931, the sense of political urgency faded.[55]

Considerable friction had existed between the 71st Congress and Hoover, in spite of Republican majorities in both houses (56 to 39 in the Senate and 267 to 167 in the House), and he had no reason to expect the 72d Congress would be easier to work with, for the election of 1930 was a disaster for Republicans. In both House and Senate, their majority dropped to one vote. By the time the first session of the 72d Congress began in December 1931, there had been special elections to replace members who had died, and Democrats picked up four seats, allowing them to organize the House. Hoover might have called a special session of Congress but had no intention of doing so. He wanted to manage without Congress as long as possible.[56] Under normal circumstances his decision might not have been harmful, but circumstances in 1931 were not normal.

RESPONSE TO MONETARY CRISIS, JUNE–DECEMBER 1931

An international monetary crisis began in Central Europe in the spring of 1931, spreading from Austria to Hungary, Germany, and Great Britain. Harrison stayed in contact with European central bankers and kept the reserve board, Treasury Department, and State Department informed of developments. Meyer, Mills, and Henry L. Stimson, secretary of State, conferred with Hoover. The president understood the possible seriousness of the situation, but his reaction was hesitant and insufficient. Even when he proposed a one-year moratorium on international debts, which required consultation with members of Congress, Hoover refused to call a special session. While the moratorium temporarily improved conditions, it did not prevent a run on the pound that forced Britain to leave the gold standard in September.[57]

Harrison began in June to advocate a resumption of moderate purchases of government securities. Exceedingly large imports of gold, caused by Europeans exchanging local currencies for assets in the United States, caused him to believe purchases might help slow the flow of gold by generating fears of inflation abroad. Between June 22 and August 3, the OMPC purchased about $80 million of government securities. At the same time, however, reserve banks allowed their acceptance holdings to mature without new purchases, and the volume of member bank discounts declined. Gold imports were largely offset by hoarding, reflected by larger amounts of currency in circulation. As a result, reserve credit outstanding rose only $6 million during the European crisis.[58]

Conditions remained unsettled during August and September. Member banks paid out more than $200 million for hoarding in August. At the OMPC meeting that month, Harrison supported a resolution authorizing purchase of $300 million of government securities. The other district bank governors thought this amount unnecessary and authorized purchase of $120 million. Harrison believed that $120 million was too little to accomplish much and provided the only vote against the smaller authorization. In the following week, the system bought $70 million of bankers' acceptances and $47 million of government securities, the largest single week's purchase since 1929. Purchases totaled $115 million of acceptances and $50 million of government securities by the end of August. Because these purchases failed to promote economic recovery or slow hoarding of currency, the OMPC decided to discontinue them in September. Even Harrison concluded that purchases of government securities would have little chance of improving conditions as long as member banks were allowing excess reserves to accumulate instead of employing them in the bond market.[59] Discussing goals for reserve action in the autumn, he suggested a policy of permitting district banks to meet member needs through buying acceptances. He thought the system should reconsider this only if changes in the financial situation made it desirable.[60]

When Great Britain left the gold standard on September 21, 1931, financial conditions changed radically. The British Commonwealth and many of England's principal trading partners also deserted gold. Pressure shifted to the United States as Europeans, led by the Bank of France, began to repatriate their capital. This reversed an inflow of gold that had increased monetary gold stock by $700 million since December 1929. Britain's abandonment of the gold standard generated fears that the United States would follow, and the nation lost more than $700 million of gold in six weeks. Gold exports reached panic proportions by the first week of October. Domestic currency hoarding added pressure on bankers, who tried to convert assets into cash and borrowed heavily from district banks.[61]

In response to the crisis, reserve banks raised discount rates, and Harrison tried to reassure European bankers. There is no evidence that any reserve board member opposed rate increases. Authorities followed a 19th-century rule of central banking, namely, raising discount rates to hold gold reserves. They thought it impossible to preserve domestic economic stability unless they protected the gold dollar, and they chose not to suspend the legal gold reserve requirement for the reserve system, even though the law permitted emergency suspension. Harrison tried to reassure the world's central bankers about the nation's commitment to gold. He sent cables emphasizing the willingness of the Treasury and his bank to sell gold at the statutory price of $20.67 per troy ounce 1,000 fine and to buy it at the same price, plus a small charge for melting and alloy. By assuring central bankers that the country had a free gold market, he hoped to make them less likely to convert holdings into gold. A week later he sent another cable declaring that a change in the law regarding the weight of the gold dollar was neither necessary nor likely.[62]

Reserve policy in the autumn of 1931 caused gold exports to decelerate but did not prevent damage to the American financial situation. Currency hoarding increased to $1 billion. Large numbers of banks failed, and bankers became so liquidity conscious that credit for business borrowers dried up. Loans of member banks fell by almost $5 billion in 1931, adding to a previous decline of almost $6 billion since October 1929. Money supply decreased by 12% between August 1931 and January 1932. Stock and bond markets suffered, too, as banks seeking liquidity dumped assets on falling markets. By December, banks in the New York district had such large losses on bond accounts that to charge losses off completely would wipe out capital funds in about 300 institutions and impair the capital in another 150 to 200. The volume of reserve bank credit outstanding increased by $1 billion in the weeks after the British left gold, when member banks borrowed to cover gold exports and hoarding, but then decreased as deposits in member banks fell, reducing their required reserves and enabling them to repay about $200 million of their indebtedness to district banks. The panic passed by the beginning of December. Gold again entered the country, and a little currency returned from hoarding. Still, the absence of open market purchases during the autumn allowed the downward trend of economic indicators to resume in 1932.[63]

As pressure on England mounted in the late summer months, Hoover had recognized that America's economic situation might deteriorate if the British left gold. He sent a letter to Meyer on September 8, 1931, which Meyer forwarded to district governors, urging that reserve officials in each district assemble bankers to discuss a solution to bank closings. On September 15, Hoover met with 14 of the nation's most respected bankers to suggest that they form a voluntary association of banks to pool $500 million in capital and lend it to banks against assets not eligible for discount at reserve banks. Bankers were wary about making a commitment. They feared that if strong banks tried to help weak ones, the effort might damage the strong without saving the weak. At the time that Britain left the gold standard, they had not agreed to support Hoover's initiative.[64]

Hoover met with prominent New York bankers on October 4 to urge them to adopt his proposal for a National Credit Corporation. To avoid speculation that might intensify panic, the meeting was secret. The president spoke earnestly, but the New Yorkers did not immediately consent. Before organizing such a corporation, they insisted that Hoover try to persuade Congress to pass an amendment to the reserve act making additional types of paper eligible for discount, a bill recreating the War Finance Corporation, and amendments to strengthen the Federal Farm Loan Bank System. He agreed, and then bankers consented on October 6 to organize the National Credit Corporation.[65]

Still not wishing to call a special session of Congress, Hoover conferred with a bipartisan group of politicians that evening to explain the situation and outline the agreement he had reached. He hoped the voluntary efforts of the credit corporation would make a significant difference to the economy. Receiving support from congressional leaders, he issued a statement that announced New York bankers would form a corporation to aid weak banks. In addition, he indicated his support for broadening eligibility provisions in the reserve act, establishing a corporation similar to the War Finance Corporation, and strengthening the Federal Land Banks.[66]

Although Hoover received much public praise for formation of the National Credit Corporation, the attitude of bankers doomed the attempt from the outset. The corporation failed to lend much money because bankers feared such loans would flood good banks with poor assets. By the time Congress convened in December, even Hoover recognized that the National Credit Corporation was inadequate and that legislative action was essential. After months of trying to end the depression on his own, he had to turn to politicians for help. When he did so, the government's depression policy entered a new and more active stage.[67]

CONCLUSION

Confusion over monetary policies in 1930–31 inhibited effective action by the Federal Reserve System. Although officers and directors of the New York reserve bank occasionally proposed greater purchases of government securities, opposition within the OMPC consistently restrained that policy. Much of the resistance to large and constant purchases of government securities resulted from an illusion that the money supply was adequate because short-term interest rates hit record lows. The persistent decline of the money supply, perhaps the most important source of contraction, went largely unnoticed by officials. Without doubt, their defense of the gold standard in the autumn of 1931 caused an abrupt decline in the money supply and a sharp increase in bank failures. Because officials were divided and followed inadequate guidelines, monetary policy did little to combat recession and contributed to deflation in the closing months of 1931.

The illusions held by Hoover in 1930–31 were many. It appeared to him that economic problems in the United States were the result of a lack of confidence in the banking system and economy. He continued to believe that voluntary effort and public works could end deflation, and he hoped to avoid federal intervention in financial mechanisms. When bankers seemed incapable of acting, he pressed them to establish the ineffective National Credit Corporation. In 1932, he bent to the inevitable and approved a more active role for government in easing the depression, but his beliefs continued to constrain him.

Given Hoover's inability to lead and confusion among the best bankers and financiers in the nation, the lack of action by Congress should not be surprising, for Congress historically has acted most effectively when consensus and compromise could be achieved. Neither consensus nor compromise developed in the first two years of the depression, whether on branch banking, the Glass bill, or other measures to end bank failures. Illusions and confusions among the nation's leaders encouraged a protracted economic decline.

NOTES

1. Barrie A. Wigmore, *The Crash and Its Aftermath* (Westport, Conn.: Greenwood, 1985), 24, 101; John Kenneth Galbraith, *The Great Crash 1929* (Boston: Houghton Mifflin, 1961 [1954]), 149–50; "R.S. Hecht of Hibernia Bank and Trust Company of New Orleans Believes Definite Indications of Economic Recovery Should Soon Appear," *Commercial and Financial Chronicle*, 132 (10 January 1931): 192; "Allard Smith of Union Trust Company of Cleveland Looks for Business Recovery in Present Year," *Commercial and Financial Chronicle*, 132 (17 January 1931): 394–5; Kathryn M. Dominguez, Ray C. Fair, and Matthew D. Shapiro, "Forecasting the Depression: Harvard versus Yale," *American Economic Review*, 78 (September 1988): 598–9; Lester V. Chandler, *America's Greatest Depression 1929–41* (New York: Harper and Row, 1970): 2–7, 72–5, 80–2; *Federal Reserve Bulletin*, 18 (March 1932): 153; "Trends of the Markets in Money, Stocks, Bonds," *Business Week* (30 December 1931): 29. Peter Temin argues convincingly that the cause of the depression and the explanation for its depth was rigid adherence to the gold standard; *Lessons from the Great Depression* (Cambridge, Mass.: MIT, 1989), 19–37, 41–87. However, there has been a recent debate over whether the deflation of the early 1930s should have been anticipated. Those scholars who argue it should have been support the view that the Federal Reserve's monetary policy should have been more expansionary. For more on this topic, see Daniel B. Nelson, "Was the Deflation of 1929–1930 Anticipated? The Monetary Regime as Viewed by the Business Press," *Research in Economic History*, 13 (1991): 1–65; Stephen G. Cecchetti, "Prices During the Great Depression: Was the Deflation of 1930–1932 Really Unanticipated?" *American Economic Review*, 82 (March 1992): 141–56; James D. Hamilton, "Was the Deflation During the Great Depression Anticipated? Evidence from the Commodity Futures Market," *American Economic Review*, 82 (March 1992): 157–78.

2. Federal Reserve Board, *Seventeenth Annual Report Covering Operations for the Year 1930* (Washington, D.C.: U.S. Government Printing Office, 1931), 17–8; H. Parker Willis, "Commercial, Investment, and Other Types of Banking," *The Banking Situation: American Post-War Problems and Developments*, H. Parker Willis and

John M. Chapman, eds. (New York: Columbia University, 1934), 196–8; Carl M. Gambs, "Bank Failures: An Historical Perspective," *Federal Reserve Bank of Kansas City Monthly Review* (June 1977): 19; David E. Hamilton, "The Causes of the Banking Panic of 1930: Another View," *Journal of Southern History*, 51 (November 1985): 585–91, 597–607; Eugene Nelson White, *The Regulation and Reform of the American Banking System, 1900–1929* (Princeton, N.J.: Princeton University, 1983), 126–7; Bert Ely, "The Big Bust: The 1930–33 Banking Collapse—Its Causes, Its Lessons," *The Financial Services Revolution: Policy Directions for the Future*, Catherine England and Thomas Huertas, eds. (Boston: Kluwer Academic, 1988): 51–6.

3. R.S. Hecht, *The Situation that Confronts Banking* (New York: American Bankers' Association, Economic Policy Committee, 1931), 6–9; "Comptroller of Currency Pole before Central Atlantic States Bank Management Conference Warns of Increased Governmental Supervision of Banks if Banks Fail in Maintaining Sound Management," *Commercial and Financial Chronicle*, 132 (7 March 1931): 1723–4; National Industrial Conference Board, *The Banking Situation in the United States* (New York: National Industrial Conference Board, 1932), 44; Elmus Wicker, "A Reconsideration of the Causes of the Banking Panic of 1930," *Journal of Economic History*, 40 (September 1980): 574–83; "Rogers Caldwell, Former President of Defunct Investment Banking Firm of Caldwell and Company, Nashville, Indicted by Davidson County, Tennessee, Grand Jury," *Commercial and Financial Chronicle*, 132 (21 March 1931): 2113; Joseph L. Lucia, "The Failure of the Bank of the United States: A Reappraisal," *Explorations in Economic History*, 22 (October 1985): 405–9; Hamilton, "Causes of Banking Panic," 591–6; R.W. Goldschmidt, *The Changing Structure of American Banking* (London: George Routledge and Sons, 1933), 225–7; Milton Friedman and Anna Jacobson Schwartz, *A Monetary History of the United States, 1867–1960* (Princeton, N.J.: Princeton University, 1963), 308–13; *Wall Street Journal*, 4 March 1931, 19. Of course, the majority of bank failures did not involve dishonesty or malfeasance by officers and directors. Careful studies, comparing assets of banks that failed to those of banks that did not fail, indicate that those banks that suspended had had problems with their assets throughout the 1920s as a result of postwar deflation and depression in farm values. For such vulnerable

institutions, the decline of farm commodity prices, further decrease in land values, and increasing demands of depositors for cash during the recession of 1929–30 were sufficient to push them into insolvency. The drought of 1930 in the Upper South also made things worse. See Hamilton, "Causes of Banking Panic," 596–607.

4. Elmus R. Wicker, "Federal Reserve Monetary Policy, 1922–33: A Reinterpretation," *Journal of Political Economy*, 73 (August 1965): 330–1; Federal Reserve Board, *Seventeenth Annual Report, 1930*, 1–9; Federal Reserve Board, *Eighteenth Annual Report Covering Operations for the Year 1931* (Washington, D.C.: U.S. Government Printing Office, 1932), 7; Karl R. Bopp, "Three Decades of Federal Reserve Policy," *Postwar Economic Studies*, 8 (November 1947): 13–4; Elmus R. Wicker, *Federal Reserve Monetary Policy, 1917–1933* (New York: Random House, 1966), 153. There is some evidence that reserve banks actually competed with one another for reserves and attempted to prevent reserve losses by keeping discount rates relatively high. This upward pressure on discount rates contributed to the decline of the money supply. Only the New York bank cut its discount rate to keep pace with market rates. See David C. Wheelock, *The Strategy and Consistency of Federal Reserve Monetary Policy, 1924–1933* (Cambridge: Cambridge University, 1991), 111–2.

5. Herman E. Krooss, *Executive Opinion: What Business Leaders Said and Thought on Economic Issues 1920s–1960s* (Garden City, N.Y.: Doubleday, 1970), 134–5; National Industrial Conference Board, *The Availability of Bank Credit* (New York: National Industrial Conference Board, 1932), 18, 122–4; *Federal Reserve Bulletin*, 17 (February 1931): 55; Ibid., 18 (March 1932): 153; memorandum, Minutes of Meeting of the Open Market Policy Conference, January 21, 1931, Box 69, General Records of the Department of the Treasury, Office of the Secretary, General Correspondence 1917–32, Record Group 56, National Archives, Washington, D.C.; Christian Saint-Etienne, *The Great Depression, 1929–1938: Lessons for the 1980s* (Stanford, Cal.: Hoover Institution, 1984), 20; Temin, *Lessons of the Great Depression*, 54.

6. Diary, v. 17, 14 May 1930, Charles Sumner Hamlin Papers, Manuscript Division, Library of Congress, Washington, D.C.; Wicker, *Federal Reserve*, 153–8, 163–9; outgoing cablegram to Moreau from Harrison, 31 July 1930, Binder 28, George Leslie Harrison Papers, Manuscript Division, Butler Library, Columbia University, New York,

N.Y.; Karl Brunner and Allan H. Meltzer, "What Did We Learn from the Monetary Experience of the United States in the Great Depression?" *Canadian Journal of Economics*, 1 (May 1968): 347–8; Eugene Nelson White, "A Reinterpretation of the Banking Crisis of 1930," *Journal of Economic History*, 44 (March 1984): 128; Ben S. Bernanke, "Nonmonetary Effects of the Financial Crisis in the Propagation of the Great Depression, *American Economic Review*, 73 (June 1983): 266; Temin, *Lessons of the Great Depression*, 52–4; Wheelock, *Monetary Policy*, 66.

7. Outgoing cablegram to Norman from Federal Reserve Bank of New York, 26 March 1930, Binder 19, Harrison Papers; Wicker, *Federal Reserve*, 150–1; outgoing cablegram to Norman from Harrison, 25 April 1930, Binder 19, Harrison Papers; memorandum, Recommendations Adopted by Open Market Investment Committee, 22 May 1930, Box 354, Hamlin Papers.

8. Wicker, *Federal Reserve*, 154–6; letter to Norris from Harrison, 3 July 1930, Box 355, Hamlin Papers; letter to Harrison from Black, 11 July 1930, Binder 53, Harrison Papers; letter to Harrison from Seay, 10 July 1930, Binder 53, Harrison Papers; Wigmore, *Crash and Its Aftermath*, 118–20. Harrison's conclusion was based on the low level of borrowing by banks in New York and other leading cities.

9. Hamlin Diary, v. 18, 2 October 1930.

10. Untitled statement by Open Market Policy Conference, 24 September 1930, Box 355, Hamlin Papers.

11. Elmus Wicker, "Reconsideration of Causes of Banking Panic," 574–83; Hamilton, "Causes of Banking Panic," 591–6.

12. Hamlin Diary, v. 18, 18 December 1930; Paul B. Trescott, "Bank Failures, Interest Rates, and the Great Currency Outflow in the United States, 1929–1933," *Research in Economic History*, 11 (1988): 74.

13. Federal Reserve Board, *Seventeenth Annual Report, 1930*, 2–3, 8; *Federal Reserve Bulletin*, 17 (February 1931): 53–5; Albert U. Romasco, *The Poverty of Abundance: Hoover, the Nation, the Depression* (New York: Oxford University, 1965), 76–7. The rise in member bank borrowing and the decline in total loans and investments was concentrated in country banks; Wigmore, *Crash and Its Aftermath*, 122–3.

14. Outgoing cablegram to Norman from Harrison, 10 January 1931, Binder 20, Harrison Papers; *Federal Reserve Bulletin*, 17 (February 1931): 53–5.

15. Memorandum: Meeting of Board of Directors December 18, 1930, Binder 56, Harrison Papers. Lucia, "Failure of the Bank of the United States," argues that the reserve acted responsibly toward the Bank of the United States, lending $19 million to try to help the bank resolve its liquidity crisis (412–5).

16. Friedman and Schwartz, *Monetary History*, 312–4; Ellis W. Hawley, *The Great War and the Search for a Modern Order: A History of the American People and Their Institutions, 1917–1933* (New York: St. Martin's, 1979), 195–7; Hamlin Diary, v. 19, 29 April 1931.

17. Joseph E. Reeve, *Monetary Reform Movements: A Survey of Recent Plans and Panaceas* (Washington, D.C.: American Council on Public Affairs, 1943), 11–2, 307–8; Joseph Dorfman, *The Economic Mind in American Civilization*, 5 v. (New York: Viking, 1946–59), V: 690, 693–4; letter to Meyer from Edie, 28 April [1931], Box 356, Hamlin Papers; Friedman and Schwartz, *Monetary History*, 409–10; Frederick A. Bradford, "Stable Money Theory and Business Depression," *Bankers Magazine*, 122 (February 1931): 169–70.

18. Chandler, *America's Greatest Depression*, 113–4; Krooss, *Executive Opinion*, 132–4; "B.M. Anderson, of Chase National Bank of New York, Views Cheap Money as Aid to Speculation But Costly to Business," *Commercial and Financial Chronicle*, 130 (19 April 1930): 2698–9; "The Financial Situation," *Commercial and Financial Chronicle*, 130 (21 June 1930): 4289–90.

19. "The Financial Situation," *Commercial and Financial Chronicle*, 132 (24 January 1931): 532.

20. Chandler, *America's Greatest Depression*, 116–7; Wheelock, *Monetary Policy*, 113–7. There is a real question, however, whether a more aggressive monetary policy could have corrected the situation. While Friedman and Schwartz argue that it could have (*Monetary History*, 391–419), Wigmore makes the case that the Federal Reserve did all that could have been reasonably asked of it and that monetary policy could not have cured the depression (*Crash and Its Aftermath*, 550–2).

21. Robert S. McElvaine, *The Great Depression: America, 1929–1941* (New York: Times Books, 1984), 65–9, 73–9; Hawley, *The Great War*, 184–95; Albert U. Romasco, "Herbert Hoover's Policies

for Dealing with the Great Depression: The End of the Old Order or the Beginning of the New?" *The Hoover Presidency: A Reappraisal*, Martin L. Fausold and George T. Mazuzan, eds. (Albany: State University of New York, 1974): 83–6; Susan Estabrook Kennedy, *The Banking Crisis of 1933* (Lexington: University of Kentucky, 1973), 25; Chandler, *America's Greatest Depression*, 87; Martin L. Fausold, *The Presidency of Herbert C. Hoover* (Lawrence: University of Kansas, 1985), 72–7; Richard Earl Edwards, Herbert Hoover and the Public Relations Approach to Economic Recovery, 1929–1932 (Ph.D. dissertation, University of Iowa, 1976), 57–60, 76–8; *Congressional Record*, 75, pt. 4: 4596, 72d Congress, 1st session; William J. Barber, *From New Era to New Deal* (Cambridge: Cambridge University, 1985), 78–86, 95–9, 104–20. Hoover did ask the Federal Reserve Board in March 1930 whether it would "consider making first mortgages" on residential property "eligible for rediscount at the Federal Reserve Banks." When the board responded negatively, Hoover allowed this idea to die without making a formal proposal to Congress. See Barber, *From New Era to New Deal*, 96–7.

22. Address by Hoover before the American Bankers' Association, Cleveland, Ohio, 2 October 1930, reprinted in *Congressional Record*, 74, pt. 1: 203, 71st Congress, 3d session.

23. Hamlin Diary, v. 18, 3 October 1930; Wicker, *Federal Reserve*, 158–9; Wicker, "Federal Reserve," 337n.

24. Wicker, *Federal Reserve*, 158–9; Wicker, "Federal Reserve," 337n; *Federal Reserve Bulletin*, 16 (October 1930): 615; *Wall Street Journal*, 5 September 1930, 12.

25. Wicker, *Federal Reserve*, 158–9; Wicker, "Federal Reserve," 337n; Hamlin Diary, v. 19, 26 July 1931; *Federal Reserve Bulletin*, 16 (December 1930): 763; Ibid., 17 (May 1931): 248; *Congressional Record*, 73, pt. 6: 5947, 71st Congress, 3d session. For an example of Meyer working more closely with the administration than with the board, see Hamlin Diary, v. 19, 2 October 1931.

26. Jordan A. Schwarz, "Hoover and Congress: Politics, Personality, and Perspective in the Presidency," *Hoover Presidency*, Fausold and Mazuzan, eds., 90.

27. Ibid., 92–3; Fausold, *Presidency of Hoover*, 49.

28. Gerald C. Fischer, *American Banking Structure* (New York: Columbia University, 1968), 18–23, 30–1; White, *Regulation and Reform*, 223.

29. Hecht, *Situation that Confronts Banking*, 14; *Federal Reserve Bulletin*, 16 (December 1930): 812–4; Goldschmidt, *Changing Structure of Banking*, 184–5; National Industrial Conference Board, *Banking Situation*, 51. The original National Bank Act was silent on the subject of branching. Prior to the passage of the McFadden Act, Congress amended the National Bank Act, permitting state banks converting into national banks to retain branches previously established and permitting a national bank with branches to consolidate with another national bank and still retain branches. The Supreme Court ruled in 1924 that national banks had no authority to establish new branches. See National Industrial Conference Board, *Banking Situation*, 50–1.

30. Hecht, *Situation that Confronts Banking*, 13; *Wall Street Journal*, 4 January 1930, 8; "Rogers Caldwell Indicted," 2113.

31. Hecht, *Situation that Confronts Banking*, 13–4; Thomas Joel Anderson, Jr., *Federal and State Control of Banking* (New York: Bankers Publishing Company, 1934), 255, 258–61.

32. Fischer, *American Banking Structure*, 72, 81–2, 95; *Federal Reserve Bulletin*, 16 (December 1930): 811, 815; Bernhard Ostrolenk, "The Revolution in Banking Theory," *Atlantic Monthly*, 145 (February 1930): 218–9; Goldschmidt, *Changing Structure of Banking*, 185–6. According to Fischer, Wisconsin was the only state to declare that any corporation, which controlled a state bank or trust company, doing business in the state was automatically engaged in the business of banking and subject to supervision by the banking department.

33. Herbert Clark Hoover, *The State Papers and Other Public Writings of Herbert Hoover*, W.S. Myers, ed., 2 v. (New York: Doubleday, 1934), I: 154–5; *Wall Street Journal*, 4 January 1930, 8; U.S., Congress, House, Committee on Banking and Currency, *Branch, Chain, and Group Banking: Hearings Pursuant to H.Res. 141*, 71st Congress, 2nd session, 25 February–11 June 1930; Thomas B. Paton, "Banking Measures in the 71st Congress," *Journal of the American Bankers Association*, 22 (February 1930): 741–2. The House authorized hearings by passing H.Res. 141 on February 10, 1930; *Congressional Record*, 72, pt. 3: 3382–3, 71st Congress, 2d session.

34. House Committee on Banking and Currency, *Branch, Chain, and Group Banking*, 1570–99, 1665–81, 1752–66, 1781–96. Also Wilbert M. Schneider, *The American Bankers Association: Its Past and Present* (Washington, D.C.: Public Affairs, 1956), 216–8.

35. House Committee on Banking and Currency, *Branch, Chain, and Group Banking*, 10–219, 787–975, 1037–168, 1174–85, 1201–42, 1259–334, 1339–49, 1464–97, 1536–40, 1607–21, 1643–64, 1689–733, 1955–96.

36. Letter to Eccles from Awalt, 25 January 1935, Box 16, Papers of Marriner S. Eccles, Manuscript Division, Special Collections Department, Marriott Library, University of Utah, Salt Lake City, Utah; House Committee on Banking and Currency, *Branch, Chain, and Group Banking*, 42–3, 746, 1598; U.S., Congress, House, Committee on Banking and Currency, *Investigation of Group, Chain, and Branch Banking: Report Pursuant to H.Res. 141*, H. Rept. 2946, 71st Congress, 3d session, 3 March 1931.

37. A copy of S.Res. 71 as introduced appears in *Congressional Record*, 71, pt. 2: 1830, 71st Congress, 1st session.

38. *Congressional Record*, 71, pt. 2: 1830, pt. 5: 4887, 71st Congress, 1st session.

39. *Congressional Record*, 72, pt. 7: 7309, pt. 8: 8335, 71st Congress, 2d session; "Inquiry Into National Banking Laws Likely by Senate—King Resolution for Probe Into Defects of Federal Reserve System To Be Taken Up After Holidays," *Commercial and Financial Chronicle*, 129 (21 December 1929): 3902; *Wall Street Journal*, 7 January 1930, 16; Ibid., 22 April 1930, 16; Ibid., 6 May 1930, 16; catalogued correspondence to Willis from Glass, 22 January 1930, Henry Parker Willis Papers, Manuscript Division, Butler Library, Columbia University, New York, N.Y.; John Douglas Lyle, The United States Senate Career of Carter Glass of Virginia, 1919–1939 (Ph.D. dissertation, University of South Carolina, 1974), 159–60; "Senate Committee Discusses Amendment to Federal Reserve Act Eliminating 15-Day Loans," *Commercial and Financial Chronicle*, 130 (25 January 1930): 568; "Senator Glass Heads Subcommittee of Senate to Investigate National and Federal Reserve Banking Systems—Inquiry to Be Undertaken in Fall," *Commercial and Financial Chronicle*, 130 (7 June 1930): 3986. The subcommittee members were Glass, Norbeck, Frederic C. Walcott (R–CONN), John G. Townsend, Jr. (R–DEL), and Sam G. Bratton (D–NM). When Congress reconvened, Bratton changed committee assignments, and Norbeck appointed Robert Bulkley (D–OH) to replace him.

40. Arthur M. Schlesinger, Jr. *The Age of Roosevelt*, 3 v. (Boston: Houghton Mifflin, 1957–60), III: 295–6; Jordan A. Schwarz, *The Interregnum of Despair: Hoover, Congress, and the Depression* (Urbana: University of Illinois, 1970), 95–6; Gilbert Courtland Fite, "Peter Norbeck: Prairie Statesman," *University of Missouri Studies*, 22, 2 (1948): 169–70.

41. For more on the real bills doctrine, see Chapter One. Lyle, Senate Career of Glass, 158–60; Alfred Cash Koeniger, "Unreconstructed Rebel:" The Political Thought and Senate Career of Carter Glass, 1929–1936 (Ph.D. dissertation, Vanderbilt University, 1980), 50; *The Reminiscences of Chester Morrill*, 201–3, Oral History Collection, Butler Library, Columbia University, New York, N.Y.; George D. Green, "The Ideological Origins of the Revolution in American Financial Policies," *The Great Depression Revisited*, Karl Brunner, ed. (Boston: Martinus Nijhoff, 1981), 227; "Senator Glass Asks Amendment to Banking Statutes—Introduces Bill for Far-Reaching Changes in Law on Federal Reserve and National Banks," *Commercial and Financial Chronicle*, 130 (21 June 1930): 4353–5; *Congressional Record*, 72, pt. 10: 10973, 71st Congress, 2d session. Commercial and investment banking were interrelated in three ways: (1) commercial bankers invested part of their deposits in investment securities, such as stocks and bonds, which they purchased from investment bankers; (2) borrowers expected commercial bankers to lend with securities as collateral; and (3) commercial banks owned investment affiliates or used their bond departments to underwrite securities. See Glenn G. Munn, "Relation of Investment to Commercial Banking," *Bankers Magazine*, 118 (March 1929): 361–2; William F. Shughart, III, "A Public Choice Perspective of the Banking Act of 1933," *The Financial Services Revolution*, England and Huertas, eds., 89–90.

42. Lyle, Senate Career of Glass, 160–6; *Wall Street Journal*, 18 June 1930, 17; Office Correspondence to Federal Reserve Board from Wingfield, 23 June 1930, Box 14, Adolph Caspar Miller Papers, Manuscript Division, Library of Congress, Washington, D.C.; "Senator Glass Asks Amendment to Banking Statutes," 4353–5.

43. Lyle, Senate Career of Glass, 160–6; *Wall Street Journal*, 18 June 1930, 17; Office Correspondence to Federal Reserve Board from Wingfield, 23 June 1930; "Senator Glass Asks Amendment to Banking Statutes," 4353–5; Ostrolenk, "Revolution in Banking Theory," 219.

44. *Federal Reserve Bulletin*, 17 (February 1931): 58–9; *Wall Street Journal*, 18 June 1930, 17; Office Correspondence to Federal Reserve Board from Wingfield, 23 June 1930; "Senator Glass Asks Amendment to Banking Statutes," 4353–5; Hamlin Diary, v. 17, 21 November 1929, 13 December 1929. This part of the bill did not appear in later versions, probably because few reserve banks had net earnings in 1931 more than sufficient to pay dividends and add to surplus. Only two paid a franchise tax.

45. *Wall Street Journal*, 15 January 1931, 6; letter to McMullan from Glass, 16 December 1930, Box 12, Willis Papers; U.S., Congress, Senate, Committee on Banking and Currency, *Operation of the National and Federal Reserve Banking Systems: Hearings before a Subcommittee Pursuant to S.Res. 71*, 71st Congress, 3rd session, 19 January–2 March 1931.

46. Senate Committee on Banking and Currency, *Operation of National and Federal Reserve Banking Systems: Subcommittee Hearings*, 1–30.

47. Ibid., 123–63; J.M. Daiger, "Wall Street or Washington: Which Shall Rule the Federal Reserve," *World's Work*, 60 (August 1931): 52.

48. Sidney Hyman, *Marriner S. Eccles: Private Entrepreneur and Public Servant* (Stanford, Cal.: Stanford University, Graduate School of Business, 1976), 441; Daiger, "Wall Street or Washington," 52; Harold Barger, *The Management of Money: A Survey of American Experience* (Chicago: Rand McNally, 1964), 50; Senate Committee on Banking and Currency, *Operation of National and Federal Reserve Banking Systems: Subcommittee Hearings*, 163–81.

49. Senate Committee on Banking and Currency, *Operation of National and Federal Reserve Banking Systems: Subcommittee Hearings*, 31–90.

50. Ibid., 191–2, 236, 248, 258, 292–4, 300–2, 307, 338–40, 356, 404–5, 416, 421, 539–41; Lyle, Senate Career of Glass, 196. Some New York banks began to divest themselves of securities affiliates late in 1931 because of economic difficulties; Wigmore, *Crash and Its Aftermath*, 239.

51. Senate Committee on Banking and Currency, *Operation of National and Federal Reserve Banking Systems: Subcommittee Hearings*, 195–6, 207, 209–25, 243–4, 269, 315–7, 323–9, 332,

361–2, 374, 378–9, 397, 404, 421–2, 576–7, 582–3, 603–4, 618, 627; Lyle, Senate Career of Glass, 195.

52. Senate Committee on Banking and Currency, *Operation of National and Federal Reserve Banking Systems: Subcommittee Hearings*, 31–90; 123–81; "Banking Inquiry Stresses Issues Awaiting Decision," *Business Week* (11 March 1931): 6. For Glass's efforts in the 72d Congress, 1st session, see Chapter Three. For passage of the Glass bill by the Senate, see Chapter Four, and for enactment of the Glass bill (combined with deposit insurance), see Chapter Five.

53. *Congressional Record*, 72, pt. 5: 4663, pt. 7: 7339, 7383, pt. 11: 11893, 71st Congress, 2d session; U.S., Congress, Senate, Committee on Banking and Currency, *Compromise of Liability of Shareholders in Failed National Banks: Report to Accompany S. 544*, S. Rept. 65, 71st Congress, 2d session, 18 December 1929; House Committee on Banking and Currency, *Compromise of Liability of Shareholders in Failed National Banks: Report to Accompany S. 544*, H. Rept. 639, 71st Congress, 2d session, 8 February 1930; House Committee on Banking and Currency, *Waiver of Notice by State Member Banks of Withdrawal from Federal Reserve System: Report to Accompany H.R. 8877*, H. Rept. 488, 71st Congress, 2d session, 23 January 1930; Senate Committee on Banking and Currency, *Waiver of Notice by State Member Banks of Withdrawal from Federal Reserve System: Report to Accompany H.R. 8877*, S. Rept. 316, 71st Congress, 2d session, 3 April 1930; House Committee on Banking and Currency, *Cancellation of Federal Reserve Bank Stock Held by Member Banks Which Have Ceased to Function in Certain Cases: Report to Accompany H.R. 6604*, H. Rept. 487, 71st Congress, 2d session, 23 January 1930; Senate Committee on Banking and Currency, *Cancellation of Federal Reserve Bank Stock Held by Member Banks Which Have Ceased to Function in Certain Cases: Report to Accompany H.R. 6604*, S. Rept. 437, 71st Congress, 2d session, 15 April 1930; Senate Committee on Banking and Currency, *Granting the Federal Reserve Board Discretionary Authority in the Matter of Assessment of Costs of Examining Member Banks Against Banks Examined: Report to Accompany S. 485*, S. Rept. 317, 71st Congress, 2d session, 3 April 1930; House Committee on Banking and Currency, *Granting the Federal Reserve Board Discretionary Authority in the Matter of Assessment of Costs of Examining Member Banks Against*

Banks Examined: Report to Accompany S. 485, H. Rept. 1656, 71st Congress, 2d session, 26 May 1930.

54. The other four bills enacted were: (1) H.R. 9046, limiting member bank discounting of paper from a single borrower to 10% of capital and surplus; (2) S. 486, concerning the security required of national banks that received deposits of public funds; (3) S. 3627, allowing national banks to surrender voluntarily trust powers previously granted by the Federal Reserve Board; and (4) S. 4096, removing an ambiguity in the Federal Reserve Act about elections of class A and class B directors for reserve banks. See *Federal Reserve Bulletin*, 16 (May 1930): 325; Ibid., 16 (August 1930): 518.

55. "Mounting Bank Failures Stimulate Movement for Inquiry by Congress," *Commercial and Financial Chronicle*, 132 (3 January 1931): 62; "The Financial Situation," *Commercial and Financial Chronicle*, 132 (7 March 1931): 1671; Gordon Wells McKinley, The Federal Reserve System in the Period of Crisis, 1930 to 1935 (Ph.D. dissertation, Ohio State University, 1948), 84. Economic historians have debated the effects of the Banking Panic of 1930. The discussion began with Friedman and Schwartz and has included publications by Temin, Wicker, Hamilton, White, and others. The controversy has focused on the causes of the crisis and its economic effects, such as influencing the currency-deposit ratio and interest rates. Since no new bank legislation resulted from the suspensions in the winter of 1930–31, I have not attempted to do justice to arguments of these writers. For more information, see Friedman and Schwartz, *Monetary History*, 308–13; Peter Temin, *Did Monetary Forces Cause the Great Depression?* (New York: Norton, 1976), 79; Wicker, "Reconsideration of Causes of Banking Panic," 571–83; James M. Boughton and Elmus R. Wicker, "The Behavior of the Currency-Deposit Ratio during the Great Depression," *Journal of Money, Credit, and Banking*, 11 (November 1979): 405–18; Elmus Wicker, "Interest Rate and Expenditure Effects of the Banking Panic of 1930," *Explorations in Economic History*, 19 (October 1982): 435–45; Hamilton, "Causes of Banking Panic," 581–608; White, "Reinterpretation of Banking Crisis," 119–37; Bernanke, "Nonmonetary Effects of Financial Crisis," 257–75; Thomas Mayer, "Money and the Great Depression: A Critique of Professor Temin's Thesis," *Explorations in Economic History*, 15 (April 1978): 127–45; Temin, *Lessons of the Great Depression*, 50–4; Lucia, "Failure of the Bank of the United States," 408–15; Trescott,

"Bank Failures and Currency Outflow," 73–4; Wigmore, *Crash and Its Aftermath*, 125–8.

56. Martin L. Fausold and George T. Mazuzan, "Introduction," *Hoover Presidency*, Fausold and Mazuzan, eds., 11; John D. Hicks, *Republican Ascendancy, 1921–1933* (New York: Harper and Brothers, 1960), 239; Hoover, *State Papers*, I: 565; Fausold, *Presidency of Hoover*, 140; Schwarz, "Hoover and Congress," 88.

57. Federal Reserve Board, *Eighteenth Annual Report, 1931*, 2; Diaries, Henry L. Stimson Papers, XVI: 108–9, 129–31, 146–7, 154–95 (microfilm edition, reel 3), Manuscripts and Archives, Yale University Library, Yale University, New Haven, Conn.; letter to McDougal from Harrison, 9 July 1931, Box 117, Eugene Meyer Papers, Manuscript Division, Library of Congress, Washington, D.C.; Theodore G. Joslin, *Hoover Off the Record* (Garden City, N.Y.: Doubleday, Doran, 1934), 117–8; Fausold, *Presidency of Hoover*, 143–5; Friedman and Schwartz, *Monetary History*, 314–5. The closeness of Harrison's contacts with the Bank of England during this crisis is evident from outgoing and incoming cablegrams in Binder 20, Harrison Papers and from summaries of conversations with central bankers, Binder 45, Harrison Papers.

58. Memorandum: Meeting of Board of Directors June 18, 1931, Binder 50, Harrison Papers; Preliminary Memorandum on Credit Conditions for the Meeting of the Open Market Policy Conference August 11, 1931, 3 August 1931, Box 356, Hamlin Papers; Friedman and Schwartz, *Monetary History*, 314.

59. Hamlin Diary, v. 19, 10 August 1931; "Trends of the Markets in Money, Stocks, Bonds," *Business Week* (19 August 1931): 41–2; Memorandum: Meeting of Executive Committee September 1, 1931, Binder 50, Harrison Papers; Memorandum: Meeting of Board of Directors September 10, 1931, Binder 50, Harrison Papers; *Federal Reserve Bulletin*, 17 (September 1931): 495.

60. Memorandum: Meeting of Board of Directors September 10, 1931, Binder 50, Harrison Papers.

61. "Trends of the Markets in Money, Stocks, Bonds," *Business Week* (7 October 1931): 41; *Federal Reserve Bulletin*, 17 (November 1931) 603–5; G. Walter Woodworth, *The Money Market and Monetary Management*, 2d ed. (New York: Harper and Row, 1972), 394; Friedman and Schwartz, *Monetary History*, 315–6.

62. Federal Reserve Board, *Eighteenth Annual Report, 1931*, 7; Hamlin Diary, v. 19, 1 October 1931, 8–9 October 1931, 14–16 October 1931; Preliminary Memorandum for the Open Market Policy Conference November 30, 1931, 27 November 1931, Box 357, Hamlin Papers; Elmer Wood, *Monetary Control* (Columbia: University of Missouri, 1963), 109; Wheelock, *Monetary Policy*, 41; Memorandum: Meeting of Board of Directors October 8, 1931, Binder 50, Harrison Papers; outgoing cablegram to Moret from Harrison, 25 September 1931, Binder 29, Harrison Papers; outgoing cablegram to Norman from Harrison, 2 October 1931, Binder 20, Harrison Papers.

63. *Federal Reserve Bulletin*, 17 (December 1931): 658; Office Correspondence to Meyer from Joy, 7 October 1931, Box 119, Meyer Papers; Friedman and Schwartz, *Monetary History*, 317–9; memorandum, Banking Situation in the Second District, 8 December 1931, Binder 53, Harrison Papers; Federal Reserve Board, *Eighteenth Annual Report, 1931*, 2–5. Reserve officials realized by October 26 that their policies had had a negative effect on the domestic economy. See Preliminary Memorandum on Credit Conditions for the Meeting of the Executive Committee of the Open Market Policy Conference October 26, 1931, Hamlin Papers, Box 356. For events in 1932, see Chapter Three. Some modern scholars have criticized the system's response to the gold drain, believing that reserve authorities should not have placed such importance on defending the gold standard. See for example, Woodworth, *Money Market*, 394. Such criticisms ignore the system's previous actions to protect the gold standard in Europe. Reserve officials may have been mistaken to concentrate on gold, but such a preoccupation was nothing new. See Wicker, "Federal Reserve," 325–43; Wigmore, *Crash and Its Aftermath*, 218–29.

64. Office Correspondence to Meyer from Joy, 17 November 1931, Box 119, Meyer Papers; Stimson Diaries, XVIII: 9 (microfilm reel 3); letter to Meyer from Hoover, 8 September 1931, Box 152, Presidential Subject File, Herbert Clark Hoover Papers, Herbert Hoover Presidential Library, West Branch, Iowa; letter to Hoover from Meyer, 9 September 1931, Box 152, Presidential Subject File, Hoover Papers; James Stuart Olson, *Herbert Hoover and the Reconstruction Finance Corporation, 1931–1933* (Ames: Iowa State University, 1977), 24–5.

65. Letter to Harrison from Hoover, 5 October 1931, Box 155, Presidential Subject File, Hoover Papers; Copy of Prepared Statement Read to Meeting of Nineteen New York Bankers Held at Secretary Mellon's Apartment, Sunday, October 4, 1931, Box 155, Presidential Subject File, Hoover Papers; Schwarz, *Interregnum of Despair*, 88–9; Romasco, *Poverty of Abundance*, 87–9; James S. Olson, "The End of Voluntarism: Herbert Hoover and the National Credit Corporation," *Annals of Iowa*, 41 (1972): 1108–9.

66. Olson, *Hoover and RFC*, 26–7; Hoover, *State Papers*, II: 4–7; Romasco, *Poverty of Abundance*, 89.

67. Romasco, *Poverty of Abundance*, 92–5; Olson, *Hoover and RFC*, 27–32; Chandler, *America's Greatest Depression*, 88.

CHAPTER THREE

BANKING REFORM IN 1932

When the 72d Congress assembled in December 1931, the country faced grave economic difficulties. President Herbert Hoover had tried to stabilize conditions by persuading bankers to form the National Credit Corporation, which pooled funds to lend to weaker banks. NCC directors proved reluctant to disburse much money, and by December 22 only $15 million had reached banks. Hoover realized that further aid was essential to prevent collapse of the banking system. As he had promised New York bankers in October, his annual message to Congress recommended broadening the definition of paper eligible for discount at reserve banks and establishing a government finance corporation to lend to banks and railroads. He also proposed that Congress investigate the desirability of expanding branch banking, increasing membership in the Federal Reserve System, and separating commercial, savings, and investment banking.[1]

Congress had few ideas for resolving the crisis. As Hoover requested, it passed the Reconstruction Finance Corporation Act on January 22 and in February approved the first Glass–Steagall Act, which broadened the definition of paper eligible for discount at reserve banks. No further legislation affecting the system passed until near the end of the session, when a provision in the Emergency Relief and Construction Act (July 16) authorized district banks to lend directly to individuals and corporations. A rider to the Home Loan Bank Act, which also passed on July 16, permitted issue of additional national banks notes. These four emergency measures were insufficient to halt bank failures but may have prevented a general collapse in 1932.[2] Congress also considered insurance of bank deposits and reform of the National Bank and Federal Reserve Acts. Such measures, which faced opposition from bankers, some members of Congress, the Hoover administration, and reserve officials, were not to become law until 1933.

The nation's attention turned to the presidential election during the autumn of 1932. Although Republican and Democratic platforms included banking planks, banking reform had no bearing on the outcome. Probably any Democrat could have defeated Hoover, and Franklin D. Roosevelt appeared flexible and moderately progressive.

Nineteen thirty-two was a year of transition. Unlike 1930–31, when no bank legislation of consequence passed, Congress enacted four emergency measures in 1932, which members hoped would combat depression. At the same time, the two most important bills, deposit insurance and reform of the banking system, did not achieve widespread political support in that year. When they did pass, in June 1933, many provisions remained from earlier versions.

EMERGENCY LEGISLATION IN 1932

The first emergency measure to pass Congress in 1932 was the Reconstruction Finance Corporation Act, which helped many banks and businesses during the Great Depression. Hoover had recommended in October 1931 the establishment of an institution similar to the War Finance Corporation of World War I. He then consulted Eugene Meyer, governor of the Federal Reserve Board, who drafted a bill with help from the board's staff. This proposal would establish a temporary agency, the RFC, which would lend to financial institutions and railroads and have the reserve board governor as one director.[3]

Because the measure had support from Hoover, Meyer, and Treasury officials, and because economic conditions were so bad, it moved rapidly through Congress. Senator Frederic Walcott (R–CONN) introduced the RFC bill (S. 1) on December 9, 1931, and the Banking and Currency Committee reported it favorably on January 6, 1932, after closed hearings. It passed five days later. Henry Steagall (D–ALA), chairman of the Banking and Currency Committee, introduced a similar bill in the House (H.R. 7360) on January 9, and it passed on January 15. The two bills differed in an important paragraph because of efforts by Senator Carter Glass (D–VA). The House would allow reserve banks to purchase or discount RFC notes and debentures and to make advances on member bank promissory notes secured by such notes or debentures, which would simultaneously broaden eligibility and tie RFC operations to the reserve system. Glass, the Senate's expert on financial and banking legislation, feared this clause would cause the system to acquire frozen assets, so Walcott's bill emerged from committee and passed without it. The conference committee accepted the Senate position, and the bill passed both houses on January 22. Hoover signed it three days later.[4]

As a result of Glass's effort, RFC operations related only indirectly to the reserve system. Meyer provided a link between the two agencies because he sat on both the reserve board and the RFC's board of directors, until Congress amended the law in July 1932. RFC loans to individual member banks, usually arranged without aid from reserve personnel, provided another link between the two. The agency helped thousands of banks and trust companies in the next months, although not all were member banks.[5] However, the liquidity of the banking system and the economy as a whole would have been better served if Glass had not insisted on severing RFC operations from the reserve banks. The RFC could raise money through the bond market, but it could not raise enough to act as the nation's lender of last resort in a true panic. If the House version of the act had passed, the reserve system would have felt a greater obligation to prevent bank failures, and the Banking Panic of 1933 might never have occurred.

The Glass–Steagall Act of 1932 concerned the reserve system intimately. Two needs led to its passage: to broaden the definition of paper eligible for discount at district banks, allowing members greater access to reserve facilities; and to alter the collateral requirement for reserve notes, permitting the use of government securities. Bankers had requested the first in October because a few banks needed emergency loans but had no eligible paper or government securities to pledge as collateral. Reserve officials suggested the second in an attempt to free gold from use as collateral for reserve notes.[6]

Two bills, introduced by Senator Arthur H. Vandenberg (R–MICH) on December 9, 1931, sought to deal with these problems. The measure to broaden eligibility (S. 546) ran into opposition from Glass and other senators who believed that member banks had sufficient eligible paper and that widening eligibility would flood the system with poor securities. Many reserve officials favored redefining eligibility, but a few shared Glass's fear.[7] Table 3A indicates total eligible paper of member banks and division of those assets between city and country banks. While most reserve city banks had sufficient assets for discounting, country banks were less well supplied. Vandenberg's other

TABLE 3A
ELIGIBLE ASSETS OF MEMBER BANKS, 1930–32

Date	Holdings of U.S. Securities* and Eligible Paper (In millions of dollars)					
	By reserve city banks			By country banks		
	Securities	Eligible Paper	Total	Securities	Eligible Paper	Total
<u>1930</u>						
Mar.	2,619	2,542	5,161	818	1,662	2,480
June	2,640	2,285	4,925	772	1,620	2,392
Sep.	2,682	2,271	4,953	764	1,541	2,305
Dec.	2,777	2,100	4,877	708	1,438	2,146
<u>1931</u>						
Mar.	3,584	2,045	5,629	776	1,373	2,149
June	3,871	1,870	5,741	836	1,328	2,164
Sep.	3,942	1,787	5,729	994	1,209	2,203
Dec.	3,706	1,505	5,211	989	1,068	2,056
<u>1932</u>						
June	3,985	1,457	5,442	994	971	1,965
Sep.	4,623	1,508	6,131	1,003	916	1,919
Dec.	4,776	1,403	6,179	987	844	1,831

* Exclusive of government securities issued against national bank note circulation.

Source: *Federal Reserve Bulletin*, 19 (March 1933): 144.

bill (S. 547) would make government securities eligible as collateral for reserve notes, as Hoover, Meyer, and Ogden Mills, now secretary of the Treasury, all wished. At the time, reserve notes' collateral had to be two-fifths gold and the rest either gold or eligible paper. In the autumn and winter of 1931–32, member banks discounted less commercial paper, so reserve bank holdings of paper declined; as more gold was tied up as collateral, less was free for export (Table 3B). Gold collateral behind each note had risen to more than 70% by February 1932. Because of his belief in real bills theory, Glass thought note issues should be connected to eligible commercial paper, not government securities, and he opposed Vandenberg's proposal.[8]

TABLE 3B
FREE GOLD OF FEDERAL RESERVE BANKS, 1931–32
(In millions of dollars)

Reserve Bank District	31 October 1931	15 February 1932
Boston	21	9
New York	437	266
Philadelphia	34	31
Cleveland	27	33
Richmond	12	12
Atlanta	10	7
Chicago	44	30
St. Louis	15	11
Minneapolis	10	2
Kansas City	21	16
Dallas	11	4
San Francisco	21	22
Total	663	444

Source: Lester V. Chandler, *American Monetary Policy, 1928–1941* (New York: Harper and Row, 1971), 187.

Reserve officials who supported the second Vandenberg bill believed the small amount of free gold available was preventing system purchases of government securities, which might counter declines in economic indicators. As early as mid-1931, reserve bank governors had worried that continued system purchases of government securities would impair their free gold positions. While they may have used this as an excuse to avoid open market operations, by February 15 free gold at the Minneapolis bank had declined to $2 million and at the Dallas bank to $4 million.[9] Foreign money on deposit in the United States or invested in short-term Treasury bills in early February was over $1 billion, while total free gold had declined to between $400 and $500 million. A change in collateral requirements for reserve notes would free $900 million for other uses. Meyer and the governor of the New York Federal Reserve Bank, George L. Harrison, expected to export gold to France in the next months. At the same time, they did not want such exports and the credit contraction that would accompany them to damage the domestic economy, as had happened the previous autumn. They wanted to counter exports and domestic hoarding by large purchases of government securities, which was not feasible unless the securities could be used as collateral for reserve notes.[10]

Hoover supported Vandenberg, but Glass effectively prevented action on either bill. The president decided to appeal directly to Glass, asking him on January 27 to introduce a measure that would take one or two provisions from his reform bill and include a section concerning collateral for reserve notes. Glass was reluctant, and his opposition continued into February. Harrison, Meyer, and Mills saw Hoover on February 9 to ask him to press Glass again. Hoover later claimed that Mills told him the nation was within two weeks of leaving the gold standard, which both regarded as the cornerstone of a sound economy.[11]

Hoover may have misunderstood exactly what Mills said, mistaking possibilities for probabilities. Mills had been confident in January that the nation would not leave gold but months later issued a statement explaining that continued drains on the nation's gold stock at the level of the previous autumn, "would have set in motion forces of destruction so great that they might overwhelm any country."[12] No matter what the president believed, reserve officials knew that the gold dollar was safe. As E.A. Goldenweiser, a member of the board's staff, said, "there was no danger of our going off the gold standard, unless the Federal Reserve authorities and the Treasury had violated the law and had failed to use the resources at their command."[13] The system could have conserved gold by reducing the number of notes in district vaults, substituting reserve notes for gold certificates in circulation, and purchasing acceptances that could be used as collateral for reserve notes, or it could have countered hoarding and gold exports by selling government securities and raising discount rates. Only if the system wished to expand bank credit while simultaneously paying out currency to hoarders and gold to foreigners, as it did, was there danger.[14]

Hoover presided over a breakfast meeting on February 10 to discuss the situation with key senators, and Glass agreed to sponsor a measure that would broaden eligibility of paper and alter collateral requirements for reserve notes.[15] The president apparently had to plead, for he remarked in private, "You have no idea how I had to demean myself before those Democratic swine before they consented to agree."[16] Apparently, he never told Glass the nation could be off gold in less than two weeks, but the senator recognized that the gold problem was "grave" and that French withdrawals "might stimulate a raid on the free gold of the Federal Reserve System which might not stop short of disaster."[17] To prevent any danger to the free gold supply, he agreed to a temporary change in collateral requirements.

The bill (S. 3616) that Glass introduced on February 11 had three parts. The first, originally in the Glass banking reform bill, added section 10(a) to the reserve act, which would allow a district bank to make an advance to a group of five or more member banks on any acceptable collateral if six members of the reserve board approved. The interest rate for such an advance had to be one percentage point higher than the discount rate. The second part, which the Senate banking committee had originally intended to place in the Glass bill, added section 10(b), which would allow district banks to discount any good asset of banks lacking eligible assets. Each discount would have to have approval of six members of the reserve board and carry an interest rate a percentage point higher than the normal discount rate. This section would expire one year after enactment. The last part of the bill amended section 16 of the reserve act to authorize use of United States government securities as collateral for note issues for one year. As a reluctant supporter, Glass restricted the bill as much as possible, limiting 10(a) to banks that had no eligible or acceptable assets and 10(b) to banks having capital of $500,000 or less.[18] The committee report declared the bill "so carefully safeguarded, the committee thinks, as to make it improbable that there can be any unwholesome inflation of the currency."[19]

After persuading Glass to act, the president conferred with House leaders, especially Steagall, whom he wanted to sponsor the bill in the House. The Alabaman was happy to agree because he believed purchasing government securities and widening eligibility would increase currency in circulation and aid recovery. Indeed, he was more willing to promote monetary expansion than either the administration or Glass, and he introduced the measure (H.R. 9203) on February 11. Mills, Meyer, and Charles G. Dawes of the RFC appeared before his committee for a short hearing the next day. Mills declared that the United States could meet all demands for gold, and Steagall told his committee the bill had nothing to do with the foreign situation. The measure reported by his committee was identical to the Senate bill, except it would limit the operation of sections 10(a) and 10(b) to one year and require consent from a majority of the reserve board. Opposition came from two groups—inflationists, who believed the bill did too little to generate purchasing power for consumers, and congressmen, some of whom disliked hasty action. Louis McFadden (R–PA), senior minority member of the Banking and Currency Committee, not only deplored the haste but also complained about changing eligibility and increasing the board's power over discounting. Nonetheless, the House passed the measure on February 15 by 350 to 15, with a few members who had voiced complaints voting in its favor because of the economic situation.[20]

Although Republicans hoped the Senate would adopt the House version, Glass insisted on his bill. As he explained to the Senate, changing eligibility requirements would have a psychological effect and altering collateral requirements for reserve notes would allow gold withdrawals without causing domestic contraction. After protests by the administration and bankers, he agreed to an amendment that changed maximum capital for banks using section 10(b) from $500,000 to $2 million, so more banks could be included. A debate arose concerning the one-year limitation placed on two portions of the measure. John Blaine (R–WIS) believed the whole bill should be limited to one year, with permanent changes made later. Glass wanted 10(a) to be permanent but thought of the other parts as emergency powers that should expire in one year. Elmer Thomas (D–OKLA) argued that the whole bill should be permanent, since no one knew when the emergency would end. Failing that, he suggested it expire in two years. The Senate approved a Thomas amendment to extend the last sections to March 3, 1934. The bill then passed the Senate on February 19 without a recorded vote.[21]

The conference committee worked swiftly. The committee's compromise dropped the time limit on 10(a) in the House bill, making it permanent, and set the expiration date on the other parts for March

3, 1933, as Glass desired. Conferees agreed to allow groups of fewer than five banks to borrow under 10(a) if they had deposits equaling 10% of total deposits in the group's reserve district. The committee decided to require approval of five members of the reserve board for use of 10(a) and (b), and they set the capital required in 10(b) at $5 million. Congress passed the measure without recorded votes the day conferees reported. Although the bill limited eligibility more than Hoover had originally hoped, he signed it on February 27.[22]

Glass had been a reluctant supporter of the act because it made important dents in the real bills theory of reserve operations. Eligibility and collateral requirements in the Federal Reserve Act had reflected a belief that note issues and reserve credit should increase as commercial paper expanded and decrease as commercial paper declined. Section 10(b) represented a step away from real bills doctrine because it allowed member bank advances on sound assets, although such loans remained carefully restricted. The change in reserve note collateral requirements freed the size of note issues from the amount of eligible paper held by reserve banks. Because the last two parts of the Glass–Steagall Act were to expire on March 3, 1933, many observers assumed deviation from real bills would be temporary. Congress later extended the sections, and eventually both became permanent. This act was a harbinger of other changes, as the process of detaching the reserve act from real bills continued in the next few years.[23]

In New York, Harrison had waited anxiously until the Glass–Steagall Act passed because economic indicators continued to decline. More than 400 bank suspensions occurred during January and February 1932 (Table 3C), member bank loans and investments fell (Table 3D), and reserve bank credit outstanding declined (Table 3E). More than $1 billion in gold left the country, hoarding remained at high levels (Table 3F), and commodity prices dropped. The bond market firmed in February, but the stock market was dull. Only open market rates in New York City did not reflect strain.[24]

Harrison wanted to purchase government securities immediately, countering expected gold exports. Not all reserve bank governors agreed, but a majority voted on February 24 to authorize $250 million for purchase of government securities at the rate of $25 million per week. Along with loans granted by the RFC, this mild expansionary program had some positive effects in March and April. Reserve bank credit outstanding decreased as money returned from hoarding and members repaid district banks. Reserve balances of member banks rose

TABLE 3C
BANK SUSPENSIONS, 1931–32

Month	All Banks	Member Banks			Non-Member Banks
		Total	National	State	
1931					
Jan.	198	25	20	5	173
Feb.	77	20	15	5	57
Mar.	86	19	18	1	67
Apr.	64	20	17	3	44
May	91	26	24	2	65
June	167	36	26	10	131
July	93	18	16	2	75
Aug.	158	41	29	12	117
Sep.	305	62	46	16	243
Oct.	522	125	100	25	397
Nov.	175	43	35	8	132
Dec.	358	81	63	18	277
1932					
Jan.	342	87	74	13	255
Feb.	121	30	24	6	91
Mar.	46	7	7	0	39
Apr.	74	11	6	5	63
May	82	20	14	6	62
June	151	48	44	4	103
July	132	24	20	4	108
Aug.	85	19	17	2	66
Sep.	67	16	12	4	51
Oct.	102	20	20	0	82
Nov.	93	25	19	6	68
Dec.	161	24	19	5	137

Source: Federal Reserve Board, *Nineteenth Annual Report, 1932*, 154.

for the first time since the summer of 1931, and bank failures slowed further. Still, member banks' total loans and investments dwindled, and general conditions remained depressed.[25]

TABLE 3D
MEMBER BANKS
CLASSIFICATION OF LOANS AND INVESTMENTS, 1930–32
(In millions of dollars)

Date	Total Loans & Invest-ments	LOANS			Investments	
		Banks	Cus-tomers	Other	U.S. Secur-ities	Other
1930						
Mar.	35,056	527	21,494	3,097	4,085	5,852
June	35,656	535	21,565	3,113	4,061	6,380
Sep.	35,472	466	21,010	3,262	4,095	6,639
Dec.	34,860	631	21,007	2,233	4,125	6,864
1931						
Mar.	34,729	446	19,940	2,454	5,002	6,886
June	33,923	457	19,257	2,103	5,343	6,763
Sep.	33,073	599	18,713	1,563	5,564	6,635
Dec.	30,575	790	17,570	901	5,319	5,996
1932						
June	28,001	573	15,267	747	5,628	5,786
Sep.	28,045	457	14,497	970	6,366	5,755
Dec.	27,469	444	13,905	855	6,540	5,726

Source: *Federal Reserve Bulletin*, 19 (March 1933): 140.

The OMPC began bolder efforts the second week of April, buying $100 million of government securities per week for a month. In early May, when gold formed 90% of collateral for reserve notes, the system began using the last section of the Glass–Steagall Act, substituting government securities as collateral. Heavier purchases forestalled criticism by inflationists, as reserve officials had hoped. To meet complaints of real bills theorists that the OMPC was flooding banks with reserves they could not use, the New York reserve bank formed a Banking and Industrial Committee to seek out loans its member banks

TABLE 3E
RESERVE BANK CREDIT OUTSTANDING, JULY 1931–1932
(In millions of dollars)

Date	Bills Dis-counted	Bills Bought	U.S. Govern-ment Secur-ities	Other	Total
1931					
July	169	79	674	32	954
Aug.	222	135	712	38	1,107
Sep.	280	259	736	38	1,313
Oct.	613	692	733	50	2,088
Nov.	695	560	727	53	2,035
Dec.	775	340	777	59	1,951
1932					
Jan.	828	221	759	57	1,865
Feb.	848	151	743	43	1,785
Mar.	714	105	809	24	1,652
Apr.	605	52	1,014	23	1,694
May	486	41	1,413	20	1,960
June	495	50	1,697	20	2,262
July	523	60	1,818	21	2,422
Aug.	451	37	1,850	15	2,353
Sep.	387	34	1,848	13	2,282
Oct.	328	34	1,851	18	2,231
Nov.	313	34	1,851	13	2,211
Dec.	282	34	1,854	22	2,192

Source: *Federal Reserve Bulletin*, 19 (January 1933): 11.

could make to businessmen. The committee's initial success led Hoover to urge other district banks to form similar committees.[26]

The economy responded positively to OMPC purchases, but country banks used the money thus generated to satisfy demands for liquidity rather than employing it in loans and investments. Reserve

TABLE 3F
CURRENCY HELD BY PUBLIC AND DEPOSITS, SEASONALLY ADJUSTED, 1931–32
(In millions of dollars)

Date	Currency Held by Public	Deposits Adjusted				
		Commercial Banks			Mutual Savings Banks	Postal Savings System
		Demand	Time	Total		
1931						
May	3,897	19,993	19,026	39,019	9,816	324
June	3,995	19,888	18,715	38,603	9,864	346
July	4,058	19,744	18,508	38,252	9,900	371
Aug.	4,177	19,252	18,145	37,397	9,944	422
Sep.	4,289	19,080	17,564	36,644	9,984	469
Oct.	4,537	18,173	16,645	34,818	10,009	537
Nov.	4,503	17,852	16,099	33,951	10,020	564
Dec.	4,604	17,290	15,445	32,735	9,970	604
1932						
Jan.	4,896	16,611	15,059	31,670	9,897	665
Feb.	4,824	16,486	14,803	31,289	9,905	691
Mar.	4,743	16,367	14,652	31,019	9,942	705
Apr.	4,751	16,131	14,543	30,674	9,924	721
May	4,746	15,785	14,360	30,145	9,894	741
June	4,959	15,490	14,031	29,521	9,890	783
July	5,048	15,104	13,979	29,083	9,874	828
Aug.	4,988	15,201	13,853	29,054	9,854	847
Sep.	4,941	15,270	13,746	29,016	9,863	857
Oct.	4,863	15,393	13,844	29,237	9,860	870
Nov.	4,842	15,713	13,756	29,469	9,876	883
Dec.	4,830	15,511	13,690	29,201	9,901	900

Source: Milton Friedman and Anna Jacobson Schwartz, *A Monetary History of the United States, 1867–1960* (Princeton, N.J.: Princeton University, 1963), 713.

bank credit outstanding rose in late April and early May, as did members' excess reserves. In spite of gold exports, currency continued to return from hoarding, and money rates in New York City dropped further. Bank suspensions remained moderate, in part because of RFC lending. Stock prices drifted lower, as did commodity prices.[27]

The OMPC's executive committee reduced its purchases in mid-May and again in June. Several OMPC members did not understand why banks were accumulating excess reserves. They assumed that members could not use the money profitably and that further purchases of government securities would not aid banks or stimulate recovery. James McDougal, Chicago's governor, was a hesitant supporter of purchases in February, and he later joined Roy A. Young, Boston's governor, in opposition. Their resistance may have related to portfolios of members in their districts, which had sacrificed earnings for liquidity by calling loans and expanding holdings of government securities, at a time when the rate of return on such securities was declining. Because members still had to pay dividends and interest on deposits, lower earnings caused a problem. McDougal and Young may have hoped that earnings on government securities would improve if OMPC purchases ended. Other governors worried about their banks' gold reserve ratios, which declined when they participated in purchases.[28] As a result of the OMPC's decision to slow purchases, hoarding and gold exports absorbed essentially all reserve credit injected in June. Member bank loans and investments dropped steeply that month, as did their excess reserves. Stock and bond markets were steady, but commodity prices continued to fall.[29]

A banking crisis then developed in Chicago in late June. It began with failures of suburban banks and spread to larger ones, as depositors caused a classic series of runs. Even though it had previously opposed OMPC purchase of government securities, the Chicago reserve bank sharply expanded purchases for its own account during the crisis, trying to aid members in distress. Dawes resigned from the RFC to assume control of Central Republic Bank and Trust Company of Chicago. He wanted to avoid a run on his bank because he believed a receiver could liquidate Central Republic's assets and pay depositors and creditors in full. After the bank underwent large withdrawals on June 23–24, he decided not to reopen the following Monday, June 27. When he warned other Chicago bankers that his bank would close, they begged him to reconsider, for they feared it might cause every bank in the city to suspend. When he refused, someone called Hoover, who consulted

Meyer, Mills, Harrison, and W. Randolph Burgess, a staff member at the New York reserve bank. Hoover decided Central Republic could not close because a general failure of Chicago banks might generate panic, perhaps even national collapse. Jesse Jones and Wilson McCarthy, RFC directors who were in Chicago for the Democratic convention, joined local RFC employees and made a rough appraisal of the bank's assets, deciding they could authorize lending up to $90 million. Dawes was reluctant to accept the loan, but eventually Jones and others persuaded him, and Central Republic opened on schedule. The loan ended runs in Chicago, after forty institutions had closed, and Dawes eventually repaid the RFC.[30]

So many OMPC members resisted continuation of an expansionary policy by mid-July that Harrison was willing to accept purchase of just enough securities to replace those reaching maturity. New York officials had tired of buying for system account without full participation by other reserve banks.[31] They might have abandoned purchases earlier, had they not feared Congress would pass inflationary bills. When Congress adjourned in July, another expansionary influence disappeared. Fortunately, gold imports began, which increased member bank reserves. Commodity prices finally rose a bit, and long-term capital interest rates fell. Even stock and bond markets showed improvement. Still, banking statistics reflected depressed conditions: member banks' loans and investments declined, 280 banks suspended in June and July, and banks continued to emphasize liquidity.[32]

The reserve's purchase of government securities between February and August could not have occurred without the Glass–Steagall Act because the system's free gold situation would have prevented it. Although one might criticize the system for not acting more decisively in March, remember that several OMPC members had supported the policy only reluctantly and Young had opposed it. Given the internal division of opinion, purchase of more than $1 billion of government securities between February 27 and July 20 was a notable achievement for Meyer and Harrison. The operation offset an increase in hoarded currency and $400 million in gold exports, while simultaneously lowering open market rates and allowing member banks to liquidate over $200 million of indebtedness to reserve banks.[33]

Throughout the congressional session, reserve officials had feared passage of proposals to inflate prices, increase currency in circulation, or raise purchasing power. They worried especially about the Goldsborough (H.R. 11499) and Fletcher (S. 4429) bills, which called for the system to reflate the commodity price index to a 1920s level and stabilize it there.[34] Congress adjourned without enacting stabilization, but pressure for inflation did lead to expansion of national bank notes in circulation and authorization for reserve banks to lend directly to individuals, partnerships, and corporations.

Yale economist Irving Fisher led stabilizationists. He believed both inflation and deflation would be avoided if prices remained stable. He knew the gold standard could not promise price stability and proposed to replace gold with a standard based on average prices of a wholesale commodity index. Conservatives disputed the practicality of Fisher's commodity dollar, but the idea appealed to many people in 1932. Fisher became a member of the Committee for the Nation, which sent material regularly to members of Congress. Farm groups and their representatives in government joined Fisher in supporting immediate reflation and stabilization, calling this an "honest dollar" or "honest money."[35]

Hoover was convinced that a sound economy required a gold standard, and congressional stabilization proposals assumed an adjustable gold value for the dollar. Such bills would order the reserve system to attempt reflation of prices to a level that varied from bill to bill and then stabilization at that level. H.R. 10517, discussed during House hearings, would give the reserve board a new legal mandate, provide it with authority to issue debentures if supplies of government securities became too small to reach or maintain stabilization, and allow it to raise or lower the official price of gold.[36]

Reserve officials adamantly opposed any stabilization bill. As Meyer told Representative T. Alan Goldsborough (D-MD), "The relationship between the operations of the Federal reserve system and the price level is indirect and dependent on a large number of developments that are beyond the control of the Federal reserve system."[37] During hearings on Goldsborough's bill before the House Banking and Currency Committee in March and April 1932, 24 witnesses appeared, but the only ones opposed were Meyer, Harrison, and Goldenweiser, who argued that the system could not control the economy sufficiently well to stabilize price levels. Harrison questioned using a commodity index, reminding the committee that commodity prices had declined slightly in 1928 and 1929. Most of the witnesses presented the viewpoint of farmers, emphasizing that no recovery could occur without revival of rural purchasing power.[38]

After the hearings Goldsborough introduced a new bill (H.R. 11499) that received committee endorsement and moved through the House quickly. This measure would add section 31 to the reserve act, investing the system and the secretary of the Treasury with responsibility for restoring and maintaining an average purchasing power of the dollar at a level to be determined from wholesale commodity prices for the years 1921–29.[39] In the House debate on May 2, Steagall led those in favor, declaring that H.R. 11499 was not "radical."[40] Opponents blasted the bill as inflationary, declared stabilization impossible, and emphasized the reluctance of Mills and reserve officials to be responsible for it. These arguments failed to convince a majority, and the Goldsborough bill passed by 289 to 60 on May 2.[41]

The Senate Banking and Currency Committee held hearings on the Goldsborough and Fletcher measures in May. The bill (S. 4429) introduced by Senator Duncan U. Fletcher (D–FLA) differed from the House measure by specifying a 1926 price level and allowing district banks to pay out reserve notes at par in exchange for government securities. Three-quarters of those testifying at the hearings believed that reflation and stabilization of prices based on some index would be the best way to end depression. Farm representatives who had appeared at House hearings repeated their testimony. Meyer and Adolph C. Miller, a member of the reserve board, opposed the bills. The Senate committee never approved a stabilization bill because of opposition from Hoover, Mills, reserve officials, and Glass. Only Blaine and Fletcher spoke in favor of stabilization in committee.[42]

Glass did not think the reserve system had a right to generate inflation or deflation and persuaded his colleagues that, if inflation of currency and credit were necessary, they should support a bill that would diffuse funds throughout the nation. He prepared a substitute for the Goldsborough measure that would allow issue of more national bank notes by increasing for five years the number of United States government bonds that could serve as collateral. According to law, national banks that deposited designated government bonds with the treasurer of the United States received bank notes equal to par value of the bonds, although a 5% redemption fund had to remain with the Treasury. In 1931, banks could use only three issues of government bonds for this purpose, all of which paid 2% interest and could be redeemed by the Treasury at any time. Glass had opposed issuance of currency other than reserve notes but preferred to increase circulation of bank notes to accepting a stabilization bill.[43]

William E. Borah (R–IDA), a believer in "honest money," determined to move the Glass bank note measure through Congress before it adjourned. He offered the proposal as an amendment to the Home Loan Bank Bill (H.R. 12280), and the rider passed by 53 to 18, after the Senate amended it to permit use only of government bonds paying 3 and 3/8% interest or less for three years. The Senate passed the whole bill on July 12.[44]

Because Congress would adjourn within days, the conference committee worked swiftly. It resolved differences about the Home Loan Banks easily but was unable to concur on the Glass–Borah rider because House conferees preferred the Goldsborough measure. When Steagall placed the report before the House, he moved that the Glass–Borah rider be further amended by adding the text of the Goldsborough bill. The House narrowly defeated Steagall's motion, killing the Goldsborough bill for 1932. After conversation with Senate conferees, Steagall asked for a vote on the Glass–Borah rider, which the House defeated soundly, probably because Hoover had threatened to veto the Home Loan Bank Bill unless the amendment were eliminated.[45] On July 16, with adjournment hours away, the Senate again refused to accept the bill without the rider. Hoover changed his mind and sent word that he would rather accept the rider than kill the measure. The bill passed both houses, and Congress adjourned. Hoover signed it on July 22, after the comptroller of the currency assured him the provision would make little difference.[46] Theoretically, the Glass–Borah amendment permitted an increase of $917 million in national bank note circulation. Actually, currency in circulation declined in the second half of 1932. National bank notes in circulation rose by $120 million between July 1 and January 1, 1933, replacing other forms of currency as reserve officials had expected.[47]

The Emergency Relief and Construction Act, which allowed reserve banks to lend to individuals, partnerships, and corporations, also passed Congress on the last day of the session. Hoover had asked for an expansion of the RFC's lending powers and recommended an omnibus plan of emergency relief and construction in early June. John N. Garner (D–TEX), speaker of the House, promoted a bill (H.R. 12445) that passed quickly because House members wanted to enact relief before the November elections. The Senate approved a relief bill (S. 4755) introduced by Robert F. Wagner (D–NY). In conference

Garner refused to compromise on a section that would allow the RFC to make unlimited and unsecured loans directly to individuals and businesses. Because this clause would inject government into private business, Hoover issued a veto on July 11.[48]

Immediately after the veto, the Senate took up another relief bill (H.R. 9642) that the House had approved, amending it to include a proposal submitted by Glass that would substitute reserve banks for the RFC in the section permitting direct loans to individuals or businesses. Reserve board member Charles S. Hamlin had suggested this to Glass, who became convinced the system should have the power on a permanent basis. He and reserve officials recognized that the clause might help economic recovery by allowing worthy borrowers to obtain funds, and Garner finally agreed to the change.[49]

While this relief bill was in conference, the committee inserted a few new clauses, one of which almost caused another veto. At Hoover's request, the committee eliminated the governor of the reserve board as a director of the RFC, for Meyer had become exhausted trying to do both jobs. Unfortunately, Garner inserted paragraphs calling for publication of RFC loans and prohibiting loans to institutions whose officers or directors had been connected with the agency in the previous year, a response to the Dawes loan. Initially, the Senate had balked at the provision for publicizing RFC loans. But after the House refused to yield, the Senate accepted the conference report and passed the relief bill on July 16. Hoover was concerned about the publicity feature until Joseph T. Robinson (D–ARK), Senate minority leader, assured everyone that no publicity would occur while Congress was not in session. The president signed the bill on July 21, in spite of lingering uncertainty about the publication clause.[50]

Authority to lend to individuals, partnerships, and corporations conflicted with the idea of the Federal Reserve System as a bankers' bank and put reserve banks into potential competition with members. Still, district banks could make such discounts only under unusual and exigent circumstances. Borrowers had to demonstrate that they could not secure credit from local banks. Reserve banks could discount only normally eligible paper. At least five board members had to approve such discounts, and Congress gave them the right to establish restrictions. Reserve officials decided not to lend to nonmember banks, which had access to the RFC, and announced that district banks would help worthy borrowers get accommodation from commercial banks. It issued in late July an authorization for reserve banks to make direct loans for six months, but they actually made such loans only when no commercial bank could be found. By January 1, 1933, reserve banks had disbursed less than $860,000 to individuals, partnerships, and corporations but had arranged many more loans between commercial banks and businesses.[51]

INSURANCE OF BANK DEPOSITS

Insurance of bank deposits became an issue during 1931–32, but both Hoover and Congress hesitated to adopt it. The collapse of several state deposit guaranty plans before 1930 explained their stance. The Hoover administration and most eastern bankers regarded failure of such plans as proof that they were unsound. They argued that insurance promoted bad banking by forcing well-managed banks to pay depositors of poorly run ones. Supporters of a federal guaranty replied that state plans had exhibited flaws a federal system could avoid. Programs in western states had covered many banks with poorly diversified assets, and when agricultural distress mounted, large numbers had failed. In a federal system, diversification was more certain. Moreover, state plans had not included adequate supervision of participating banks. With better regulation, bad management could be minimized and would not endanger better-run banks.[52]

Although both believed deposit guaranty plans were unsound, Hoover and Glass wanted to help depositors in closed banks by speeding liquidation. Glass included provisions for a liquidating corporation in his reform bill (S. 3215). His corporation would accelerate liquidation but would pay out only what a bank's assets would bring, often less than 100%. He did his utmost to oppose deposit insurance bills in the banking committee and prevented Senate action during 1932.[53]

Steagall, a long-time supporter of deposit insurance, introduced his bill (H.R. 10241) on March 7, 1932. It would establish a Federal Bank Liquidating Board to pay depositors of a failed member bank of the reserve system part of their money within 60 days and the remainder within a year, repaying depositors in full. The liquidating board would appoint agents to assess liabilities and assets of closed banks. To make payments to depositors, agents could borrow on a bank's assets from a fund drawn from the Treasury, reserve banks, and members banks. The liquidating board could demand continuing contributions from members.[54]

Steagall's bill included other banking reforms. Since small banks had been more prone to fail, it would require newly organized or consolidated member banks to have $50,000 capital plus 10% surplus. It would end the comptroller of the currency's authority to assess stockholders for double par value of their stock (known as double liability), which had provided poor protection for depositors and had made bank stocks an unattractive investment. The measure would allow member banks to charge fees for remitting checks drawn on other banks because Steagall thought par clearance had unjustifiably damaged earnings of small banks.[55]

The House Banking and Currency Committee held hearings on Steagall's bill in March and April. John Pole, comptroller of the currency, sympathized with the desire to aid small banks but "unequivocally and unalterably opposed" any guaranty because it would put a "premium upon incompetency and irresponsibility."[56] He worried that increasing minimum bank capital to $50,000 for new banks would inhibit his emergency ability to organize an institution to replace a failing one. Bankers from across the country testified against deposit insurance. Supporters, including a few bankers and members of Congress, emphasized that no depositor had lost money under state guaranty programs, that problems affecting state plans, such as lack of diversification and regulation, could be avoided in federal legislation, and that enacting deposit insurance would end bank failures and hoarding.[57]

Steagall introduced a revised bill (H.R. 11362), reported by the committee on April 19, that differed from the original. This version would allow more banks to be insured by permitting banks not members of the reserve system to participate in the guaranty program and by lowering initial contributions from banks. It would authorize the liquidating board to borrow up to $500 million from the RFC if necessary. To make administration easier, first payments to depositors would occur after 90 days instead of 60, and payments would stretch over 18 months instead of 12. To protect the public and the guaranty fund, a section would allow the liquidating board to remove officers or directors of national banks if their work had become detrimental to their banks. Heeding Pole's complaint, Steagall amended the clause on capital so that new banks organized to take over the business of failing ones could have minimum capital of $25,000. The new bill would limit interest paid by members on deposits to 4% because Steagall wished to prevent banks from bidding for deposits.[58]

The House began consideration of Steagall's revised bill on May 25. McFadden led the opposition; he and other congressmen noted that state guaranties of bank deposits had collapsed and that the bill would penalize sound banking. A few feared banks that did not or could not join the liquidating fund would go out of business as depositors rushed to insured banks. Others wondered whether $500 million would suffice to protect deposits totaling $54 billion. Several congressmen disputed Steagall's claim that the bill relied on insurance principles because assessments on banks were based on total deposits, not on quality of management. A few spoke against eliminating double liability because it had given partial protection to depositors, and the House amended the measure to preserve double liability. Steagall and William Stevenson (D–SC) led the floor fight. They believed the bill would restore confidence in banks. Stevenson and Fiorello LaGuardia (R–NY) emphasized that opposition to the bill resulted from concern about what was best for banks from the viewpoint of bankers. Proponents denied that failure of state plans had any relevance to a federal measure. McFadden offered an amendment that would have deleted the liquidating board from the bill, but it failed. The bill then passed on May 27.[59]

The Senate Committee on Banking and Currency did not consider Steagall's bill or similar legislation during the 1931–32 session, focusing instead on the Glass reform measure. Conflicts about deposit insurance led Peter Norbeck (R–SD), committee chairman, to appoint a subcommittee to study proposals, perhaps hold hearings, and report when Congress reconvened in December 1932.[60]

GLASS BANKING REFORM BILL, 1932

Glass had continued to work on his bill to reform the banking system throughout 1931, preparing a lengthy and complex measure (S. 3215) based on earlier testimony before his subcommittee. He introduced it January 21, 1932. Originally, he had hoped to unify commercial banking by requiring all banks to join the reserve system, but the attorney general informed him this would probably be unconstitutional. His bill would separate commercial banking from savings and investment banking, prohibit member banks from using reserve funds in securities markets, control group banking, regulate bank affiliates, expand branch banking by national banks, establish a corporation to liquidate closed banks, and increase powers of the reserve board.[61] Much of his concern about speculation, investment banking, and securities affiliates was a result of his belief in the misleading real bills theory. He was sure that investment and commercial banking had become unduly mixed. Because he thought member banks should concentrate on short-term commercial loans, he perceived changes in bank portfolios during the 1920s as destabilizing. He believed that crises could be avoided only if banks were forced to confine their portfolios to short-term loans.[62]

Several provisions of the Glass bill attempted to ensure separation of commercial banking from investment or savings banking. The measure would forbid underwriting and distribution of stocks and bonds by member banks. It would impose an interest rate at least a percentage point higher than the discount rate for advances to member banks. It would regulate member bank lending to customers who used stocks or bonds as collateral and prohibit loans to stockbrokers by other than national banks. Such loans by others had complicated reserve efforts to restrain the stock market boom in 1929. The bill would direct the reserve system to prevent use of its credit for speculation; Glass believed the reserve authorities already had power to stop such "misuse" of their credit, but Harrison had disagreed at hearings in 1931. Because Glass believed bankers had used demand deposits to invest in long-term loans and securities, one section would require member banks to separate assets purchased with savings deposits from assets purchased with demand deposits.[63]

The Glass bill would restrict group banking to improve safety of member banks. To regulate holding companies owning stock in members, the comptroller of the currency would receive authority to examine and call for periodic reports from all bank affiliates. The bill would forbid use of identical stock certificates for member banks and affiliates, common in the 1920s. One paragraph would restrict loans by member banks to affiliates—including holding companies—to 10% of the banks' capital stock.[64]

Other provisions in the Glass bill would strengthen the banking system. The measure would establish a corporation to liquidate assets of closed member banks. The corporation would send accountants to a newly failed bank, buy the assets, and pay depositors as much of their money as possible. Capital would come from the Treasury, reserve banks, and member banks. The bill would allow national banks to open state-wide branches in states permitting it because Glass believed branching could solve many problems of small banks. The measure would require member banks to have capital equal to at least 15% of deposits.[65]

A few sections concerned the reserve board's powers and structure. The bill would eliminate the secretary of the Treasury as a member of the board, because Glass thought former secretaries had exercised too much power, and would require two of the six appointed members to have banking experience. The measure recognized authority of the Open Market Policy Conference, making the existing committee statutory under the board's regulation. The 12 reserve bank governors, plus the reserve board governor, would be its members. Glass included a provision allowing the reserve board to supervise dealings of reserve banks with foreign banks because some officials had disliked contacts between European central bankers and the New York Federal Reserve Bank.[66]

When the full Banking and Currency Committee began to consider the Glass bill, bankers, reserve authorities, and others complained so much that the committee sent it back to the subcommittee. Bankers and reserve officials were convinced the bill might destroy an already weak securities market, cause some banks to close, and lead many others to drop out of the reserve system. Unit bankers protested the branch banking section. Group bankers complained about clauses on holding companies and affiliates. Many bankers suggested appointing a bipartisan commission to study conditions and the bill. The American Bankers' Association began lobbying to stop, or at least delay, consideration. Controversy surrounding the measure, along with its technical nature, ended the senator's hope for swift action. When he agreed to introduce the emergency Glass–Steagall measure in February, his reform bill was delayed.[67]

At Senator Walcott's request, reserve experts Goldenweiser and Burgess began working with the subcommittee. They generally represented the views of Meyer and Mills, but the reserve board had not approved their recommendations to the subcommittee. Glass thought they represented the board and was disappointed later to learn that they did not. Burgess and Goldenweiser suggested over two dozen changes in the bill. Concerning member banks, they recommended: (1) prohibiting member banks from lending to their holding company affiliates upon stock of the holding company; (2) striking out the section that imposed a penalty rate on advances to member banks; (3) omitting the clause imposing segregation of assets acquired with savings deposits; (4) increasing bank capital but not by requiring an arbitrary 15% of total deposits, as in the bill; and (5) allowing branch banking in trade areas, sometimes across state lines. They recommended that Glass eliminate section 3, which would obligate the system to monitor excessive use of reserve credit by member banks that made or carried loans covering investments or that traded in stocks and bonds. Both agreed with Harrison that reserve officials could not control money released to banks by discounts or open market purchases. Finally, they asked Glass to add new sections to protect bank safety, one prohibiting the spreading of malicious rumors about banks and another allowing the board to remove bank officers and directors who violated its rules and regulations.[68] Willis thought these suggestions would remove the measure's more important provisions.[69]

Glass apparently agreed because only a few of the changes recommended by Goldenweiser and Burgess appeared in his revised bill (S. 4115) of March 17. Because of objections to the provision that national banks have capital equal to 15% of gross deposits, the revised bill would require new national banks to have $100,000 capital, with two exceptions: in localities with fewer than 6,000 people, a bank could open with $50,000 capital; and when a new bank succeeded to the business of a failed bank, it could have as little as $25,000 capital. Following a suggestion of Burgess and Goldenweiser, the measure would allow state-wide branch banking, plus branching across state lines within a distance of 50 miles from the home bank. At Robert J. Bulkley's (D–OH) suggestion, the bill would require separation of affiliates from member banks within three years, instead of regulating those affiliates. Although it would impose a penalty rate for advances, the subcommittee heeded previous criticism, and the measure would permit a member bank to make loans to customers with securities as collateral while an advance was outstanding, unless its district bank or the board had issued a warning. The subcommittee would give the comptroller of the currency and reserve officials authority to remove member banks' officers and directors who had persistently pursued unsound practices, as requested.[70]

This bill did not meet with universal acclaim. The day Glass introduced it, Senators Walcott and John G. Townsend, Jr. (R–DEL) announced opposition to some provisions. Members of the full committee wished to schedule hearings, which began on March 23 with the appearance of the president of the Investment Bankers' Association, Allan M. Pope, and the president of the American Bankers' Association, Harry J. Haas.[71] Witnesses objected to many provisions, but generally complained about the bill's "extreme deflationary character."[72] Pope and others thought the penalty rate on 15-day advances would cause depreciation of government bonds. They asserted that provisions prohibiting underwriting and distribution of securities would depress securities markets because they would require national banks to sell several billion dollars of stocks and bonds. They believed that separation of affiliates within three years would force many securities distributors out of business. Most witnesses, including Pope and Haas, admitted they preferred no legislation.[73]

Comptroller Pole complained that the bill would unnecessarily burden national banks. He presented no opposition to divorce of securities affiliates but saw little reason to restrict other affiliates. He thought provisions regarding group banking would be harmful because they applied only to groups owning national bank stock, not those owning state member banks. He complained that restrictions on loans to securities dealers did not cover state member banks. A supporter of branch banking, he argued the bill did not sufficiently extend it and still preferred trade-area branching.[74]

Governor Meyer presented the reserve board's views of the Glass bill. Although Meyer and Mills thought the bill should be postponed at least a year, they compromised their position to attain unanimity among board members. The board suggested changes in almost all sections, but Meyer assured Glass the bill deserved to pass, if amended as indicated. To protect member banks, board members supported a prohibition on loans by a member to any affiliate that owned or controlled that member and on loans using the stock of such an affiliate as collateral. They would limit loans to any other affiliate to 10% of the bank's capital and surplus but allow loans to all affiliates to equal 20% in aggregate (excluding loans on government securities or paper eligible for discount). They were against mandatory separation of affiliates, preferring to receive authority to obtain reports and make examinations. To improve supervision, they proposed forcing nonmember state banks that were affiliates of member banks to join the reserve system or divorce themselves from members. They thought the Treasury should provide capital for the liquidating corporation instead of reserve and member banks. They opposed a penalty rate on advances to member banks because such advances had little connection with speculation. Meyer even suggested that member bank advances be for 90 days, instead of 15. The board opposed formation of any bank with capital less than $50,000 and suggested that branch banking be permitted beyond 50 miles from the home city regardless of state lines. Meyer told Glass the open market committee should be nonstatutory, with mechanisms for deciding upon open market policy left to the board, which would give it greater authority and freedom of action. He advocated clarification of the board's powers over reserve banks' relations with foreign banks and over the OMPC, which had been more definite in the previous bill.[75]

The Federal Advisory Council's statement was much more critical of the measure, calling it an "inopportune time" to reform the banking system. The council said the bill "would necessitate a wholesale liquidation of securities" when there was "no justification whatsoever for such drastic action."[76] It criticized a dozen sections, and many of its comments contradicted the board's. District bank governors agreed with the council, indicating a division between regional reserve authorities and the board.[77]

Once hearings had concluded, Chester Morrill and Walter Wyatt of the board's staff aided the subcommittee in drafting yet another measure. The new bill received only one negative vote in committee. It was cast by Blaine, who opposed removal of a section concerning regulation of private banks and thought another one, prohibiting bank loans to brokers and dealers of securities, was weak. Glass introduced the newest version (S. 4412) on April 18, and the committee reported it the same day. This bill included most of the reserve board's suggestions but would still take the liquidating corporation's capital from the Treasury, reserve banks, and member banks. Because of Glass's opposition, the committee did not agree to 90-day member bank advances, but it did strike out the penalty rate on 15-day advances, which everyone had criticized. To ease enforcement, the committee redefined affiliates, treating holding company affiliates separately, a suggestion by Norbeck. The measure would set up a statutory open market committee composed only of 12 reserve bank governors, leaving out the reserve board governor, but Glass adopted Meyer's suggestion to strengthen the board's authority over foreign transactions of reserve banks. Glass submitted the banking committee's report, and Norbeck filed a minority report opposing branch banking.[78]

Most bankers had opposed older versions of the bill, and many opposed this one. The secretary of the Pennsylvania Bankers'

Association decided to form an organization to combat the branch banking provision. Wall Street bankers complained about the section requiring divorce of securities affiliates within three years. The American Bankers' Association announced it would accept the bill with elimination of sections forcing member banks to provide part of the capital for the liquidating corporation, requiring members to end participation in underwriting and distribution of investment securities within three years, insisting on divorce of securities affiliates, and violating state autonomy with regard to branch banking.[79]

The Senate steering committee placed S. 4412 on the calendar late in April, and Senator Hamilton Kean (R–NJ) announced he would seek amendments to prevent branching across state lines and to extend the time for divorcing securities affiliates to five years. Glass agree to these changes on May 4, apparently because of banker protests. Senate debate began on May 9, with the Virginian making a long speech that justified the need to correct abuses. Walcott was the primary Republican defender, and he and Bulkley led discussion about affiliates. Norbeck and Blaine opposed state-wide branch banking, while Fletcher defended the amended branching provision. Senators introduced more than 50 amendments, and it became evident that the measure would not pass quickly. The Senate voted to lay it aside and take up a tax bill on May 12. The Glass bill came up again on June 1 but was put aside for an appropriations measure. Glass was ill in the summer and autumn of 1932, and while he was not in attendance, senators voted to make the Agricultural Marketing Act the next business, displacing the Glass bill. Debate resumed only after Congress reconvened in December.[80]

Thus, the most comprehensive and controversial banking bill of 1932 failed to pass, in part because bankers, reserve officials, and banking committees were unable to agree. Glass had altered controversial points but failed to convince Congress or the administration to support his bill. Although the senator remained committed to the measure, significant banking reform awaited new circumstances.

ELECTION OF 1932

When the Republican national convention met in Chicago in June, Hoover's renomination was a foregone conclusion, and so was most of the platform, which he had sent from Washington. Delegates focused on the vice presidential nomination and prohibition, adopting the plank on banking without debate. They agreed that bank laws should establish more rigorous regulation and supported requiring examinations of and periodic reports from member banks' affiliates. Republicans promised a sound dollar, meaning adherence to the gold standard.[81]

The Democratic convention convened in Chicago two weeks later. Although Governor Franklin D. Roosevelt of New York was the front-runner, he lacked sufficient votes on the first three ballots. Alfred E. Smith and others had organized a stop-Roosevelt effort that succeeded until Garner, who controlled the Texas and California delegations and did not want the convention to become deadlocked, released his delegates. Nominated on the next ballot, Roosevelt then offered Garner the vice presidential place. Glass composed the banking and monetary planks of the platform, which the delegates adopted without debate. Democrats emphasized more supervision of banks, separating investment from commercial banking, preventing use of bank funds for speculation, and speeding efforts to liquidate assets in closed banks.[82] They advocated "a sound currency to be preserved at all hazards."[83]

Hoover believed his administration had done everything feasible to end depression and start recovery. His speeches defended his record and charged that FDR's election would ruin the nation. Hoover and his supporters thought an economic corner had been turned in the summer of 1932, but full recovery did not materialize, perhaps because the administration had focused only on financial remedies and had ignored the service, production, merchandising, and investment sectors of the economy. Although economic indicators, including industrial production and commodity prices, began to rise in August, improvement was modest, bank suspensions continued, and Americans waited for the elections to bring change.[84]

Roosevelt and his managers ran a better organized campaign, as James A. Farley kept in close touch with state, county, and precinct workers. Each of FDR's addresses dealt with a single topic, and none was long, a contrast to the interminable and rambling speeches of his opponent. Ever the practical politician, Roosevelt knew Americans were disappointed because Hoover seemed more concerned with saving railroads and banks than with feeding and clothing the needy. Attacks on Hoover showed little consistency, but as long as FDR appeared more willing than the president to use government authority to combat the depression, his election was assured.[85]

The main issue was the depression, and banking and monetary reform occasionally came up. The RFC loan to Central Republic Bank during the Democratic convention received severe criticism. Hoover wanted to avoid panic, so he concealed the facts behind the loan. This may have been politically unwise, for the public saw it as another example of the president's willingness to aid the powerful but not the desperate, assuming the bank had received millions because its chairman, Dawes, had been an RFC director. When Hoover finally released information about the loan in early November, few voters paid attention.[86]

Roosevelt made his only speech about commercial and investment banking at Columbus, Ohio, in August. To protect banks and investors, he favored publicity concerning new securities, regulation of holding companies selling securities in interstate commerce, regulation of securities and commodities exchanges, more thorough supervision of national banks, and separation of investment from commercial banking. This speech followed the Democratic platform but also expressed FDR's beliefs about banking.[87]

The most serious election exchange regarding banking and monetary matters occurred as a result of Hoover's address in Des Moines on October 4, when he claimed that Mills had told him in February that the nation was within two weeks of going off the gold standard. This speech infuriated Glass, who made a statement blaming Hoover's policies for causing the gold drain, arguing that the president had done nothing to prevent the country from leaving gold, and accusing him of exaggerating the situation. Senator James Watson (R–IND) charged that Glass himself had known of a gold crisis. Glass's rebuttal quoted public testimony by Mills and Meyer to show that the gold standard had been in no danger, and when this failed to quiet Republican claims that Hoover had saved the country, Glass notified Democratic National Headquarters that he would be willing to make a radio speech. In the course of an hour-long address, he attacked Hoover on many issues and accused Republicans of causing the depression and inventing a gold crisis. He denied that FDR's administration would adopt inflation, endanger the gold standard, or approve a federal guaranty of bank deposits. Having obtained an advance copy of the speech, Mills followed Glass on the radio and attempted to answer each claim.[88]

These charges enlivened the last month of the campaign but made no difference to the outcome. Roosevelt had had a tougher fight for the

Democratic nomination than he did afterward against Hoover. Even if he had proclaimed his willingness to attempt inflation, Roosevelt probably would have won. Since he was uncertain whether abandoning the gold standard would be necessary for recovery, he said as little as possible about inflation or gold. He won by an overwhelming majority.[89]

An era of Republican rule thus had ended. The era of Democratic rule, however, had to wait until March 4, 1933. In the meantime, the banking system deteriorated, and the lame-duck Congress floundered without leadership in the nation's most distressing interregnum period since 1860–61.

CONCLUSION

Party affiliation had meant little in the congressional banking debates of 1932, for the RFC and the Glass–Steagall Act received bipartisan support in Congress. Stabilization had support not only of such Democrats as Fletcher and Goldsborough but also of Republicans such as Norbeck. Deposit insurance similarly appealed to members of both parties. Even the modified Glass bill received support from such a Republican as Walcott.

Instead of party, Carter Glass was the key to banking reform in 1932. When he agreed with Hoover and reserve officials, a proposal became law. This was true of all four emergency measures affecting member banks. His opposition sufficed to block the Goldsborough stabilization bill and Steagall's deposit insurance bill. At the same time, Glass could not push through his modified reform measure because bankers attacked it, because he never persuaded Hoover to endorse it without qualification, and because reserve officials divided over it.

The RFC and the Glass–Steagall Act may have prevented a banking collapse in 1932. RFC loans provided cash to shaky banks, and the OMPC's purchases, made possible by the Glass–Steagall Act, slowed deflation. Bank failures in Chicago and other cities did not cause a national bank panic.

A program to ease the fear of depositors might have stabilized the situation. The proposed Glass liquidating corporation would have helped Americans having deposits in closed banks. Steagall's deposit guaranty bill had the potential to ease hoarding and reduce bank failures. Unfortunately, Hoover, Glass, and Steagall were unable to agree on a suitable measure to aid depositors.

Because Glass believed in real bills theory, many provisions in his original reform bill would have had a deflationary effect, especially those restricting loans on securities collateral, charging a penalty rate on member bank advances, and prohibiting member banks from underwriting and distributing stocks and bonds. Several of the most deflationary provisions were left out of his modified bill, but Glass was determined to separate investment and commercial banking because real bills doctrine misled him into thinking that banks should confine their portfolios to short-term commercial loans. Regulation alone would have sufficed to avoid abuses of the 1920s, as reserve officials recognized.

Division among reserve officials ended the program of buying government securities in the summer of 1932 because OMPC members misinterpreted effects of previous purchases. The modified Glass reform bill would have done little to resolve the structural limitations on reserve action because it would have left the 12 reserve bank governors as members of the open market committee. By making the OMPC both statutory and permanent, Glass would have deprived the reserve board of existing authority to reorganize the committee and have continued the possibility that division of opinion could handicap the board.

Glass, Steagall, the reserve board, and Hoover wanted to increase federal supervision over member banks and give the comptroller and reserve board additional power, but lack of consensus on other parts of bills introduced by Glass and Steagall prevented action. Because bank regulation was a technical subject and few experts concurred, reform took a long time. Only after the crisis of 1933 did a consensus emerge, and by then it was too late to save hundreds of banks.

NOTES

1. James Stuart Olson, *Herbert Hoover and the Reconstruction Finance Corporation, 1931–1933* (Ames: Iowa State University, 1977), 28–32; outgoing cablegram to Moret from Harrison, 22 December 1931, Binder 29, George Leslie Harrison Papers, Manuscript Division, Butler Library, Columbia University, New York, N.Y.; Herbert Clark Hoover, *The State Papers and Other Public Writings of Herbert Hoover*, W.S. Myers, ed., 2 v. (New York: Doubleday, 1934), II: 46–51.

2. Robert S. McElvaine, *The Great Depression: America, 1929–1941* (New York: Times Books, 1984), 89; Milton Friedman and Anna Jacobson Schwartz, *A Monetary History of the United States, 1867–1960* (Princeton, N.J.: Princeton University, 1963), 323; Lester V. Chandler, *America's Greatest Depression 1929–41* (New York: Harper and Row, 1970), 87.

3. Olson, *Hoover and RFC*, 25–9; Merlo J. Pusey, *Eugene Meyer* (New York: Alfred A. Knopf, 1974), 217; *The Reminiscences of Chester Morrill*, 178–80, Oral History Collection, Butler Library, Columbia University, New York, N.Y. [hereafter cited as Morrill, OHRO]; Chandler, *America's Greatest Depression*, 88. The first RFC directors were Eugene Meyer (governor of the Federal Reserve Board), Ogden Mills (secretary of the Treasury), H. Paul Bestor (commissioner of the Federal Farm Loan Board), Charles G. Dawes, Harvey C. Couch, Jesse H. Jones, and Wilson McCarthy.

4. Olson, *Hoover and RFC*, 34–41; *Congressional Record*, 75, pt. 1: 187, pt. 2: 1348, 1416-39, 1472–98, 1562–73, 1581-3, 1644-5, 1657–1705, 1727–53, 1816–49, 1902–29, 1954–81, 2049–81, 2133–54, 2271–3, pt. 3: 2526–37, 2389–92, 2507–14, 72d Congress, 1st session; Alfred Cash Koeniger, "Unreconstructed Rebel:" The Political Thought and Senate Career of Carter Glass, 1929–1936 (Ph.D. dissertation, Vanderbilt University, 1980), 32–3; *New York Times*, 6 January 1932, 1, 16. Conferees also authorized up to $200 million for aid to banks in process of liquidation or rehabilitation, in spite of Treasury opposition.

5. Pusey, *Meyer*, 220; Olson, *Hoover and RFC*, 43; Gordon Wells McKinley, The Federal Reserve System in the Period of Crisis, 1930 to 1935 (Ph.D. dissertation, Ohio State University, 1948), 215. According to member Charles Hamlin, the board did not discuss the

RFC bill before it went to Congress; Diary, v. 20, 17–19 December 1931, Charles Sumner Hamlin Papers, Manuscript Division, Library of Congress, Washington, D.C. Hamlin felt Meyer neglected his job as governor while he served at the RFC; Hamlin Diary, v. 20, 21 May 1932, 31 May 1932.

6. Olson, *Hoover and RFC*, 28–32; Lester V. Chandler, *American Monetary Policy, 1928–1941* (New York: Harper and Row, 1971), 188–9.

7. *Congressional Record*, 75, pt. 1: 196, 72d Congress, 1st session; C. David Tompkins, *Senator Arthur H. Vandenberg: The Evolution of a Modern Republican, 1884–1945* (East Lansing: Michigan State University, 1970), 69–70; John Douglas Lyle, The United States Senate Career of Carter Glass of Virginia, 1919–1939 (Ph.D. dissertation, University of South Carolina, 1974), 202–7; *Wall Street Journal*, 27 October 1931, 6; S. 546, Box 66, General Records of the Department of the Treasury, Office of the Secretary, General Correspondence 1917–32, Record Group 56, National Archives, Washington, D.C. [Except where noted, all citations to RG 56 in this chapter refer to the Office of the Secretary, General Correspondence 1917–32.] For more on the attitudes of reserve officials, see statement by Federal Advisory Council, Office Correspondence to Board from McClelland, 15 September 1931, Box 84, Records of the Federal Reserve System, Subject File, 1914–54, Record Group 82, National Archives, Washington, D.C.; Hamlin Diary, v. 20, 11 January 1932; *Wall Street Journal*, 3 December 1931, 8. [All citations to RG 82 refer to Subject File, 1914–54.]

8. Letter to Willis from Walcott, 23 December 1931, Box 11, Henry Parker Willis Papers, Manuscript Division, Butler Library, Columbia University, New York, N.Y.; Harold Barger, *The Management of Money: A Survey of American Experience* (Chicago: Rand McNally, 1964), 101–2; Hamlin Diary, v. 20, 28 January 1932; S. 547, Box 9, Bill Records, Committee on Banking and Currency, Records of the United States Senate, Record Group 46, National Archives, Washington, D.C. [All citations to RG 46 in this chapter refer to Bill Records, Committee on Banking and Currency, 72d Congress.] Mills became secretary of the Treasury in February after Andrew Mellon resigned to become ambassador to the Court of St. James, but Hoover had relied on him for months before his nomination. See Lawrence Leo Murray, III, Andrew W. Mellon, Secretary of the

Treasury, 1921–1932: A Study in Policy (Ph.D. dissertation, Michigan State University, 1970), 190–2, 278–80; Martin L. Fausold, *The Presidency of Herbert C. Hoover* (Lawrence: University of Kansas, 1985), 44–5.

9. Chandler, *American Monetary Policy*, 186–9; Memorandum: Meeting of Executive Committee January 4, 1932, Binder 50, Harrison Papers; Minutes of the Meeting of the Open Market Policy Conference, January 11 and 12, 1932, Box 3, General Records of the Department of the Treasury, Office of the Secretary, List of Individual Files, RG 56; Minutes of the Meeting of the Open Market Policy Conference, August 11, 1931, Box 69, RG 56; letter to McDougal from Harrison, 21 August 1931, Binder 53, Harrison Papers. A vigorous academic debate has raged over whether free gold was a serious constraint on action between September 1931 and February 1932. Friedman and Schwartz in *Monetary History* argue that free gold was not a constraint even in January 1932 (399–406). I agree with Chandler's viewpoint: "A shortage of free gold was certainly not the only reason for the failure of the Federal Reserve to make large purchases in the open market during this period." Reserve officials had many reasons to oppose "easy money" in the autumn of 1931, when gold withdrawals reached panic proportions. Still, "Meyer and Harrison knew that a marked improvement in free-gold positions was a necessary requisite to getting the assent of the governors to large open-market purchases" (*American Monetary Policy*, 186). Harrison favored amending the collateral provisions as early as April 1931; Hamlin Diary, v. 19, 7 April 1931.

10. *New York Times*, 14 February 1932, II: 7; Extension of Glass–Steagall Act: Memorandum Transmitted by Governor Meyer to Chairman Steagall of the House Committee on Banking and Currency, 23 January 1933, Box 85, Eugene Meyer Papers, Manuscript Division, Library of Congress, Washington, D.C.; Hamlin Diary, v. 20, 19 January 1932; Chandler, *American Monetary Policy*, 186–9.

11. Jordan A. Schwarz, *The Interregnum of Despair: Hoover, Congress, and the Depression* (Urbana: University of Illinois, 1970), 95; Joseph E. Reeve, *Monetary Reform Movements: A Survey of Recent Plans and Panaceas* (Washington, D.C.: American Council on Public Affairs, 1943), 17; Susan Estabrook Kennedy, *The Banking Crisis of 1933* (Lexington: University of Kentucky, 1973), 46–7; Memo on Passage of Glass–Steagall Act of 1932, Box 157, Presidential Subject File, Herbert Clark Hoover Papers, Herbert Hoover Presidential

Library, West Branch, Iowa; William Starr Myers and Walter H. Newton, *The Hoover Administration: A Documented Narrative* (New York: Charles Scribner's Sons, 1936), 78–9, 165, 169–71; Arthur Krock, *Memoirs: Sixty Years on the Firing Line* (New York: Funk and Wagnalls, 1968), 132–3. [All references to Hoover Papers in this chapter are to Presidential Subject File.] An exact date for Mills's alleged statement cannot be determined from contemporary evidence. Hoover had a number of conferences about an emergency bank bill, and Mills attended nearly all. Hoover originally believed that Mills said this on February 9, but no other participant heard it. Hoover later claimed the meeting with Mills occurred when they were alone on February 7. See Memo on Passage of Glass–Steagall Act of 1932, Box 157, Hoover Papers; Herbert Clark Hoover, *The Memoirs of Herbert Hoover*, 3 v. (New York: Macmillan, 1951–52), III: 115–6.

12. "Reply of Secretary of Treasury Mills to Senator Glass," *Commercial and Financial Chronicle*, 135 (5 November 1932): 3095. See also letter to Stokes from Mills, 23 January 1932, Box 110, Ogden Livingston Mills Papers, Manuscript Division, Library of Congress, Washington, D.C.; *The Reminiscences of Eugene Meyer*, III: A86, Oral History Collection, Butler Library, Columbia University, New York, N.Y. [hereafter cited as Meyer, OHRO].

13. Untitled memorandum, 5 October 1932, Box 2, Emanuel Alexandrovich Goldenweiser Papers, Manuscript Division, Library of Congress, Washington, D.C. Goldenweiser was chief of the Research Division.

14. Ibid.; Chandler, *American Monetary Policy*, 182–4; Hamlin Diary, v. 21, 14 October 1932; *Federal Reserve Bulletin*, 18 (March 1932): 144.

15. Myers and Newton, *Hoover Administration*, 171; *New York Times*, 11 February 1932, 1–2.

16. Meyer, OHRO, III: A28–9.

17. Letter to Kemmerer from Glass, 13 February 1932, Box 285, Carter Glass Papers, Alderman Library, University of Virginia, Charlottesville, Va. See also Koeniger, "Unreconstructed Rebel," 38–9, 73–4; Rixey Smith and Norman Beasley, *Carter Glass: A Biography* (New York: Longmans, Green, 1939), 316–20.

18. *Congressional Record*, 75, pt. 4: 3734–5, 72d Congress, 1st session; *New York Times*, 13 February 1932, 1, 4; U.S., Congress, Senate, Committee on Banking and Currency, *Improvement of Facilities*

of the Federal Reserve System: Report to Accompany S. 3616, S. Rept. 237, 72d Congress, 1st session, 12 February 1932.

19. Senate Committee on Banking and Currency, *Improvement of Facilities: Report on S. 3616.*

20. Myers and Newton, *Hoover Administration*, 172; Jack Brien Key, "Henry B. Steagall: The Conservative as a Reformer," *Alabama Review*, 17 (July 1964): 202–3; *New York Times*, 12 February 1932, 1, 14; Ibid., 13 February 1932, 1, 4; Ibid., 16 February 1932, 1, 12; *Congressional Record*, 75, pt. 4: 3801, 3890, 3962–4003, 72d Congress, 1st session.

21. *New York Times*, 16 February 1932, 1, 12; Ibid., 18 February 1932, 3; Ibid., 19 February 1932, 4; Ibid., 20 February 1932, 1–2; *Congressional Record*, 75, pt. 4: 4134–45, 4223–44, 4310–35, 72d Congress, 1st session. For protests from bankers, see Box 252, Glass Papers.

22. *New York Times*, 21 February 1932, 6; Ibid., 25 February 1932, 29, 33; Ibid., 27 February 1932, 1, 4; Ibid., 28 February 1932, 1–2; *Congressional Record*, 75, pt. 4: 4335, 4415, pt. 5: 4761–2, 4783–7, 4940, 72d Congress, 1st session; Memo on Passage of Glass-Steagall Act of 1932, Box 157, Hoover Papers; Federal Reserve Board, *Nineteenth Annual Report Covering Operations for the Year 1932* (Washington, D.C.: U.S. Government Printing Office, 1933), 191–2.

23. See Chapter One for an explanation of real bills doctrine. Chandler, *American Monetary Policy*, 188; E.A. Goldenweiser, *American Monetary Policy* (New York: McGraw-Hill, 1951), 124–5; Howard H. Hackley, *Lending Functions of the Federal Reserve Banks: A History* (Washington, D.C.: Board of Governors of the Federal Reserve System, 1973), 100–2, 106–9; McKinley, Federal Reserve, 344–5. Section 10(b) became permanent with the passage of the Banking Act of 1935. Government securities became permanently eligible as collateral for reserve notes during World War II. Congress eliminated all gold collateral requirements for reserve notes in 1968, so government securities now form the primary basis for such notes. Although the reserve system used the last section of the Glass–Steagall Act extensively, banks used sections 10(a) and (b) less. The reserve board decided not to issue rules or regulations for implementing these clauses because loans would be granted only in exceptional circumstances. By January 1933, reserve banks had disbursed $28,965,000 under section 10(b) and none under section 10(a). See

Chandler, *American Monetary Policy*, 189–90; Office Correspondence to Boatwright from Van Fossen, 27 March 1934, Box 85, RG 82. By March 14, 1934, reserve banks had lent $300,910,000 under section 10(b); confidential memoranda, 24 March 1934, Box 360, Hamlin Papers.

24. "Money Market in January," *Monthly Review of Credit and Business Conditions, Second Federal Reserve District* (1 February 1932): 9–10; "Money Market in February," *Monthly Review of Credit and Business Conditions, Second Federal Reserve District* (1 March 1932): 17–9; "Trends of the Markets in Money, Stocks, Bonds," *Business Week* (17 February 1932): 38; James Daniel Paris, *Monetary Policies of the United States, 1932–1938* (New York: Columbia University, 1938), 83.

25. Memorandum: Meeting of Board of Directors February 18, 1932, Binder 50, Harrison Papers; Minutes of the Meeting of Governors, February 24 and 25, 1932, Box 69, RG 56; Memorandum: Meeting of Board of Directors February 25, 1932, Binder 50, Harrison Papers; Olson, *Hoover and RFC*, 49–50; "Money Market in March," *Monthly Review of Credit and Business Conditions, Second Federal Reserve District* (1 April 1932): 25; *Federal Reserve Bulletin*, 18 (April 1932): 227; Ibid. (May 1932): 290; "Money Market in April," *Monthly Review of Credit and Business Conditions, Second Federal Reserve District* (1 May 1932): 33–5.

26. Memorandum, Meeting of Joint Conference of the Federal Reserve Board and the Open Market Policy Conference, 12 April 1932, Box 69, RG 56; "Money Market in April," 33–5; *Wall Street Journal*, 14 May 1932, 1, 7; "Cheap Money Policy of Reserve Heads Off More Drastic Plans," *Business Week* (27 April 1932): 5–6; folder on Banking and Industrial Committee, Box 1, Harrison Papers; Hamlin Diary, v. 20, 21 May 1932.

27. *Federal Reserve Bulletin*, 18 (June 1932): 350; Ibid. (July 1932): 410–3; "Money Market in May," *Monthly Review of Credit and Business Conditions, Second Federal Reserve District* (1 June 1932): 41–2; Olson, *Hoover and RFC*, 49–50.

28. Chandler, *American Monetary Policy*, 197; Olson, *Hoover and RFC*, 56–7; Friedman and Schwartz, *Monetary History*, 384–9; Gerald Epstein and Thomas Ferguson, "Monetary Policy, Loan Liquidation, and Industrial Conflict: The Federal Reserve and the Open Market Operations of 1932," *Journal of Economic History*, 44

(December 1984): 968–73, 977. Epstein and Ferguson also suggest that New York City banks became fearful of the magnitude of gold exports in June and July because such withdrawals came from their deposits and reduced both earnings and safety. The authors imply that this concern over exports of foreign balances caused the New York reserve bank to abandon its position in favor of buying government securities, but most of the directors and staff members of that bank wanted purchases to continue, as the authors admit in footnote 54 on page 975. Much of their argument rests on Harrison's suggestion at the June 16 meeting of the executive committee that the system try to "maintain the excess reserves of member banks at a figure somewhere between $250,000,000 and $300,000,000 until there was some expansion of credit which would make it desirable to reconsider the program." (976) I agree with Epstein and Ferguson that "Harrison's decision to place the target in these terms probably reflects the increasing difficulty in getting more expansionary policies passed" (976–7), but that statement relates more to opposition from the executive committee than to fears of members about gold withdrawals. Without doubt, gold exports put severe pressure on New York City banks, but Epstein and Ferguson fail to demonstrate that this factor influenced the policy of Harrison or his directors. Harrison felt on June 30 that the system should continue its purchases at the existing level or, perhaps, even buy a little more. Harrison's main concerns were to make a more equitable distribution of government securities bought for the system's account and to end bank failures by greater RFC efforts. See Memorandum: Meeting of Board of Directors June 30, 1932, Binder 50, Harrison Papers.

29. "Trends of the Markets in Money, Stocks, Bonds," *Business Week* (22 June 1932): 34; *Federal Reserve Bulletin*, 18 (July 1932): 411–2.

30. "The Financial Situation," *Commercial and Financial Chronicle*, 135 (12 November 1932): 3204–5; Bascom N. Timmons, *Portrait of an American: Charles G. Dawes* (New York: Henry Holt, 1953), 315–21; Jesse H. Jones and Edward Angly, *Fifty Billion Dollars: My Thirteen Years with the RFC* (New York: Macmillan, 1951), 74–8; Olson, *Hoover and RFC*, 58–60; Pusey, *Meyer*, 223–4.

31. Friedman and Schwartz, *Monetary History*, 388–9; Chandler, *American Monetary Policy*, 196–7; Memorandum: Meeting of Board of Directors June 30, 1932, Binder 50, Harrison Papers; Memorandum: Meeting of Executive Committee July 5, 1932, Binder 50, Harrison

Papers; Memorandum: Meeting of Board of Directors July 7, 1932, Binder 50, Harrison Papers.

32. Friedman and Schwartz, *Monetary History*, 386, 389; *New York Times*, 17 April 1932, II: 7; *Wall Street Journal*, 29 July 1932, 8; *Federal Reserve Bulletin*, 18 (September 1932): 559–61, 563; "Trends of the Markets in Money, Stocks, Bonds," *Business Week* (3 August 1932): 34. Hoarding was concentrated in the Northeast, Chicago district, and San Francisco district in 1932; Paul B. Trescott, "Bank Failures, Interest Rates, and the Great Currency Outflow in the United States, 1929–1933," *Research in Economic History*, 11 (1988): 58. Banking failures and liquidity problems were not always in the same areas. In addition to strains in the Chicago and San Francisco districts, there were significant difficulties in the Richmond and Cleveland districts, while banks in New York were particularly liquid; Barrie A. Wigmore, *The Crash and Its Aftermath* (Westport, Conn.: Greenwood, 1985), 318–9. On the reserve system's fear of inflationary bills, see also note 34 below.

33. Federal Reserve Board, *Nineteenth Annual Report Covering Operations for the Year 1932* (Washington, D.C.: U.S. Government Printing Office, 1933), 16; Extension of Glass–Steagall Act: Memorandum Transmitted by Governor Meyer to Chairman Steagall, Box 85, Meyer Papers; Schroeder Boulton, "Open-Market Policy of the Federal Reserve in 1932," *The Banking Situation: American Post-War Problems and Developments*, H. Parker Willis and John M. Chapman, eds. (New York: Columbia University, 1934), 767–79.

34. Chandler, *American Monetary Policy*, 195–7, 202–3; Memorandum: Meeting of Executive Committee March 29, 1932, Binder 50, Harrison Papers; Memorandum: Meeting of Executive Committee April 4, 1932, Binder 50, Harrison Papers; letter to Glass from Seay, 16 May 1932, Box 7, Glass Papers; Memorandum: Meeting of Board of Directors May 26, 1932, Binder 50, Harrison Papers. The stabilization bills were H.R. 20, H.R. 21, H.R. 49, H.R. 128, H.R. 5078, H.R. 7800, H.R. 8026, H.R. 8246, H.R. 10280, H.R. 10487, H.R. 10517, H.R. 11499, S. 197 and S. 4429. Other inflationary bills included H.R. 12497, which would have reduced the gold content of the dollar from 25.8 to 16.5 grains nine-tenths fine; S. 2487 and H.R. 6712, which would have established a bimetallic standard; and S. 125, which would have abolished the gold dollar. None of these bills emerged from committee. Bills to issue emergency bond currency or

increase the number of government bonds that could act as collateral for national bank notes were common in the early months of the session; see H.R. 5857, H.R. 6704, H.R. 6720, H.R. 8495, H.R. 11251, and S. 2675.

35. Reeve, *Monetary Reform*, 24–6, 162–79; Henry William Spiegel, *The Growth of Economic Thought*, 2d ed. (Durham, N.C.: Duke University, 1981), 625; David Dean Webb, Farmers, Professors and Money: Agriculture and the Battle for Managed Money, 1920–1941 (Ph.D. dissertation, University of Oklahoma, 1978), 178–82; Joseph Dorfman, *The Economic Mind in American Civilization*, 5 v. (New York: Viking, 1946–59), V: 678–80; John L. Shover, "Populism in the Nineteen-Thirties," *Agricultural History*, 39 (January 1965): 17–9.

36. Edward Owings Guerrant, *Herbert Hoover, Franklin Roosevelt: Comparisons and Contrasts* (Cleveland: Howard Allen, 1960), 49. H.R. 21 would have raised the commodity price level to the debt incurrence stage and stabilized it there. Early versions of Goldsborough's bill used the 1926 price level, as did S. 4429 and H.R. 10280. H.R. 10517, a copy of which appeared on the first page of the House hearings cited below, mentioned no precise date.

37. Letter to Goldsborough from Meyer, 12 February 1932, Box 119, Meyer Papers.

38. U.S., Congress, House, Committee on Banking and Currency, *For Increasing and Stabilizing the Price Level of Commodities: Hearings on H.R. 10517*, 72d Congress, 1st session, 16 March–14 April 1932.

39. *Congressional Record*, 75, pt. 8: 8646, 72d Congress, 1st session; U.S., Congress, House, Committee on Banking and Currency, *Restoring and Maintaining the Purchasing Power of the Dollar: Report to Accompany H.R. 11499*, H. Rept. 1103, 72d Congress, 1st session, 22 April 1932.

40. *Congressional Record*, 75, pt. 9: 9410, 72d Congress, 1st session.

41. Ibid., pt. 9: 9410–33.

42. Ibid., pt. 8: 8459; U.S., Congress, Senate, Committee on Banking and Currency, *Restoring and Maintaining the Average Purchasing Power of the Dollar: Hearings on H.R. 11499 and S. 4429*, 72d Congress, 1st session, 12–18 May 1932; Webb, Farmers, 187; *Wall Street Journal*, 2 June 1932, 11.

43. Letter to Jenkins from Glass, 22 September 1931, Box 278 and 279, Glass Papers; "Glass 'More Money' Bill Seems Useful Only in Grave Emergency," *Business Week* (15 June 1932): 8; McKinley, Federal Reserve, 236–8; *Federal Reserve Bulletin*, 18 (August 1932): 478; *Congressional Record*, 75, pt. 11: 11704, 72d Congress, 1st session.

44. Hoover supported a system of mortgage banks in his annual address to Congress; see Hoover, *State Papers*, II: 49. The House version (H.R. 12280) passed on June 10, but the Senate debate did not start until July. Claudius O. Johnson, *Borah of Idaho* (New York: Longmans, Green, 1936), 456–7, 472; *Congressional Record*, 75, pt. 11: 12628–9, pt. 13: 14231, 14380–1, pt. 14: 14852–7, 14862–72, 14957–73, 15004–9, 15095–6, 72d Congress, 1st session.

45. *Congressional Record*, 75, pt. 14: 15258–9, 15379–80, 15453–5, 15469–81, 72d Congress, 1st session; *New York Times*, 17 July 1932, 1, 14; Gilbert Y. Steiner, *The Congressional Conference Committee: 70th to 80th Congresses* (Urbana: University of Illinois, 1951), 33–5; *Wall Street Journal*, 12 July 1932, 1, 7. The Home Loan Bank System was unrelated to the operations of reserve banks.

46. *New York Times*, 17 July 1932, 1, 14; Steiner, *Congressional Conference Committee*, 35; *Congressional Record*, 75, pt. 14: 15600–5, 15631–41, 15664, 15731–5, 15746–53, 72d Congress, 1st session; Hoover, *State Papers*, II: 240.

47. *Federal Reserve Bulletin*, 18 (August 1932): 479; Federal Reserve Board, *Nineteenth Annual Report, 1932*, 23; Arthur Whipple Crawford, *Monetary Management under the New Deal: The Evolution of a Managed Currency System* (Washington, D.C.: American Council on Public Affairs, 1940), 15–6. When this provision expired in 1935, the Treasury Department called all government bonds bearing interest of 3 3/8% or less, ending issue of national bank notes, which had begun during the Civil War; U.S., Treasury Department, *Annual Report of the Secretary of the Treasury for the Fiscal Year Ended June 30, 1935* (Washington, D.C.: U.S. Government Printing Office, 1936), 22–3.

48. There were fifteen relief bills in this congressional session. "President Hoover's Program to Hasten Economic Recovery," *Commercial and Financial Chronicle*, 134 (18 June 1932): 4429–30; "For Public Relief, the R.F.C.: For Industry, Federal Reserve," *Business Week* (20 July 1932): 3; Olson, *Hoover and RFC*, 66–71;

Congressional Record, 75, pt. 11: 11942, 12128, 12189–244, 12275, pt. 12: 12943, 13277, 13437–43, 13446–56, 13472–84, 13499–500, 13559–77, 13580–99, 13642–92, 13694–714, 13765–86, pt. 13: 13876–9, 14780–9, 14809–21, 72d Congress, 1st session; Ellis W. Hawley, *The Great War and the Search for a Modern Order: A History of the American People and Their Institutions, 1917–1933* (New York: St. Martin's, 1979), 209. Meyer also opposed RFC loans to private individuals; Pusey, *Meyer*, 221.

49. Kennedy, *Bank Crisis*, 48–9; Hamlin Diary, v. 21, 9 July 1932; Ibid., 12–13 July 1932; *Congressional Record*, 75, pt. 14: 14944–57, 14981, 15027–8, 15040–2, 15095–131, 15233–4, 72d Congress, 1st session; Olson, *Hoover and RFC*, 72; Office Correspondence to Hamlin from Wyatt, 22 July 1932, Box 357, Hamlin Papers.

50. Pusey, *Meyer*, 225–6; Olson, *Hoover and RFC*, 72–3; *New York Times*, 16 July 1932, 1–2; Ibid., 17 July 1932, 1, 14; Ibid., 22 July 1932, 1; *Congressional Record*, 75, pt. 14: 15032, 15390–2, 15489–92, 15605–21, 72d Congress, 1st session; "Representative Rainey Says Publicity of Reports of Loans by RFC Under Emergency Relief Act Will Be Mandatory," *Commercial and Financial Chronicle*, 135 (23 July 1932): 544.

51. Hackley, *Lending Functions*, 128–30; *Federal Reserve Bulletin*, 18 (August 1932): 518–20, 523; *Wall Street Journal*, 18 July 1932, 1; American Institute of Banking, *Banking and the New Deal* (New York: American Institute of Banking, 1933), 112; *Federal Reserve Bulletin*, 18 (August 1932): 518–20, 523. The board eventually extended authorization to make such loans until July 31, 1936. Although the section is still part of the reserve act, it has not been used since. Susan Kennedy contends in *Banking Crisis* that the system's narrow interpretation "defeated the intent of the direct loan amendment and ended hopes for a positive, aggressive Federal Reserve program to release credit." (49) This explanation misrepresents facts. Garner had intended RFC direct loans to be inflationary. As soon as Glass's substitute received support, the intent of the direct loan amendment changed because it required all direct discounts to involve eligible paper and have security. Reserve banks refused over 500 loans between August 1932 and January 1933, but in each case one or both of these conditions had not been met. Hope for an aggressive program of credit

expansion ended when the OMPC stopped purchasing large amounts of government securities.

52. I use guaranty of deposits and insurance of deposits interchangeably. Letter to Norbeck from Mills, 9 March 1932, Box 38, RG 46; Thomas B. Paton, "16 Deposit Guaranty Bills in Congress: The Idea Persists Despite Past Attempts," *Journal of the American Bankers Association*, 24 (April 1932): 621, 652; Arthur Crawford, "Deposit Guaranty in Congress," *Burroughs Clearing House* (July 1932): 15–6; James Goodwin Hodgson, comp., "Federal Regulation of Banking with Guaranty of Deposits: Briefs, References, Reprints," *Reference Shelf*, 8 (November 1932): 151–83; Jack Brien Key, The Congressional Career of Henry B. Steagall of Alabama (M.A. thesis, Vanderbilt University, 1952), 77–8. For opinions of New York bankers, see letters in Box LE198, Robert Ferdinand Wagner Papers, Georgetown University Library, Georgetown University, Washington, D.C.

53. Letter to Norbeck from Mills, 12 March 1932, Box 43, RG 46; *New York Times*, 25 January 1932, 14; Lyle, Senate Career of Glass, 213, 255, 271–2, 300. The administration bill to aid depositors in closed banks was known as the Thomas–Beedy bill (S. 2810 and H.R. 7370). For differences between Glass's and Hoover's proposals, see Memorandum, Comparison of the Thomas Bill, S. 2810, and Section 12-B of the Glass Bill, S. 3215, Dealing with Relief for Creditors of Closed Banks, Box 16, RG 56.

54. *New York Times*, 8 March 1932, 16; Key, Career of Steagall, 74–7.

55. *New York Times*, 8 March 1932, 16; U.S., Congress, House, Committee on Banking and Currency, *To Provide Guaranty Fund for Depositors in Banks: Hearings on H.R. (10241) 11362*, 72d Congress, 1st session, 14 March–8 April 1932, 2; *Congressional Record*, 75, pt. 10: 11211–3, 72d Congress, 1st session. Par clearance did damage earnings of banks, but federal officials thought the trade-off between earnings and ease of clearance justifiable.

56. House Committee on Banking and Currency, *Guaranty Fund: Hearings*, 6.

57. Ibid., 6–235. No reserve official testified, but the board was familiar with provisions of H.R. 10241; Summary of the Provisions of H.R. 10241, Prepared by George Vest, 8 March 1932, Box 150, RG 82.

58. *Congressional Record*, 75, pt. 8: 8273, 8539, 72d Congress, 1st session; U.S., Congress, House, Committee on Banking and Currency, *To Amend the National Banking Act and the Federal Reserve Act and to Provide a Guaranty Fund for Depositors in Banks: Report to Accompany H.R. 11362*, H. Rept. 1085, 72d Congress, 1st session, 19 April 1932; Memorandum, Principle Differences Between H.R. 11362 and H.R. 10241, by George Vest, 19 April 1932, Box 16, RG 56.

59. *Congressional Record*, 75, pt. 10: 11211–39, 11319–49, 11432–53, 72d Congress, 1st session; "House Passes Steagall Bill for Guarantee of Deposits in National Banks," *Commercial and Financial Chronicle*, 134 (4 June 1932): 4088–90.

60. Letter to Graham from Norbeck, 28 June 1932, Box 53, RG 46; letter to Jones from Blount, 30 September 1932, Box 1, Peter Norbeck Papers, Richardson Archives, I.D. Weeks Library, University of South Dakota, Vermillion, S.D.; "Senate Sidetracks Steagall Bill for Guarantee of Bank Deposits," *Commercial and Financial Chronicle*, 134 (25 June 1932): 4598.

61. Helen M. Burns, *The American Banking Community and New Deal Banking Reforms, 1933–1935* (Westport, Conn.: Greenwood, 1974), 17; *New York Times*, 22 January 1932, 1; Smith and Beasley, *Glass*, 306; S. 3215, Box 37, RG 46.

62. Chandler, *American Monetary Policy*, 270–1; Morrill, OHRO, 200–3; "Glass Bill Promotes Deflation and Bank Control of Business," *Business Week* (3 February 1932): 5; Koeniger, "Unreconstructed Rebel," 49; Preliminary Analysis of Glass Bill, Division of Research and Statistics and Division of Bank Operations, 24 January 1932, Box 149, RG 82. Glass failed to realize that loan and investment portfolios had changed because the nature of commercial banking had shifted during and after World War I, and he ignored the long history of intermixed commercial and investment banking in this country; Golembe Associates, Inc., *Commercial Banking and the Glass–Steagall Act* (Washington, D.C.: American Bankers Association, 1982), 26–36. For more on real bills theory, see Chapter One.

63. H. Parker Willis, "The Glass Bill," *The Banking Situation*, Willis and Chapman, eds., 62–4, 67–72; Lyle, Senate Career of Glass, 216–7; Smith and Beasley, *Glass*, 301.

64. Willis, "Glass Bill," 78–80. Apparently, Norbeck insisted on these provisions as a condition for continued toleration of group banking.

65. Willis, "Glass Bill," 64–7, 81; *New York Times*, 27 January 1932, 1,8.

66. *Congressional Record*, 75, pt. 3: 3000–1, 72d Congress, 1st session; "Glass Bill Promotes Deflation," 5–6; Hamlin Diary, v. 18, 26 March 1931. Willis said the committee wanted the OMPC made statutory to be certain the board would not change it in future; Willis, "Glass Bill," 83.

67. *New York Times*, 27 January 1932, 1, 8; Ibid., 28 January 1932, 10; Ibid., 2 February 1932, 37; Preliminary Analysis of Senate Bill 3215, 24 January 1932, Box 149, RG 82; *Congressional Record*, 75, pt. 5: 5084, 72d Congress, 1st session; for suggestions that the measure be delayed, see S. 3215, Box 37, RG 46.

68. Hamlin Diary, v. 20, 1 February 1932, 10 February 1932, 13 February 1932, 21–22 March 1932, 25–26 March 1932; Comments and Recommendations on Glass Bill (S. 3215) by W. Randolph Burgess and E.A. Goldenweiser, 7 February 1932, Box 149, RG 82; Comments and Recommendations on Sections of Glass Bill (S. 3215) Dealing with Affiliates by W. Randolph Burgess and E.A. Goldenweiser, 29 February 1932, Box 149, RG 82.

69. Letter to Glass from Willis, 9 February 1932, catalogued correspondence, Willis Papers.

70. *New York Times*, 18 March 1932, 16–7; Preliminary Memorandum, Confidential Committee Print of March 17, 1932: Changes from Print of January 21, 1932, Box 148, RG 82; *Congressional Record*, 75, pt. 6: 6329, 72d Congress, 1st session; newspaper clipping, 11 May 1932, Box 43, Robert Johns Bulkley Papers, Western Reserve Historical Society Collections, Cleveland, Ohio. The legal capital requirements of national banks in 1932 were $25,000 in communities with fewer than 3,000 people, $50,000 in those with fewer than 6,000 people, and $100,000 in larger towns; "Our Banking Situation—A Suggestion for Reducing Bank Failures," *Commercial and Financial Chronicle*, 134 (19 March 1932): 2031.

71. *New York Times*, 18 March 1932, 1, 17; Ibid., 19 March 1932, 23, 28; Ibid., 22 March 1932, 2; Ibid., 23 March 1932, 2; Lyle, Senate Career of Glass, 254.

72. U.S., Congress, Senate, Committee on Banking and Currency, *Operation of the National and Federal Reserve Banking Systems: Hearings on S. 4115*, 72d Congress, 1st session, 23–30 March 1932, 17.

73. Ibid., 16–70, 95–354, 441–545.

74. Ibid., 422–37.

75. Ibid., 357–402; Hamlin Diary, v. 20, 22–23 March 1932, 26–28 March 1932; Morrill, OHRO, 203–5; *Federal Reserve Bulletin*, 18 (April 1932): 206–22.

76. *Federal Reserve Bulletin*, 18 (April 1932): 222–5.

77. Ibid.; letter to Meyer from McDougal, 12 April 1932, Box 148, RG 82; *New York Times*, 30 March 1932, 8; letter and memorandum to Norbeck from Harrison, 7 April 1932, Box 148, RG 82.

78. Morrill, OHRO, 204–6; letter to Willis from Glass, 19 April 1932, Box 46, Glass Papers; *New York Times*, 17 April 1932, 1, 20; letter to Wood from Norbeck, 4 April 1932, Box 46, RG 46; *Wall Street Journal*, 18 April 1932, 6; U.S., Congress, Senate, Committee on Banking and Currency, *Operation of National and Federal Reserve Banking Systems: Report to Accompany S. 4412*, S. Rept. 584, 72d Congress, 1st session, 22 and 30 April 1932.

79. *New York Times*, 21 April 1932, 37; Ibid., 24 April 1932, II: 7, 10; Ibid., 25 April 1932, 27; Ibid., 27 April 1932, 27; Ibid., 1 May 1932, II: 7, 14; Ibid., 3 May 1932, 35.

80. *Wall Street Journal*, 26 April 1932, 1; *New York Times*, 5 May 1932, 28; *Congressional Record*, 75, pt. 9: 9824–5, 9882–916, 9973–87, 9996–10007, 10051–61, 10068–72, pt. 11: 11728, 12748–9, 13001–4, 72d Congress, 1st session. Copies of more than fifty amendments are in S. 4412, Box 49, RG 46.

81. Roy V. Peel and Thomas C. Donnelly, *The 1932 Campaign: An Analysis* (New York: Farrar and Rinehart, 1935), 47–9, 89–91; Frank Freidel, "Election of 1932," *History of American Presidential Elections, 1789–1968*, Arthur M. Schlesinger, Jr. and Fred L. Israel, eds. (New York: McGraw-Hill, 1971), III: 2712–5, 2747.

82. Peel and Donnelly, *1932 Campaign*, 91–103; Freidel, "Election," III: 2716–29, 2742–3; Cordell Hull, *Memoirs of Cordell Hull*, 2 v. (New York: Macmillan, 1948), I: 151; Lionel V. Patenaude, "The Garner Vote Switch to Roosevelt: 1932 Democratic Convention," *Southwestern Historical Quarterly*, 79 (October 1975): 194–204.

83. Freidel, "Election," III: 2742.

84. Peel and Donnelly, *1932 Campaign*, 108–10, 128–49; Freidel, "Election," III: 2712, 2732–3, 2735; Wigmore, *Crash and Its Aftermath*, 313; "The Financial Situation," *Commercial and Financial Chronicle*, 135 (1 October 1932): 2207; Fausold, *Presidency of Hoover*, 212.

85. Peel and Donnelly, *1932 Campaign*, 110–7, 128–49, 157–79; Freidel, "Election," III: 2733–7; Steven Skowronek, "Presidential Leadership in Political Time," *The Presidency and the Political System*, Michael Nelson, ed. (Washington, D.C.: Congressional Quarterly, 1984), 91; Richard Earl Edwards, Herbert Hoover and the Public Relations Approach to Economic Recovery, 1929–1932 (Ph.D. dissertation, University of Iowa, 1976), 220–8.

86. McElvaine, *Great Depression*, 90; Olson, *Hoover and RFC*, 59; "President Hoover in St. Louis Speech Relates Incidents Bearing on Loan by Reconstruction Finance Corporation to Dawes Bank," *Commercial and Financial Chronicle*, 135 (12 November 1932): 3266; see also note 30 above. Hoover was not more concerned about businesses than people, and he abandoned volunteerism for passage of the RFC and Emergency Relief and Construction Acts. His problem was inability to use publicity to generate an image of concern.

87. *Wall Street Journal*, 23 August 1932, 8; Daniel R. Fusfeld, *The Economic Thought of Franklin D. Roosevelt and the Origins of the New Deal* (New York: Columbia University, 1956), 188–9; Rexford G. Tugwell, *The Democratic Roosevelt: A Biography of Franklin D. Roosevelt* (Garden City, N.Y.: Doubleday, 1957), 344.

88. Hoover, *State Papers*, II: 298–306; "Senator Glass Disputes President Hoover's Statement that United States Was in Peril of Being Forced Off Gold Standard," *Commercial and Financial Chronicle*, 135 (15 October 1932): 2588–90; "Senator Glass Declares Statements of President Hoover Are 'Flagrantly Contrary' to Facts," *Commercial and Financial Chronicle*, 135 (5 November 1932): 3089–93; "Reply of Secretary of Treasury Mills," 3093–5.

89. Peel and Donnelly, *1932 Campaign*, 179, 220–2; Freidel, "Election," III: 2731-2, 2738–9, 2806; Edward L. Schapsmeier and Frederick H. Schapsmeier, *Henry A. Wallace of Iowa, 1910–1965*, 2 v. (Ames: Iowa State University, 1968), I: 154–5; Ernest K. Lindley, *The Roosevelt Revolution: First Phase* (New York: Viking, 1933), 37–8. FDR received conflicting advice about gold and inflation during

the campaign; see letters in Box 107, Raymond Moley Papers, Hoover Institution on War, Revolution, and Peace, Stanford University, Stanford, Cal.

CHAPTER FOUR

BANKING REFORM DURING THE INTERREGNUM AND THE BANKING CRISIS OF 1933

When the lame-duck session of the 72d Congress convened in December 1932, its leaders lacked a program, were reluctant to follow President Herbert Hoover, and were uncertain about the intentions of President-elect Franklin D. Roosevelt. The Senate approved the Glass banking reform bill in January 1933, but the House Banking and Currency Committee never acted on it. The Steagall deposit insurance measure, passed by the House in May 1932, never received the Senate committee's support. The session's only substantive bank legislation empowered the comptroller of the currency to extend to national banks all privileges held by state banks. This allowed national banks to close whenever local or state authorities declared a bank "holiday."

The economic situation, which had improved during August and September 1932, became unstable late in the year when bank failures accelerated and hoarding resumed. Local moratoria or holidays had saved scattered banks throughout 1932. The governor of Nevada proclaimed the first state-wide holiday in October. The Reconstruction Finance Corporation resolved local crises until the governor of Michigan declared a bank holiday on February 14, 1933, which started a national panic. Hoover then sought joint action with Roosevelt to calm the public, but FDR refused to cooperate. It was the worst situation ever to afflict national banks, and most of them were closed when he took office on March 4.

Roosevelt delegated the task of devising an emergency program to William Woodin, his secretary of the Treasury, who worked with Republican holdovers in the Treasury, the new assistant secretary of

State, the new attorney general, and the reserve board's general counsel. They quickly produced a bill and a plan to reopen banks. Their Emergency Banking Act retained private ownership of banks, expanded power of the Treasury over them, and broadened discount facilities of reserve banks. FDR's fireside chat of March 12 explained the crisis, described the schedule for reopening banks, and restored public confidence. A hastily constructed measure, the Emergency Banking Act had not attempted fundamental reform, which remained for the "Hundred Days."

GLASS BANKING REFORM BILL

Senator Carter Glass (D–VA) had been trying since 1931 to reform the federal reserve and national banking systems. When the lame-duck session convened in December 1932, he was determined to maneuver his most recent measure (S. 4412) through the Senate. This bill would separate commercial from investment banking, prevent member banks from using reserve system funds in securities markets, control group banking, regulate bank affiliates, expand the ability of national banks to organize branches, and establish a corporation to liquidate closed banks.[1]

After Hoover had emphasized the desirability of bank reform in his annual message to Congress on December 6, 1932, Glass received cooperation from Senators Frederic C. Walcott (R–CONN) and John G. Townsend, Jr. (R–DEL). The bill became privileged business on January 5, 1933.[2] By then, Glass had shown willingness to amend two controversial sections. He agreed to change the time limit for divorcing securities affiliates of member banks from three years to five and to modify the provision on branches so that national banks could establish branches only in states permitting them and could not open branches across state lines. A few members of the Senate Committee on Banking and Currency hoped to permit branches wherever not legally prohibited, since not all states had laws about branches. Peter Norbeck (R–SD), the committee chairman, and others opposed any extension of branching because it might damage small banks. When debate on the bill began, this issue remained unresolved.[3]

Bankers' opinions of the Glass measure remained divided. The American Bankers' Association still believed regulation of securities affiliates would cause less disruption of stock markets than separation would. Some bankers did not want to contribute capital to the corporation that would liquidate closed institutions, since member bank earnings were already low. Because bankers could not concur on branching, the national association allowed state groups to make separate recommendations. Most bankers still opposed the bill, but a few agreed to support it late in 1932, if amended as Glass had indicated. In part, these men recognized that they could not stop the Senate; in part, they believed they could make do with the bill.[4]

Reserve officials were as divided over the bill as were bankers. Eugene Meyer, governor of the Federal Reserve Board, wanted to strengthen the banking system by permitting more branches and by requiring state banks to join the reserve system. George L. Harrison, governor of the New York reserve bank, and Ogden Mills, secretary of the Treasury, apparently hoped to shelve the measure, probably because it might disrupt stock and bond markets. The Federal Advisory Council sent a letter to Norbeck suggesting that the liquidating corporation be financed solely by the Treasury instead of taking funds from reserve and member banks. The council agreed with the American Bankers' Association that member banks' investment affiliates should not be outlawed. As representatives of district banks, the council wanted the reserve board to be restricted to supervision rather than management of the system.[5] Perhaps because reserve officials disagreed, such suggestions had little effect.

FDR's attitude toward the Glass bill was ambiguous. Soon after the 1932 election Rexford Tugwell, a member of the Brains Trust, arranged a meeting between Roosevelt and H. Parker Willis, who had advised Glass on earlier drafts of his bill. According to Tugwell, Willis lectured FDR about finance, but according to Willis, Roosevelt was interested in improving bank safety by segregating assets purchased with savings and demand deposits, increasing reserve requirements for savings deposits, and permitting the liquidating corporation to recapitalize and reopen failed institutions immediately. He also wanted to limit branch banking to a single county, perhaps fearing concentration of wealth. He told Willis he hoped Glass's measure would pass during the lame-duck session.[6] After Hoover's address to Congress, John N. Garner (D–TEX), speaker of the House, and Joseph T. Robinson (D–ARK), Senate minority leader, met with FDR to discuss the bill. At that time he approved passage, but within days he told Garner he had changed his mind. This unexplained reversal made little difference to senators, although it may have influenced House Democrats.[7]

Senate debate began January 5, 1933 and concentrated on branch banking. Huey Long (D–LA), who feared the possibility of large banks dominating the nation, started a filibuster against branches beyond county lines. Glass argued that branching was the only way to prevent another wave of bank failures. He added that an amendment suggested by Senator Arthur H. Vandenberg (R–MICH), would prevent cut-throat competition from metropolitan banks by permitting them to establish branches in communities served by an independent bank only by buying the local bank. After days of delay, Long accepted a unanimous consent agreement to limit debate.[8] The Senate on January 21 adopted a compromise branch banking provision offered by Sam G. Bratton (D–NM), which allowed any national bank receiving the comptroller of the currency's permission to "establish and operate new branches within the limits of the city, town, or village, or . . . State in which said [national banking] association is situated, if such establishment and operation are at the time expressly authorized to State banks by the law of the State in question."[9] Although Glass believed in allowing statewide branches for national banks, he accepted this provision, for he did not want to jeopardize the whole bill. Hugo L. Black (D–ALA) presented an amendment to maintain the status quo by striking the entire branching section, but the Senate defeated it 45 to 17.[10]

Reflecting sentiment that had increased in the West, Midwest, and South throughout 1932, a group of senators hoped to revise the Glass bill by increasing the value of silver and cheapening the gold dollar. Long presented a proposal by Representative O.H. Cross (D–TEX) that would direct the secretary of the Treasury to purchase silver bullion and pay for it by issuing paper money called silver certificates. Burton K. Wheeler (D–MONT) offered a substitute amendment that would reestablish a bimetallic standard at the mid-nineteenth-century ratio of sixteen-to-one. Wheeler incorrectly believed that remonetizing silver would raise commodity prices by increasing the supply of metal available as collateral for currency in circulation. Glass and David Reed (R–PA) led the opposition, arguing against inflation of prices in general and against revaluing silver at the ratio of sixteen-to-one in particular. When the Senate was about to vote on Wheeler's substitute, Glass made a motion to table both. The vote was 56 to 18 in favor, which killed hope that an inflationary bill would pass during the session.[11]

The Senate adopted other amendments before approving the Glass bill. It changed the provisions for capitalization of the liquidating corporation, allowing the Treasury Department to subscribe to capital stock, although Glass still opposed a federal guaranty of deposits. Hamilton Kean (R–NJ) proposed that reserve banks provide the corporation's capital. Glass vigorously opposed this, complaining that the corporation would benefit depositors, not the reserve system. The amendment failed, 43 to 25. Without debate the Senate altered the time limit for divorcing affiliates from three to five years and agreed to give holding company affiliates five years instead of three to build a reserve for double liability. Thomas P. Gore (D–OKLA) presented a proposal, written by the office of the comptroller of the currency, that would prevent executive officers of member banks from borrowing from their own banks and would require a report whenever a brother, sister, spouse, or child of an executive officer borrowed from the officer's bank. The Senate accepted Gore's amendment on a voice vote and subsequently approved the bill, 54 to 9, on January 25. Several senators opposing branch banking, including Long, Norbeck, John J. Blaine (R–WIS), and Smith W. Brookhart (R–IOWA), paired with senators favoring the measure and did not vote.[12]

When the Glass bill reached the House Banking and Currency Committee, few observers expected passage before Congress adjourned. Many members of the House opposed any extension of branch banking. Others—including the committee chairman, Henry B. Steagall (D–ALA)—wanted the Senate committee first to approve the Goldsborough bill to reflate and stabilize prices, which the House had passed in May 1932. Many members preferred a full guaranty of deposits, as provided by the Steagall deposit insurance measure, to the liquidating corporation in the Glass bill, which would pay depositors and creditors only the amount realized by sale of a closed bank's assets. The Goldsborough stabilization measure and the Steagall deposit insurance bill had remained in the Senate banking committee for months because of opposition from Glass. These antagonisms, Roosevelt's vacillation, and the bank panic of late February 1933 insured that the Glass bill would die in the House committee when the session adjourned.[13]

BANKING CRISIS OF 1933

Although banking statistics had shown improvement during August and September 1932, bank failures increased (Table 4A), hoarding resumed (Table 4B), and member banks' loans and investments

TABLE 4A
BANK SUSPENSIONS, OCTOBER 1932–1933

Date	Total	Members			Non-Members
		Total	National	State	
1932					
Oct.	97	20	20		77
Nov.	95	25	19	6	70
Dec.	153	23	19	4	130
1933					
Jan.	242	59	44	15	183
Feb.	154	27	20	7	127
Mar. 1–4	24				24
Mar. 5–15	42	3	2	1	39
Mar. 16–31	39				39
Apr.	36	6	2	4	30
May	18	1	1		17
June	15	1	1		14
July	13	3	3		10
Aug.	18				18
Sep.	15	2	1	1	13
Oct.	22	1	1		21
Nov.	18				18
Dec.	27	1		1	26

Source: *Federal Reserve Bulletin*, 19 (February 1933): 77; Ibid., 20 (April 1934): 251.

TABLE 4B
CURRENCY HELD BY PUBLIC AND DEPOSITS,
SEASONALLY ADJUSTED, SEPTEMBER 1932–1933
(In millions of dollars)

Date	Currency Held by Public	Deposits Adjusted				
		Commercial Banks			Mutual Savings Banks	Postal Savings System
		Demand	Time	Total		
1932						
Sep.	4,941	15,270	13,746	29,016	9,863	857
Oct.	4,863	15,393	13,844	29,237	9,860	870
Nov.	4,842	15,713	13,756	29,469	9,876	883
Dec.	4,830	15,511	13,690	29,201	9,901	900
1933						
Jan.	4,979	15,648	13,527	29,175	9,899	941
Feb.	5,588	14,394	12,625	27,019	9,837	1,005
Mar.	5,509	13,543	10,918	24,461	9,740	1,112
Apr.	5,202	13,837	10,708	24,545	9,688	1,158
May	5,019	14,430	10,651	25,081	9,616	1,178
June	4,949	14,283	10,855	25,138	9,586	1,185
July	4,886	14,201	11,073	25,274	9,561	1,176
Aug.	4,850	14,265	11,077	25,342	9,534	1,177
Sep.	4,830	14,341	11,090	25,431	9,534	1,179
Oct.	4,803	14,510	11,074	25,584	9,516	1,187
Nov.	4,844	14,714	11,005	25,719	9,520	1,196
Dec.	4,839	14,920	11,048	25,968	9,532	1,206

Source: Milton Friedman and Anna Jacobson Schwartz, *A Monetary History of the United States, 1867–1960* (Princeton, N.J.: Princeton University, 1963), 713–4.

declined in November, December, and January. Money markets were unstable, and member banks had acquired excess reserves of $500 million by December (Table 4C) because they feared withdrawals by depositors and sought liquidity. The RFC worked diligently to provide

TABLE 4C
MEMBER BANK EXCESS RESERVES,
SEPTEMBER 1932–JUNE 1933
(Averages of daily figures, in millions of dollars)

Date	Total—All Member Banks	New York City	Other Reserve Cities
1932			
Sep.	345.5	193.4	119.6
Oct.	435.9	241.6	160.5
Nov.	482.2	266.8	181.8
Dec.	525.8	283.2	206.9
1933			
Jan.	583.8	286.2	254.2
Feb.	417.3	74.5	291.0
Mar.	n/a	n/a	n/a
Apr.	379.1	150.2	129.4
May	319.1	106.0	132.0
June	363.1	68.9	198.0

Source: *Federal Reserve Bulletin*, 19 (August 1933): 477.

that liquidity but was hampered by the requirement that its loans be fully secured. Still, by December 31, 1932, the RFC had lent more than $1.25 billion to 6,648 financial institutions.[14]

The first state-wide holiday occurred on October 31, 1932, after a chain of banks in Nevada owned by George Wingfield desperately requested additional RFC aid. Examiners decided the chain lacked sufficient collateral. Because most of the state's public funds were on deposit in Wingfield banks, Nevada Governor Fred B. Balzar declared a bank holiday, hoping that Wingfield and the RFC would reach agreement. Wingfield negotiated until his chain suspended on December 14. Like moratoria in Midwestern towns that autumn, the Nevada holiday did not alarm most Americans, who continued to regard bank problems as isolated.[15] Still, Nevada was undoubtedly a "rehearsal for the disaster which overcame the nation's financial structure in February and March of 1933."[16]

Banks faced both liquidity and solvency problems by January 1933, as anyone reading newspapers could discover. More than 240 banks suspended that month, increases of currency in circulation indicated widespread hoarding, and moderate gold losses began. Iowa adopted a measure allowing its superintendent of banking to operate banks in receivership on a restricted basis, while the RFC aided banks undergoing runs in Memphis, Little Rock, Mobile, Kansas City, Chattanooga, Cleveland, and St. Louis. Confidence in banks declined, and they were having greater difficulties meeting needs by borrowing. The money supply fell during February, as currency held by the public climbed more than $600 million and bank deposits declined by more than $2 billion.[17]

The RFC suffered from ineffective leadership and publicity during January and February. Hoover had appointed Atlee Pomerene as its chairman and Charles A. Miller as president during the congressional recess, but Senate Democrats refused to approve his appointees. The agency's problems were compounded by publication of RFC loan reports, which named banks that had required aid. Since July 1932, the clerk of the House had published such reports. Garner supported a resolution (H.Res. 335) to require publication of monthly loan reports issued before that date, which passed the House after little debate. He believed any agency lending government funds should be publicly accountable.[18] No "rash of failures accompanied" publication, but debate in Congress about the wisdom of publishing RFC loans "contributed materially to public fear and consequently to the weakness of the banking system."[19]

Federal reserve officials based policy on erroneous beliefs when they met on January 4. They expected gold imports to continue and a seasonal return of currency to banks after the Christmas holidays. The Open Market Policy Conference wished to maintain member banks' excess reserves at $500 million. The OMPC feared excess reserves might rise to $800 million in January unless they sold government securities. It authorized the executive committee to sell such securities to offset a return flow of currency so long as excess reserves remained more than $500 million. At the same time, it authorized the purchase of government securities to maintain excess reserves at $500 million, as long as reserve holdings of such securities did not rise above the then current level of $1,851 million.[20]

To carry out these instructions, the executive committee allowed $88 million of government securities to mature without replacement over the next three weeks, while excess reserves of member banks remained above $500 million. The public's lack of confidence in banks, reflected in currency and gold hoarding, then caused a decline in excess reserves to $340 million on February 15. The committee reversed policy and began purchasing securities, but it had little room for action when panic began, because system holdings of government securities were less than $20 million below the ceiling adopted on January 4. The committee could have called a new OMPC meeting, but Harrison thought members would be reluctant to leave their reserve banks during the panic.[21]

February began with banking problems in the news. During the first week, bank failures averaged ten a day. On February 4, Louisiana Governor Oscar K. Allen declared a state-wide holiday to protect Hibernia Bank and Trust Company of New Orleans, one of the largest in the state, until it could borrow $20 million from the RFC. This holiday ended quickly, but distrust of banks grew, and withdrawals nationally jumped to $15 million a day in mid-February. No sooner had Louisiana banks reopened than problems arose in Baltimore, Nashville, San Francisco, and Detroit.[22]

The crisis in Detroit, where two holding companies dominated banking, preoccupied the RFC during the second week of February. The Ford family controlled the Guardian Detroit Union group, and other auto makers controlled Detroit Bankers' Company. Trouble began in the Guardian group, at Union Guardian Trust Company, which had previously borrowed $12 million from the RFC. The trust company was insolvent in early February and, without new capital, would have to close. The RFC knew that if the trust company failed, it could cause the other 20 institutions in the group to suspend and force a general closing in Michigan. Still, the Guardian group offered collateral worth $35 million for a loan of $65 million. RFC directors tentatively approved the loan on February 6, with the stipulation that the group raise $5 million in new capital and reduce liabilities by persuading depositors to subordinate claims, giving the group and the RFC certainty that those deposits would not be withdrawn. RFC directors soon realized that many members of Congress would criticize the agency for accepting a paper loss of $30 million. By February 9, they were proposing to lend the group $50 million and to acquire $15 million for the group from other sources.[23]

Hoover met with Senator James Couzens (R–MICH), Vandenberg, Miller, Mills, Arthur Ballantine (undersecretary of the Treasury), and Roy Chapin (secretary of Commerce) to discuss the Detroit situation. Not a supporter of the RFC, Couzens was determined to oppose any RFC loan beyond the value of collateral offered. Once other participants concurred, Hoover revealed that Edsel Ford had agreed to subordinate $7.5 million of deposits and that Alfred P. Sloan (General Motors) and Walter P. Chrysler had agreed to deposit $1 million each in the Guardian group. He then asked Couzens, a multi-millionaire and former Ford partner, to place $1 million in the group. On poor terms with Henry Ford, Couzens refused to pull Ford's chestnuts out of the fire. When the Union Guardian Trust Company shut on Friday, February 10, no one knew if it would reopen.[24]

Hoover, RFC officials, and bankers realized they had three days to work out a solution, since Monday, February 13, was a legal holiday for Lincoln's birthday. Hoover sent Ballantine and Chapin to Detroit on February 11 to assist in raising money, but they were unable to find even $1 million. The president decided that an additional $4.5 million would have to come from the Fords, and on February 12 he telephoned Henry Ford, who refused to contribute more money. Chapin and Ballantine met him in person next day, but he was obdurate. Faced with the possibility that failure of the Guardian group would bring down the Detroit Bankers' group and might set off a national panic, Ford was willing to let a crash occur. He even threatened to withdraw $25 million from First National Bank, the largest member of Detroit Bankers' Company. No one could find more capital, so Ford's actions forced suspension of both bank holding companies. Because many state banks kept part of their reserves in Detroit banks, the suspensions imperiled dozens of banks. To protect banks and depositors, Governor William Comstock declared an eight-day state holiday, taking effect February 14, in the hope that Detroit banks could reorganize and reopen. The Michigan holiday shocked the nation and began the Panic of 1933.[25]

While his administration desperately sought a way to reopen Detroit's banks, Hoover began to blame the crisis on the election and impending inauguration of Roosevelt. Claiming that fear fed panic, he hoped to force FDR to issue a declaration favoring a balanced budget and opposing inflation. He genuinely believed that one bracing statement from FDR would restore confidence. The president wrote FDR on February 17, outlining the situation in Michigan. Implying that silence caused the panic, Hoover asked for a statement. Roosevelt was uncertain about his commitment to gold and had no intention of making a declaration about his plans. He did not intend to take any responsibility before March 4, believing that cooperation would limit his effectiveness.[26]

Vandenberg worried because a state governor had no authority to close national banks by proclamation. F. Gloyd Awalt, acting comptroller of the currency, did not intend to keep national banks in Michigan open and agreed to Vandenberg's proposal that the comptroller of the currency be allowed to extend to national banks any privileges conveyed by state laws to state banks. After receiving support from Mills and the reserve board, Vandenberg suggested that Couzens, the senior senator, introduce such a resolution. Because Glass had doubt about granting such undefined authority, he delayed the resolution until the banking committee met, when senators approved it 8 to 4 in spite of his opposition. Couzens reported the resolution to the Senate on February 21, when it passed by unanimous consent.[27] The resolution moved through the House just as quickly. The banking committee, which met February 22–23 to question Vandenberg and discuss the resolution, reported it on February 24. The Rules Committee approved holding a vote the following day, when the resolution passed 241 to 4. Hoover signed it that evening. In this case, Democrats and Republicans had worked with Hoover's administration to aid national banks, but the bank panic was spreading so rapidly that Awalt had difficulty determining the situation in each state.[28]

All the while a Senate investigation into stock exchange practices was contributing to public distrust of banks. This inquiry had begun in 1932 and continued under Norbeck's direction. Hearings in 1932 had disclosed that manipulation of company stock by directors was common but revealed little that was illegal about stock exchange practices. Norbeck hired Ferdinand Pecora, a tenacious lawyer from New York, as counsel in January 1933. Pecora launched a hearing on the Insull utility empire on February 15. For the first time commercial bankers became implicated in stock manipulation. Charles G. Dawes, president of Central Republic Bank of Chicago, testified that his bank had lent nearly 90% of its assets to various Insull companies even though Illinois law limited loans to a single borrower to 10% of assets. Such revelations became front-page news.[29]

Norbeck and Pecora next looked into the affairs of National City Bank of New York and its investment affiliate, National City Company.

Norbeck chose these institutions because their salesmen had sold bonds and securities that had become worthless to banks and individuals in South Dakota. Roosevelt had also received a tip about National City Company. Pecora went to New York to look at their records and within four days found enough to shake the financial community.[30]

Hearings on National City began February 21 and ended March 2, keeping pace with the developing panic. First to testify was Charles E. Mitchell, chairman of the board of both institutions, who revealed that National City Company, although owned by stockholders, was controlled by a board of three trustees who had never accounted for operations, kept minutes of meetings, or made reports until 1931, when they began issuing earnings' statements and balance sheets. The trustees had established a management fund, withdrawing a fifth of the company's net annual profits after 8% went to capital, surplus, and undivided profits. The fund had disbursed millions to Mitchell and other insiders. After the stock market crash, National City Bank lent more than $2 million to officers of both companies to cover losses. Many such loans had no collateral and earned no interest. National City Company had sold nearly two million shares of National City Bank stock, while borrowing from the bank on the basis of worthless Cuban sugar loans. When bank examiners criticized these loans, National City Company sold them as bonds to investors. This testimony crystallized public sentiment in favor of separating commercial and investment banking.[31]

The panic worsened each day between February 21 and March 3. Currency and gold went into hoarding, and state after state declared holidays (Table 4D). Pressure concentrated on New York City banks, which had to face currency drains from correspondent banks and gold drains as depositors and foreigners moved assets abroad. Even in the worst stages of the panic, domestic hoarders accepted reserve notes in exchange for deposits; only a small percentage insisted on gold coin or certificates. The New York reserve bank had tried to ease the pressure by lowering its rate for buying acceptances to .5% on February 16. Six days later it had acquired $149 million of acceptances and began to raise its rate, which reached 3.25% on March 3. New York and Chicago reserve banks also raised discount rates in a classical response to monetary panic. Member banks became deeply indebted to reserve banks (Table 4E), as excess reserves dwindled.[32]

TABLE 4D
BANK HOLIDAYS IN 1933*

Date	States
Jan. 20	Iowa
Feb. 4	Louisiana
Feb. 14	Michigan
Feb. 24	Maryland
Feb. 27	Arkansas, Ohio
Mar. 1	Alabama, Kentucky, Tennessee
Mar. 2	Arizona, California, Georgia, Idaho, Louisiana, Mississippi, Missouri, Nevada, New Mexico, Oklahoma, Oregon, Texas, Utah, Washington, Wisconsin
Mar. 3	Colorado, Connecticut, Delaware, Maine, Minnesota, Montana, Nebraska, New Hampshire, North Dakota, Rhode Island, South Dakota, Vermont, Virginia
Mar. 4	Illinois, Iowa, Massachusetts, New Jersey, New York, Pennsylvania

* Not all banks in states with holidays observed them, and some banks only restricted withdrawals.

Source: James S. Olson, *Saving Capitalism: The Reconstruction Finance Corporation and the New Deal, 1933–1940* (Princeton, N.J.: Princeton University, 1988), 26–35; *New York Times*.

The panic in Michigan put pressure on banks in nearby states. Indiana next declared a holiday. A holiday in Maryland was necessary

TABLE 4E
MEMBER BANKS
CLASSIFICATION OF LOANS AND INVESTMENTS, 1932–33
(In millions of dollars)

Date	Total Loans and Invest-ments	Loans			Investments	
		Banks	Custo-mers	Other	U.S. Secur-ities	Other
1932						
June	28,001	573	15,267	747	5,628	5,786
Sep.	28,045	457	14,498	970	6,366	5,755
Dec.	27,469	444	13,905	855	6,540	5,726
1933						
June	24,786	330	11,337	1,191	6,887	5,041
Oct.	24,953	297	11,523	1,238	6,801	5,093
Dec.	25,220	287	11,315	1,231	7,254	5,132

Source: Federal Reserve Board, *Twentieth Annual Report, Covering Operations for the Year 1933* (Washington, D.C.: U.S. Government Printing Office, 1934), 174.

because of problems in Baltimore, and an Ohio moratorium saved the situation in Cleveland and other cities. Banks in these locations had suffered liquidity problems for months, but a bank holiday in one location caused depositors elsewhere to fear similar holidays and to withdraw as much currency as possible while local banks were still open. Thus, individual depositors seeking cash to make purchases in case of a bank holiday caused the bank runs that made holidays necessary. By the first three days of March the strain on banks in money market centers was becoming significant and had become unbearable for many country banks.[33]

When Governor Comstock had extended the Michigan bank holiday on February 21, Hoover recognized that panic would not end easily. Believing that the reserve board had not aided Detroit's banks sufficiently, he wrote to the board for advice. Despite serious problems in the Cleveland and Chicago districts, the board offered no proposals.[34] It promised only to study "all aspects of the situation."[35]

The Federal Advisory Council joined other bankers in urging Roosevelt to make a statement about the budget and gold standard. It drafted a resolution, which Mills apparently wished to send to FDR, but Charles Hamlin and perhaps other board members believed the council was attempting to embarrass Roosevelt. Consequently, the council tore up the resolution and sent a representative to FDR to stress the desirability of making such a statement. He was no more likely to respond to this appeal than to others.[36]

Rumors that Roosevelt intended to leave the gold standard and inflate prices increased during the final week of February. Widespread knowledge that Glass had declined the Treasury portfolio fed such rumors. Although he issued a statement emphasizing his health as his reason for declining, Glass in truth had been unable to secure assurance that FDR would not pursue inflationary efforts to raise prices. These rumors prompted a run on the dollar in foreign exchange markets, which caused the primary drains of the nation's gold holdings.[37]

Roosevelt answered a request in Hoover's letter of February 17 when on February 21 he nominated Woodin, a New York industrialist and member of the board of directors of the New York reserve bank, as secretary of the Treasury. Mills went to New York and talked to Woodin on February 22–23. Under instruction from Hoover, he stressed the need for joint action in the crisis. Woodin faithfully returned FDR's answer: Hoover was free to do as he wished, but FDR would not participate. This answered another part of Hoover's letter of February 17. Woodin repeated this answer February 27, when he saw Mills and Meyer in Washington.[38]

While the public became increasingly alarmed, Roosevelt remained calm and confident. Raymond Moley, his assistant secretary of State, later wondered if FDR comprehended the seriousness of the situation. Roosevelt probably knew the system was collapsing and assumed a national bank holiday would be necessary. Tugwell on February 25 told James Rand, a manufacturer, member of the Committee for the Nation, and Roosevelt supporter, that FDR would direct his attention to rehabilitating the banks because there would be a collapse within a few days. Rand telephoned and left a message for Hoover outlining this conversation. Concluding that the incoming administration wanted to blame Republicans for the banking crisis, Hoover worked even harder to commit FDR to joint action, while trying to prevent a general collapse.[39]

Hoover could not have expected a positive response when he wrote FDR again on February 28. He repeated that "a declaration even now on the line I suggested . . . would contribute greatly to restore confidence and would save losses and hardships to millions of people."[40] He mentioned the need for Congress to meet promptly after March 4 and offered to call a special session so members would have time to arrive. He assured FDR that he desired to cooperate. Roosevelt replied the following day, enclosing two letters, one dated February 20 and another March 1. Internal evidence indicates he wrote both after he received Hoover's letter of February 28. Again he refused to act prior to inauguration. He believed "that on present values very few financial institutions anywhere in the country are actually able to pay off their deposits in full, and the knowledge of this fact is widely held." As for calling Congress into session, he agreed that an early meeting would be required, adding that he had not decided "on a definite time."[41]

The Treasury Department had been working on legal means to end the panic. Awalt consulted Walter Wyatt, the reserve board's legal counsel, and between February 14 and 17 they drafted a bill to appoint conservators instead of receivers to speed reorganization or liquidation of banks. Known as the Bank Conservation Bill, the measure gained Mills' support, but Hoover refused to push it during the last weeks of the session. The president was equally reluctant to support other measures designed by Awalt and Wyatt. They drafted a bill to allow the RFC to purchase preferred stock from banks, which would provide institutions with capital. Wyatt prepared an executive order declaring a national bank holiday on the basis of a 1917 statute known as the Trading-with-the-Enemy Act, which permitted the president to embargo gold, and he drafted a joint resolution for Congress to ratify the order.[42]

Hoover remained uncertain of his authority to declare a bank holiday based on the act of 1917. Congress had repealed parts of the act during the 1920s, and the question of whether the president still had authority to embargo gold rested on a technicality—whether a whole paragraph had been repealed or just part of it down to a semicolon. William D. Mitchell, attorney general, had doubt about the legality of action based on the act and reinforced Hoover's reluctance to declare a holiday without FDR's consent. Roosevelt became aware that the

Trading-with-the-Enemy Act might be used to embargo gold and asked Tugwell to look into the matter. Tugwell spoke to Herbert Feis, economic adviser to the State Department, who found a heavily marked copy of the statute in the Treasury. Tugwell examined clauses Awalt and Wyatt had used to draft the bank holiday order. He reported to FDR, who asked Senators Key Pittman (D–NEV) and James F. Byrnes (D–SC) to investigate whether the president still had authority to embargo gold. Neither man would venture an opinion; Roosevelt and his nominee for attorney general, Homer Cummings, debated using the 1917 statute until inauguration day. In the meantime, Hoover refused to act alone.[43]

Hoover wrote the reserve board again on February 28, asking whether it would support a federal guaranty of deposits or the issue of emergency scrip by clearing house associations. For the first time he was willing to agree to a guaranty of up to half of bank deposits, even though no one knew how much it might cost. Meyer and other board members continued to oppose deposit guaranty and scrip plans. Although they did not like the situation, they replied on March 2 that they opposed both ideas and had no other recommendation. Historian Susan Kennedy believes that neither the board nor Hoover wanted responsibility for deciding what to do. Hoover and Mills consulted Woodin as to whether Roosevelt would support a guaranty of deposits. The lame-duck Congress would adjourn within days, and they did not want to submit a proposal without FDR's approval. Roosevelt believed deposit insurance was unsound, as Woodin told Mills on March 1.[44]

While Roosevelt and his entourage traveled from New York City to Washington on March 2, Hoover, Mills, and Ballantine still hoped for a joint program. Hoover spoke to Glass and Robinson in an effort to discover FDR's intentions, but the senators did not know what he had in mind and confirmed that Congress would not act without his approval. Since Roosevelt had told Garner he preferred Congress not to pass hasty measures, legislative action before March 4 became impossible.[45]

News on March 2 was bad, as more states declared bank holidays or restricted withdrawals. Pressure on New York banks had led to higher interest rates on call loans, bankers' acceptances, time loans on stock market collateral, and commercial paper. The New York reserve bank raised its discount rate from 2.5% to 3.5%. In spite of selling acceptances and government securities to other reserve banks on February 28, March 1, and March 2, the New York bank dropped below the required 40% gold reserve for federal reserve notes. The board had power to suspend such requirements for 30 days and reluctantly did so on March 3. Harrison complained that this still left district banks open for gold and currency withdrawals, and the New York reserve bank was down to only $381 million in gold by March 4, having lost $330 million in gold since March 1. He thought a national bank holiday essential. The board debated the idea for hours on March 2–3, agreeing to accept a bank holiday between March 3 and 5 if FDR would concur.[46]

Accepting a suggestion from the board, Mills spoke to Woodin on the evening of March 2 about a bank holiday proclamation based on the Trading-with-the-Enemy Act. Roosevelt would not agree to a joint proclamation, but Woodin suggested that Hoover declare a holiday until noon, March 4. Then FDR would assume responsibility. This eminently sensible suggestion received little consideration, for Hoover became angry when he learned of it. He wanted a joint proclamation and was willing to use the Trading-with-the-Enemy Act only to limit hoarding of coin and currency. He insisted on relaying his position to Woodin and Roosevelt, who responded that he could do as he chose.[47]

Hoover still hoped Roosevelt would join in a proclamation to stop hoarding and restrict currency withdrawals. FDR and his family arrived at the White House on Friday, March 3, to pay a customary courtesy call, only to discover that Hoover intended to discuss the panic. Roosevelt sent for Moley who joined the conversation along with Mills and Meyer, both of whom wanted Hoover to declare a holiday with or without FDR's support. Although Roosevelt refused joint action prior to the inauguration, he thought the president had authority to act. Hoover and FDR spoke by telephone twice on the evening of March 3; both times Roosevelt made clear that he would not support a holiday lasting beyond noon on March 4. He had decided to use the Trading-with-the-Enemy Act, for he told Glass he would close the banks after he took office, and he did not oppose a proclamation by Hoover as long as it did not remain in force beyond the inauguration.[48]

The reserve system faced tremendous strain on March 3. Depositors across the nation withdrew more than $100 million in gold that day. The New York reserve bank alone lost more than $300 million in gold and currency to individuals and interior banks. Its gold reserve fell to 24%, and it would have needed $250 million from other reserve banks if the board had not suspended legal requirements. The Chicago reserve bank suffered acute gold losses, apparently because bankers there did not want gold to be used to bolster the New York bank. Panic was so great that Chicago officials expected to lose $100 million in gold during the two hours the reserve would be open on Saturday morning, March 4, and others thought New York could lose up to $500 million in gold and currency. Directors of both districts wired the board to recommend a national bank holiday.[49]

The reserve board was willing to support more radical action than Hoover was willing to take in the closing day of his administration. Given the withdrawals of March 3, board members felt compelled to seek a national holiday and began preparing a letter to Hoover urging a declaration. By the time the board approved a letter, it was after midnight. When the messenger reached the White House, he had to awaken Hoover, who refused to act. Just before the inauguration, Hoover wrote a blistering reply, calling the board's letter unjustified and unnecessary and complaining that Roosevelt had not wanted a holiday, that the attorney general had doubted validity of the 1917 statute, and that the governors of New York and Illinois had been prepared to act.[50]

Once it became clear that Hoover would not issue a holiday proclamation, Treasury and reserve officials began to ask state governors to close the banks. Most urgent were those states having reserve banks, especially New York and Illinois. After Roosevelt retired for the night, Woodin and Moley went to the Treasury Department to help reach the governors. In New York, Harrison had been in touch with Governor Herbert Lehman since early evening and now urged Lehman to issue a state proclamation. New York clearing house bankers asked to keep banks open, but Harrison insisted that Lehman act. Finally, at 3:30 a.m., March 4, after the clearing house and state superintendent of banks had agreed, Lehman closed New York's banks. Governor Henry Horner of Illinois had agreed earlier to declare a holiday if Lehman would. Wyatt finally woke up Governor Gifford Pinchot of Pennsylvania, who spoke to his attorney general and declared a moratorium. By dawn most states had closed their banks, although ten had merely set limits on withdrawals.[51]

Saturday, inauguration day, was dreary and cold, reflecting the mood of the retiring president. Roosevelt was cheerful and confident. His inaugural address conveyed both a sense of seriousness and a willingness to act. Most Americans who heard it were reassured and heartened. Having promised action, FDR's administration went to work immediately. The Senate confirmed his cabinet selections that afternoon, and the individuals took office the same day. Cummings missed the inaugural parade so he could study the Trading-with-the-Enemy Act. He later assured FDR of its validity. Roosevelt and several advisers reviewed the situation and approved a plan that led to a national bank holiday, a special session of Congress to validate the moratorium and reopen banks, and an invitation to bankers in New York, Chicago, Philadelphia, Baltimore, and Richmond to come to Washington the next day.[52]

FDR's plan for the emergency was conservative, perhaps because its origin lay in the Hoover administration. Mills, Awalt, Ballantine, and Wyatt worked with Moley, Cummings, and Woodin during the critical days of March 4–9. They drafted the proclamation that declared a national holiday. When Roosevelt issued it after midnight on the morning of March 6, it closed all banks through March 9 and gave the secretary of the Treasury authority to issue regulations permitting necessary transactions. The proclamation embargoed gold exports, except under license from the secretary of the Treasury. Although Mills gradually faded from the scene, cooperation continued as officials prepared regulations for limited bank transactions. One more critical decision remained—whether to issue scrip or emergency currency. Debate continued until March 7, when Woodin decided to rely on federal reserve bank notes, which would require a 5% reserve of any asset normally eligible for purchase by or discount at district banks.[53]

Woodin also faced the problem of reopening the banks. He promised Roosevelt that he would have emergency legislation ready by Thursday, March 9. He had learned about the bills and resolutions previously prepared, and Mills gave Woodin a plan to reopen banks by classifying them into three categories. Those in the first group would be solvent banks capable of immediate reopening; the second group would include those that lacked capital, liquidity, or solvency but could be reorganized and reopened; those in the third group were insolvent and would be liquidated. This plan became part of the emergency banking bill, with conservators to be appointed for banks in group two. Awalt initially estimated that 2,200 national banks were solvent and could reopen immediately. Information available to the Treasury about solvency of nonmember state banks was sketchy, and no one was certain how many could reopen. Roosevelt accepted the Mills proposal because it would reopen only the best banks, but he ruled out deposit insurance, which he regarded as promoting unsound banking practices.[54]

The reserve board was not asked for its opinion of the emergency legislation, in spite of the system's importance for reopening banks. It learned of the administration's plan on March 8. Members agreed to allow Woodin, as board chairman, to ask officials at each reserve bank to certify solvent member state banks, and Awalt promised to identify sound national banks. He appraised assets on "normal" values, without regard to capital structure, and on March 8 estimated that 4,000 national banks could reopen. Next day he decided that 5,500 national banks were solvent. Woodin instructed reserve personnel to use Awalt's criteria for judging state member banks. Reserve banks found their task difficult because the most recent information about state banks was as of December 31, 1932. Nevertheless, they provided the requested lists. Woodin later asked reserve banks to issue recommendations about the solvency of national banks as well.[55]

The emergency bill went through many hands between March 5 and 9. Wyatt pulled together legislation he had drafted earlier. Awalt, Ballantine, Woodin, Cummings, Moley, and Roosevelt reviewed Wyatt's draft and made changes. Glass began working with the administration on March 7. He wanted to insure that the measure was sound and demanded that states, not the Treasury, be responsible for reopening nonmember banks. Roosevelt invited key congressmen and senators to the White House on the evening of March 8 to discuss the bill. Most of those attending learned details of the measure for the first time, and some did not grasp it fully.[56] Still, "it was clear on Capitol Hill that what President Roosevelt wants in the way of emergency legislation will be granted."[57]

Final changes in the measure came from congressional suggestions. Several progressive legislators had hoped Roosevelt would nationalize banks, but his goal was to restore confidence, and he preferred to rely on bankers. At the White House meeting, FDR rejected using scrip as unnecessary and opposed insuring deposits as unsound. After the meeting Wyatt prepared another draft of the bill, completed at 3:00 a.m., March 9, hours before Congress convened. That morning Glass inserted a few changes on a confidential print of the bill prepared for the banking committee, and it went to the printer to become S. 1 and H.R. 1491.[58]

The emergency bill combined a hodgepodge of ideas, many proposed in February 1933. Title I would legalize FDR's actions by authorizing the president to restrict banking operations during a national liquidity crisis. It would authorize the secretary of the Treasury both to license member banks for reopening and to require delivery of all privately held gold or gold certificates to the treasurer of the United States. Title II was based on the Bank Conservation Bill, first prepared by Awalt and Wyatt in February. It would allow the comptroller of the currency to appoint national bank conservators with wide powers to manage banks that might be reorganized. Conservators would serve until the secretary of the Treasury licensed banks or the comptroller of the currency appointed receivers. Title III would permit national banks to issue preferred stock without double liability and allow the RFC (at the request of the secretary of the Treasury) to purchase such stock from state and national banks, aiding either reopening or recapitalization. Title IV would allow issuance of federal reserve bank notes to meet emergency currency needs and authorize district banks to make 90-day advances to any individuals, partnerships, or corporations that offered government securities as collateral. It would amend the authority of reserve banks to make advances under section 10(b) of the reserve act, removing restrictions that Glass had insisted upon in 1932, including the $5 million capital maximum and the requirement that five reserve board members approve each loan. The bill's final title would appropriate $2 million to carry out the statute.[59]

Congress met at noon on March 9, prepared to act. Both houses spent time organizing committees and selecting party floor leaders, until the president's brief message arrived. In the House, which acted more quickly than the Senate, Steagall as chairman of the banking committee introduced the emergency measure. The committee briefly considered the bill, and Joseph W. Byrns (D–TENN), now majority leader, asked that debate be limited to 40 minutes with no amendment. This motion received support from Bertrand Snell (R–PA), minority leader, who said he did not know what was in the bill but intended to give the president everything he asked. The clerk of the House read the measure, Steagall spent a few minutes explaining it, and a few representatives spoke about the emergency. A little after 4:00 p.m., the House voted unanimously to approve it.[60]

The Senate acted more deliberately but with speed. Because Glass, ranking Democrat of the banking committee, had chosen to be chairman of the Appropriations Committee, Duncan U. Fletcher (D–FLA) had become the banking chairman, and he introduced the Senate bill. Glass had asked Wyatt to prepare a memorandum, which Glass used to explain the bill to the committee, and Ballantine and Awalt answered questions. William G. McAdoo (D–CAL), former secretary of the Treasury but a new member of the Senate, protested that the measure did too little to inflate prices, but William E. Borah (R–IDA) was the only one to vote against reporting the bill. When printed copies of the measure arrived, around 4:30 p.m., it had passed the House. Debate lasted longer than in the House because a few senators insisted on introducing amendments. Long wanted to authorize the president to permit nonmember banks to become members of the reserve system without subscribing to district banks' capital stock. Gore offered a substitute for Long's amendment that would have allowed state banks to become associates of the reserve system, again without subscribing to stock. Gore's suggestion limited associate membership to two years and gave the comptroller of the currency power of approval. The Senate rejected Long's amendment and Gore's substitute because Glass argued they would be unfair to state banks that had joined the reserve system by subscribing to stock. Conservatives such as Glass and Reed admitted they would have opposed sections of the measure if the emergency had not been so great, but the vote in the Senate was 73 to 7. Six of those voting against it were western progressives who wished to nationalize banks. Roosevelt signed the measure that evening.[61]

Both the public and the financial community welcomed the law. The *New York Times* summarized the prevailing view when it concluded that the "bill's provisions do not go beyond what the situation has appeared to demand."[62] The public looked forward to reopenings. When Roosevelt issued a proclamation continuing the bank holiday over the weekend, many people were surprised, for everyone had assumed solvent banks would resume business on Friday, March 10. Woodin explained that sorting applications to reopen thousands of banks would take time. Roosevelt issued an executive order on March 10 that allowed the Treasury to license member banks and state authorities to license nonmembers.[63]

Reserve banks were open March 10–11, operating under Treasury regulations, and the reserve board authorized them to make advances for payroll or other essential purposes to individuals, partnerships, or corporations that had notes with government securities as collateral. After reopening began on March 13, the board would allow district banks to make such advances for any purpose. Unlike 1932, when the board excluded banks from its definition of corporations for reserve banks' direct loans, the board made no effort to prescribe restrictions.

Both member and nonmember banks could now borrow for 90 days, placing the strength of the reserve system behind all solvent institutions. The board also issued blanket permission for member banks to discount paper acquired from nonmember banks.[64]

Over the weekend the administration prepared to reopen solvent banks, although Woodin announced that a few solvent institutions might not be licensed immediately because the Treasury wished to check with state authorities and clearing house associations and to examine any bank that did not belong to a clearing house or had undergone no recent examination. Roosevelt issued a statement on March 11 explaining the staggered reopening. Beginning Monday, March 13, licensed member banks in reserve cities would resume operation on an unrestricted basis, and state authorities could license solvent state banks in those cities. Banks in clearing house cities would receive licenses on Tuesday, March 14, and on Wednesday the remainder not needing examination would open. Roosevelt spoke to the nation in his first fireside chat on March 12. He presented a clear picture of fractional reserve banking to average Americans, explaining the importance of confidence and the danger of hoarding. He assured people their money would be safe in banks. He emphasized that some banks that had not received a license by March 16 would open later. He did not promise that every bank would resume business or that individual depositors would not suffer losses. Historians have agreed that FDR's radio speech ended the crisis of confidence, but no one then could be certain of public response.[65]

Reserve officials were essential to reopening banks. District banks had to issue a recommendation for every member bank before Woodin would grant a license, and New York directors felt morally obligated to keep licensed banks in operation. They worried that too many banks with poor assets would open and thought they might have to lend to such banks on questionable collateral. Harrison asked that the administration guarantee that any loss from such loans would be absorbed by the government.[66] Roosevelt instead wrote to Woodin that he recognized the federal government's obligation to repay the reserve banks for losses on the emergency loans. He promised to ask Congress to indemnify district banks if money were lost.[67] This left reserve officials freer to evaluate assets liberally and to certify more banks as solvent. For the board, reopening meant stacking telegrams with recommendations from district banks into approved and disapproved piles and sending approvals to Woodin. Inevitably a few mistakes were made, as when an insolvent bank received a license because two telegrams had stuck together, but reserve banks and the board made the process easier and faster for the administration.[68]

Reopenings went smoothly. On Monday, March 13, banks in reserve cities resumed business on an unrestricted basis, except that FDR's executive order of March 10 prohibited hoarding and paying out gold. In most cases state banks in reserve cities also opened. In New York City all but nine institutions reopened. In Chicago five major banks and 29 smaller ones, having 97% of the city's resources, reopened. On Tuesday the story was much the same, except in Detroit where Awalt appointed conservators to Guardian National Bank and First National Bank. People in small communities finally discovered whether their local banks would reopen on March 15. Sometimes state authorities took longer to license nonmember banks, and a few allowed state banks to operate on a restricted basis. A member bank that had not received a license by March 16 could continue limited transactions under regulations promulgated during the holiday. Woodin issued statements emphasizing that banks not receiving a license or that received a conservator might still reopen on an unrestricted basis in the near future.[69]

The economy soon responded to the end of the crisis, in spite of deflationary effects from insolvent banks that remained closed. Millions in currency and gold flowed into district banks, which caused currency in circulation to decline by more than $1 billion in the last half of March. Return of hoarded currency allowed banks to improve reserve positions and reduce borrowings from district banks. Stock exchanges reopened March 15, money market rates eased, and retail buying increased. The government bond market scored gains in all issues in heavy trading. The Treasury Department licensed gold exports, declining no requests in March. Many assumed gold regulations and licensing of exports would be temporary, so the dollar remained strong in exchange markets. Banking business was near normal in New York by March 16, but in the Chicago and Cleveland districts fewer than 60% of banks had resumed operation. Arkansas, Illinois, Iowa, Michigan, Minnesota, Mississippi, Ohio, Washington, and Wisconsin had hundreds of closed banks—more than 1,000 national and 4,000 state banks had not reopened. Nevertheless, 90% of member bank deposits were available on an unrestricted basis, and the economic outlook was improving at the end of March. The nadir of the Great Depression had passed.[70]

Congress remained concerned about nonmember banks. Robinson introduced a bill (S. 320) on March 13 that would amend the emergency act to allow state nonmember banks to borrow from district banks for one year. The reserve board discussed this bill and prepared a letter to Glass suggesting its improvement. The board hoped that loans would be granted only at the discretion of district banks, after examination of applying institutions, and if collateral met requirements set for member banks. But the Senate banking committee had reported Robinson's bill before reserve officials could act. Under unanimous consent, Robinson brought the measure up for discussion on March 14. He added an amendment to make explicit the ability of conservators to borrow from the RFC. Both amendment and bill passed the Senate by unanimous consent after debate about whether it did enough for state banks.[71]

Woodin, Meyer, Miller, and Glass saw FDR about Robinson's bill on the evening of March 14 and explained how unfair it would be to state member banks that had complied with the obligations of membership. To lend to nonmembers without restriction would be to put them on the same level as state member banks, which would then have no reason to remain in the system. Roosevelt thought the bill necessary, politically and economically, but was willing to compromise on changes the board and Glass desired.[72]

Steagall introduced a revised measure (H.R. 3757) on March 17, with approval of reserve officials. Although this version would allow nonmembers to borrow from district banks, it made explicit the reserve's power to decline collateral offered. The measure would require state banking authorities to approve each loan and obligate a borrowing nonmember to comply with the Federal Reserve Act and regulations of the board applying to state member banks, with one exception—a nonmember indebted to a district bank would not have to subscribe to reserve bank stock. This measure represented a simultaneous attempt to aid nonmember banks in difficulty and to adhere to the idea that reserve credit should be limited to members. When Steagall introduced it, he hoped the House would act by unanimous consent, but Snell asked for delay until the following Monday to give members a chance to study it. Steagall issued a favorable report on the measure on March 20, and the House considered it that day. He moved to suspend the rules and pass the bill, and it passed by a two-thirds vote after debate over its implications.[73]

This bill moved through the Senate quickly, although the banking committee reported a substitute on March 22. The newest version contained the Steagall bill but included provisions from another bill (S. 334), introduced by Robert J. Bulkley (D–OH), that had passed the Senate March 16. The Bulkley measure permitted the RFC to purchase capital notes or debentures as well as preferred stock in state banks. The Senate debated the substitute for Steagall's bill on March 22–23. Alva B. Adams (D–COL) wanted an amendment to eliminate the required examination before a reserve bank could grant an advance, but members of the banking committee attacked the proposal, and it failed to pass. Members of the committee helped defeat a suggestion by Long that would have allowed the RFC to use up to 90% of estimated value of collateral from nonmember banks for lending purposes. The Senate then passed the bill without a recorded vote, and the House agreed to the Senate's amendments the same day. Roosevelt signed it March 24.[74]

Reserve banks accepted their new authority cautiously, advancing only $560,000 to nonmembers by November 15, 1933. The New York bank's directors and others still believed the RFC should care for nonmember banks. Ultimately, the RFC did so, although reconstruction started slowly and continued for years. RFC aid to banks came in two forms after the crisis; both were necessary to rehabilitate the financial system. It purchased preferred stock or capital notes and debentures from licensed institutions to strengthen their capital and from conservators to permit reorganization and reopening of unlicensed banks. Two thousand institutions that operated before the panic never reopened, and many borrowed from the RFC to speed liquidation of assets. Both RFC programs released deposits in unlicensed banks, either through reorganization or liquidation, but the purpose of preferred stock purchases was to increase the capital/deposit ratio in licensed banks.[75]

Because the reserve system was little involved in liquidation, recapitalization, or reorganization, there is no reason to recount these efforts here. At the end of 1934, 946 national banks were still in receivership, and 1,093 had been reorganized. The last conservatorship ended in February 1935. By September 3, 1934, the RFC had authorized more than $1 billion to purchase or lend on capital notes or preferred stock of banks, aiding more than 6,600 institutions.[76] Roosevelt and Treasury officials had recognized that the bank holiday had presented an opportunity to reestablish the solvency and liquidity of the country's banks. By the end of 1935, the administration had largely accomplished this work.

The crisis also gave Roosevelt an opportunity to suspend the gold standard and decide about devaluation of the dollar. FDR's bank holiday proclamation of March 6 called hoarding unwarranted and prohibited reserve and other banks from paying out, withdrawing, or earmarking gold if it would facilitate hoarding. It forbade export of gold without a license from the secretary of the Treasury. One of Woodin's first regulations allowed reserve banks to perform limited services for member banks if the banks delivered all their gold coin, bullion, and certificates to district banks. On March 8, the reserve board asked district banks to prepare lists identifying people who had withdrawn gold during the crisis and not redeposited it before March 13. Title I of the Emergency Banking Act had given the secretary of the Treasury authority to require the delivery of gold to the treasurer of the United States.[77]

Roosevelt took the United States off the gold standard and began to remove gold from private hands in April 1933. He issued an executive order on April 5 calling in holdings larger than $100. Another order issued on April 20 prohibited gold exports and curtailed the authority of the secretary of the Treasury to issue export licenses. Later FDR revoked the $100 exemption, and by December 28, 1933, no gold was legally in private possession. More than $800 million in gold coin and certificates returned to reserve banks between March 5 and December 31.[78] Such steps were the first in a policy of inflating prices and devaluing the dollar (described in Chapter Six). Without the banking emergency, FDR's gold policies certainly would have faced more intense resistance from economic conservatives.

CONCLUSION

The interregnum of 1932–33 was the most difficult presidential transition of this century, and it inspired a constitutional amendment to inaugurate presidents on January 20 rather than March 4. Republicans were giving the reigns of power to Democrats in 1933, but more important Hoover was leaving the presidency to a man whom he profoundly distrusted. Beginning to defend his record as president during the 1932 campaign, Hoover remained a critic of the New Deal long after Roosevelt had died. During the financial panic, he attempted to blame everyone else—FDR, the reserve board, his attorney general—for the problems. Unfortunately, Roosevelt, too, was influenced by politics. Deciding soon after the election not to undertake joint action with Hoover, he held steadfast even in the face of banking collapse. Partisanship was a factor in the government's inability to halt the panic, and both Hoover and Roosevelt undoubtedly had played a political game.

Partisanship had hampered congressional action, too. Republicans nominally controlled the Senate in January 1933, but whenever the party's progressives voted with Democrats, they could defeat a proposal. Democrats supposedly controlled the House but were disunited. Hoover had little hope of congressional cooperation, and FDR's attitude toward several bills, including the Glass bill, was ambiguous. Given this appalling situation, the lame-duck session's inaction was irresponsible but hardly surprising. Politics also appeared in the debate on the Garner resolution for publishing RFC monthly loan reports, which could not have passed the House without Democratic votes. Democrats apparently believed Republicans had used RFC aid on a partisan basis and suspected the agency had lent more to large banks than small ones.

Although partisanship dramatically affected the banking system during the interregnum, the panic would never have happened if the financial structure had not been so weak or if the reserve system had responded less timidly. The RFC aided hundreds of financial institutions, but limits on its powers restricted its success to small crises. When Congress had passed the Federal Reserve Act in 1913, it had assumed it had made the banking system panic proof. The public sadly discovered otherwise in 1933. The reserve system should have acted to counter the liquidity crisis by purchasing large amounts of government securities and acceptances. The Open Market Policy Conference acted on a false premise in January. Unfortunately, the executive committee failed to seek a new policy when conditions changed. Each district bank tried to cope with withdrawals in its area. At the same time, Meyer refused to ask the reserve banks to provide liquidity by purchasing $100 million of government securities because he believed $100 million was too little to dent the panic.[79] The board's only contributions during the crisis were to compel reserve banks outside New York to buy securities from the New York bank on March 1–2, to suspend legal reserve requirements on March 3, and to ask Hoover to declare a national bank holiday on the morning of March 4.

Reserve officials did assist in reopening banks, but that hardly compensated for their appalling inaction during the panic.

The three pieces of legislation that passed in February and March—the Couzens resolution, the Emergency Banking Act, and the Robinson–Steagall Act—had two points in common. First, they had nonpartisan support. This was essential for passage of the Couzens resolution in February, which a Republican introduced with approval from the administration and which passed the Democratic House with only four opposing votes. Second, all three measures increased the power of federal authorities. The Couzens resolution temporarily granted the comptroller of the currency power that could have permitted much greater competition between state and national banks. The Emergency Banking Act allowed the secretary of the Treasury to determine solvency of member banks and to ask the RFC to buy preferred stock in state and national banks. Never had the Treasury had such control over banks. Title IV expanded reserve banks' ability to lend under section 10(b) and to make 90-day advances secured by government bonds to individuals, partnerships, and corporations. This continued the trend toward widening the definition of eligible paper and expanding reserve banks' ability to lend, which had begun in 1932. The Robinson–Steagall Act perpetuated the arrangement by temporarily allowing reserve banks to lend to nonmembers. The pattern of greater regulation by federal authorities continued in the Banking Acts of 1933 and 1935.

The fear that gripped average depositors during the panic has never been fully understood. Polling techniques were in their infancy, and the connection between lack of confidence in banks, the Michigan holiday, and National City revelations may never be known. Why did few depositors insist on withdrawing gold, while most people settled for currency? Were gold hoarders more frightened or better informed? How many of them feared inflation? Not all depositors withdrew their money even during the panic. Were they poorly informed and less afraid? Did they understand fractional reserve banking better or assume the government or the reserve system would cope? The panic presented a psychological situation that is now difficult to understand in its complexity and confusion.

Without doubt, public confidence revived after Roosevelt took office, and his administration deserves credit for rehabilitating the financial system. The crisis demonstrated FDR's ability to make decisions quickly, his political savvy, and his confidence. In years ahead, he would rely on these traits to push legislation through Congress and sustain public support. Just as the Nevada bank holiday presented a glimpse of the coming panic, FDR's actions during the crisis revealed the personal style that would dominate his presidency. In that sense the banking crisis opened a new chapter in American history.

NOTES

1. For a more detailed description of the bills Glass introduced in 1932, including S. 4412, see Chapter Three. For his efforts in 1931, see Chapter Two.

2. Wall Street Journal, 7 December 1932, 4; Ibid., 9 December 1932, 1; Ibid., 16 December 1932, 1; *New York Times*, 16 December 1932, 14.

3. *New York Times*, 14 December 1932, 12; *Wall Street Journal*, 17 December 1932, 5; Ibid., 4 January 1933, 11.

4. *New York Times*, 13 November 1932, IV: 1; *Wall Street Journal*, 13 December 1932, 4; Ibid., 22 December 1932, 4; Susan Estabrook Kennedy, *The Banking Crisis of 1933* (Lexington: University of Kentucky, 1973), 72; letter to Glass from Norris, 3 October 1932, Box 299, Carter Glass Papers, Alderman Library, University of Virginia, Charlottesville, Va.

5. *New York Times*, 20 November 1932, IV: 1; Diary, v. 21, 18 November 1932, Charles Sumner Hamlin Papers, Manuscript Division, Library of Congress, Washington, D.C.; Ibid., v. 22, 9 December 1932; letter to Norbeck from Smith, 19 December 1932, Box 150, Records of the Federal Reserve System, Subject File, 1914–54, Record Group 82, National Archives, Washington, D.C. [All citations to RG 82 refer to Subject File, 1914–54.]

6. Diary, 17 November 1932, Rexford Guy Tugwell Papers, Franklin Delano Roosevelt Library, Hyde Park, N.Y.; Rexford G. Tugwell, *To the Lesser Heights of Morningside: A Memoir* (Philadelphia: University of Pennsylvania, 1982), 239; H. Parker Willis, Memorandum of conference with Franklin D. Roosevelt, Rexford Guy Tugwell, H. Parker Willis, and James Harvey Rogers, 17 November 1932, Box 274, Glass Papers; letter to Glass from Willis, 19 November 1932, Box 274, Glass Papers.

7. Kennedy, *Banking Crisis*, 73; Bascom N. Timmons, *Jesse H. Jones: The Man and the Statesman* (New York: Henry Holt, 1956), 178; *New York Times*, 8 December 1932, 17.

8. *Congressional Record*, 76, pt. 2: 1330–6, 1404–21, 1449–69, 1572–81, 1623–36, 1646–57, 1724–56, 1935–43, 1993–2027, 2074–96, 72d Congress, 2d session. At this time Thomas supported any scheme

to inflate the currency; Eric Manheimer, The Public Career of Elmer Thomas (Ph.D. dissertation, University of Oklahoma, 1952), 102.

9. *Congressional Record*, 76, pt. 2: 2205–8, 72d Congress, 2d session.

10. Alfred Cash Koeniger, "Unreconstructed Rebel:" The Political Thought and Senate Career of Carter Glass, 1929–1936 (Ph.D. dissertation, Vanderbilt University, 1980), 84; *New York Times*, 22 January 1933, 1, 14; *Congressional Record*, 76, pt. 3: 2511–2, 72d Congress, 2d session.

11. *Congressional Record*, 76, pt. 2: 2293–4, pt. 3: 2349–75, 2380–93, 72d Congress, 2d session; *Wall Street Journal*, 4 January 1933, 12; *New York Times*, 24 January 1933, 5; Ibid., 25 January 1933, 1, 7; David Dean Webb, Farmers, Professors and Money: Agriculture and the Battle for Managed Money, 1920–1941 (Ph.D. dissertation, University of Oklahoma, 1978), 202, 221–8; Joseph E. Reeve, *Monetary Reform Movements: A Survey of Recent Plans and Panaceas* (Washington, D.C.: American Council on Public Affairs, 1943), 272–3.

12. *Congressional Record*, 76, pt. 2: 2262–93, pt. 3: 2393, 2399–2408, 2511–7, 72d Congress, 2d session; *New York Times*, 26 January 1933, 1–2.

13. *New York Times*, 27 January 1933, 2; Ibid., 20 February 1933, 3; *Wall Street Journal*, 21 January 1933, 1; Ibid., 27 January 1933, 4; Ibid., 6 February 1933, 6; Harris Gaylord Warren, *Herbert Hoover and the Great Depression* (New York: W.W. Norton, 1967 [1959]), 282; James L. Walsh, "Banking Laws Will Be Changed," *Bankers Monthly*, 49 (December 1932): 714; John Douglas Lyle, The United States Senate Career of Carter Glass of Virginia, 1919–1939 (Ph.D. dissertation, University of South Carolina, 1974), 300. For more detail about the Goldsborough stabilization bill and the Steagall deposit insurance measure, see Chapter Three. A bill to insure deposits (S. 5291), introduced by Arthur Vandenberg on December 23, 1932, also died in the Senate committee.

14. Memorandum, Business and Credit Conditions, 3 January 1933, Box 358, Hamlin Papers; Milton Friedman and Anna Jacobson Schwartz, *A Monetary History of the United States, 1867–1960* (Princeton, N.J.: Princeton University, 1963), 348; James Stuart Olson, *Herbert Hoover and the Reconstruction Finance Corporation, 1931–1933* (Ames: Iowa State University, 1977), 96–7; James S.

Olson, *Saving Capitalism: The Reconstruction Finance Corporation and the New Deal, 1933–1940* (Princeton, N.J.: Princeton University, 1988), 26–7; Barrie A. Wigmore, *The Crash and Its Aftermath* (Westport, Conn.: Greenwood, 1985), 423. William Starr Myers and Walter H. Newton were incorrect when they said in *The Hoover Administration: A Documented Narrative* (New York: Charles Scribner's Sons, 1936), 332, that banks were stronger in December than in June 1932. According to Eugene Stevens of the Chicago reserve bank, about 179 member banks and 650 nonmembers in his district were restricting deposit withdrawals in some manner in November 1932; Minutes of Federal Reserve Agents Conference, Washington, D.C., November 1932, Box 118, Eugene Meyer Papers, Manuscript Division, Library of Congress, Washington, D.C.

15. James Stuart Olson, "Rehearsal for Disaster: Hoover, the R.F.C., and the Banking Crisis in Nevada, 1932–1933," *Western Historical Quarterly*, 6 (April 1975): 149–61; Olson, *Hoover and RFC*, 94–5; Kennedy, *Banking Crisis*, 67; Cyril B. Upham and Edwin Lamke, *Closed and Distressed Banks: A Study in Public Administration* (Washington, D.C.: Brookings Institution, 1934), 10–2.

16. Olson, "Rehearsal for Disaster," 159.

17. Lester V. Chandler, *American Monetary Policy, 1928–1941* (New York: Harper and Row, 1971), 209–13; Kennedy, *Banking Crisis*, 74; Olson, *Hoover and RFC*, 100–1; Jesse H. Jones and Edward Angly, *Fifty Billion Dollars: My Thirteen Years with the RFC* (New York: Macmillan, 1951), 16–7; Friedman and Schwartz, *Monetary History*, 349.

18. Timmons, *Jones*, 176–7; *Congressional Record*, 76, pt. 2: 1361–2, 72d Congress, 2d session; Frank Freidel, *Franklin D. Roosevelt: Launching the New Deal* (Boston: Little, Brown, 1973), 180–1. The clerk acted under authority granted by the Emergency Relief and Construction Act passed in July 1932; for more information, see Chapter Three.

19. Olson, *Hoover and RFC*, 100.

20. Memorandum, Meeting of Board of Directors December 22, 1932, Binder 50, George Leslie Harrison Papers, Manuscript Division, Butler Library, Columbia University, New York, N.Y.; Chandler, *American Monetary Policy*, 217–8; Friedman and Schwartz, *Monetary History*, 389–90.

21. Chandler, *American Monetary Policy*, 218–9; Friedman and Schwartz, *Monetary History*, 390; *Wall Street Journal*, 13 January 1933, 1; Memorandum: Meeting of Board of Directors February 16, 1932, Binder 50, Harrison Papers.

22. Lawrence Sullivan, *Prelude to Panic: The Story of the Bank Holiday* (Washington, D.C.: Statesman, 1936), 51; Olson, *Hoover and RFC*, 101; Kennedy, *Banking Crisis*, 75–6; Harold Wolfe, *Herbert Hoover, Public Servant and Leader of the Loyal Opposition* (New York: Exposition, 1956), 344; Jones and Angly, *Fifty Billion Dollars*, 16–7.

23. Upham and Lamke, *Closed and Distressed Banks*, 152–4; Timmons, *Jones*, 180; Kennedy, *Banking Crisis*, 84–5; Olson, *Hoover and RFC*, 102–3; Presidential Log and Documents, 9 February 1933, Box 33, Post-Presidential Subject File, Herbert Clark Hoover Papers, Herbert Hoover Presidential Library, West Branch, Iowa. A cogent explanation of how the Detroit banks had gotten into difficulties starting in 1929 appears in Wigmore, *Crash and Its Aftermath*, 434–9.

24. Presidential Log and Documents, 9 February 1933, Hoover Papers; Kennedy, *Banking Crisis*, 87–8; Harry Barnard, *Independent Man: The Life of Senator James Couzens* (New York: Charles Scribner's Sons, 1958), 224–7; Olson, *Hoover and RFC*, 103.

25. Presidential Log and Documents, 12–13 February 1933, Hoover Papers; Kennedy, *Banking Crisis*, 88–95; Roy D. Chapin and A.A. Ballantine, Statement of Interview with Mr. Henry Ford, 13 February 1933, Box 3, Arthur Atwood Ballantine Papers, Herbert Hoover Presidential Library, West Branch, Iowa; Olson, *Hoover and RFC*, 103–4; Jones and Angly, *Fifty Billion Dollars*, 61–5.

26. Myers and Newton, *Hoover Administration*, 338–40; Martin L. Fausold, *The Presidency of Herbert C. Hoover* (Lawrence: University of Kansas, 1985), 229–32; Kennedy, *Banking Crisis*, 136–9; Frank Freidel, "The Interregnum Struggle Between Hoover and Roosevelt," *The Hoover Presidency: A Reappraisal*, Martin L. Fausold and George T. Mazuzan, eds. (Albany: State University of New York, 1974): 145–9; Diary, 21 February 1933, Raymond Moley Papers, Hoover Institution on War, Revolution, and Peace, Stanford University, Stanford, Cal. Wigmore, *Crash and Its Aftermath*, argues that Hoover's diagnosis of the problems was correct (447). For an account of negotiations to reopen Detroit's banks prior to March 4, see Kennedy, *Banking Crisis*, 96–102.

27. Memorandum, Summary of Michigan's "Bank Holiday," scrapbook V, Arthur H. Vandenberg Papers, Michigan Historical Collections, Bentley Historical Library, University of Michigan, Ann Arbor, Mich.; Presidential Log and Documents, 15 February 1933, Hoover Papers; letter to Couzens from Mills, 18 February 1933, Box 111, Ogden Livingston Mills Papers, Manuscript Division, Library of Congress, Washington, D.C.; C. David Tompkins, *Senator Arthur H. Vandenberg: The Evolution of a Modern Republican, 1884–1945* (East Lansing: Michigan State University, 1970), 78–9; *Congressional Record*, 76, pt. 5: 4691, 72d Congress, 2d session.

28. Memorandum, Summary of Michigan's "Bank Holiday," Vandenberg Papers; Tompkins, *Vandenberg*, 79; U.S., Congress, House Committee on Banking and Currency, *Power of the Comptroller of the Currency over National Banks: Report to Accompany S.J. Res. 256*, H. Rept. 2111, 72d Congress, 2d session, 24 February 1933; *Congressional Record*, 76, pt. 5: 5012, 5022–6, 72d Congress, 2d session; Walter Wyatt, "Federal Banking Legislation," *Banking Studies*, E.A. Goldenweiser, Elliott Thurston, and Bray Hammond, eds. (Washington, D.C.: Board of Governors of the Federal Reserve System, 1941): 54. The resolution as amended by the House limited the exercise of such authority so that it expired six months from approval by the president but could be extended another six months. The House also added an amendment to exclude any possible automatic extension of branch banking. Undoubtedly part of the resolution's strength in the House can be attributed to the declaration of state-wide holidays in Indiana and Maryland as well as the extension of Michigan's holiday.

29. The investigation began under authority of S.Res. 84, 72d Congress, 1st session, and it continued throughout the lame-duck session under authority of S.Res. 239. "Senate Adopts Resolution to Investigate Stock Market Trading," *Commercial and Financial Chronicle*, 134 (5 March 1932): 1680; *Congressional Record*, 75, pt. 12: 13558, 72d Congress, 1st session; Kennedy, *Banking Crisis*, 104–7; Gilbert Courtland Fite, "Peter Norbeck: Prairie Statesman," *University of Missouri Studies*, 22, 2 (1948): 172–9; Vincent P. Carosso, *Investment Banking in America: A History* (Cambridge, Mass.: Harvard University, 1970), 322–8.

30. Kennedy, *Banking Crisis*, 126–7; Barnard, *Couzens*, 205–6; Carosso, *Investment Banking*, 329–30.

31. Thomas L. Stokes, *Chip Off My Shoulder* (Princeton, N.J.: Princeton University, 1940), 355–7; Thomas Joel Anderson, Jr., *Federal and State Control of Banking* (New York: Bankers Publishing Company, 1934), 280, 282; Carosso, *Investment Banking*, 330–5; Kennedy, *Banking Crisis*, 103; Ron Chernow, *The House of Morgan: An American Banking Dynasty and the Rise of Modern Finance* (New York: Atlantic Monthly, 1990), 355–6. George J. Benston argues that these apparent abuses were not illegal and were only peripherally related to separating commercial from investment banking; *The Separation of Commercial and Investment Banking: The Glass–Steagall Act Revisited and Reconsidered* (New York: Oxford University, 1990), 47–76.

32. Friedman and Schwartz, *Monetary History*, 325–6; Gordon Wells McKinley, The Federal Reserve System in the Period of Crisis, 1930 to 1935 (Ph.D. dissertation, Ohio State University, 1948), 95–6, 289; Chandler, *American Monetary Policy*, 218–9. The hoarding of so little gold would indicate that the panic had more to do with instability of banks than with fear for the gold dollar; Federal Reserve Board, *Twentieth Annual Report Covering Operations for the Year 1933* (Washington, D.C.: U.S. Government Printing Office, 1934), 1; Chandler, *American Monetary Policy*, 222–4; Kennedy, *Banking Crisis*, 224; Wigmore, *Crash and Its Aftermath*, 448.

33. Chandler, *American Monetary Policy*, 215; Olson, *Hoover and RFC*, 104–5; Hamlin Diary, v. 22, 26 December 1932; Jones and Angly, *Fifty Billion Dollars*, 69–70; George A. Selgin, "Accommodating Changes in the Relative Demand for Currency: Free Banking vs. Central Banking," *Cato Journal*, 7 (Winter 1988): 638; Wigmore, *Crash and Its Aftermath*, 448–9.

34. *Wall Street Journal*, 22 February 1933, 4; Myers and Newton, *Hoover Administration*, 355–7; Sullivan, *Prelude to Panic*, 94–6.

35. Myers and Newton, *Hoover Administration*, 357.

36. Hamlin Diary, v. 22, 21 February 1933; Tugwell Diary, 18 February 1933. Bankers had begun to urge FDR to act as early as February 17; Herman E. Krooss, *Executive Opinion: What Business Leaders Said and Thought on Economic Issues 1920s–1960s* (Garden City, N.Y.: Doubleday, 1970), 164; Office Correspondence to Confidential Files from Harrison, 17 February 1933, Binder 46, Harrison Papers.

37. Lyle, Senate Career of Glass, 279–84; Koeniger, "Unreconstructed Rebel," 82–3; Myers and Newton, *Hoover Administration*, 340–2; Raymond Moley, *The First New Deal* (New York: Harcourt, Brace and World, 1966), 80–6; Barrie A. Wigmore, "Was the Bank Holiday of 1933 Caused by a Run on the Dollar?" *Journal of Economic History*, 47 (September 1987): 741–4. According to Rexford G. Tugwell, *In Search of Roosevelt* (Cambridge, Mass.: Harvard University, 1972), 239, FDR had not definitely decided on inflation in February 1933 but was considering it. Wigmore firmly believes that the banking panic might not have occurred if there had been no discussion in the Roosevelt camp about leaving the gold standard; *The Crash and Its Aftermath*, 423, 445–7.

38. Kennedy, *Banking Crisis*, 140–1; Myers and Newton, *Hoover Administration*, 343–4; Presidential Log and Documents, 22 February 1933, Hoover Papers; Merlo J. Pusey, *Eugene Meyer* (New York: Alfred A. Knopf, 1974), 20.

39. Raymond Moley, *After Seven Years* (New York: Harper and Brothers, 1939), 143; Myers and Newton, *Hoover Administration*, 356; Freidel, *Roosevelt: Launching the New Deal*, 184–6; Presidential Log and Documents, 25 February 1933, Hoover Papers. Daniel Roper, soon to be secretary of Commerce, claimed FDR told him a week before that it might be necessary to act on inauguration day; Daniel C. Roper and Frank H. Lovette, *Fifty Years of Public Life* (Durham, N.C.: Duke University, 1941), 267–8.

40. Myers and Newton, *Hoover Administration*, 360.

41. Ibid., 344–5, 360; Sullivan, *Prelude to Panic*, 110. Hoover had already issued a proclamation calling for the Senate to convene at noon on March 4; Presidential Press Release, 14 February 1933, Box 111, General Records of the Department of the Treasury, Office of the Secretary, General Correspondence 1917–32, Record Group 56, National Archives, Washington, D.C.

42. Olson, *Hoover and RFC*, 111–3; *The Reminiscences of Walter Wyatt*, Interview I: 14–7, Oral History Collection, Butler Library, Columbia University, New York, N.Y. [hereafter Wyatt, OHRO]; Timmons, *Jones*, 188. According to E.A. Goldenweiser, Mills asked Awalt to draft a bill using conservators; letter to Ballantine from Wyatt, 1 August 1944, Box 3, Ballantine Papers. Drafts of the executive order and joint resolution are in Box 6, Records of the Office of the Comptroller of the Currency, Banking Emergency Records,

Record Group 101, National Archives, Washington, D.C. The comptroller's office had also drafted a resolution to establish currency issues by clearing house associations and a bill to protect bank depositors against the creation of preferences during runs and failures; Box 1, Banking Emergency Records, RG 101. [All citations to RG 101 in this chapter refer to Banking Emergency Records.]

43. Wyatt, OHRO, Interview I: 14–5; Tugwell Diary, 27 February 1933; Helen M. Burns, *The American Banking Community and New Deal Banking Reforms, 1933–1935* (Westport, Conn.: Greenwood, 1974), 33–4.

44. Pusey, *Meyer*, 232–3; Hamlin Diary, v. 22, 1 March 1933; Myers and Newton, *Hoover Administration*, 359–63; Kennedy, *Banking Crisis*, 146; Sullivan, *Prelude to Panic*, 112.

45. *New York Times*, 3 March 1933, 1–2; Presidential Log and Documents, 2 March 1933, Hoover Papers; Freidel, *Roosevelt: Launching the New Deal*, 192.

46. *Wall Street Journal*, 2 March 1933, 1; *New York Times*, 3 March 1933, 1–2, 25, 27; Chandler, *American Monetary Policy*, 216, 219–20; Burns, *American Banking Community*, 32–3, 36–7; Hamlin Diary, v. 22, 2 March 1933; Olson, *Saving Capitalism*, 33; Wigmore, "Bank Holiday Caused By Run on Dollar," 745, 747–8.

47. Myers and Newton, *Hoover Administration*, 363–5; Freidel, *Roosevelt: Launching the New Deal*, 191–2; Presidential Log and Documents, 2 March 1933, Hoover Papers; Moley, *After Seven Years*, 144.

48. Moley, *First New Deal*, 148–51, 159; David Burner, *Herbert Hoover, a Public Life* (New York: Alfred A. Knopf, 1979), 323; Kennedy, *Banking Crisis*, 147–9; Presidential Log and Documents, 3 March 1933, Hoover Papers; Rixey Smith and Norman Beasley, *Carter Glass: A Biography* (New York: Longmans, Green, 1939), 341–2; Olson, *Saving Capitalism*, 34.

49. Freidel, *Roosevelt: Launching the New Deal*, 189–90; "American Banking," *Banker*, 26 (April 1933): 50; Presidential Log and Documents, 3 March 1933, Hoover Papers; Chandler, *American Monetary Policy*, 220–1; Memorandum, Meeting of the Federal Reserve Board, from 10 p.m. March 3rd to 4 a.m. March 4th, Box 7, Emanuel Alexandrovich Goldenweiser Papers, Manuscript Division, Library of Congress, Washington, D.C.; Hamlin Diary, v. 22, 3 March 1933.

50. Hamlin Diary, v. 22, 3 March 1933; Pusey, *Meyer*, 20–1; letter to Meyer from Hoover, 4 March 1933, Box 173, Presidential Personal File, Hoover Papers. Adolf Berle told Charles Hamlin that Roosevelt had never said he did not want Hoover to issue a proclamation; Hamlin Diary, v. 22, 6 March 1933. Hoover cannot have definitely known at 1:30 a.m. that New York and Illinois would both declare holidays. According to Morrill, it was 2:22 a.m. when Mills told the board that probably Illinois and New York would agree to bank holidays; Box 359, Hamlin Papers (attached to letter to Hamlin from Stevens, 11 August 1933). Apparently Hoover had feared he might continue to receive last-minute appeals for action. According to James Stringfellow, a White House guard, Hoover had left orders not to be disturbed, and Mrs. Lou Hoover was angry with those who decided to wake the president so he could read the board's letter; Memorandum to Meyer from Fahy, 7 April 1933, Box 28, Meyer Papers.

51. Freidel, *Roosevelt: Launching the New Deal*, 193–4; Memorandum: Special Meeting of Board of Directors March 3, 1933, Binder 50, Harrison Papers; Moley, *First New Deal*, 128n; Kennedy, *Banking Crisis*, 149–51; Kenneth S. Davis, *FDR: The New Deal Years, 1933–1937, A History* (New York: Random House, 1986), 26. Wigmore, "Bank Holiday Caused by Run on Dollar," says that the New York Clearing House banks were in exceptionally liquid condition and that the banks needed the holiday less than the New York Federal Reserve Bank did (748–9).

52. Robert S. McElvaine, *The Great Depression: America, 1929–1941* (New York: Times Books, 1984), 139–40; Edgar Eugene Robinson, *The Roosevelt Leadership, 1933–1945* (Philadelphia: J.B. Lippincott, 1955), 102; Burns, *American Banking Community*, 40–1; Freidel, *Roosevelt: Launching the New Deal*, 214–5; Kennedy, *Banking Crisis*, 157. The bankers in Washington could agree on little beyond a national bank holiday. Finally they recommended deposit insurance and the issuance of scrip. Woodin accepted neither, and the bankers departed without having any influence. See Kennedy, *Banking Crisis*, 168–70.

53. Freidel, *Roosevelt: Launching the New Deal*, 220; Arthur M. Schlesinger, Jr. *The Age of Roosevelt*, 3 v. (Boston: Houghton Mifflin, 1957–60), II: 5; Kennedy, *Banking Crisis*, 159–60, 164–8, 172–5; Franklin Delano Roosevelt, *The Public Papers and Addresses of Franklin D. Roosevelt*, Samuel I. Rosenman, comp., 13 v. (New York:

Random House, 1938–45), II: 17, 24–6. FDR also issued a proclamation calling Congress into session at noon on Thursday, March 9. Davis, *FDR: The New Deal*, claims that FDR pressured Treasury officials to avoid scrip by proposing the highly inflationary plan of allowing holders of government bonds to cash them at par value (a total of $21 billion). Davis believes that FDR intended to horrify Treasury officials so that they would finally agree on their own plan to provide currency in the aftermath of the bank holiday (52). E.A. Goldenweiser claimed credit for originating the idea of using federal reserve bank notes; letter to Ballantine from Wyatt, 1 August 1944, Box 3, Ballantine Papers. Most of the federal reserve bank notes that the Treasury printed were not needed in 1933 and were not issued until World War II, when scarce materials led to their use. These notes have not been issued since 1945. Some of the more important Treasury regulations were as follows: banks could make change, complete settlements not involving cash, allow access to safety deposit boxes, continue certain transactions for trust accounts, accept deposits in segregated accounts, provide usual salaries and wages, and permit withdrawals to cover food, medicine and other essentials. Paying out gold or gold certificates was prohibited, and the banks were to discourage withdrawals for hoarding. Banks in each locality interpreted the regulations to the best of their abilities and forwarded questions to district banks, which also operated under instructions issued by the reserve board. See *Federal Reserve Bulletin*, 19 (March 1933): 122–30. Originals of the regulations, instructions, and interpretations signed by Roosevelt and Woodin are in Box 9, RG 101.

54. Kennedy, *Banking Crisis*, 157, 170–1; James Edward Sargent, The Hundred Days: Franklin D. Roosevelt and the Early New Deal, 1933 (Ph.D. dissertation, Michigan State University, 1972), 142–4. Mills considered using either preferred stock purchases or a 50% guaranty of deposits to aid banks in the second group. He did not realize the strength of FDR's opposition to deposit insurance. For more on Roosevelt and guaranty of deposits, see Chapter Five.

55. Hamlin Diary, v. 22, 8–9 March 1933; Kennedy, *Banking Crisis*, 182–3; telegram to Federal Reserve Agents from Woodin, 8 March 1933, Box 5, RG 101; Memorandum: Executive Session of Special Meeting of Board of Directors March 8, 1933, Binder 50, Harrison Papers; telegram to Federal Reserve Bank Governors from Woodin, 10 March 1933, Box 9, RG 101.

56. Freidel, *Roosevelt: Launching the New Deal*, 220–1, 225–6; Kennedy, *Banking Crisis*, 175; Moley, *First New Deal*, 176–7; *New York Times*, 9 March 1933, 2.

57. *New York Times*, 9 March 1933, 2.

58. Wyatt, OHRO, Interview I: 30–3; Ronald Allen Mulder, *The Insurgent Progressives in the United States Senate and the New Deal, 1933–1939* (New York: Garland, 1979), 42; *New York Times*, 9 March 1933, 1-2. Copies of both the committee print and S. 1 are in Box 3, Ballantine Papers. Comparison reveals that the most significant changes were in Titles I and IV. In Title I, power to require the return of gold or gold certificates was shifted from the reserve board to the secretary of the Treasury and the obligation to return gold was extended to include individuals and corporations as well as member banks. In Title IV, Glass made explicit that advances under the authority of section 10(b) as amended still had to carry an interest rate one percentage point above the normal discount rate. Glass also limited the expanded authority to lend under section 10(b) to "March 3, 1934 or after the expiration of such additional period not exceeding one year as the President may prescribe."

59. *New York Times*, 10 March 1933, 2.

60. *Wall Street Journal*, 10 March 1933, 5; Roosevelt, *Public Papers*, II: 45–6; William E. Leuchtenburg, *Franklin D. Roosevelt and the New Deal, 1932–1940* (New York: Harper and Row, 1963), 43–4; *Congressional Record*, 77, pt. 1: 76–81, 89, 73d Congress, 1st session; Jack Brien Key, "Henry B. Steagall: The Conservative as a Reformer," *Alabama Review*, 17 (July 1964): 204–5.

61. Wyatt, OHRO, Interview I: 30–3; Memorandum, Monday Night, March 6, 1933, Box 7, Goldenweiser Papers; Memorandum, Emergency Banking Act of 1933, Box 543, William Gibbs McAdoo Papers, Manuscript Division, Library of Congress, Washington, D.C.; Kennedy, *Banking Crisis*, 176–7; *Congressional Record*, 77, pt. 1: 49–67, 85, 73d Congress, 1st session; Ronald A. Mulder, "Reluctant New Dealers: The Progressive Insurgents in the United States Senate, 1933–1934," *Capitol Studies*, 2 (Winter 1974): 7–8; Ronald L. Feinman, *Twilight of Progressivism: The Western Republican Senators and the New Deal* (Baltimore: Johns Hopkins University, 1981), 58.

62. *New York Times*, 10 March 1933, 14.

63. Ibid., 1; Pamela Webb, "Business as Usual: The Bank Holiday in Arkansas," *Arkansas Historical Quarterly*, 39 (Autumn 1980): 259; *Federal Reserve Bulletin*, 19 (March 1933): 126–7; Roosevelt, *Public Papers*, II: 54–6. The authority of the secretary of the Treasury to license member banks remained in effect until April 8, 1947.

64. *Federal Reserve Bulletin*, 19 (March 1933): 127–8; Howard H. Hackley, *Lending Functions of the Federal Reserve Banks: A History* (Washington, D.C.: Board of Governors of the Federal Reserve System, 1973), 120, 131; *New York Times*, 14 March 1933, 8. Reserve banks lent more than $4 million under the direct loan provisions between July 1932 and November 1933; Confidential Memoranda, Division of Bank Operations, 17 November 1933, Box 359, Hamlin Papers.

65. *New York Times*, 11 March 1933, 3; Ibid., 12 March 1933, 1; Roosevelt, *Public Papers*, II: 61–5. For the effects of FDR's fireside chat, see Kennedy, *Banking Crisis*, 181–2; Freidel, *Roosevelt: Launching the New Deal*, 230–1; Leuchtenburg, *Roosevelt*, 44.

66. Memorandum: Special Meeting of the Board of Directors March 10, 1933, Binder 50, Harrison Papers; Memorandum: Special Meeting of Board of Directors March 11, 1933, Binder 50, Harrison Papers; Kennedy, *Banking Crisis*, 183–4.

67. Letter to Woodin from Roosevelt, 11 March 1933, Box 5, RG 101. Woodin read a draft of this letter to the reserve board, which approved it; Hamlin Diary, v. 22, 11 March 1933.

68. Memorandum, Special Meeting of Board of Directors March 11, 1933, Binder 50, Harrison Papers; Wyatt, OHRO, Interview I: 55–6. FDR's letter may be one reason J.U. Calkins, governor of the San Francisco reserve bank, backed down on his original recommendation that Bank of America not reopen on March 13. In a telephone call to Woodin, who wanted to open the bank, Calkins would not take sole responsibility for keeping this bank and its 410 branches closed. See Kennedy, *Banking Crisis*, 186–7; Moley, *After Seven Years*, 154; Freidel, *Roosevelt: Launching the New Deal*, 232–3.

69. *New York Times*, 15 March 1933, 6, 8; Ibid., 16 March 1933, 5–6; Kennedy, *Banking Crisis*, 185–7; *Federal Reserve Bulletin*, 19 (March 1933): 130. Copies of the authorizations Woodin sent to the reserve banks are in Box 12, RG 101. Woodin revoked the authority

of unlicensed banks to make distributions for emergency needs on March 18 since enough institutions were fully open.

70. *New York Times*, 17 March 1933, 4; Ibid., 18 March 1933, 19; *Wall Street Journal*, 16 March 1933, 1; Ibid., 18 March 1933, 5; Federal Reserve Board, *Twentieth Annual Report, 1933*, 14–7; Timmons, *Jones*, 190; *Federal Reserve Bulletin*, 19 (April 1933): 209, 219; Frederick A. Bradford, *Monetary Developments since 1932* (New York: Longmans, Green, 1934), 5. Awalt had placed another 1,000 national banks in receivership by March 16.

71. *Congressional Record*, 77, pt. 1: 247, 331–5, 73d Congress, 1st session; Kennedy, *Banking Crisis*, 199–200; letter to Glass from Meyer, 14 March 1933, Box 358, Hamlin Papers; Hamlin Diary, v. 22, 14 March 1933; *New York Times*, 15 March 1933, 4.

72. *The Reminiscences of Eugene Meyer*, III: A103, Oral History Collection, Butler Library, Columbia University, New York, N.Y.; Hamlin Diary, v. 22, 14–18 March 1933; *Wall Street Journal*, 17 March 1933, 10.

73. *Congressional Record*, 77, pt. 1: 600–7, 630–41, 73d Congress, 1st session; telegram to Federal Reserve Agents and Governors from Morrill, 17 March 1933, Box 358, Hamlin Papers; U.S., Congress, House, Committee on Banking and Currency, *Loans to State Banks by Federal Reserve Banks: Report to Accompany H.R. 3757*, H. Rept. 10, 73d Congress, 1st session, 20 March 1933.

74. U.S., Congress, Senate, Committee on Banking and Currency, *Direct Loans to State Banks and Trust Companies: Report to Accompany H.R. 3757*, S. Rept. 4, 73d Congress, 1st session, 22 March 1933; *Congressional Record*, 77, pt. 1: 540–1, 651, 707–22, 789–814, 849–50, 73d Congress, 1st session; *Wall Street Journal*, 25 March 1933, 7; *New York Times*, 24 March 1933, 31. The act expired on March 24, 1934.

75. Confidential Memoranda, Division of Bank Operations, 17 November 1933, Box 359, Hamlin Papers; Kennedy, *Banking Crisis*, 201; letter to Black from Harrison, 26 May 1933, Binder 51, Harrison Papers; Friedman and Schwartz, *Monetary History*, 330, 426. Two other minor changes in the Emergency Banking Act aided the process of reconstruction. An amendment to the bank conservation title (S. 1410) passed Congress in May. It struck out "national banking association" in section 207 and replaced it with "bank" to make it consistent with the definition of banks in section 202, allowing the

comptroller of the currency to reorganize trust companies and savings banks in the District of Columbia. FDR signed an amendment to Title III of the emergency act (S. 1425) on June 15, 1933. This change, which passed at the RFC's request, clarified the ability of national banks to issue one *or more* classes of preferred stock and altered the paragraph concerning dividend payments to eliminate the priority given to preferred stock in the emergency act. Congress also passed an amendment to the National Banking Act (S. 1415) that permitted national banks to lend amounts larger than 10% of their capital and surplus for the purpose of aiding in the liquidation of unlicensed state or national banks.

76. Ross M. Robertson, *The Comptroller and Bank Supervision: A Historical Appraisal* (Washington, D.C.: Office of the Comptroller of the Currency, 1968), 123–5; letter to Roosevelt from Jesse Jones, 3 September 1934, Box 2, Official File 643, Franklin Delano Roosevelt Presidential Papers, Franklin Delano Roosevelt Library, Hyde Park, N.Y.; press release, Treasury Department, 13 May 1935, Box 9, Official File 21b, FDR Papers. On liquidation, reorganization, and recapitalization, see Olson, *Saving Capitalism*, 66–89; James Francis Thaddeus O'Connor, *The Banking Crisis and Recovery under the Roosevelt Administration* (Chicago: Callaghan, 1938), 28–60.

77. Federal Reserve Board, *Twentieth Annual Report, 1933*, 26–7.

78. Ibid., 27–8; untitled memorandum, 30 January 1934, Box 2448, RG 82. The Treasury Department was integrally involved in drafting the proclamations and executive orders regarding gold, but the reserve board was less often consulted. The board had most influence on the executive order of April 5. See documents in Box 5, General Records of the Department of the Treasury, Office of the Secretary of the Treasury, Office of Domestic Gold and Silver Operations, Record Group 56, National Archives, Washington, D.C.

79. Olson, *Saving Capitalism*, 32.

CHAPTER FIVE

THE BANKING ACT OF 1933

During the first Hundred Days of Franklin D. Roosevelt's presidency, a combination of his dynamic personality, a new Congress, and intense public pressure brought forth a rush of legislation, including the Banking Act of 1933. That act was the work of Representative Henry M. Steagall (D–ALA) and Senator Carter Glass (D–VA), who combined separate reform measures introduced during 1932 to produce a bill that included divorce of commercial from investment banking and deposit insurance.

Roosevelt and most bankers believed the Glass–Steagall bill had both good and bad points. They accepted the division of commercial from investment banking because of revelations by Charles Mitchell, president of National City Bank of New York, during the Pecora hearings of February 1933. Still, FDR and eastern bankers opposed deposit insurance because they thought it would force sound bankers to pay for mistakes of unsound ones. The public wholeheartedly endorsed a deposit guaranty, and legislators' efforts to fulfill constituents' demands led to an increase of federal authority over financial institutions and to establishment of the Federal Deposit Insurance Corporation, which began operation January 1, 1934.

The Banking Act of 1933 imposed many new rules and restrictions on members of the Federal Reserve System. Bankers complained about parts of the act, and their lobbying led to minor changes in 1934–35. Still, they did not succeed in altering the substance of the act and eventually accepted provisions they had not wanted, especially establishment of the Federal Deposit Insurance Corporation. Since 1970, Congress has repealed some restrictions on member banks and may make other changes to erase the legal barrier between commercial and investment banking. After more than fifty years, bankers accept the

FDIC but seek to amend sections of the act they agreed to with little protest in 1933.

PERSONNEL CHANGES

The elections of 1932 moved Democrats into and Republicans out of Washington. Electoral realignments such as this one promoted sweeping rather than incremental change because there were many new representatives and because parties became polarized and homogeneous. In the House of Representatives, 131 Democrats achieved election for the first time, and the Democratic majority increased to more than 190 seats. They captured a solid majority in the Senate, too, 60 to 35. On average, new Democrats reflected the socio-economic status of their constituents, many of whom were first-time voters brought out by the depression. Democrats had won in 1932 because they persuaded such voters that government in their hands would deal actively with economic problems, while voters had perceived the recovery efforts of Republicans as inadequate. The 73d Congress was as eager to experiment and take action as was Roosevelt.[1] FDR "made the Democratic party the party of the new agenda in the eyes of the electorate" with the "congressional party" as a "willing partner."[2] Perhaps this explains the rapid passage of the Banking Act of 1933, a measure that had stalled in Congress during Herbert Hoover's administration.

House leadership underwent considerable turnover in March 1933. The former speaker had become vice president, so Henry T. Rainey (ILL), former majority leader, became speaker. Democrats chose Joseph W. Byrns (TENN) as majority leader. Turnover in House membership led to changes in the Banking and Currency Committee that enhanced Steagall's power as chairman. Only two Republicans, Robert Luce (MASS) and Carroll L. Beedy (ME), had served on the committee before. Six Republicans replaced four who had not been reelected and two others who were elected but not reassigned to the banking committee. Eight Democrats who were members in 1932 and eight new Democrats completed the committee, which was enlarged from 21 to 24.[3]

Since only one-third of Senate seats are filled in any election, the effect of the balloting in 1932 was less noticeable than in the House. John N. Garner (TEX) was vice president, and Joseph T. Robinson

(ARK) became majority leader. The Senate Committee on Banking and Currency underwent fewer changes than its counterpart in the House. Glass possessed seniority on this committee and on Appropriations. Because he chose to become chairman of Appropriations, a staunch Roosevelt supporter, Duncan U. Fletcher (FLA), became chairman of Banking and Currency. Glass may have assumed that he would still be able to dominate banking legislation through his knowledge and personality. Fletcher allowed such domination by appointing the Virginian chairman of the subcommittee on banking. Other subcommittee members were Robert J. Bulkley (D–OH), William G. McAdoo (D–CAL), Frederic C. Walcott (R–CONN), and John G. Townsend, Jr. (R–DEL). All save McAdoo, a former secretary of the Treasury and a newly elected senator, had been on the committee since 1930. Increased from 19 to 20 members, the full committee had other changes because three Republicans had been defeated and Cordell Hull (D–TENN) left to join FDR's cabinet. Leaders assigned a new Republican and four new Democrats to the committee.[4]

Because the Democratic party had substantial majorities in both houses, the battle for New Deal programs was fought among conservative, moderate, and liberal factions within the party. Not strictly regional, these groups were often separated by generational and socio-economic differences. A few southern Democrats were liberals who joined men of like mind from other areas to support Roosevelt even in the late 1930s, when there was strong conservative opposition to his program. Other southerners doubted the wisdom of the New Deal in 1933 and later turned to opposition. Most Democrats stood between these extremes, and as party leader Roosevelt sought to conciliate moderates. Congress provided FDR with overwhelming support during 1933–34, giving him almost everything he asked. Near the end of the Hundred Days and during the second session, some signs of congressional revolt emerged, usually from members trying to secure greater change rather than from conservatives.[5]

Although the banking bill of 1933 dealt with the Federal Reserve Act, the board made no new attempt to amend or oppose it because of instability in the board's membership. Eugene Meyer had tendered his resignation as governor in late March because he disagreed with FDR's policies, but he remained in office, without attempting to lead the board, while FDR sought a successor. Eugene R. Black, governor of the Atlanta reserve bank, finally accepted the position in May, on a temporary basis. He had been in office little more than a month before passage of the Banking Act of 1933. Just before Congress adjourned in June, Roosevelt filled two vacancies left by the Hoover administration, naming politicians M.S. Szymczak and J.J. Thomas. The former had been city controller of Chicago and a friend of the late Mayor Anton J. Cermak. A lawyer and farmer, Thomas had been chairman of the Nebraska Democratic State Committee. William Woodin, as secretary of the Treasury, became an ex officio member and chairman of the board. The comptroller of the currency, a post that had been vacant since autumn, was also an ex officio member. F. Gloyd Awalt, deputy comptroller of the currency, had been acting comptroller but did not sit with the board. When FDR appointed J.F.T. O'Connor as comptroller in April 1933, Awalt remained as deputy because officials appreciated his work during the financial emergency. O'Connor had aided FDR's campaign in California and was a lawyer and associate of McAdoo and A.P. Giannini (Bank of America). Only Adolph C. Miller, Charles S. Hamlin, and George R. James were board members all of 1932–33. Such change made it difficult for the board to reach a consensus about anything.[6]

PASSAGE OF THE BANKING ACT OF 1933

The banking crisis of February and early March 1933 persuaded the public that a federal guaranty of deposits was necessary to restore confidence in banks. Senators and congressmen received scores of letters from constituents asking for this reform. Roosevelt resisted such sentiment successfully during the bank holiday, but members of Congress realized that no other change could as easily restore confidence. Such legislators as Steagall and Fletcher had long believed in a deposit guaranty, and the groundswell of support for it convinced Glass that he had to accept it if he wanted the rest of his reforms to pass. When he announced he would introduce a bill that included deposit insurance, Woodin and FDR became concerned. They believed that any attempt to guarantee deposits would encourage irresponsible bankers to take excessive risks, since losses to depositors would be covered. Glass warned Roosevelt that because of public pressure Congress would amend the bank bill to attach deposit insurance, whether or not FDR approved.[7]

Glass introduced his measure (S. 245) on March 11. It was similar to the Senate bill that had passed during January 1933.

Roosevelt told Glass he approved of most of the bill, including sections to divorce commercial from investment banking. He agreed that state and national banking should be unified under one regulatory authority but thought Congress should limit branch banks to a single county, instead of adopting the bill's provision permitting state-wide branching in accord with state law. Of course, he and Woodin opposed deposit insurance. Woodin also feared the measure would dampen recovery by preventing banks from underwriting securities, and he opposed the removal of the secretary of the Treasury (himself) from the reserve board. Later he expressed concern that reserve banks could not safely contribute $150 million from surplus to the insurance fund and that state banks not meeting insurance qualifications would be driven out of business. The banking subcommittee discussed the bill for the remainder of March, while Glass negotiated with Steagall for a similar measure in the House. Since the senator accepted the inevitability of including deposit insurance, Steagall cooperated. With advice from reserve board employees Walter Wyatt and Chester Morrill, the Glass subcommittee was finishing the measure in early April, when the reservations of Woodin and Roosevelt caused a delay.[8]

Since Glass wanted his bill to pass, he tried to be reasonable about administration complaints. As a supporter of state-wide branch banking, he chose to ignore FDR's opinion about branches, and he refused to divide the bill into segments to be addressed separately, as FDR had suggested. The most important subcommittee concession concerned deposit insurance. Roosevelt had refused to approve a 100% guaranty of deposits, so subcommittee members agreed to insure fully deposits up to $10,000, protect three-fourths of deposits between $10,000 and $50,000, and guarantee half of those above $50,000. They limited to $150 million the Treasury's contribution to the insurance corporation's capital, adopting FDR's advice. Also at his suggestion, the insurance plan would not operate until July 1, 1934. To pacify Woodin, the subcommittee struck the section that would have eliminated the secretary of the Treasury from the reserve board. Glass then introduced his new bill (S. 1631) on May 10 with unenthusiastic approval from Roosevelt and Woodin.[9]

In addition to deposit insurance, subcommittee members included a few provisions that had not appeared in previous Glass bills. A paragraph suggested by Winthrop W. Aldrich of Chase National Bank would extend separation of commercial and investment banking by requiring private banks, which had been unregulated, either to cease accepting deposits or to stop underwriting, issuing, and distributing stocks. If they chose to receive deposits, private banks would have to submit to examination by the comptroller of the currency or a reserve bank and would have to publish reports of their condition. Another provision, derived from an older Steagall deposit insurance bill, would curb bank competition by prohibiting member banks from paying interest on demand deposits. Because the subcommittee believed that interest rate competition had injured bank earnings in the 1920s, it included a related section allowing the reserve board to set a maximum rate that member banks could pay on savings deposits. This provision replaced one from earlier versions of the Glass bill, which would have limited the interest rate on savings deposits to no more than 3%.[10]

The subcommittee measure included three sections from a Glass bill introduced in 1932 that had not appeared in the measure passed by the Senate in January 1933. The first would allow the reserve board, upon affirmative vote of six members, to fix the percentage of a bank's capital and surplus that could be invested in loans secured by stocks or bonds and to change such percentage to prevent undue use of bank loans for securities speculation. Another provision would amend the Clayton Anti-Trust Act of 1914 so that no director, officer, or employee of a national bank could hold a similar position in a corporation or be a member of a partnership that made loans secured by stocks or bonds (except loans to its own subsidiaries). A third paragraph would prohibit any officer or director of a member bank from also being an officer, director, or manager of a securities company after January 1, 1934 and would outlaw correspondent relationships between member banks and securities dealers.[11]

Glass believed dividing commercial from investment banking would increase the safety of banks, and this emphasis remained evident in the new measure, which would divorce securities affiliates within two years, instead of the five allowed by the Senate bill of January 1933. All three sections taken from a Glass bill of 1932 served to separate commercial and investment banking, as did the new section regarding private banks. The subcommittee measure retained a related provision that would require the reserve board to discourage undue speculation through regulating the use of money lent to member banks. After revelation at the Pecora hearings of February 1933 that National City Bank had made loans to its investment affiliate secured by collateral that became worthless, popular sentiment crystallized in favor of reform. This sentiment was only strengthened by the Pecora investigation of J.P. Morgan and Company, the premier private banking firm on Wall Street, during May and June 1933.[12] For this reason the subcommittee was able to include sections that Glass had given up hope of having enacted a year earlier.

The Glass bill would increase the power of the reserve board in several ways. As mentioned, the board would receive authority to set interest rates that member banks paid on savings deposits and would have a duty to prevent speculation by regulating member bank loans secured by stocks or bonds. The board would also receive explicit authority to oversee relations between reserve banks and foreign banks, which reflected a belief of Glass and board members that foreign bankers had relied excessively on New York reserve officials. The board would gain authority to issue permits to holding companies that owned member banks, which would allow the companies to vote reserve bank stock held by affiliated member banks. The board could revoke a permit if a holding company did not live up to conditions named in the bill. The board would receive the right to assess a monetary penalty on any member bank that did not cease to be affiliated with companies issuing or underwriting stocks and bonds.[13]

When the full Senate banking committee met on May 13 to consider the subcommittee bill, it added a few sections. One would prohibit bank officers from writing insurance, separating the two businesses. Another would protect rights of minority stockholders. McAdoo wished the section on deposit insurance to go into effect immediately, but the committee decided against it. Glass submitted the committee report on May 17.[14]

Steagall on May 16 introduced his measure (H.R. 5661), which was not identical to the Senate version, and the House Committee on Banking and Currency reported it three days later. Unlike the Glass bill, Steagall's measure had language to prohibit reserve banks from engaging in open market operations except in accord with resolutions first adopted by the Federal Open Market Committee—established as a statutory body—and approved by the reserve board. The House measure would set a maximum interest rate of 3% that member banks could pay on time deposits, while the Senate bill would leave the board to set maximum rates. Unlike Glass, Steagall had never been an advocate of branch banking and did not want to change the statute concerning branches. Steagall had always sought to protect nonmember banks, so his insurance program would allow banks unaffiliated with the reserve system to participate and would establish a new corporation to administer the plan. Glass hoped to use deposit insurance to achieve unified banking under the Federal Reserve System, so his bill would leave administration to the reserve and limit participation to member banks or those that had applied for membership.[15]

The House began considering Steagall's bill on May 20, after he obtained a resolution from the Rules Committee confining debate to four hours.[16] Steagall defended the provisions drawn from the Glass bill:

> The purpose of the regulatory provisions of this bill is to call back to the service of agriculture and commerce and industry the bank credit and the bank service designed by the framers of the Federal Reserve Act.
>
> The purpose is to strengthen the banking structure, to establish adequate capital requirements, to provide more effective regulation and supervision, to eliminate dangerous and unsound practices, and to confine banks of deposit to legitimate functions and to separate them from affiliates or other organizations which have brought discredit and loss of public confidence. We propose to see to it that hereafter the credit facilities of the Federal Reserve System shall be devoted primarily to the purposes to which that great act was dedicated at the outset.[17]

Debate focused on deposit insurance, which Steagall defended. Because of public support for a guaranty, few members opposed that part of the bill, but several feared it would not protect state banks because it would put them "at the mercy of a Federal agency," which might discriminate in its authority to issue rules and regulations.[18] The House adopted a few changes, starting with a committee amendment that would allow the board of directors of the deposit insurance corporation to choose its chairman. The members also accepted Wright Patman's (D–TEX) amendment to alter the corporation's board of directors by eliminating a member chosen from the reserve board in favor of another presidentially appointed member, so the corporation would not be directly connected to the reserve system. The House approved an amendment introduced by Beedy that would exclude from insurance coverage banks in receivership or liquidation on the day the corporation began operation.[19] The House accepted an amendment by John Y. Brown (D–KEN) to change the effective date of insurance from one year after enactment to whenever the president might proclaim after "examinations provided in section 302-a of all State banks applying within thirty days from the enactment of this act have been completed and said applications approved or rejected."[20]

Overwhelming support for Steagall's measure was apparent on May 23, when members voted 262 to 19 to pass it. Criticism had come from southern and western congressmen who desired to protect state banks and from such farm-state progressives as William Lemke (R–ND), who preferred greater governmental authority over national and state banks. Conservative opposition remained muted; Republicans supported the bill in hope of improving the banking system.[21]

Senate proceedings, which began May 19, reflected the general consensus about the need to restore depositors' confidence. Arthur H. Vandenberg (R–MICH) had already introduced an amendment that would provide an immediate guaranty of deposits in all state and national banks up to $2,500. Vandenberg had supported insurance during the previous session and now spoke to members of the administration, bankers, senators, and congressmen, in an effort to gain their support. He received encouragement from constituents and Michigan bankers because their institutions had suffered more than most during the banking crisis. Another advocate of an immediate guaranty was McAdoo, who had tried to put such a provision into subcommittee and committee bills.[22]

Glass began debate by describing how this bill differed from the one passed by the Senate in January. He explained that he thought the secretary of the Treasury should not be a member of the reserve board, but that the subcommittee had eliminated that proviso because Woodin had protested. Glass told senators he had no objection to an amendment that would require the divorce of securities affiliates within one year instead of two as the bill provided. He claimed the section prohibiting member banks from paying interest on demand deposits would end reliance on correspondent banks that paid interest on bankers' balances, which he assumed would halt the movement of money from smaller to larger cities, leaving more in rural communities to meet local needs. He added that prohibiting interest on demand deposits would make it easier for banks to pay assessments to support the insurance fund. He thought the reserve board should have power to adjust interest rates that member banks could pay on savings because he believed members had paid excessive interest during the 1920s, which had forced them to seek higher rates of return on riskier assets. Finally, Glass defended deposit insurance, saying it would lead to better banking because strong banks would have incentive to prevent competitors from failing. He emphasized that member banks would contribute to the fund and that executive departments would not control the program, so the plan was not a government guaranty of deposits. He justified requiring insured banks to join the reserve system before July 1935 by extolling a unified banking system that would end regulatory competition between states and the federal government.[23]

Senate debate ended May 25, after Glass surprisingly announced that his subcommittee had met with Vandenberg and decided to accept his amendment for immediate insurance. Considering that amendment first, the Senate approved it by voice vote. Smaller alterations also passed without recorded votes; the most important would change from two years to one the time limit for member banks to separate from securities affiliates and for private banks to be examined or cease accepting deposits. Another extensively debated alteration concerned a paragraph on postal savings deposits. Because bankers had complained for years about competition from the Postal Savings System, the Senate amendment would allow such deposits to draw interest only when a saver gave a 60-day notice of withdrawal, although postal depositors would be able to withdraw money on demand without interest. Senators then approved the Glass bill by voice vote. Members of the subcommittee became conferees, while Steagall, T. Alan Goldsborough (D–MD), and Luce represented the House.[24]

Bankers, especially those in areas that had experienced few failures, were appalled when the House passed a bill containing deposit insurance and alarmed when the Senate followed with a plan for an immediate guaranty. The well-publicized opposition of Roosevelt and Woodin had lulled bankers into believing that deposit insurance, which they regarded as unsound, had no chance. Several state banking associations, the American Bankers' Association, and the Association of Reserve City Bankers now came out against the Glass and Steagall bills. Francis H. Sisson, president of the ABA, said that instead of trying to insure deposits, Congress should establish fewer banks that were better capitalized, supervised, and managed and should standardize laws and methods.[25] He sent telegrams to bankers calling attention to the bill, labeling it a serious threat to banks, and urging them to send their protests to President Roosevelt.[26] Aldrich of Chase National told FDR that enactment of the insurance section in the Glass bill would be unfortunate unless changes in the insurance provisions could be made that would increase the responsibility of depositors.[27]

Not all bankers opposed insurance. Country bankers, especially those in the South and West, often supported it because it would protect small banks from unnecessary runs.[28]

Federal reserve officials were dismayed when the Steagall and Glass bills passed. They, too, believed deposit insurance would lead to irresponsible banking. Members of the Federal Advisory Council announced on May 16 that they were completely opposed to the guaranty of bank deposits and preferred additional study of the issue.[29] Directors of the New York Federal Reserve Bank agreed. They particularly wanted to avoid an insurance fund that reserve officials would have to administer in addition to their other duties, as the Glass bill proposed. They also feared that large state member banks might withdraw from the reserve system to avoid insurance and that national banks might convert to state charters to do the same.[30]

James P. Warburg, a Wall Street banker who was currently a presidential adviser, told Woodin on May 27 that New York bankers were threatening to withdraw from the reserve system if the Glass bill became law. Woodin told Warburg that he would try to convince the president to veto the bill, adding that banks ought to telegraph opinions of the measure to Roosevelt. Warburg repeated this conversation to the governor of the New York reserve bank, George L. Harrison, and suggested that he inform other reserve banks, which the governor agreed to do. Like other New York bankers, Warburg regarded deposit insurance as an erroneous idea that would have significantly negative consequences.[31]

When the Senate passed the Glass bill with the Vandenberg amendment attached, FDR's opposition increased. Because of public pressure, he had been prepared to accept an insurance fund with capital provided by member banks, reserve banks, and the Treasury. He now refused to accept Vandenberg's proposal for an immediate though temporary guaranty for all licensed banks (without examination or qualification) to be paid for entirely by the federal government. He sought to influence the conference committee to reject Vandenberg's amendment at a White House meeting on June 1, which Glass, Steagall, Woodin, Black, O'Connor, and Dean Acheson, the undersecretary of the Treasury, attended.[32] The *New York Times* announced on June 6 that Roosevelt had threatened to veto the measure if changes in insurance provisions were not made, but the next day

FDR wrote privately that some form of deposit insurance would pass Congress, which he was trying to make as "sound as possible."[33]

Roosevelt was able to modify the Vandenberg amendment, in part because Glass opposed it, but was unable to persuade the conference committee to reject it. Public support had been mounting since the Senate approved the Glass bill, possibly because the Pecora hearings had resumed with testimony from J.P. Morgan and George Whitney that made front-page news.[34] At another White House meeting on June 7, which Glass, Woodin, Acheson, Black, and O'Connor attended, Glass received a more accurate impression of provisions FDR might accept. Roosevelt would approve a temporary insurance plan administered by the reserve system that would cover both state and national banks and begin on January 1, 1934, and he would prefer that insured state banks have until 1936 to join the reserve system.[35]

Negotiations between Glass and House members of the conference committee proved difficult. The emergency session of Congress would end within days, important legislation was on the calendar, and Steagall remained concerned about the treatment of state banks. He and Glass thought of leaving the measure for the next session, but Steagall decided he preferred to work out a compromise. If Glass had been reluctant, he agreed when Representative John E. Rankin (D–MISS) announced that House members were signing a round robin pledging to stay in session until a deposit insurance bill passed.[36]

The conference committee filed its report soon after Roosevelt, Steagall, and Goldsborough met on June 12. The permanent insurance plan followed provisions from Steagall's bill, which would establish an independent agency, known as the Federal Deposit Insurance Corporation, to administer insurance and would require the Treasury, reserve banks, and member banks to furnish capital. The FDIC could increase capital stock up to three times the original amount by issuing bonds—obligations of the corporation, not the federal government. A three-person board of directors—two presidential appointees and the comptroller of the currency—would administer both temporary and permanent insurance. The temporary plan applied to any solvent bank seeking membership and would begin January 1, 1934, unless the president fixed an earlier date. A state bank could join if a state banking authority issued a certificate of solvency, which the FDIC would accept after examination. Deposits up to $2,500 would have full coverage under the temporary plan. Insured state banks would have until July 1, 1936 to join the reserve system or withdraw from the

FDIC. Glass and McAdoo had insisted that insured banks must become members of the system, and Steagall agreed to this provision as better than the one in the Senate bill, which would allow only a year to join.[37]

Except for sections on deposit insurance, the conference committee adopted most of the Senate bill, including provisions to separate banks from securities affiliates within a year, to regulate private bankers who chose to accept deposits, to direct the board to curb the use of reserve funds for speculation, to prohibit payment of interest on demand deposits, to extend branch banking, and to forbid loans by banks to their own officers. The decisions on branch banking and on requiring all insured banks to become members of the reserve system by 1936 went against Goldsborough's beliefs, but he agreed not to deadlock the conference committee.[38]

In addition to deposit insurance, the compromise bill drew three sections from the Steagall measure. One provision would repeal all double liability on stock issued after passage of the measure. Prior to this, the comptroller of the currency could assess holders of national bank stock up to twice the face value of the stock if the bank failed or needed to increase its capital. Known as double liability, this restriction had not protected depositors during the depression and had become a deterrent to the issue and sale of new bank stock. The conference report also adopted the more specific House language regarding the Federal Open Market Committee. Finally, the bill would increase substantially the shares that each director of a member bank was required to own, in an attempt to impose greater accountability on directors.[39]

Some observers believed Vandenberg and Long might try to prevent Senate passage of the conference report. To forestall such a move, O'Connor telephoned Long on June 13, hours before the vote. Because of confidence in O'Connor, who would be a member of the FDIC board, Long agreed to announce his lack of opposition when the report reached the Senate floor for consideration. Vandenberg also announced acceptance of the conference committee bill. For him the important feature was a clause allowing the president to start the insurance program before January 1. The Senate approved the Banking Act of 1933 by voice vote on June 13.[40]

The conference report met no opposition in the House, and Steagall's speech in favor of deposit insurance brought prolonged applause. He called it a "great step toward economic recovery and revival of business," and the "greatest measure for the elevation of banking to a place worthy of a great civilization that has ever been undertaken in the history of the United States."[41] He made a long exposition of the report because the conference had adopted much of the Senate version. Luce, the only House Republican on the committee, made it clear that he accepted the major features of the bill but feared that machinery establishing the FDIC might not be adequate. Goldsborough defended compromises on such issues as the 1936 deadline to join the reserve system, extension of branch banking, and starting deposit insurance in January 1934, saying that otherwise no bill would both pass Congress and receive FDR's approval. One a division demanded by Harold McGugin (R–KAN), only six members voted against the measure.[42]

Roosevelt signed the Banking Act of 1933 on June 16, with Glass, Steagall, O'Connor, and others present. He complimented Glass for his perseverance.[43] Roosevelt had bowed to public demands for deposit insurance, in spite of doubt about the program, just as Glass had done. Congress recognized the level of constituent support for insurance and forced the president to compromise on this issue, which indicated its greater willingness to experiment on this issue.

AFTERMATH

Bankers who had sought to prevent passage of the act did not give up, for many provisions would not take effect until July 1934. They hoped to persuade Congress to alter several sections, especially those concerning deposit insurance. Reflecting the views of eastern bankers, the *Wall Street Journal* indicated that banks would try to make deposit insurance work because they recognized the "strength of the popular demand . . . to make all banks safe" and because "under extremely cautious management, this ill-conceived insurance scheme" probably would not cause "serious harm during the few months which must elapse before Congress can eliminate its worst features."[44] The American Bankers' Association convention adopted a resolution in September recommending that Roosevelt postpone deposit insurance and expressing concern that there would be insufficient time to examine banks before January 1. City bankers criticized the permanent insurance program, which would begin July 1, 1934, because FDIC assessments would not be limited, would be based on total deposits instead of insured deposits, and would be called for only when the fund was depleted. Since the temporary plan provided for immediate, but strictly limited, assessments based on insured deposits, bankers sought to make the temporary plan permanent.[45] Country bankers also disliked the provision for unlimited assessments, but because most of their accounts were smaller than $2,500, they had no objection to assessments on total deposits instead of insured deposits. They feared that forcing insured banks to join the reserve system would doom many small banks, which would have difficulty meeting the reserve's requirements for membership.[46]

The administration worked diligently in the autumn of 1933 to ensure that deposit insurance would not disrupt the banking system. With the appointment in September of Walter J. Cummings, a Democrat who had been serving as executive assistant to the secretary of the Treasury, and E.G. Bennett, a Republican banker from Utah, the FDIC's board began to function. It decided that banks could join the corporation if their assets met 90% of liabilities, without regard to capital. These terms pleased many state bankers, as did FDR's announcement that he would not start insurance coverage until January 1. Roosevelt insisted that members of the reserve system join the FDIC without further examination, which reduced to 8,000 the number of banks needing examination. O'Connor gathered names of more than 1,500 qualified examiners and promised that each state would receive an examiner familiar with local values.[47]

As the FDIC began to admit banks, Roosevelt asked the Reconstruction Finance Corporation to help nonmember banks qualify. The RFC initiated a program of lending to licensed banks that were at or near insolvency. Such loans were part of a broader effort to clean up remnants of the banking crisis by reopening or liquidating unlicensed banks and by increasing capital in operating ones. Jesse Jones began this effort at the American Bankers' Association convention in September, when he urged bankers to participate. FDIC examiners discovered that 1,000 state banks had assets insufficient to cover 90% of their liabilities. Even more institutions lacked capital. The RFC provided loans to these banks as quickly as possible, and the program continued even after temporary insurance began.[48]

When deposit insurance became effective on January 1, 1934, it covered 13,201 institutions: 5,153 national banks, 856 state member banks, 6,978 other state banks, and 214 other financial institutions. Approximately 1% of state banks applying could not qualify before

January 1, but the number of insured banks continued to increase slowly throughout 1934. Under the temporary plan the FDIC insured all funds for 97% of depositors. Bankers in general were happy with the transition to temporary insurance because deposits increased as public confidence rose.[49]

Roosevelt and Steagall had hoped Congress would make no changes in the act during the next session, but legislators recognized that bankers' concerns about the permanent plan were legitimate. Vandenberg suggested in January 1934 that the temporary plan replace permanent insurance, and his bill (S. 2520) would eliminate the clause requiring insured banks to join the reserve system by July 1, 1936. Other legislators introduced bills to amend the permanent insurance plan, and Roosevelt realized by mid-February that to prevent unilateral congressional action he would have to present a measure.[50]

The administration proposed on February 14 that Congress extend the temporary program until July 1, 1935. This suggestion resolved several problems. It reduced banker pleas for immediate amendments to the act, allowed FDIC directors time to become familiar with its weaknesses, and permitted the RFC time to help banks temporarily insured become eligible for the permanent plan. Roosevelt sent Steagall and Fletcher a draft bill written by FDIC directors and staff, which also had the support of the reserve board and Treasury Department. Shortly thereafter both men introduced bills (S. 2789 and H.R. 8016) to extend the temporary insurance plan for one year. These measures would also make clear FDIC authority to act as receiver for insured banks that had closed under the temporary plan. To make FDIC bonds more marketable, the bills would place a government guaranty behind such bonds and make them eligible for reserve open market operations.[51]

The Glass subcommittee considered the Fletcher bill during late February and early March. Glass disliked the section placing a government guaranty behind FDIC obligations. He told the secretary of the Treasury that he had not opposed the Treasury's original purchase of FDIC stock but had never wanted the government to become the primary stockholder of the corporation because he had always opposed a Treasury guaranty of deposits. The bill that the subcommittee and full committee approved eliminated this provision. Glass introduced the committee version as a new bill (S. 3025) and reported it for the committee on March 12. The Senate passed it by unanimous consent the same day.[52]

The House banking committee did not move so rapidly. Steagall wished to increase deposit coverage from $2,500 to $10,000 and thought that one authority should examine all insured banks. If these changes were adopted, he had no objection to making the temporary plan permanent, as Vandenberg suggested. Not all committee members agreed; 13 of the newest members had pledged to vote against reporting the FDIC bill. As April neared, the committee had not acted on the Senate's or Steagall's version. Roosevelt telegraphed Rainey and Steagall, urging them to report and pass a bill substantially the same as the Senate's. Later FDR told Steagall that he wanted the deposit insurance bill passed with the $2,500 limit and teased the congressman about selling out to the rich, since 97% of depositors were covered already. Steagall replied that his committee had scheduled hearings on the bill to begin the next day. He added that a measure (H.R. 7908) by Clarence J. McLeod (R–MICH), which would order the RFC to pay depositors all funds tied up in failed member banks, had dominated committee attention. Roosevelt, the Treasury, and the RFC opposed the McLeod bill as too costly.[53]

Unfortunately the effort to extend temporary deposit insurance became entwined with the McLeod measure. Legislators were unhappy with the slow liquidation of institutions that had remained closed since the banking crisis. The McLeod bill provided an easy and politically attractive way to increase purchasing power and end criticism among depositors of closed banks. After supporters began circulating a petition to force its discharge, the House banking committee held hearings and reported on April 12 a much revised bill, which deleted provisions of McLeod's measure and substituted sections of a bill (H.R. 9043) previously introduced by Prentiss M. Brown (D–MICH). The Brown version would have the RFC assume ownership of remaining assets in state, national, and private banks closed on or after January 1, 1930 and pay depositors all balances up to $2,500. Although the McLeod/Brown measure never passed, it delayed consideration of the FDIC bill and led to a change in its provisions.[54]

At House hearings on the FDIC bill, opposition came from committee members who feared the proposal was an attempt by bankers to prevent insurance from becoming a permanent program. Leo T. Crowley, a Wisconsin banker who had replaced Cummings as chairman of the FDIC's board, insisted that his board wanted to make the corporation stronger by postponing the permanent plan and had no wish to destroy it. Bennett described the bill's drafting to assure committee members that bankers had not written it. O'Connor brought a presidential message indicating that insurance of bank deposits had become a permanent part of the New Deal. The persistent belief that extension of the temporary plan was part of a campaign to aid bankers led Crowley to suggest that it was unfortunate the American Bankers' Association had supported the measure. In the end FDIC directors persuaded the committee that banks needed time to strengthen their capital.[55]

The House committee reported the FDIC bill on May 21, and debate began a few days later. This measure was somewhat different from the one passed by the Senate. Committee members had compromised on Steagall's desire to increase insurance coverage by raising the maximum to $5,000 for commercial banks. To meet demands of McLeod bill supporters, the committee measure would increase the FDIC's power to lend to receivers and liquidators or to buy assets of closed banks. To cover increased payments to depositors, other sections would allow the FDIC to issue bonds equal to five times initial capital and place a government guaranty behind the bonds, as the administration suggested. The bill would eliminate a phrase in the Banking Act of 1933 that required insured banks to join the reserve system by July 1, 1936. House debate reflected many of the same concerns that had appeared in the hearings. Steagall assured congressmen that the measure was not an attempt to prevent permanent insurance. No one spoke in opposition, although McLeod made a plea for his payoff measure. After a few hours of discussion and minor amendment on May 24, the House passed the bill unanimously.[56]

The conference committee on the FDIC bill had limited time to agree and might have reached an impasse if the administration had not suggested a compromise. Congressional leaders hoped to adjourn by mid-June, yet not until May 31 did the House name Steagall, Goldsborough, and Luce as conferees. Fletcher headed the Senate group—Glass, Bulkley, Townsend, and Walcott. Glass was determined to fight several House changes, especially elimination of the requirement that insured banks join the reserve system, on which he had insisted in 1933. The committee had not agreed when officials from the Treasury Department, RFC, FDIC, and reserve system discussed the FDIC bill on June 4–5. They recommended that the RFC, not the FDIC, should lend to receivers on the assets of closed banks and that the $5,000 maximum for insured deposits in the House bill be accepted. The conference committee included these compromises in its report of

June 11. Glass insisted that insured banks join the reserve system by July 1, 1937, two years after permanent insurance would begin. Both House and Senate passed the conference report on June 14, and Roosevelt signed it two days later.[57]

Deposit insurance provisions of the Banking Act of 1933 were not the only parts bankers and legislators sought to change. A section in the FDIC act of 1934 repealed a provision of the 1933 act concerning stock that individuals had to own to qualify as directors of member banks. The act of 1933 required directors in small banks to double the stock they owned, from $500 to $1,000, by July 1, 1934 and in medium-sized banks from $1,000 to $2,500. Bankers had complained that directors would have trouble meeting this requirement, either because they did not have money to purchase more or because stock was widely distributed. The House banking committee inserted repeal of this section into the FDIC measure, and Senate conferees agreed, probably because it would have weighed heavily on small banks.[58]

Reserve officials and legislators suggested other changes in the Banking Act of 1933. The Federal Advisory Council and directors of the New York reserve bank advocated reform of sections preventing member banks from underwriting securities. They feared disruption of the investment banking industry in July 1934, when member banks would complete divorce of their securities affiliates. Among amendments proposed by members of Congress were a reduction of capital required for national banks, the publication of state member banks' reports of their condition, the end of double liability on national bank shares issued before June 1933, a postponement of the date by which private bankers had to decide whether or not to accept deposits, additional time for banks to dispose of securities affiliates, and permission for banks to underwrite some securities. None of these proposals passed in 1934.[59]

The comptroller of the currency prepared the most comprehensive set of amendments to the act of 1933, which Steagall (H.R. 9720) and Bulkley (S. 3748) introduced late in the session. This measure would make clearer the language and intent of Congress. One section would give legal definition to the term "executive officer," used in the act without definition, and another would amend the prohibition against the "business of dealing in investment securities" to forbid the "business of dealing in stocks, bonds, or securities."[60] Because neither bill emerged from committee until June, the rush of other legislation prevented passage. Still, O'Connor hoped to amend the Banking Act of 1933 when the 74th Congress convened in January 1935.[61]

CONCLUSION

The Banking Act of 1933 was the first major alteration of the Federal Reserve Act since 1913. Unfortunately Glass had based much of it on a faulty analysis of economic problems. His wish to separate commercial from investment banking stemmed from his belief in the antiquated real bills theory of banking. He thought commercial banks should confine their business to accepting deposits and making short-term loans based on production and marketing of commodities. He saw that investment affiliates of member banks had participated in underwriting more than half of stock and bond issues in 1930 (the peak year) and assumed that the market boom and crash had been caused by plentiful bank credit that borrowers used to purchase securities. He thought losses from such activities had contributed to bank failures after 1929. Because of his beliefs, the act of 1933 required the reserve board to regulate loans for speculation, member banks to divorce securities affiliates, and commercial and investment banks to end interlocking directorates. The Pecora hearings of 1933 intimated that big-city banks had foisted poor bonds on unsuspecting correspondent banks and lent money on exceedingly favorable terms to securities affiliates and to customers buying stocks and bonds from affiliates. Such revelations convinced the public and many bankers that Glass was correct to insist on separating commercial from investment banking.[62]

Problems disclosed by Pecora were caused by conflicts of interest, which Congress might have solved by placing investment affiliates under strict federal regulation instead of requiring divorce. Banks themselves had owned less than 1% of corporate stock available in 1929, although they held more than 12% of corporate bonds. The act of 1933 placed both holding company affiliates and other member bank affiliates under the examining authority of the reserve system and comptroller of the currency. Congress could have included investment affiliates in the same category. In fact, earlier versions of the Glass bill had called for regulation rather than separation of investment affiliates, and the reserve board had supported that proposal. Congress wished to make banks safe, but there is no evidence that owning securities affiliates or purchasing corporate bonds caused the bank failures of the early 1930s. Probably federal regulation of relations between insured banks and investment affiliates would have protected banks sufficiently, especially since the divorce did not end dependence of investment bankers on commercial banks for financing. Regulation would have had the advantage of not forcing a reorganization of facilities for securities underwriting and distribution during a depression.[63]

Recently economists and big-city bankers have questioned the rationale for separating different kinds of financial institutions. There is "virtually no evidence to support the popular impression that the suspension and failure of commercial banks after 1929 was the result of their prior involvement in financing stock market 'speculation,'" and apparently no affiliate affected the solvency of its parent bank.[64] Driven by competition, bankers since the 1970s have used holding companies to test the artificial lines between types of financial institutions. Banks have arranged with limited-service institutions to finance corporate issues of stocks and bonds, offered financial advice to companies, helped with mergers and acquisitions, and run discount stock brokerages. Banks are trying to enter such new businesses as insurance and real estate to meet competition from nonbank institutions such as Prudential-Bache and Sears, Roebuck and Company. The Banking Act of 1933 has prevented integration of financial markets in the United States and reduced the ability of the banking system to innovate and compete in money and capital markets, leaving nonbank institutions to originate "near moneys" such as money market and cash management accounts. The act may have inhibited competition abroad, where such restrictions have never applied and where corporate customers may rely on a single institution as a depository for surplus cash and as an investment bank for new issues of stocks and bonds. Congress, the Treasury Department, the FDIC, and reserve officials now recognize that the Banking Act of 1933 needs revision, although debate continues about the extent of change. Perhaps soon this relic of the 1930s will disappear.[65]

Faulty economic analysis by Congress also explains enactment of limits on interest payments to depositors. Glass and Steagall assumed that rate competition had squeezed banks' earnings. Not until after 1960 did economists look at interest rates actually paid on deposits and at rates of return earned by banks' assets in the 1920s. Banks had suffered a squeeze, but this had little relation to rates paid on deposits, which remained stable throughout the decade. Congress had no good reason to forbid interest payments, although bankers themselves had complained about excessive rate competition. The prohibition of interest on demand deposits unnecessarily disrupted correspondent banking relations, leading bankers to withdraw deposits from institutions in financial centers and depriving large banks of funds they could have used more effectively than could the smaller banks that withdrew them. The limits on interest for savings deposits had little importance until market rates rose above the ceilings in the 1950s. Over the next two decades, interest rate regulation handicapped banks that competed for funds with other financial institutions. Recently, Congress has eliminated federal controls on savings rates, and the Depository Institutions Deregulation and Monetary Control Act of 1980 permits limited interest on demand deposits. Now market competition determines most interest payments.[66]

The Banking Act of 1933 did not include two reforms widely recommended by analysts—state-wide branch banking, and unification of state and federal banking systems—that could have prevented the chartering of many small, weak banks. Glass had tried to achieve both changes but was forced to compromise by representatives of unit bankers in the House and Senate. Branch banking could have solved many difficulties by eliminating small banks, which were vulnerable to local economic disasters and could not afford to hire the best managers. Because of opposition from Norbeck, Long, and others, Glass agreed in January 1933 to permit state law to determine federal policy on branches, and this section remained unchanged in the act adopted in June 1933. National banks could establish branches only to the extent permitted by state law, which meant that those in California could have branches state-wide, while those in Texas could establish none. Fortunately, several states had adopted branch banking between 1930 and 1933 (Table 5A), a trend that has continued. The act made state boundaries the ultimate geographic extension of branch banking, and only recently have barriers to interstate banking begun to fall.[67]

Glass believed the act of 1933 provided for unification of banking systems because banks joining the FDIC would have to join the Federal Reserve System by the summer of 1936. Steagall was a champion of small state banks and had supported deposit insurance as a way to save the unit banking system. With support from bankers, Congress in 1934 postponed to 1937 the deadline to join the reserve system. The Banking Act of 1935 again postponed it, and after Glass died Congress repealed this requirement. The reason analysts favored the unification of banking was the confusion of regulatory authority prior to 1933. States

TABLE 5A
SUMMARY OF STATE LAWS RELATING TO BRANCH BANKING, DEC. 31, 1933

		Total
States Permitting State-wide Branch Banking	Arizona, California, Connecticut, Delaware, Idaho, Maryland, Michigan, Nevada, North Carolina, Oregon, Rhode Island, South Carolina, South Dakota, Utah, Vermont (1), Virginia, Washington	17
States Permitting Branch Banking Within Limited Areas	Georgia (2), Indiana (3), Iowa (4), Louisiana (5), Maine (6), Massachusetts (7), Mississippi (8), Montana (9), New Jersey (10), New York (11), Ohio (12), Pennsylvania (13), Tennessee (14), Wisconsin (15)	14
States Prohibiting Branch Banking	Alabama, Arkansas, Colorado, Florida, Illinois, Kansas, Minnesota, Missouri, Nebraska, New Mexico, Texas, West Virginia	12
States Having No Legislation On Branch Banking	Kentucky (16), New Hampshire, North Dakota, Oklahoma, Wyoming	5

(1) Provisions permit state-wide establishment of "agencies." (2) City or municipality. (3) Same County. (4) "Offices" in contiguous counties if no bank already located there. (5) Municipality or parish. (6) County or adjoining county. (7) Same town. (8) Same city. (9) Consolidating banks can continue operation in same or adjoining counties. (10) Same city, town, township, borough, or village. (11) City limits. (12) Same county. (13) Corporate limits of same place. (14) Same county. (15) Same corporate limits with "stations" permitted in same county. (16) No provisions on branches, but court decisions permit establishment of additional offices to receive deposits and pay checks.

Source: Horace White, *Money and Banking*, rev. ed. (Boston: Ginn, 1935), 682–4.

examined state banks, the comptroller of the currency regulated national banks, reserve banks could examine any member bank, and the RFC required every institution in which it had an investment to furnish a biannual report of condition. The FDIC only increased the existing regulatory confusion because it could examine nonmember insured banks and, with permission of the reserve board or comptroller of the currency, could examine insured member banks. Because state laws were often more lax than federal law, the possibility remained that state and federal authorities would compete in chartering banks.[68]

Contrary to the fears of bankers in 1933, establishment of the FDIC was for many years a most effective provision for preventing bank failures. It increased the safety and stability of the banking system because it reduced the possibility that frightened depositors would cause runs on solvent institutions. More than 90% of commercial banks have been members of the FDIC since 1934, providing some unification to American banking. Since 1933 the corporation has gained extensive power to regulate establishment of new banks and supervise insured banks. The FDIC succeeded because it tried to prevent failures by supervising closely problem banks and merging endangered institutions with stronger ones. As a result, the number of failed banks remained low, and the corporation had no trouble paying losses to depositors. A higher rate of failure since 1980 led officials to suggest that assessments not be based on deposits but on the level of risk associated with banks' assets, placing the burden on institutions most likely to fail. Such a suggestion has merit, especially if a fair way to rate the riskiness of assets could be found. Most recently the Bush administration has proposed that assessments be based on the amount of capital a bank has, with the lowest assessments given to banks with the largest capital to deposits ratio. Congress adopted this idea in 1991.[69]

The Banking Act of 1933 increased the reserve board's power and independence in several ways. The board received new authority to regulate bank holding companies, other affiliates of member banks, interest rates on savings deposits, member bank loans based on securities, and relations between reserve banks and foreign bankers. It increased the system's autonomy from Congress and the Treasury by giving the board discretion over reserve bank earnings and permitting the board to control its budget. The act lengthened the terms of office for board members, from ten to twelve years, which enhanced their lack of dependence on the executive branch. Glass had wished to increase reserve independence by removing the secretary of the Treasury as an ex officio member, but Woodin's opposition postponed that reform for two years.[70] The Banking Act of 1935 extended the power of the reserve board, continuing a trend begun by the Glass–Steagall Act of 1932.

Throughout the 73d Congress, legislators were more willing than the president to protect depositors. The Banking Act of 1933 was not an administration measure. Roosevelt had even threatened to veto it because of the Vandenberg amendment. The act represented a triumph for Glass and Steagall, and its passage was a result of constituent pressure in favor of a deposit guaranty, which FDR was unable to ignore. In 1934, however, Roosevelt told Congress that deposit insurance had become a permanent part of the New Deal.[71] In spite of the popularity of deposit insurance, FDR had no plan to aid depositors whose banks had closed previously. During the second session of the 73d Congress, persistent congressional support for the McLeod payoff measure forced him to accept RFC aid to depositors in closed banks. Thus, in both 1933 and 1934 it was constituent pressure, recognized first by Congress and only later by Roosevelt, that caused changes in public policy toward depositors.

NOTES

1. Glenn R. Parker, "Congressional Change," *Studies of Congress*, Glenn R. Parker, ed. (Washington, D.C.: Congressional Quarterly, 1985): 485; Richard B. Morris and Jeffrey B. Morris, eds., *Encyclopedia of American History*, 6th ed. (New York: Harper and Row, 1982), 1213; Michael R. King and Lester G. Seligman, "Critical Elections, Congressional Recruitment and Public Policy," *Elite Recruitment in Democratic Politics: Comparative Studies across Nations*, Heinz Eulau and Moshe M. Czudnowski, eds. (New York: Halstead, 1976): 286–93; David W. Brady, "Elections, Congress, and Public Policy Changes: 1886–1960," *Realignment in American Politics: Toward a Theory*, Bruce A. Campbell and Richard J. Trilling, eds. (Austin: University of Texas, 1980), 188–92; Everett Carll Ladd, Jr. and Charles D. Hadley, *Transformations of the American Party System: Political Coalitions from the New Deal to the 1970s*, 2d ed. (New York: W.W. Norton, 1978), 35–6; Kristi Andersen, *The Creation of a Democratic Majority, 1928–1936* (Chicago: University of Chicago, 1979), 34–8, 66–72.

2. Barbara Sinclair, *Congressional Realignment, 1925–1978* (Austin: University of Texas, 1982), 34.

3. Alvin M. Josephy, Jr., *On the Hill: A History of the American Congress* (New York: Simon and Schuster, 1979), 320; J.M. Galloway, "Speaker Joseph W. Byrns: Party Leader in the New Deal," *Tennessee Historical Quarterly*, 25 (Spring 1966): 73; Richard Franklin Bensel, *Sectionalism and American Political Development, 1880–1980* (Madison: University of Wisconsin, 1984), 173; Brady, "Elections, Congress, and Public Policy," 179, 183, 193–6; *Congressional Directory*, 72d Congress, 2d session, January 1933, 192; *Congressional Directory*, 73d Congress, 1st session, June 1933, 163–73, 192.

4. Political scientists have been less interested in analyzing the Senate for changes in 1933, perhaps because the six-year Senate term blurred realignment shifts. Josephy, *On the Hill*, 320; U.S., Congress, Senate, Committee on Banking and Currency, *Fiftieth Anniversary, 63d Congress, 1913, to 88th Congress, 1963*, S. Doc. 15, 88th Congress, 1st session, 15 March 1963; Susan Estabrook Kennedy, *The Banking Crisis of 1933* (Lexington: University of Kentucky, 1973), 204. Members of the Senate Committee on Banking and Currency were

Fletcher, Glass, Bulkley, Robert F. Wagner (D–NY), Alben W. Barkley (D–KEN), Thomas P. Gore (D–OKLA), Edward P. Costigan (D–COL), Robert R. Reynolds (D–NC), James F. Byrnes (D–SC), John H. Bankhead (D–ALA), McAdoo, Alva B. Adams (D–COL), Peter Norbeck (R–SD), Walcott, Townsend, James Couzens (R–MICH), Frederick Steiwer (R–ORE), and Hamilton F. Kean (R–NJ).

5. James Walter Hilty, Voting Alignments in the United States Senate, 1933–1944 (Ph.D. dissertation, University of Missouri, Columbia, 1973), 134; Galloway, "Byrns," 72; George Brown Tindall, *The Emergence of the New South: 1913–1945* (Baton Rouge: Louisiana State University, 1967), 611–9; Albert U. Romasco, *The Politics of Recovery: Roosevelt's New Deal* (New York: Oxford University, 1983), 34–5; Herman E. Krooss, *Executive Opinion: What Business Leaders Said and Thought on Economic Issues 1920s–1960s* (Garden City, N.Y.: Doubleday, 1970), 164–5; Randall B. Ripley, *Majority Party Leadership in Congress* (Boston: Little, Brown, 1969), 73–5.

6. *Wall Street Journal*, 13 April 1933, 15; Ibid., 10 May 1933, 5; Diary, v. 23, 21 April 1933, 26 April 1933, Charles Sumner Hamlin Papers, Manuscript Division, Library of Congress, Washington, D.C.; *New York Times*, 11 May 1933, 25; Ibid., 3 June 1933, 17; Ibid., 4 June 1933, II: 9. Hamlin thought the board was being overrun by politicians; Diary, v. 23, 14 June 1933.

7. Joseph Anthony Imler, The First One Hundred Days of the New Deal: The View from Capitol Hill (Ph.D. dissertation, Indiana University, 1975), 225–6, 232–3; Gordon Wells McKinley, The Federal Reserve System in the Period of Crisis, 1930 to 1935 (Ph.D. dissertation, Ohio State University, 1948), 312; Alfred Cash Koeniger, Carter Glass and the New Deal: From the Presidential Campaign of 1932 through the Hundred Days Session of Congress (M.A. thesis, Vanderbilt University, 1974), 70; William James Wells, Duncan Upshaw Fletcher: "Florida's Grand Old Man" (M.A. thesis, Stetson University, 1942), 157; *New York Times*, 4 April 1933, 31; Ibid., 8 April 1933, 1; Ibid., 12 April 1933, 1, 3. Glass was never happy about having to include deposit insurance in his bill; *The Reminiscences of Walter Wyatt*, Interview II: 76–7, Oral History Collection, Butler Library, Columbia University, New York, N.Y. [hereafter cited as Wyatt, OHRO].

8. Kennedy, *Banking Crisis*, 204; *Wall Street Journal*, 18 March 1933, 1; Ibid., 30 March 1933, 1–2; Ibid., 11 April 1933, 1; Ibid., 12 April 1933, 1, 7; letter to Glass from Woodin, 9 April 1933, Box 61, General Records of the Department of the Treasury, Office of the Secretary, General Correspondence 1933–56, Record Group 56, National Archives, Washington, D.C.; Hamlin Diary, v. 22, 17 March 1933; Ibid., v. 23, 31 May 1933. [All citations to RG 56 in this chapter refer to the Office of the Secretary, General Correspondence 1933–56.] Kennedy incorrectly says that S. 245 was introduced on March 9. According to Wyatt (OHRO, Interview I: 34–9, Interview II: 58, 72–5), Morrill and Wyatt drafted the provisions for the deposit insurance plan in the Glass bill, and Wyatt also drafted sections forbidding member banks to pay interest on demand deposits and permitting the reserve board to regulate interest payments on savings deposits. Woodin asked a few directors of the Federal Reserve Bank of New York for their views on deposit insurance. None of them favored a deposit guaranty, and all wanted any such program to be as restricted as possible. See Memorandum: Meeting of Executive Committee April 10, 1933, Binder 50, George Leslie Harrison Papers, Manuscript Division, Butler Library, Columbia University, New York, N.Y. For more on the Glass bills introduced in 1932, see Chapter Three, and for the bill passed by the Senate in January 1933, see Chapter Four.

9. *New York Times*, 12 April 1933, 3; Ibid., 14 April 1933, 33; *Wall Street Journal*, 13 April 1933, 1; Ibid., 25 April 1933, 1; Ibid., 6 May 1933, 1; letter to McAdoo from Glass, 25 April 1933, Box 383, William Gibbs McAdoo Papers, Manuscript Division, Library of Congress, Washington, D.C.; Alfred Cash Koeniger, "Unreconstructed Rebel:" The Political Thought and Senate Career of Carter Glass, 1929–1936 (Ph.D. dissertation, Vanderbilt University, 1980), 101; John Douglas Lyle, The United States Senate Career of Carter Glass of Virginia, 1919–1939 (Ph.D. dissertation, University of South Carolina, 1974), 305–8.

10. *New York Times*, 10 May 1933, 23; Ibid., 11 May 1933, 3; *Wall Street Journal*, 11 May 1933, 1, 9; Ibid., 10 March 1933, 8.

11. Synopsis of the Glass Banking Bill, 11 May 1933, Box 275 and 276, Carter Glass Papers, Alderman Library, University of Virginia, Charlottesville, Va.; Summary of Glass Bill S. 1631 As Reported on May 15, 1933, Box 176, Records of the Federal Reserve System, Subject File, 1914–54, Record Group 82, National Archives,

Washington, D.C. [All citations to RG 82 refer to Subject File, 1914–54.]

12. Kennedy, *Banking Crisis*, 212–3; Karl R. Bopp, "Three Decades of Federal Reserve Policy," *Postwar Economic Studies*, 8 (November 1947): 10–1, U.S., Congress, Senate, Committee on Banking and Currency, *Operation of National and Federal Reserve Banking Systems: Report to Accompany S. 1631*, S. Rept. 77, 73d Congress, 1st session, 17 May 1933, especially sections entitled, "Inflation of Bank Credit," "Stock-Exchange Speculation," and "Analysis of Present Banking Problem"; W. Nelson Peach, *The Security Affiliates of National Banks* (Baltimore: Johns Hopkins University, 1941), 157–9; Ron Chernow, *The House of Morgan: An American Banking Dynasty and the Rise of Modern Finance* (New York: Atlantic Monthly, 1990), 360–77.

13. Senate Committee on Banking and Currency, *Operation of Banking Systems: Report on S. 1631*; Lawrence E. Clark, *Central Banking under the Federal Reserve System with Special Consideration of the Federal Reserve Bank of New York* (New York: Macmillan, 1935), 278–80, 344–5; William O. Weyforth, *The Federal Reserve Board: A Study of Federal Reserve Structure and Credit Control* (Baltimore: Johns Hopkins University, 1933), 165–70. The bill would also increase the reserve system's autonomy by giving it complete discretion over its own funds and budgets and by eliminating the franchise tax reserve banks had paid on earnings.

14. *New York Times*, 14 May 1933, 6; Senate Committee on Banking and Currency, *Operation of Banking Systems: Report on S. 1631*.

15. Koeniger, Carter Glass and the New Deal, 72–3; Jack Brien Key, The Congressional Career of Henry B. Steagall of Alabama (M.A. thesis, Vanderbilt University, 1952), 90–2; U.S., Congress, House, Committee on Banking and Currency, *Banking Act of 1933: Report to Accompany H.R. 5661*, H. Rept. 150, 73d Congress, 1st session, 19 May 1933; Kennedy, *Banking Crisis*, 218–9. Steagall clearly hoped that deposit insurance would protect unit banking; Carter H. Golembe and David S. Holland, *Federal Regulation of Banking, 1983–1984* (Washington, D.C.: Golembe Associates, 1983), 44. Steagall had introduced H.R. 5598, his version of the Glass bill, on May 10. After the House Committee on Banking and Currency met, he introduced H.R. 5661, which included committee amendments.

16. *Congressional Record*, 77, pt. 4: 3834, 73d Congress, 1st session; *Wall Street Journal*, 20 May 1933, 1.

17. *Congressional Record*, 77, pt. 4: 3835, 73d Congress, 1st session.

18. Ibid., 3835–42, 3903–28 (quotation on 3903); *New York Times*, 21 May 1933, 5.

19. *Congressional Record*, 77, pt. 4: 4028–54, 73d Congress, 1st session; *Wall Street Journal*, 23 May 1933, 6; *New York Times*, 23 May 1933, 27; Ibid., 24 May 1933, 29.

20. *Congressional Record*, 77, pt. 4: 4054, 73d Congress, 1st session.

21. Ibid., 4058; *New York Times*, 24 May 1933, 29; Imler, First Hundred Days, 228–9. See also notes 19 and 20 above.

22. *New York Times*, 19 May 1933, 4; C. David Tompkins, *Senator Arthur H. Vandenberg: The Evolution of a Modern Republican, 1884–1945* (East Lansing: Michigan State University, 1970), 85–6, 88–90. Clippings from Michigan newspapers indicating widespread support for the amendment are in scrapbook V, especially pages 76B, 77A, and 79B, Arthur H. Vandenberg Papers, Michigan Historical Collections, Bentley Historical Library, University of Michigan, Ann Arbor, Mich. Jesse Jones, chairman of the Reconstruction Finance Corporation and a consistent supporter of deposit insurance, suggested in March that full coverage for deposits up to $2,500 would protect most Americans.

23. *Congressional Record*, 77, pt. 4: 3725–31, 4168, 73d Congress, 1st session; *New York Times*, 20 May 1933, 1; Wyatt, OHRO, Interview II: 75; Helen M. Burns, *The American Banking Community and New Deal Banking Reforms, 1933–1935* (Westport, Conn.: Greenwood, 1974), 84–5. Chase National Bank announced that it would be separating from its securities affiliate in March 1933, and by June the bank had almost completed the process. This speed impressed members of Congress, who decided one year for such proceedings should be sufficient time; Benjamin J. Klebaner, *Commercial Banking in the United States: A History* (Hinsdale, Ill.: Dryden, 1974), 140. All states that had previously had deposit guarantees had limited interest payments on time deposits to prevent aggressive rate competition; Klebaner, *Commercial Banking*, 139.

24. *Congressional Record*, 77, pt. 4: 4148, 4159–82, pt. 5: 4399, 73d Congress, 1st session; *New York Times*, 26 May 1933, 1–2. Lionel Patenaude, "Vice President John Nance Garner: A Study in the Use of Influence during the New Deal," *Texana*, 11, 2 (1973): 127–8, and Bascom N. Timmons, *Jesse H. Jones: The Man and the Statesman* (New York: Henry Holt, 1956), 194–5, both emphasize that Garner helped Vandenberg place his amendment before the Senate, but more important to the amendment's passage was the subcommittee's decision to support it.

25. *New York Times*, 19 May 1933, 27; Ibid., 20 May 1933, 19; Ibid., 21 May 1933, II: 7; telegram to Wagner from Irish, 23 May 1933, Box LE215, Robert Ferdinand Wagner Papers, Georgetown University Library, Georgetown University, Washington, D.C.; Joseph J. Schroeder, *They Made Banking History: The Association of Reserve City Bankers* (Chicago: Rand McNally, 1962), 131–3.

26. Telegram to First Savings Bank (Ogden, Utah) from Sisson, 26 May 1933, Box 218, Marriner S. Eccles Papers, Manuscript Division, Special Collections Department, Marriott Library, University of Utah, Salt Lake City, Utah.

27. Letter to Roosevelt from Aldrich, 22 May 1933, Official File 230, Box 2, Franklin Delano Roosevelt Presidential Papers, Franklin Delano Roosevelt Library, Hyde Park, N.Y.

28. Burns overemphasizes banker unity in opposition to deposit insurance in *American Banking Community*, 86–8, possibly because her sources dealt with northeastern banks; Krooss gauges bankers' opinions correctly in *Executive Opinion*, 167.

29. Statement of the Federal Advisory Council, 16 May 1933, Box 359, Hamlin Papers.

30. Memorandum: Meeting of Board of Directors May 11, 1933, Binder 50, Harrison Papers; Memorandum: Meeting of the Board of Directors May 25, 1933, Binder 50, Harrison Papers.

31. *The Reminiscences of James Paul Warburg*, 841, 863, 871, Oral History Collection, Butler Library, Columbia University, New York, N.Y.; memorandum to Moley from J.P.W., 1 June 1933, Box 6, James Paul Warburg Papers, John F. Kennedy Library, Waltham, Mass.

32. Burns, *American Banking Community*, 90; Tompkins, *Vandenberg*, 90–1; Diary, v. 1, 1 June 1933, James Francis Thaddeus O'Connor Papers, Bancroft Library, University of California, Berkeley,

Cal.; *New York Times*, 2 June 1933, 4; letter to Glass from Roosevelt, 2 June 1933, Official File 21b, Box 10, FDR Presidential Papers.

33. *New York Times*, 6 June 1933, 1; letter to Pierce from Roosevelt, 6 June 1933, Official File 230, Box 2, FDR Presidential Papers. It is possible that O'Connor's strong position in favor of deposit insurance helped to change FDR's mind between June 1 and June 6; O'Connor Diary, v. 1, 22 June 1933. FDR's willingness to compromise may also have resulted from a comment of Vandenberg, who said that if his amendment did not appear in the conference bill, he would attach it as a rider to the next administration bill. See Tompkins, *Vandenberg*, 92–3; *New York Times*, 6 June 1933, 1.

34. O'Connor Diary, v. 1, 1 June 1933; Donald A. Ritchie, "The Legislative Impact of the Pecora Investigation," *Capitol Studies*, 5, 2 (1977): 91–2; Kennedy, *Banking Crisis*, 212–3; *New York Times*, 24 May 1933, 1, 16; Ibid., 25 May 1933, 1, 13; U.S. Congress, Senate, Committee on Banking and Currency, *Stock Exchange Practices: Hearings on S.Res. 84 (72d Congress), S.Res. 56 (73d Congress), and S.Res. 97 (73d Congress)*, 73d Congress, 1st and 2d sessions, 23 May 1933–5 April 1934, 3-226, 307–773; Chernow, *House of Morgan*, 360–74.

35. O'Connor Diary, v. 1, 7 June 1933; *New York Times*, 8 June 1933, 35.

36. Imler, First Hundred Days, 230–1; *New York Times*, 9 June 1933, 3; Ibid., 12 June 1933, 1, 4; *Wall Street Journal*, 10 June 1933, 6; Gilbert Y. Steiner, *The Congressional Conference Committee: 70th to 80th Congresses* (Urbana: University of Illinois, 1951), 37.

37. Kennedy, *Banking Crisis*, 220; Steiner, *Congressional Conference Committee*, 37–8; *Congressional Record*, 77, pt. 6: 5769–83, 5861–3, 73d Congress, 1st session; *Wall Street Journal*, 13 June 1933, 11; Wyatt, OHRO, Interview II: 77–8. Wyatt told McAdoo he thought country banks would have the political power to postpone the date of joining the reserve system, and Steagall privately expressed hope that this would happen. See Wyatt, OHRO, Interview II: 77–8; Key, Career of Steagall, 96.

38. *Congressional Record*, 77, pt. 6: 5769–83, 5891–8, 73d Congress, 1st session; *Wall Street Journal*, 13 June 1933, 11; *New York Times*, 13 June 1933, 1, 6. Glass told a partner of J.P. Morgan and Company that Roosevelt had insisted on the provision requiring regulation of private banks. Glass himself was more friendly to the

Morgan bank than most members of Congress. See Chernow, *House of Morgan*, 356, 375.

39. *Congressional Record*, 77, pt. 4: 3945–7, pt. 6: 5769–83, 5862, 73d Congress, 1st session; *New York Times*, 13 June 1933, 1, 6.

40. O'Connor Diary, v. 1, 13 June 1933; *New York Times*, 13 June 1933, 1, 6; Ibid., 14 June 1933, 1, 8; *Congressional Record*, 77, pt. 6: 5862–3, 73d Congress, 1st session.

41. *Congressional Record*, 77, pt. 6: 5895, 73d Congress, 1st session.

42. Ibid., 5891–8; *New York Times*, 14 June 1933, 1; *Federal Reserve Bulletin*, 19 (June 1933): 385–401.

43. *New York Times*, 17 June 1933, 1; Lyle, Senate Career of Glass, 317.

44. *Wall Street Journal*, 17 June 1933, 6.

45. Telegram to Roosevelt from American Bankers' Association, 6 September 1933, Official File 230, Box 2, FDR Presidential Papers; *New York Times*, 28 June 1933, 1, 14; Ibid., 7 September 1933, 1, 14; Ibid., 27 December 1933, 18; William E. Johnson, "Deposit Guarantee—Now That We Have It, What Are We Going to Do About It?" *Northwestern Banker*, 38 (July 1933): 7–8; Association of Reserve City Bankers, *The Guaranty of Bank Deposits: A Report of the Commission on Banking Law and Practice* (Chicago: Association of Reserve City Bankers, 1933), 5–30; letter to Laubengayer from Reichert, 6 October 1933, Box 3, Rudolph Edward Reichert Papers, Michigan Historical Collections, Bentley Historical Library, University of Michigan, Ann Arbor, Mich.

46. Robert Henry Myers, The Politics of American Banking: The Dual System, 1929–1939 (Ph.D. dissertation, University of Chicago, 1956), 69–70; *New York Times*, 7 September 1933, 14.

47. *New York Times*, 8 September 1933, 1, 13; Franklin D. Roosevelt, *Complete Presidential Press Conferences*, 25 v. (New York: Da Capo, 1972), II: 249, 257–8; Memorandum: Meeting of Executive Committee December 18, 1933, Binder 51, Harrison Papers.

48. *New York Times*, 6 September 1933, 38; Jesse H. Jones and Edward Angly, *Fifty Billion Dollars: My Thirteen Years with the RFC* (New York: Macmillan, 1951), 28–33; Raymond P. Kent, "Dual Banking between the Two World Wars," *Banking and Monetary Studies*, Deane Carson, ed. (Homewood, Ill.: Richard D. Irwin, 1963), 61–2; Federal Deposit Insurance Corporation, Division of Research and

Statistics, *History of the Federal Deposit Insurance Corporation* (Washington, D.C.: U.S. Government Printing Office, 1951), 2–3; Federal Deposit Insurance Corporation, *Annual Report, 1934* (Washington, D.C.: U.S. Government Printing Office, 1935), 50–1.

49. Federal Deposit Insurance Corporation, *Annual Report, 1935* (Washington, D.C.: U.S. Government Printing Office, 1936), 55–62; letter to Roosevelt from Cummings, 1 January 1934, Official File 2911, Box 1, FDR Presidential Papers; memorandum to Morgenthau from Smith, 2 January 1934, and memorandum to Morgenthau from Smith, 4 January 1934 [misdated 1933], Correspondence, Alphabetical File, Box 254, Henry Morgenthau, Jr., Papers, Franklin Delano Roosevelt Library, Hyde Park, N.Y.; *New York Times*, 14 February 1934, 29.

50. *New York Times*, 19 October 1933, 29; Ibid., 31 January 1934, 30; Franklin D. Roosevelt, *The Public Papers and Addresses of Franklin D. Roosevelt*, Samuel I. Rosenman, comp., 13 v. (New York: Random House, 1938–45), II: 550–1; letter to Fletcher from Gibbons, 6 March 1934, Records of the United States Senate, Committee on Banking and Currency, Bill Records, S. 2520, Box 28, Record Group 46, National Archives, Washington, D.C. [All citations to RG 46 in this chapter refer to Bill Records, 73d Congress, Senate Committee on Banking and Currency.] Bills to amend the permanent insurance plan included S. 2520, S. 2756, S. 2767, S. 2781, S. 2789, S. 2849, S. 3025, H.R. 7757, H.R. 8016, H.R. 8805, H.R. 9368, and H.R. 9915. Several of these measures postponed the effective date of the permanent plan from July 1, 1934 to July 1, 1935.

51. Letters to Fletcher and Steagall from Roosevelt, 14 February 1934, Official File 2911, Box 1, FDR Presidential Papers; memorandum by Leo T. Crowley, 15 March 1934, Official File 2911, Box 1, FDR Presidential Papers; letter to Roosevelt from Bennett, 10 February 1934, Official File 2911, Box 1, FDR Presidential Papers; *New York Times*, 15 February 1934, 31; Ibid., 16 February 1934, 34.

52. Letter to Fletcher from Morgenthau, 8 March 1934, S. 2789, Box 32, RG 46; O'Connor Diary, v. 2, 2 March 1934; *New York Times*, 11 March 1934, 10; letter to Cudlip from Vandenberg, 16 March 1934, Box 8, William Byrnes Cudlip Papers, Michigan Historical Collections, Bentley Historical Library, University of Michigan, Ann Arbor, Mich.; Diary, v. I, 4 April 1934, Morgenthau

Papers; *Congressional Record*, 78, pt. 4: 4229, 73d Congress, 2d session.

53. O'Connor Diary, v. 2, 23 February 1934; letter and memo to McIntyre from Crowley, 18 April 1934, Official File 2911, Box 1, FDR Presidential Papers; telegrams to Rainey and Steagall from Roosevelt, 27 March 1934, Official File 2911, Box 1, FDR Presidential Papers; memorandum, The President's Conference with the Senators, Saturday Afternoon, April 14, 1934, President's Secretary's File Box 188, FDR Presidential Papers; memorandum, The President's Conference with the Members of the House of Representatives at 8:30 p.m., Sunday evening, April 15, 1934, Official File 419, Box 1, FDR Presidential Papers; Morgenthau Diary, v. 1, 14 April 1934; *Wall Street Journal*, 10 April 1933, 1, 9.

54. Letter to Cudlip from Vandenberg, 16 March 1934, Box 8, Cudlip Papers; *Wall Street Journal*, 10 April 1934, 6; Ibid., 13 April 1934, 13; Ibid., 18 May 1934, 12; *New York Times*, 13 April 1934, 6; U.S., House, Committee on Banking and Currency, *For Relief of Depositors in Closed Banks: Report to Accompany H.R. 7908*, H. Rept. 1235, 73d Congress, 2d session, 12 April 1934; Cyril B. Upham and Edwin Lamke, *Closed and Distressed Banks: A Study in Public Administration* (Washington, D.C.: Brookings Institution, 1934), 182–6.

55. U.S., Congress, House, Committee on Banking and Currency, *Extension of Temporary Plan for Deposit Insurance: Hearings on S. 3025*, 73d Congress, 2d session, 16 April–15 May 1934, 1–52, 79–96, 103–26, 134–46.

56. Clipping from Detroit *News*, [dateline] 22 May 1934, scrapbook I, Box 23, Prentiss Marsh Brown Papers, Michigan Historical Collections, Bentley Historical Library, University of Michigan, Ann Arbor, Mich.; U.S., Congress, House, Committee on Banking and Currency, *Extension For 1 Year of the Temporary Plan For Deposit Insurance and Other Amendments to the Federal Reserve Act: Report to Accompany S. 3025*, H. Rept. 1724, 73d Congress, 2d session, 21 May 1934; *Congressional Record*, 78, pt. 9: 9205, 9423, 9519–39, 73d Congress, 2d session; letter to Fead from Brown, 15 May 1934, Box 1, Brown Papers; *New York Times*, 25 May 1934, 1–2. Steagall had introduced another version of this bill (H.R. 9368) on April 26, which would have increased insurance coverage from $2,500 to $10,000, eliminated the requirement that all insured banks join the

reserve system, provided a government guarantee on the principal and interest of obligations issued by the FDIC, allowed the FDIC to issue such bonds up to five times the corporation's capital, and increased FDIC power to lend to receivers or liquidators of banks that failed between December 31, 1929 and January 1, 1934. See memorandum to McIntyre from Crowley, 30 April 1934, Official File 2911, Box 1, FDR Presidential Papers.

57. *Congressional Record*, 78, pt. 9: 9667, 10136, pt. 10: 11065–8, 11114–6, 73d Congress, 2d session; Memorandum: Meeting of Board of Directors May 31, 1934, Binder 51, Harrison Papers; O'Connor Diary, v. 2, 4–5 June 1934; *New York Times*, 17 June 1934, 26. Those attending the meetings on June 4–5 included Treasury officials Henry Morgenthau, Jr., Herbert Gaston, Thomas J. Coolidge, Herman Oliphant, and Marriner S. Eccles. Also attending were Jesse Jones and Stanley Reed of the RFC, Black of the reserve board, Crowley and Bennett of the FDIC, and O'Connor.

58. Letter to Glass from McFadden, 7 December 1933, Box 273, Glass Papers; letter to Roosevelt from Haines, 12 January 1934, Box 58, RG 56; letter to Steagall from Morgenthau, 20 February 1934, S. 2601, Box 29, RG 46; *Congressional Record*, 78, pt. 2: 2014, pt. 6: 5947, pt. 9: 9519–22, pt. 10: 11065–8, 73d Congress, 2d session.

59. Federal Reserve Board, *Twentieth Annual Report Covering Operations for the Year 1933* (Washington, D.C.: U.S. Government Printing Office, 1934), 258; Office Correspondence to Confidential Files from Harrison, 4 May 1933, Binder 46, Harrison Papers; Memorandum: Meeting of Executive Committee May 21, 1934, Binder 51, Harrison Papers. Bills that sought to amend the Banking Act of 1933 included H.R. 7758, S. 2565, S. 2870, S. 3134, S. 3316, S. 3422, and S. 3600.

60. H.R. 9720, Box 2, Records of the Office of the Comptroller of the Currency, Banking Emergency Records, Record Group 101, National Archives, Washington, D.C.; S. 3748, Box 43, RG 46.

61. *Congressional Record*, 78, pt. 10: 10557, 10908, 73d Congress, 2d session; letter to O'Connor from Couzens, 2 July 1934, v. 9, O'Connor Papers.

62. "A Landmark Law that Boxes in the Banks: Reform Act of 1933," *Business Week* (19 April 1976): 56–7; Kennedy, *Banking Crisis*, 223; Joseph Ernest Goodbar, *Managing the People's Money: An Analysis of Banking Policies and Banking Control and Their Relation*

to Economic Stability (New Haven, Conn.: Yale University, 1935), 125–30. The reserve board has never enforced the provision restricting bank loans with securities as collateral; Lester V. Chandler, *American Monetary Policy, 1928–1941* (New York: Harper and Row, 1971), 271. Beliefs like those of Glass were so widespread after the Pecora hearings that the securities markets actually had increased stability after the passage of the Banking Act of 1933 and the Truth-in-Securities Act; Barrie A. Wigmore, *The Crash and Its Aftermath* (Westport, Conn.: Greenwood, 1985), 451–2.

63. Joseph Auerbach and Samuel L. Hayes, III, *Investment Banking and Diligence: What Price Deregulation?* (Boston: Harvard Business School, 1986), 14–5; Lawrence S. Ritter and William L. Silber, *Principles of Money, Banking, and Financial Markets*, 3d ed. (New York: Basic Books, 1980), 122; William G. Shepherd and Claire Wilcox, *Public Policies Toward Business*, 6th ed. (Homewood, Ill.: Richard D. Irwin, 1979), 483, 486–7; George D. Green, "The Economic Impact of the Stock Market Boom and Crash of 1929," *Consumer Spending and Monetary Policy: The Linkages*, George D. Green, ed. (Boston: Federal Reserve Bank of Boston, 1971), 206; Roger W. Valentine, "Investment Banking—History and Regulation," *American Financial Institutions*, Herbert V. Prochnow, ed. (New York: Prentice–Hall, 1951): 404; Vincent P. Carosso, *Investment Banking in America: A History* (Cambridge, Mass.: Harvard University, 1970), 368–75; Klebaner, *Commercial Banking*, 141; Mark J. Flannery, "An Economic Evaluation of Bank Securities Activities before 1933," *Deregulating Wall Street: Commercial Bank Penetration of the Corporate Securities Market*, Ingo Walter, ed. (New York: John Wiley and Sons, 1985): 70–87; Eugene Nelson White, "Before the Glass–Steagall Act: An Analysis of the Investment Banking Activities of National Banks," *Explorations in Economic History*, 23 (January 1986): 40–51; William F. Shughart, II, "A Public Choice Perspective of the Banking Act of 1933," *The Financial Services Revolution: Policy Directions for the Future*, Catherine England and Thomas Huertas, eds. (Boston: Kluwer Academic, 1988): 92–7. Shughart argues that although there was no economic justification for the division of investment and commercial banking, it probably did serve the interests of those involved in both industries as well as the Treasury Department (96–103). I find his argument more convincing than that of Jonathan R. Macey, who says that only investment bankers benefited; "Special

Interest Groups Legislation and the Judicial Function: The Dilemma of Glass–Steagall," *Emory Law Journal*, 33 (Winter 1984): 16–21. Thomas Mayer and Monojit Chatterji argue in "Political Shocks and Investment: Some Evidence from the 1930s," *Journal of Economic History*, 45 (December 1985): 920–4, that the low level of investment during the rest of the 1930s should not be attributed to the legislation passed under Roosevelt.

64. Green, "Economic Impact of Boom and Crash," 206. See also White, "Before the Glass–Steagall Act," 33–55.

65. Ibid., Golembe and Holland, *Federal Regulation*, 80–3; "Merchant Banking: Is the U.S. Ready for It?" *Business Week* (19 April 1976): 54–7, 60, 64; Richard Sylla, "Monetary Innovation in America," *Journal of Economic History*, 42 (March 1982): 30; George J. Benston, *The Separation of Commercial and Investment Banking: The Glass–Steagall Act Revisited and Reconsidered* (New York: Oxford University, 1990), 146–9, 159–62, 212–5; *Wall Street Journal*, 23 March 1984, 1; Ibid., 20 November 1984, 2; Ibid., 29 December 1986, 1, 15; *Washington Post National Weekly Edition*, 21 January 1985, 17; *New York Times*, 31 March 1986, D1, D5; Ibid., 15 January 1987, D1, D17; Ibid., 5 May 1987, D8; Ibid., 23 June 1987, A1, D6; Ibid., 16 July 1987, D15; Ibid., 10 November 1987, D1, D24; Ibid., 31 March 1988, A1, D8; Ibid., 15 September 1988, D1; Ibid., 5 April 1990, D7; Ibid., 26 September 1990, D1–2; Ibid., 1 December 1990, 1, 37; Ibid., 6 February 1991, A1, D6; Ibid., 20 November 1991, D1, D24; Ibid., 22 November 1991, D1–2; Ibid., 7 February 1992, D1, D6. For a more thorough discussion of recent desires to reform several aspects of the 1933 act, see Chapter Eight.

66. Ritter and Silber, *Principles of Money*, 88; Golembe and Holland, *Federal Regulation*, 84–6; Chandler, *American Monetary Policy*, 271; Brian C. Gendreau, "Bankers' Balances, Demand Deposit Interest and Agricultural Credit before the Banking Act of 1933: A Note," *Journal of Money, Credit, and Banking*, 11 (November 1979): 506–13; Charles F. Haywood and Charles M. Linke, *The Regulation of Deposit Interest Rates* (Chicago: Association of Reserve City Bankers, 1968), 16–25; Albert H. Cox, Jr., "Regulation of Interest on Deposits: An Historical Review," *Journal of Finance*, 22 (May 1967): 277–86; John J. Holland, Jr., "The Misinterpretation of the Causes of the Banking Collapse of 1933 and its Retarding Influence on Commercial Banking Innovation," *Bank Structure and Competition:*

Proceedings of a Conference (Chicago: Federal Reserve Bank of Chicago, 1975), 97–101.

67. Klebaner, *Commercial Banking*, 141; Howard Spencer Dye, Federal Banking Legislation from 1930 to 1938: Its History, Consequences and Related Issues (Ph.D. dissertation, Cornell University, 1949), 150, 162; Eugene Nelson White, "The Political Economy of Banking Regulation, 1864–1933," *Journal of Economic History*, 42 (March 1982): 39–40; Golembe and Holland, *Federal Regulation*, 119; *Wall Street Journal*, 26 April 1983, 4; *New York Times*, 16 December 1986, D10.

68. Kennedy, *Banking Crisis*, 211–2; Myers, Politics of American Banking, 78; C.D. Bremer, *American Bank Failures* (New York: Columbia University, 1935), 139–40; Milton Friedman and Anna Jacobson Schwartz, *A Monetary History of the United States, 1867–1960* (Princeton, N.J.: Princeton University, 1963), 435–6; Robert F. Leonard, "Supervision of the Commercial Banking System," *Banking Studies*, E.A. Goldenweiser, Elliott Thurston, and Bray Hammond, eds. (Washington, D.C.: Board of Governors of the Federal Reserve System, 1941): 207.

69. Friedman and Schwartz, *Monetary History*, 434, 437; John A. Cochran, *Money, Banking and the Economy*, 3d ed. (New York: Macmillan, 1975), 123; Kennedy, *Banking Crisis*, 222–3; Harlan M. Smith, *The Essentials of Money and Banking* (New York: Random House, 1968), 105; *Wall Street Journal*, 11 June 1984, 21; Ibid., 21 March 1984, 10; Ibid., 14 December 1984, 5; *Washington Post National Weekly Edition*, 21 January 1985, 5; *New York Times*, 5 January 1987, D2; Ibid., 28 December 1987, D1; Ibid., 28 November 1991, A1, D5; Frederic S. Mishkin, "An Evaluation of the Treasury Plan for Banking Reform," *Journal of Economic Perspectives*, 6 (Winter 1992): 143–9. The Banking Act of 1935 further strengthened the powers of the FDIC over insured banks; see Chapter Seven.

70. Senate Committee on Banking and Currency, *Operation of Banking Systems: Report on S. 1631*. In spite of these changes, the Federal Reserve System is not truly independent of Congress or the executive branch.

71. Kennedy, *Banking Crisis*, 222; Tompkins, *Vandenberg*, 94–5.

CHAPTER SIX

CHANGES IN FEDERAL RESERVE POWER DURING 1934

The 73d Congress between January and July 1934 passed three pieces of legislation that significantly affected the Federal Reserve System. Through bureaucratic maneuvering, officials of the system, Treasury Department, Reconstruction Finance Corporation, and Federal Trade Commission tried to protect their respective agency interests. Negotiation between Congress and the administration caused extensive change in two of the three measures. President Franklin D. Roosevelt remained sensitive to signs of opposition and provided some direction for executive agencies and legislators.

The Gold Reserve Act, signed on January 30, 1934, culminated FDR's efforts to raise prices of farm commodities by manipulating exchange rates and the cost of gold in terms of dollars. The act exchanged reserve banks' gold for certificates redeemable in gold when necessary to maintain parity of reserve notes. Roosevelt had intended simply to order district banks to surrender their gold, but reserve officials insisted on congressional approval. The law also established a stabilization fund, which gave the Treasury effective control over monetary policy.

Although the Gold Reserve Act moved through Congress swiftly, the Securities Exchange Act ran into stiff opposition. Protests by stock exchange members led the administration to rewrite the measure. The reserve board then asked for authority to regulate bank loans to brokers. In the original bill this responsibility had resided in the FTC, along with the right to regulate margin accounts maintained by brokers. In the act passed on June 1, 1934, the reserve board received both powers.

The third bill affecting the reserve system began as a proposal to establish regional intermediate credit banks and ended as an act to permit both reserve banks and the RFC to lend to industrialists who met credit requirements. The Industrial Loan Act, passed June 16, 1934, was part of an administration effort to provide additional money to businesses and encourage bank lending. Governor Eugene R. Black of the reserve board sponsored the intermediate credit bill, but the act was essentially a victory for Jesse H. Jones, chairman of the RFC.

MONETARY POLICY AND GOLD

President Roosevelt used special monetary authority conferred by Congress in 1933–34 to circumvent the Federal Reserve System. He entered office convinced that purchasing power of farmers had to increase before the country's economy could recover. Part of his program to aid agriculture took crops and livestock out of production; another provided for refinancing farm mortgages. During the spring and summer of 1933, FDR also allowed the gold dollar to depreciate on foreign exchange markets in an attempt to raise farm commodity prices by stimulating exports. When the strategy failed, he depreciated the dollar and finally devalued it. Reserve officials disagreed that raising prices would stimulate recovery, believing changes in economic activity stimulated price increases, not vice versa. The result of conflict between the system and Roosevelt was that during 1933–34 he seized responsibility for monetary policy.[1]

FDR's gold policy was heavily influenced by George F. Warren, an agricultural economist at Cornell University, who met regularly with the president between his election and January 1934. Warren's research on price movements since the 1840s had led him to conclude that whenever prices increased, the cost of gold rose and whenever they decreased, gold declined. Believing the dollar had become overvalued during the depression, he recommended a devaluation of 50% to restore commodity prices to the 1926 level. Roosevelt never fully adopted Warren's view that prices and the gold dollar would vary inversely, but he did believe that manipulating the dollar on exchange markets would affect export prices of such farm products as wheat, corn, and cotton.[2]

Roosevelt moved cautiously to control the nation's gold supply. His proclamation of March 6, 1933 declared the bank holiday, prohibited banks from paying out gold to prevent hoarding, and forbade gold exports without permission of the Treasury. During the bank holiday Secretary William Woodin allowed reserve banks to aid members only if they had delivered their gold to a reserve bank. An executive order of April 5, which Treasury and reserve officials helped draft, required delivery of gold held by individuals in amounts above $100.[3] Roosevelt told reporters he was acting "on the general theory that the U.S. Government is going to control all the gold in the country."[4] An executive order of April 20 prohibited gold exports and curtailed Woodin's authority to issue export licenses. This action caused speculation in dollars on world exchange markets and officially took the United States off the gold standard, although the country had lacked gold convertability since March 6.[5]

As the dollar depreciated in foreign markets during late April and May, domestic prices rose, which appeared to confirm Warren's theory that a less valuable dollar would increase farm prices by stimulating exports. Actually the dollar's depreciation resulted from a widespread belief that the United States would pursue inflation of the money supply and prices, a conclusion fostered by the prohibition of gold exports and by Congress. In mid-April its members had introduced more than forty bills to encourage inflation, supported by a bloc of congressmen mostly from the South and West, by such economists as Warren (who believed in a direct link between gold and commodity prices) and Irving Fisher of Yale University (who thought the supply of money determined prices), by such farm groups as the American Farm Bureau, and by lobbyists known as the Committee for the Nation led by James H. Rand, Jr., of Remington Rand, Vincent Bendix of Bendix Aviation, and General Robert E. Wood of Sears, Roebuck and Company.[6]

During debate on the bill (H.R. 3835) that eventually became the Agricultural Adjustment Act of 1933, Senator Elmer Thomas (D–OKLA) proposed an amendment that could produce inflation of the money supply and prices in several ways: issuance in unlimited quantities of unsecured United States notes (greenbacks) to retire the public debt or cover new expenses; remonetization and free coinage of silver at a ratio to gold determined by the president; devaluation of the gold dollar; and establishment of a stabilization board to fix the purchasing power of the dollar at 1920s levels. Thomas hoped to unite behind this proposal everyone favoring monetary action to counter the depression. Senators Robert J. Bulkley (D–OH) and James F. Byrnes (D–SC) phoned Raymond Moley, now assistant secretary of State, to warn that the Thomas amendment might pass the Senate. Wanting farm prices to rise but disapproving of unsecured paper money, Roosevelt decided to approve the amendment if Thomas would let it be rewritten. Byrnes, Moley, and Senator Key Pittman (D–NEV) began drafting a version reducing the possibility of uncontrolled price inflation. Thomas agreed to withdraw his proposal until the revision was ready.[7]

Pittman, Byrnes, James P. Warburg (a New York banker and economic adviser), and others met Moley on April 19 and finished drafting a more limited amendment. The Treasury would be unlikely to increase the money supply by issuing greenbacks because this version would authorize the president to order the secretary of the Treasury to negotiate purchase of up to $3 billion of government securities by reserve banks either in the open market or directly from the Treasury. Only if the system refused to do either, or if such action proved ineffective, could the president order the issue of $3 billion in greenbacks. Roosevelt insisted on including a sinking fund to retire at a rate of 4% annually any greenbacks issued, which would increase public confidence in the notes. The amendment would permit the president to devalue the gold dollar by no more than 50% and allow foreign nations to pay war debts in silver for six months. Finally, FDR's advisers deleted clauses regarding remonetization of silver and a price stabilization fund.[8]

Because the amendment had more to do with money than agriculture, the Senate referred it to the Banking and Currency Committee when Thomas introduced it on April 20. Senator Carter Glass (D–VA) opposed issuing greenbacks and devaluing the dollar. He feared the Treasury would force reserve officials to avoid the issue of greenbacks by purchasing government securities against their better judgment. He attempted to persuade his colleagues to report the amendment negatively or, failing that, to omit the section concerning devaluation. The vote on the latter provision was ten to ten, so it remained in the bill. The committee inserted a new clause to prevent uncontrolled increases in the money supply by allowing the Federal Reserve Board, with five affirmative votes and presidential approval, to raise or lower reserve requirements of member banks.[9]

The Senate debated the Thomas amendment in late April. Inflationists, including Thomas, Huey P. Long (D–LA), Tom Connally (D–TEX), and William E. Borah (R–IDA), hoped the measure would expand the money supply, which might aid farmers by raising prices. Staunchly opposing passage, Glass supported a proposal introduced by David A. Reed (R–PA) and Roscoe C. Patterson (R–MO) to delete the devaluation clause. Glass called devaluation an "immoral" repudiation of the Democratic party platform of 1932 and of the gold standard. Reed charged that devaluation would unconstitutionally impair existing contracts without due process of law. The Senate rejected conservative arguments by 53 to 35; 44 Democrats, 8 Republicans, and 1 Farmer–Laborer were in favor, while 11 Democrats and 24 Republicans opposed. Members who wished to help silver producers restored the provision remonetizing silver by a vote of 41 to 26. The Senate passed the Thomas proposal, 64 to 21, on April 28. Democrats Bulkley, Glass, and Joseph Bailey (SC) voted against, as did many conservative Republicans. Such progressive Republicans as Robert M. La Follette, Jr. (WIS), Peter Norbeck (SD), and Borah joined Democrats in favor.[10]

With a strong majority favoring inflation, the House voted to accept the Thomas amendment, 307 to 86. Insisting on a conference, representatives forced the Senate to exclude from the farm bill a "cost-of-production" clause to provide farmers a minimum income. The conferees reported on May 8, and both houses quickly approved the bill. Roosevelt signed the Agricultural Adjustment Act, including the Thomas amendment, on May 12.[11]

Gold clauses that required payment in dollars representing gold of the "present standard of weight and fineness" had long appeared in federal debt agreements and many private contracts. The administration knew that if FDR wanted to devalue the dollar, the law would have to change.[12] The reserve board reviewed a proposal by Dean G. Acheson, undersecretary of the Treasury, that would abrogate gold clauses in public and private contracts and make legal tender of all coins and currency issued in the United States. Although Black considered this "repudiation of a sacred promise," other members agreed that Congress should act.[13] Roosevelt sent Congress the resolution (S.J. Res. 56; H.J. Res. 192) on May 26.[14]

The resolution moved through both houses in spite of Glass, who thought it poor policy and who tried to amend the Senate measure to exclude outstanding government obligations. Most legislators knew that citizens could not pay contracts in gold because the government held almost all gold. Those voting in favor of the resolution based their action on the constitutional power of Congress to "coin money" and "regulate the value thereof." Opponents such as Representative Robert Luce (R–MASS) were mostly from the Northeast and were particularly unhappy with language calling for the Treasury to pay government obligations in legal tender, which they regarded as repudiation of a public trust. In all, only 20 senators and 57 representatives voted against the joint resolution, which Roosevelt signed on June 5.[15]

Abandonment of the gold standard and passage of the Thomas amendment and gold clause resolution encouraged a decline of the dollar on foreign exchange markets, and the World Economic Conference in London led to further depreciation. When Roosevelt had met with representatives of foreign governments in April and May 1933, he indicated willingness to stabilize the dollar soon. American, British, and French monetary experts in London began discussing the dollar's temporary stabilization in terms of foreign currencies on June 10. Roosevelt may not have realized the contradictory nature of his gold policies and international stabilization. He became uneasy when inflationists, reacting to reports of an agreement, urged him to reject stabilization. In London the American delegation continued to seek a draft resolution that would permit short-term stabilization without committing the United States to a long-term policy. The delegation cabled Roosevelt several proposals, but none satisfied him, as he remained concerned that farm prices would cease to rise if he stabilized the dollar. He finally rejected temporary stabilization in his "bombshell" message of July 3. Roosevelt was willing to stabilize the dollar only if it would not depress domestic prices or slow economic recovery.[16]

FDR's refusal to stabilize the currency drove the dollar down on exchange markets. It took $4.865 to purchase an English pound by July 19, compared with $3.41 at the end of February, and $.057275 to buy a French franc, compared with $.0394 in February. Roosevelt decided that the slide in the dollar was so rapid it might cause a collapse of international confidence in the United States. He talked to Black about marking $20 million in gold for export to the Bank of England to prevent the pound from rising above $4.86. Black spoke to George L. Harrison, governor of the New York Federal Reserve Bank, who agreed to handle the transaction. The president granted a license to export gold for two weeks so Harrison could establish credit with the Bank of England, which would purchase dollars in exchange markets for the New York bank. The dollar rose on exchanges as soon as purchases began, and commodity prices fell, so FDR refused to extend the license beyond two weeks.[17]

Roosevelt remained dissatisfied with the extent of economic recovery in the autumn of 1933. Farm commodity prices had broken in the third week of July and remained low the next two months. The Federal Open Market Committee was trying to stimulate the economy and avoid the issue of greenbacks under the Thomas amendment by purchasing $595 million of government securities between May 17 and November 29. Its purchases increased member bank reserves to $450 million by mid-July and to $794 million in November (Table 6A) but did not lead bankers to expand significantly their loans and investments (Table 6B).[18]

TABLE 6A
MEMBER BANK EXCESS RESERVES,
APRIL 1933–JUNE 1934
(averages of daily figures in millions of dollars)

Date	Total	New York City	Other Reserve Cities	Country Banks
1933				
Apr.	379.1	150.2	129.4	99.5
May	319.1	106.0	132.0	81.2
June	363.1	68.9	198.0	96.2
July	435.7	43.2	252.9	139.6
Aug.	565.5	101.8	312.3	151.3
Sep.	674.5	155.2	371.5	147.8
Oct.	758.4	149.0	437.9	171.5
Nov.	794.1	129.8	474.7	189.6
Dec.	765.7	96.0	472.6	197.1
1934				
Jan.	865.7	146.8	476.6	242.4
Feb.	890.8	118.3	509.1	263.4
Mar.	1,375.1	432.2	645.5	297.4
Apr.	1,541.0	454.6	736.4	350.1
May	1,623.5	484.7	778.4	360.4
June	1,684.6	532.2	799.6	352.8

Source: *Federal Reserve Bulletin*, 20 (June 1934): 349; Ibid., (September 1934): 585.

TABLE 6B
REPORTING MEMBER BANKS IN LEADING CITIES,
LOANS AND INVESTMENTS, APRIL 1933–JUNE 1934
(average of weekly figures in millions of dollars)

Date	Total	Loans on Secur-ities	All Other Loans	Investments	
				Total	U.S. Secur-ities
1933					
Apr.	15,935	3,606	4,658	7,671	4,621
May	16,341	3,700	4,714	7,928	4,932
June	16,619	3,764	4,741	8,114	5,141
July	16,710	3,835	4,762	8,113	5,147
Aug.	16,600	3,768	4,773	8,059	5,111
Sep.	16,566	3,728	4,831	8,007	5,067
Oct.	16,536	3,636	4,944	7,956	4,990
Nov.	16,688	3,574	4,990	8,124	5,135
Dec.	16,620	3,595	4,862	8,163	5,210
1934					
Jan.	16,589	3,542	4,732	8,315	5,334
Feb.	17,267	3,567	4,713	8,987	6,040
Mar.	17,484	3,539	4,663	9,282	6,251
Apr.	17,526	3,570	4,648	9,308	6,229
May	17,328	3,516	4,555	9,257	6,256
June	17,542	3,553	4,511	9,478	6,442

Source: *Federal Reserve Bulletin*, 19 (October 1933): 624; Ibid., 20 (September 1934): 588.

Roosevelt's interest in the Warren theory led him to wonder whether some agency other than the Treasury might be able to buy gold legally at a price higher than the statutory cost of $20.67. Although Warburg, Woodin, Acheson, and other officials opposed this idea in August, their arguments were less important to FDR than were declining commodity prices, rising unrest in farm areas, and increasing pressure from congressional inflationists. He had decided by October to experiment with Warren's plan, using the RFC to purchase newly mined domestic gold as well as gold on the world market to force down the dollar. The president announced the program on October 22 during a fireside chat. Most inflationists backed him, insisting the dollar was overvalued and that gold buying would raise farm prices.[19]

Bankers, economists, and others had opposed Roosevelt's monetary policy since March, but during the autumn their complaints reached a peak. They predicted that gold purchases would not affect domestic prices and argued that currency tampering could lead to uncontrolled price inflation, impaired government credit, and slower recovery of business confidence. The Federal Advisory Council joined the chorus of criticism when it adopted resolutions calling for monetary stabilization and warning against inflationary experiments.[20]

Opposition also existed within the administration. O.M.W. Sprague, a monetary economist who had worked as an adviser to the Treasury, resigned on November 21 to protest the gold program, and Warburg opposed the policy publicly. A lawyer with Wall Street connections, Acheson thought that buying gold above the statutory price was illegal, but he attempted to carry out FDR's decision. The president suspected him of confiding his opinion to reporters, however, and on November 15 demanded his resignation. Before he could reply, Roosevelt announced Acheson's departure. Woodin disapproved of the president's monetary program and was suffering from cancer of the throat, so he took a leave of absence the same day. Roosevelt appointed Henry Morgenthau, Jr., a friend who had served on the Federal Farm Board and believed in Warren, as acting secretary of the Treasury.[21]

Critics of Warren's theory proved more accurate than did his supporters. Although farm prices rose slightly between mid-October 1933 and the end of the year, the rise did not reflect a one-to-one relation to increases in the price of gold. The London gold price on October 21 was $29.01 an ounce. Gold purchases began October 25 and were confined to domestic gold until November 1, when the RFC started buying on the world market with the New York reserve bank as its agent. Between October 25 and November 14 the price for gold offered by the RFC increased from $31.36 to $33.56, while farm prices rose fractionally. Hoping for no more than moderate rises in the prices of wheat, cotton, and corn, FDR told reserve officials he was satisfied with initial results.[22]

Harrison, Woodin, Black, and others warned the president that gold purchases had caused weakness in government bond prices and might cause a collapse of investors' faith, which would make it difficult for the Treasury to raise money needed during the next nine months and could damage banks that held large portfolios of government securities. Roosevelt agreed the RFC should make no purchases on November 13 and 15, and later he approved sales as well as purchases to prevent the dollar, then above $35 per ounce of gold, from staying above $34. He also mandated less frequent increases in the domestic price of gold; the RFC price was $34.01 on December 1 and $34.06 on December 31. Farm commodity prices declined a little during the second half of November, discouraging FDR, who became willing to discuss permanent stabilization at a new dollar-gold ratio, possibly revaluing before Congress convened in January. He explored stabilizing the dollar-sterling rate, but when the British refused to cooperate he proceeded with plans to devalue the dollar.[23]

Because the administration wanted the government to receive windfall profits from devaluation, Roosevelt decided to require return of the remaining gold in the nation. Attorneys for the Treasury Department drafted an executive order to revoke the $100 exemption and require surrender of gold coin and certificates owned by individuals. Morgenthau released this order on December 28. While many individuals kept a coin or two, the public returned more than $800 million in gold and gold certificates between March 5 and December 31, 1933.[24]

Finding a legal way to acquire gold belonging to the reserve system proved difficult for Roosevelt. As early as September, he had asked if the government could require district banks to deposit their gold in the Treasury. Attorney General Homer Cummings believed that FDR could use orders against hoarding to require federal reserve agents to deliver gold to the treasurer of the United States. As long as the treasurer returned gold certificates, there would be no violation of the Federal Reserve Act. When Black discovered the administration's plan, he told Morgenthau and Roosevelt that the government could obtain possession of but not title to system gold, that district banks could hardly be termed hoarders, and that the Thomas amendment was probably unconstitutional. He thought profits from devaluation should go to the government through legislation but wished the system to retain its gold. Board members discussed the plan and concluded that they could not legally tell district banks to exchange gold for certificates that the Treasury would not redeem in gold because such an action might violate the reserve act and the Gold Standard Act of 1900. A stalemate persisted, with Black imploring Roosevelt to submit legislation and the president urging reserve officials to surrender their gold without congressional action. FDR gave in on December 29 and agreed to refer the question to Congress.[25]

The administration was drafting the bill that became the Gold Reserve Act when Congress reconvened in January 1934. The president saw Warren, Cummings, and Morgenthau to discuss the measure on January 11. Roosevelt decided that legislation should require delivery of reserve gold and permit a dollar equal to 50–60% of previous value, which he thought would establish reasonable exchange rates with foreign countries. A few days later he sent the Treasury proposal with a message to Congress and announced an increase in the price for domestically mined gold to $34.45, a 60% rise above former mint price. The bill as introduced would end circulation of gold and gold certificates, give the government title to all monetary gold, require district banks to surrender gold and gold certificates at the old mint price in exchange for new certificates that only reserve banks could hold, and empower the president to revalue the dollar within 50–60% of its previous value. The proposal would obligate the Treasury to redeem the new certificates held by district banks with gold whenever necessary to maintain the parity of reserve notes with other legal tender. It would also allow the secretary of the Treasury to buy and sell gold at home and in world markets and deal in foreign exchange and government securities through a stabilization fund.[26]

Roosevelt asked the reserve board to issue a statement indicating support of the bill. The board revealed it had urged the president to let Congress decide the question of title to reserve gold and emphasized that all profit from devaluation should go to the government.[27] The board issued the statement because the measure was "much better" than relying on executive orders, which might not have permitted redemption in gold of the system's certificates.[28]

The House acted quickly. The Committee on Coinage, Weights, and Measures approved the gold bill (H.R. 6976), which Andrew L. Somers (D–NY) had introduced, 15 to 1 on January 18. The next day Harold McGugin (R–KANS) and Ralph R. Eltse (R–CAL) issued a minority report arguing against depriving the system of gold collateral to protect its notes and giving such unlimited power over the stabilization fund to one man in the Treasury. Somers had intended to invite monetary economists and reserve officials to make statements, but the Democratic leaders forestalled him by scheduling debate almost immediately and limiting it to four hours. The House considered and passed the bill, 360 to 40, on January 20. Only seven Democrats voted against.[29]

The Senate Committee on Banking and Currency held brief hearings on the gold bill. First to testify in executive session was Cummings, who said the measure would be a constitutional way to regulate the value of money. Then reserve officials argued that the Treasury Department could have the profit without confiscating the system's gold. Subsequently, Duncan U. Fletcher (D–FLA), committee chairman, introduced S. 2366, on which public hearings lasted less than a week. Rand and former Senator Robert L. Owen, both of whom supported stabilization of purchasing power, expressed no criticism. Economist B.M. Anderson of Chase Manhattan Bank disagreed with nearly every section, believing that gold should circulate as coin and currency and that devaluation was unnecessary. Warren assured the committee that he had not written the bill but insisted that devaluation would not hurt creditors because otherwise debtors would be unable to repay. E.W. Kemmerer of Princeton University and H. Parker Willis of Columbia thought the reserve system, not the Treasury, should run the stabilization fund.[30]

The Senate committee reported the House bill with a few amendments on January 23. The most important would substitute a five-person board to handle the stabilization fund—secretary of the Treasury, comptroller of the currency, governor of the reserve board, and two others appointed by the president and confirmed by the Senate. A change suggested by James Couzens (R–MICH) would limit the Treasury's power by allowing the fund to operate only two years, with possible extension to a third by presidential proclamation.[31] Another clause proposed by Frederic C. Walcott (R–CONN) would narrow the Treasury's authority by permitting use of the fund only to stabilize the "exchange value of the dollar in relation to the currencies of foreign governments."[32]

Senate debate started January 24, when Fletcher explained committee amendments. Glass took the floor to claim that the government lacked authority to confiscate the reserve system's gold and substitute certificates that were not redeemable. He complained that devaluation would lead to uncontrollable price inflation. He defended the committee amendment establishing a five-person stabilization board, but the Senate rejected it 54 to 36 because Roosevelt preferred to rely on Morgenthau. Presidential pressure led to removal of the Walcott provision that limited the Treasury to influencing exchange rates. A few Republicans questioned the measure's constitutionality, claiming Congress would be surrendering authority to coin money and regulate its value, but the Senate passed the bill, 66 to 23, on January 27. Glass was the only Democrat to vote against. The House agreed to the measure as passed by the Senate on January 29, and Roosevelt signed the Gold Reserve Act of 1934 the next afternoon.[33]

Morgenthau immediately sent Black a letter asking about the total gold held by the reserve at the close of business on January 30. The board's secretary, Chester Morrill, replied that the system had gold equal to $1,761,468,965.79 and requested a receipt for that amount as quickly as possible, since the new certificates had not been printed. In one stroke, gold ceased to be the basis for federal reserve notes and the system's reserves. Certificates that could not circulate nor be redeemed, except to settle international trade balances or to maintain parity of federal reserve notes, replaced gold in system vaults.[34]

Roosevelt revalued the gold dollar by proclamation on January 31. Harrison had suggested that a devaluation as small as possible under the law (a dollar worth 60% of its former value) would disrupt foreign exchange markets least. After discussion with advisers, FDR decided that $35 should purchase an ounce of gold, which was 59.06% of the previous mint price or a devaluation of 40.94%. The government's profit was $2.808 billion. Beginning February 1, the Treasury bought gold at $35 an ounce, although the world price did not reach $35 until March. These actions placed the United States on a gold bullion standard under Treasury regulation. American citizens could not own gold except for industrial purposes nor export gold except in bullion form to settle foreign trade balances.[35]

Reestablishment of the gold dollar quieted complaints from sound-money advocates, although they worried that before 1937 the president would alter the gold content of the dollar within 50–60% of its former value. Congress stimulated unnecessary anxiety by extending the authority to 1943, when it expired unused. The Treasury's price for gold was $35 an ounce until the early 1970s. President Richard M. Nixon let the dollar float on foreign exchange markets in 1973, and the nation has not returned to the gold standard since then.[36]

Devaluation did not satisfy many silver advocates, who wanted the president to aid American silver producers, including Henry B. Steagall

(D–ALA) who chaired the House Banking and Currency Committee. In June 1934 such congressmen succeeded in passing the Silver Purchase Act, which directed the Treasury to obtain a stock of silver equal to one-fourth of the nation's total monetary stock or buy silver until the market price reached $1.2929 per ounce. To cover its large purchases, the Treasury issued silver certificates in various denominations. Acquisitions under this program, more than $1.6 billion by the end of 1941, pacified silverites, although the purchases had no economic justification.[37]

Some inflationists were not content with the silver program. Warren and the Committee for the Nation urged Roosevelt to devalue the dollar to $41 an ounce of gold or more. The Committee for the Nation began to press for a Federal Monetary Authority that would assume the monetary authority of the reserve system and Treasury and would have a mandate to restore prices to the 1926 level. Thomas and a few others continued to support additional issues of currency. Roosevelt was aware of inflationist pressure but pursued a course of stabilizing the dollar in terms of gold after January 1934.[38]

The president's gold policy did seem to achieve one of its goals. Commodity prices rose, and prices of farm products increased by 40%. Not all of the change in farm prices was a result of the gold program. The activities of the Agricultural Adjustment Administration reduced the size of crops in 1933–34, as did a regional drought. Still, Roosevelt had reason to be satisfied with price rises in such agricultural products as cotton, wheat, and corn.[39]

The most important effect of the president's decision to revalue the gold dollar at $35 an ounce was to stimulate an avalanche of gold imports, which increased the money supply. The nation's monetary gold stock in 1932 averaged below $4 billion, averaged $9 billion in 1935, and rose to $16 billion in 1939 as a consequence of imports. The Treasury Department issued gold certificates to district banks on the basis of previous gold purchases, receiving a credit on its accounts. Whenever the Treasury wished to buy more gold or pay for other purchases, it wrote a check, which expanded the money supply and member bank reserves. To the extent that monetary expansion fueled recovery after 1933, Roosevelt could have achieved the same result through encouraging the Treasury to issue and the system to purchase large amounts of government securities. Such a policy would have expanded member bank reserves in the same way that gold imports did, and Roosevelt had ample authority under the Thomas amendment to maneuver reserve officials into making large-scale purchases. Instead the system slowed open market operations in November 1933, and for the remainder of the decade its holdings of government securities were stable.[40]

If the president had pursued a policy of massive open market purchases, the world economy might have suffered less dislocation. The large gold imports and the worldwide increase of gold production were mostly due to an undervaluing of the dollar in comparison to other currencies. European nations still on the gold standard faced a difficult time after the American devaluation. They had to decide whether to revalue their currencies or permit internal prices to adjust downward while losing gold to the United States. Led by France, gold bloc nations initially tried deflation, but in 1936 they gave up and revalued. After that, a Tripartite Agreement between the United States, Britain, and France kept foreign exchange rates within a narrow range. Gold imports did not cease, however, perhaps because Adolf Hitler aroused fears of war and led Europeans to invest their money in safer places.[41]

Roosevelt was less concerned about the world economy than about conditions in the United States. To ensure his ability to influence domestic recovery, he seized control of monetary policy in March and April 1933. The Thomas amendment gave him power to use a range of mechanisms to produce expansion of the money supply. FDR and the Treasury thus undermined the reserve system as the determinant of monetary policy and bank reserves. Devaluation and gold and silver purchases expanded the monetary stock and were followed by an enormous increase in bank reserves. In addition, Roosevelt still had authority to insist that reserve banks buy up to $3 billion of government securities or order the issue of a similar amount of greenbacks. The president and Treasury remained in control of the monetary situation until after World War II.[42]

FDR's political acumen led him to adopt monetary policies that balanced the demands of inflationists and sound-money advocates. From the time he entered office, he was beset by conflicting advice, for both groups had popular support. To control the political pressures imposed by each group, Roosevelt sought a middle ground that would give him flexibility. Because he believed that economic recovery depended on a rise in farm prices, he first sided with inflationists. Still, he did not want uncontrolled price inflation, did not believe in issuing unsecured greenbacks, and did not revalue the gold dollar at $41.34 as many inflationists wished. His public support remained steady, and even after passage of the Gold Reserve Act he retained control of the monetary situation. If the political influence of inflationists had increased after 1934, FDR had the power to forestall serious criticism. As it developed, the president had little to fear from inflationists after 1934 and never used all the authority given him by Congress.[43]

SECURITIES EXCHANGE ACT

Roosevelt had announced during the election campaign of 1932 that he favored stock exchange regulation to avoid abuses of the 1920s, and he pursued that goal until the Securities Exchange Act passed in June 1934. Soon after taking office, he asked a group led by John Dickinson, assistant secretary of Commerce, to draft proposals. FDR received the group's report in January 1934. In the meantime Moley had asked lawyers Benjamin Cohen and Thomas Corcoran to formulate a bill that would regulate stock exchanges. Along with James M. Landis, who became head of the Federal Trade Commission in 1933 and who was a member of the Dickinson committee, Cohen and Corcoran had drafted the Truth-in-Securities Act of 1933. Subsequently, the three conferred with Fletcher and Ferdinand Pecora, the counsel for the Senate Committee on Banking and Currency. They agreed upon a measure that would use the FTC to regulate securities exchanges. Fletcher introduced it (S. 2692) on February 9, and Chairman Sam Rayburn (D–TEX) of the House Committee on Interstate and Foreign Commerce introduced it (H.R. 7852) the next day.[44]

The exchange bill made no mention of the reserve board but would prohibit dealers, brokers, and exchange members from using as collateral any security registered on an exchange in the United States, except to borrow from member banks of the reserve system. The same section would limit such borrowing by requiring loan values to be equal to (a) 40% of the current market price (60% margin), or (b) 80% of the stock's lowest price during the previous three years (20% margin), whichever was higher. This would permit lower margins on stable stocks and require larger ones on securities with rising prices. The purpose was to prevent pyramiding of credit when price increases had generated paper profits that could be used to purchase additional stock without using more cash. While some exchanges had adopted margin requirements by 1934, many smaller ones had not.[45]

House committee hearings began February 14, and Senate hearings on February 27. Wall Street investment houses, brokers, and exchange members protested against the Cohen–Corcoran measure. Their testimony questioned whether Congress had constitutional authority to regulate exchanges. If the legislators were determined to act, these men sought an independent commission with seven members, including the secretary of the Treasury, secretary of Commerce, and two exchange members, and they suggested the commission receive administrative flexibility to regulate margin requirements. The tactics of financiers angered Fletcher, who claimed Wall Street had begun a propaganda campaign.[46]

Both committees heard Corcoran testify that regulating margins would protect the economy from stock market instability by limiting borrowed money. He admitted to House members that clauses on margins and bank loans to brokers needed clarification. He noted that margin sections would not become effective until October 1, allowing time for brokers and banks to adjust. If committee members believed this period too short, Corcoran was willing to support an amendment that would prevent wholesale liquidation of existing accounts. He agreed that government securities and possibly municipal bonds should be excluded from margin requirements and indicated willingness to give the FTC additional flexibility to lower margins.[47]

E.A. Goldenweiser, director of research and statistics for the reserve board, presented detailed testimony to both committees about the influence of credit availability on securities speculation. He thought the sections that put lending on securities by bankers and brokers "under more reasonable control" would limit securities exchanges to "legitimate" functions and moderate or eliminate activities "definitely injurious and undesirable from the social point of view, and the economic point of view."[48] He believed the margin clause would cause credit contraction and recommended that the provision apply only to future loans. He agreed that regulatory authorities should have discretion to alter margins.[49]

Testifying before the House committee, Dickinson complained that the bill would require loan liquidation when new margins took effect and would limit stock market credit less efficiently than more flexible margins. Recognizing that regulating short-term credit used to finance securities purchases was necessary, the earlier Dickinson report had suggested reserve banks receive authority to prescribe margins, a view

Dickinson reaffirmed. He also disclosed a split among FDR's advisers regarding the extensive power that would be delegated to the FTC.[50]

Rayburn, Pecora, and others recognized the need to amend the measure, including sections on margins and brokers' loans. The committees began considering changes, even as hearings continued. Black seized this opportunity to persuade Roosevelt that the reserve board should regulate bank loans to brokers, and members of the board's staff began meeting with Pecora and others to revise the bill. At the same time Morgenthau asked a St. Louis banker who was then his assistant, Tom K. Smith, to look into the measure's effect on banks and the Treasury. Smith sought more moderate and flexible margin requirements. By March 15 the reserve board was willing to accept the additional responsibility of setting margins between brokers and their customers.[51]

The administration sent the revised version of the bill to Rayburn and Fletcher on March 19, and Rayburn introduced it as a new bill (H.R. 8720). The redrafted clauses vested authority with the reserve board to set and alter margins between banks and brokers and between brokers and customers. The bill set a standard initial loan value of whatever would be higher: 40% of the current price (60% margin); or 100% of the lowest price quotation in the previous three years, but under no circumstances more than 75% of current market price (25% margin). The reserve board would receive authority to lower the loan value, and in extraordinary circumstances the board could raise it above 40%. These levels would apply to new loans granted after August 1, 1934; outstanding loans would not have to meet the requirements until 1939.[52]

The revised bill did not satisfy brokers and exchange members. Richard Whitney, president of the New York Stock Exchange, called the changes inadequate because the measure would promote government control of exchanges, commerce, and industry. He said margins were rigid and complicated and suggested the reserve board receive power to set margins at any rate appropriate for economic conditions. Lothrop Withington, who represented New England securities dealers and brokers, and Robert K. Cassatt, who represented investment bankers in Philadelphia, agreed. Dickinson suggested that the reserve board receive power to authorize nonmember banks as well as members to lend to brokers.[53]

A few witnesses were satisfied with the new margin sections. Corcoran defended them, explaining that they had been revised so that margins on stocks with volatile prices would not change, while loan values on more stable issues would be relaxed. Winfield Riefler, an economist who was on the reserve board's staff, argued that the board should have authority to alter margins and should have guidance from Congress. Landis supported this view, indicating that a legislative guidepost provided advantages to administrators. Black preferred the board to have unlimited authority to alter margins, but he and the board were willing to accept the bill's limits.[54]

As the committees listened to final witnesses in late March, Roosevelt sought to keep the measure moving through Congress. He sent Fletcher and Rayburn letters noting his commitment to higher margins and regulation of securities exchanges. He cited persistent opposition from exchanges and declared he did not want the bill "weakened in any shape, manner or form."[55] In another letter he remarked, "Frankly, I am sick and tired of all the complaint against the Stock Exchange and Securities Bills."[56]

Criticism from stock exchange members poured into Congress, and Rayburn realized his committee would revise the measure before reporting it. The group designated a subcommittee to draft a satisfactory margin formula, which was reported on April 12. The provision would set as standard loan value the highest of 55% of the current market price (45% margin), or 100% of the lowest price during the previous three years but not more than 85% of the current market price (15% margin). The subcommittee draft would allow the reserve board greater flexibility to alter loan values. The full committee adopted an amendment that would allow the board to make arrangements with nonmember banks to lend on margin. The committee approved the amended stock exchange measure on April 25, and Rayburn introduced it as a new bill (H.R. 9323).[57] The report emphasized that margin provisions were to give the reserve system an "effective method of reducing the aggregate amount of the nation's credit resources" used for stock speculation.[58]

Although the Senate committee believed speculative credit had contributed to the stock market boom and crash of 1928–29, Fletcher expected members to present amendments to margin sections. Some wanted to permit the reserve board flexibility to alter margins. Glass argued against involving the reserve system at all because he doubted its officials knew enough about stock exchange operations to regulate margins effectively. He proposed an amendment to omit the words Federal Trade Commission and Federal Reserve Board and substitute an administrative agency known as the Federal Securities Exchange Commission. Committee members adopted this proposal, ten to eight, with Democrats split evenly. Black then informed Glass that the reserve board would prefer jurisdiction over margin lending by member banks. He persuaded the senator that the provision in the Banking Act of 1933 authorizing district banks to curb speculative loans could be effective only when members borrowed from district banks. As long as members' excess reserves remained large, they would not borrow. Glass presented Black's views to the committee, and on April 11 members deleted all statutory standards for margins and divided authority to regulate margins between the board and the five-member commission. They chose to delay the date for new margin requirements to October 1. Fletcher introduced and reported the greatly revised bill (S. 3420) on April 20, after his committee approved it eleven to eight.[59]

Debate on the Rayburn measure began April 30, after the House adopted a rule that allowed seven hours of discussion and unlimited amendment. Primary opposition came from a few Republicans who protested against placing such power with any public commission and predicted that enactment would slow economic recovery and restrict credit. Voting revealed that opponents enjoyed little support from House members, even other Republicans. Margin provisions passed without revision. The House decided the FTC was adequate to administer the bill, rejecting an amendment to establish another regulatory commission. On May 4, the bill passed, 280 to 84.[60]

Senate debate began three days later, with Fletcher speaking for two hours about abuses the measure would correct. Conservative Republicans claimed the bill would affect the internal affairs of corporations and restrict corporate financing. Because he thought brokers had made loans carelessly, Bulkley introduced an amendment to abolish margin trading on exchanges after April 1, 1935, a proposal that Senators Long, Edward P. Costigan (D–COL), and Burton K. Wheeler (D–MONT) supported. Glass spoke and voted for this amendment because he considered speculation in stocks evil. Bulkley's proposal would have kept the reserve board out of the bill, but it failed, 30 to 48. Couzens introduced an amendment that would restore the FTC as the administrative body, which failed, 29 to 51. The Senate approved the stock exchange bill on May 12, 62 to 13. Only one Democrat (Thomas P. Gore of Oklahoma) opposed its passage, and more Republicans voted for than against (15 to 12).[61]

The House and Senate stock exchange bills had only two notable differences. While the House measure would name the FTC, which administered the Truth-in-Securities Act, as the agency to regulate stock exchanges, the Senate version would establish a securities commission to administer both exchange regulation and the Truth-in-Securities Act. The House had adopted a margin section to provide a standard for the reserve board whenever it set margins for loans by brokers or banks, although the board would have flexibility to meet the needs of commerce and industry by raising or lowering requirements. The Fletcher bill would divide authority for setting margins between the reserve board for banks and the securities commission for brokers and would not limit the two agencies by providing a formula.[62]

The conference committee was hampered initially by a conflict over senators named to serve. Fletcher apparently hoped to persuade the conferees to adopt the FTC as the administrative agency. Ignoring seniority, he left off the list of conferees three supporters of an independent commission—Glass, Robert F. Wagner (D–NY), and John G. Townsend, Jr. (R–DEL). Alben W. Barkley (D–KEN) and Byrnes, the two Democrats named instead, offered to resign, but Glass dissuaded them. Roosevelt aggravated the situation by choosing this moment to announce that he preferred the more definite House provision on margins and the FTC as the administrative agency because of its expertise with securities. Normally an administration supporter, Barkley felt pledged to support Senate amendments. He asked Fletcher to allow him to withdraw from the conference committee, but the chairman refused. The incident inspired Senate conferees' defense of their version when the committee began meeting on May 17.[63]

After the conference started, progress was steady, and on May 26 the committee reached agreement. The bill reported three days later would establish a five-member independent commission to administer both this measure and the Truth-in-Securities Act, as in the Senate version. Margin requirements followed the House measure and would provide on listed securities an initial loan value of 55% of current cost or 100% of the lowest market price of the stock for the previous 36 months but not more than 75% of current market price. The reserve board would have authority to raise or lower loan values and power to issue rules and regulations concerning undermargined accounts, transfer of accounts, and setting of margin requirements for short sales, arbitrage transactions, and loans by other than brokers and stock exchange members for the purpose of carrying securities. Brokers, dealers, and exchange members could borrow on listed securities only from member banks or from nonmember banks that had filed an agreement with the reserve board, which the board could terminate after notice. Provisions on margins (including reserve board rules and regulations) would not apply until July 1, 1937 to maintenance, renewal, or extension of loans made prior to enactment. The Senate passed the bill without a recorded vote on the morning of June 1, and that afternoon the House did the same. Roosevelt signed the Securities Exchange Act on June 6, 1934.[64]

Wall Street's reaction was positive, but those connected to stock exchanges wondered who would fill positions on the SEC. According to R.E. Desverine, counsel for the Association of Stock Exchange Firms, the act would be "practicable if skillfully administered."[65] After much consideration Roosevelt decided that Joseph P. Kennedy, a Boston financier, would be the ideal chairman of the commission. He believed that as a previous stock speculator, Kennedy would be effective because he knew all the tricks of the trade and would not be corrupted by Wall Street because he had made his fortune. Other members nominated by FDR were George C. Mathews (member of the FTC), Landis, Judge Robert Healy (FTC counsel), and Pecora, all of whom had experience in drafting the Securities Exchange Act or in administering the Truth-in-Securities Act. These selections became public July 1, and shortly thereafter the commission took up its duties.[66]

A reserve board member, Charles S. Hamlin, had confided to his diary in April 1934 that giving the board control of margins "would be a grant of power greater than ever before given to any group of men in this country."[67] While this assessment is exaggerated, the Securities Exchange Act of 1934 did increase board authority over financial markets by providing a selective or qualitative control over securities loans. The reserve board and its staff considered the rules and regulations necessary to implement margin requirements, consulting reserve bankers, the SEC, and the Treasury. The board issued Regulation T setting margins for brokers on September 28, 1934. The requirements were those in the act, and many margins were 25% because of the level of stock prices that autumn. Regulation T also prescribed the way in which nonmember banks could become eligible to make loans.[68] The board issued Regulation U in 1936 to cover loans for purchasing or carrying stocks made by banks and raised the requirements to 55% (45% loan value). Since that time margins have varied, between 100% and 40%, depending on the market. Although the board and the Treasury asked Congress in 1985 to permit securities exchanges to set their own margin requirements under regulation of the SEC, Congress has shown no interest. To the present day, the reserve board sets margins for trading in securities.[69]

INDUSTRIAL LOAN ACT

The RFC and comptroller of the currency made steady progress in 1933 with efforts to reopen and recapitalize banks, while district banks purchased government securities that increased members' excess reserves. Still, lending by commercial banks rose little, and Roosevelt remained dissatisfied with the pace of recovery. In the autumn, he became convinced that bankers were refusing to lend on good collateral and inhibiting recovery because they disliked the Banking Act of 1933 and his gold program. He began to consider extending federal aid to businessmen unable to acquire bank loans with adequate security.[70] Early in 1934, two agencies, the reserve board and the RFC, responded to his desire to increase business activity, devising plans that would permit them to make or participate in loans providing industries with working capital.

Black had the reserve board's staff draft a proposal to establish 12 intermediate credit banks, connected with reserve banks, to lend small amounts to businesses for up to five years. He discussed this measure with the board and Federal Advisory Council in February 1934. Some reserve officials doubted the need for government assistance, but council members promised to discuss the plan with directors. Black then met with FDR and Treasury officials, reaching agreement on a bill by mid-March.[71]

Simultaneously RFC officials had been preparing amendments to the corporation's act, including one that would authorize the agency to lend for up to five years to industries meeting codes established under the National Recovery Act. Jones on March 13 sent his bill to Fletcher and Steagall. The move surprised Roosevelt, who had not seen the proposal. After Jones testified in executive session, the Senate banking committee agreed that Fletcher should introduce a measure containing most of the RFC amendments, but the committee insisted that the industrial loan provision and a section to establish an import-export bank each become a separate bill.[72]

Black's intermediate credit measure reached Congress on March 19, when the president requested passage. Introduced by Fletcher (S. 3101) and Steagall (H.R. 8717), the bill would permit the reserve board to issue charters to intermediate credit banks in reserve cities. The new banks would have authority to discount for or purchase from financial institutions any obligations with maturities of less than five years contracted for lending working capital to established businesses. Participating financial institutions would assume at least 20% of any loss from such transactions. Whenever financial intermediaries could not be found, credit banks could lend directly. To provide capital for credit banks, the secretary of the Treasury would purchase the stock owned by reserve banks in the Federal Deposit Insurance Corporation, using profit from the devaluation of the dollar. Each reserve bank would give the credit bank in its district an amount equal to the price of those shares. Thus, each would become a stockholder of a credit bank and—subject to the reserve board's approval—select a board of directors, a majority of whom had to be industrialists within the district. With the reserve board's approval, credit banks might issue preferred stock, notes, debentures, bonds, or other obligations, none of which would be a liability of the federal government.[73]

The Senate committee decided on March 21 to refer this bill to the subcommittee on banking chaired by Glass, which would also consider a measure (S. 3137) introduced by Fletcher authorizing direct loans to businesses by the RFC. Subcommittee members adopted a substitute for both bills drafted by Glass, who was angry that the administration had not consulted him. His measure would amend section 13 of the Federal Reserve Act by permitting a reserve bank to lend working capital directly to industrial and commercial businesses in its district for up to five years, if firms had deserved but been unable to find accommodation from more usual sources. It would allow district banks to discount for or purchase from financial institutions obligations with maturities of less than five years that had been contracted to provide working capital to businesses. Financial institutions would be liable for 20% of any loss sustained. In essence, Glass substituted reserve banks for credit banks in the original bill. Money for such loans would come from a district bank's surplus, and with the reserve board's approval each could issue notes, bonds, debentures, or other obligations up to five times its surplus on the day the bill became law. To administer the working capital program, each district bank would select an industrial advisory committee having three to five members engaged in industry.[74]

Reserve board members discussed this substitute on April 3 and decided to support it for two reasons. Glass had intimated that his subcommittee would not approve establishment of 12 new banks, and the board preferred that the reserve system, not the RFC, have authority to lend to industry. The board hoped that Congress would ask the Treasury Department to buy reserve banks' stock in the FDIC, which would double their surplus, estimated at $140 million. Black spoke to Glass about that possibility, and the senator promised to consult Roosevelt.[75]

Revising his substitute bill, Glass consulted Harrison of the New York reserve bank. He told the senator he was disturbed by the possibility that district banks would issue debentures.[76] Glass said he had copied the proviso from the credit bank measure but would strike it from his bill. Realizing that reserve banks would need capital to finance industrial loans, he proposed to direct the Treasury, using profit from devaluation of the dollar, to return to reserve banks the amount collected as a franchise tax between 1915 and 1933 under the original provisions of the Federal Reserve Act, about $150 million. He believed Congress should never have imposed this tax. If district banks were to make industrial loans, Harrison agreed that their surplus would have to be increased but suggested that they be permitted to sell their stock in the FDIC. Glass objected because that would leave the government as sole guarantor of bank deposits, which he had always opposed. Harrison also believed the industrial loan committees provided for in the bill would not work. The senator replied that Roosevelt had suggested that section.[77]

Glass worked during April to complete a bill satisfactory to the administration. He met with FDR, who gave tentative approval to industrial loans by reserve banks, pending another conference between Black and Glass. A compromise bill (S. 3487) introduced by Glass on April 28 would permit a district bank to lend working capital directly to commercial and industrial businesses in its district, for up to five years, whenever concerns could not secure funds from other institutions. To encourage banks to make loans, district banks could discount for or purchase from financial institutions any obligation that had a maturity of less than five years that they acquired by providing firms with capital. Such industrial loans or discounts could equal twice a district bank's surplus, which the Treasury would increase by lending to reserve banks $139 million, to be repaid at 1% per annum.[78]

Proposals permitting both the RFC and reserve banks to lend to businesses moved through the Senate during late April and early May. The banking committee approved the Glass measure without change and voted seven to five to reject a plan that would allow the RFC to make industrial loans. Senate debate began May 2. The primary question concerned whether the RFC as well as district banks should have authority to make industrial loans. Many members of Congress feared district banks would lend insufficient amounts to aid the economy and wished to supplement that plan with RFC loans. Fletcher held this view and introduced a new version of the RFC's bill (S. 3520) that would permit the agency to make or participate in direct loans to businesses for up to five years, whenever credit was not available from commercial or reserve banks. Fletcher's bill would limit this authority to the period before January 31, 1935 and allow the RFC to lend $250 million. During Senate consideration of the Glass bill, Barkley introduced a similar amendment that would authorize the RFC to lend $280 million to businesses until January 31, 1935, for the purpose of sustaining or increasing employment, which the Senate accepted. The amended Glass measure passed on May 14.[79]

The House adopted a measure similar to the Senate bill. Steagall held brief hearings at which Jones and Black appeared. On May 21 the banking committee reported an amended bill that would alter the RFC act in several ways and authorize direct loans to industry by the RFC and reserve banks.[80] The measure would permit the RFC to lend to firms "for the purpose of maintaining or increasing employment" and allow district banks to make loans to provide businesses with capital.[81] The House measure assumed the RFC would make more loans, giving it permanent power to lend $300 million, while reserve banks could lend only their surplus of $140 million. Debate began May 22, and the bill passed without much change the next day.[82]

The conference committee took several weeks to work out differences in the House and Senate measures. Glass, the senior senator on the committee, was disappointed by the House version. He had sponsored a bill so that district banks instead of the RFC would lend working capital to businesses. The Senate and House, fearing reserve banks would lend little, had passed versions empowering the RFC to lend to corporations, which defeated his purpose, and the House had not included the $139 million loan to district banks that Glass had added so more industrial loans could be made. He and other senators insisted that House members yield on several points. Morgenthau and

Roosevelt became active in promoting a compromise that would adopt most features of the Senate bill yet appease Steagall and the House. The version reported by the conference committee on June 16 followed the Senate measure by leaving out a proposed import-export bank and limiting RFC authority to the period before January 31, 1935. Committee members compromised on two other sections; one would allow the RFC to lend only $500,000 to a single firm, and the other would authorize but not require the secretary of the Treasury to give reserve banks up to $139 million, which would be repaid at 2% per annum. Both the House and Senate passed the measure the day the conference committee reported, and Roosevelt signed it June 19.[83]

Lending started slowly, perhaps because neither commercial nor reserve bankers wanted to make such loans. Reserve officials had authorized commitments totaling $1.6 million by mid-August but disbursed only $234,000 because of delays in paperwork and because some applicants did not need funds instantly. By January 1, 1934, district banks had received more than 5,000 applications for working capital loans equaling $190 million. They had approved only 1,020 applications for a total of $52 million, rejecting the rest as poor risks. RFC loan commitments had reached $9 million by August 31, and the agency authorized almost 600 loans for $30.5 million by January 1935. In 1935 reserve officials approved another 973 applications for a total of $72 million. Money lent by reserve banks declined after 1935, when $60 million was outstanding.[84]

In retrospect it seems obvious that there was no need for both the RFC and reserve banks to make industrial loans for working capital. Disbursements were small, and either could have handled them. That both agencies gained similar authority in 1934 was due more to politics within the executive branch and Congress than to logic or economic necessity. When Jones heard about Black's intermediate credit bill, the RFC chairman moved to capture such lending for his agency. He found it fairly easy to promote his program because many members of Congress believed reserve banks would never lend enough to aid the economy. Glass tried to derail RFC lending but found himself incapable of preventing amendment of his bill to include the agency. Thus, a bill to create 12 intermediate credit banks evolved into a measure authorizing both the RFC and reserve banks to make industrial loans.[85]

After a weak beginning, the district bank program of lending to businesses fizzled out. When the law of 1934 passed, the RFC's power was temporary, while reserve authority was permanent. Before the RFC's right to make such loans expired on January 13, 1935, Congress extended it. Legislators relaxed many of the limits originally placed on the RFC in granting such loans. By World War II, the RFC had made 12,000 loans to businesses for $848 million, becoming the primary agency making such loans. Because many reserve officials were reluctant to use their surplus for loans to industry, they were probably relieved that the RFC assumed the role. After the RFC ceased to function in the 1950s, district banks had a short-lived opportunity to expand loans in this field, until Congress repealed their authority in 1959. In the end, the money reserve banks lent, whether in connection with banks or directly, helped individual companies. Still, amounts were too small to stimulate much production, and a few firms failed in spite of assistance.[86]

The law of 1934 violated the reserve tradition of discounting only for banks, yet continued a trend toward broadening system facilities begun by the Glass–Steagall Act of 1932, the Emergency Relief and Construction Act of 1932, and the Robinson amendment to the Emergency Banking Act of 1933. The system abandoned eligibility requirements in 1935, when a new law permitted reserve banks to lend on any sound collateral.

CONCLUSION

Federal reserve officials formed only one group among many trying to extend and protect their influence during the growth of relief and regulatory organizations under Roosevelt. The Treasury Department, reserve system, and RFC all had a stake in the nation's financial affairs. The Treasury provided money for the rising expenditures of FDR's administration and, after January 1934, could influence the money supply through the stabilization fund. The reserve system regulated member banks and provided the country's circulating medium through issuing federal reserve notes. The RFC by 1934 had invested millions of dollars in state and national banks as well as in such financial intermediaries as savings and loan associations, insurance companies, and mortgage associations. Even the FTC, which in 1933 had begun regulating securities issued by investment bankers and others, attempted to protect its position during debate on the Securities Exchange Act. The ability of these agencies to defend themselves and extend their influence depended on support from Congress and the president.

Partisanship was not important in passing legislation affecting the reserve in 1934, for Republicans were few and divided into progressives and conservatives. Democrats passed the measures by large majorities. A few Democrats may have opposed the administration, but conservatives of both parties were too few to stop legislation that Roosevelt favored.

While Roosevelt's gold policies stripped the reserve system of control over the money supply, he supported increasing the system's power in the Securities Exchange Act and Industrial Loan Act, giving it responsibility for margin accounts and authority to aid business directly or through intermediaries. The apparent contradiction in FDR's attitude toward the system should be explained by board cooperation with the administration's monetary policy in 1933–34, despite members' doubts about its wisdom. Adolph C. Miller, who had been on the board since 1914, expressed fear in the autumn of 1933 that the system's actions might be closely watched. He cautioned directors of the New York reserve bank not to arouse any doubt as to their real support for the government's policy. Then if inflation failed, the reserve could not be blamed.[87] If the system had been on trial during 1933 and early 1934, Roosevelt must have acquitted the defendant, since the changes of June enhanced its influence over financial institutions. Apparently, FDR had decided that he could trust the system to accept his policies and follow his direction. After devaluation he told Black and Harrison the reserve banks had acted satisfactorily and that he would do nothing to decrease the system's influence or its power.[88] The next year he went farther, supporting a bill that became the Banking Act of 1935, which augmented the board's authority over member and reserve banks.

Normally the party in the White House loses supporters in Congress during off-year elections, but Democrats increased their majorities in both houses in November 1934. The change signaled the beginning of the New Deal coalition and revealed that the Democratic party had become the majority party. The 73d Congress passed a record number of laws affecting the financial system and convinced voters that they had been right to sweep Democrats into office. Still, the most important reform of the Federal Reserve Act did not pass until 1935, when FDR's new governor of the reserve board, Marriner S.

Eccles, squared off against Glass, whose power in the Senate had diminished during the first two years of the New Deal.

NOTES

1. John C. Adams, Franklin D. Roosevelt's Gold Policies in a Farm Sector Strategy, 1933 (Ph.D. dissertation, Indiana University, 1976), 48–50, 160–1; Elmus R. Wicker, "Roosevelt's 1933 Monetary Experiment," *Journal of American History*, 57 (March 1971): 864–6; *New York Times*, 23 October 1933, 1, 3; Lester V. Chandler, *American Monetary Policy, 1928–1941* (New York: Harper and Row, 1971), 272.

2. G.F. Warren and F.A. Pearson, "Relationship of Gold to Prices," *Journal of the American Statistical Association*, 28, sup. (March 1933): 118–26; F.A. Pearson, W.I. Myers, and A.R. Gans, "Warren as Presidential Adviser," *Farm Economics*, 211 (December 1957): 5598–669; Adams, Roosevelt's Gold Policies, 73–4.

3. Federal Reserve Board, *Twentieth Annual Report Covering Operations for the Year 1933* (Washington, D.C.: U.S. Government Printing Office, 1934), 26–7. Numerous drafts and memoranda concerning the April 5 executive order are in Box 7, Emanuel Alexandrovich Goldenweiser Papers, Manuscript Division, Library of Congress, Washington, D.C.; and Box 1, Adolph Caspar Miller Papers, Manuscript Division, Library of Congress, Washington, D.C.

4. Franklin D. Roosevelt, *Complete Presidential Press Conferences*, 25 v. (New York: Da Capo, 1972), I: 115–6.

5. Federal Reserve Board, *Twentieth Annual Report, 1933*, 27–8; Pearson, Myers, and Gans, "Warren," 5614–5; Wicker, "Roosevelt's Experiment," 873. Barrie A. Wigmore argues that the gold embargo and foreign exchange controls were absolutely necessary to restore stability to the banking system, as was devaluation of the gold dollar; "Was the Bank Holiday of 1933 Caused by a Run on the Dollar?" *Journal of Economic History*, 47 (September 1987): 753–4. Ron Chernow, *The House of Morgan: An American Banking Dynasty and the Rise of Modern Finance* (New York: Atlantic Monthly, 1990) attributes the timing of leaving the gold standard to Russell Leffingwell of J.P. Morgan and Company (358). Leffingwell encouraged columnist Walter Lippmann to publish an editorial calling for an end to the overvalued gold dollar, and FDR announced the suspension of gold exports shortly after the column appeared.

6. Adams, Roosevelt's Gold Policies, 160; Joseph Anthony Imler, The First One Hundred Days of the New Deal: The View from Capitol Hill (Ph.D. dissertation, Indiana University, 1975), 129; Milton Friedman and Anna Jacobson Schwartz, *A Monetary History of the United States, 1867–1960* (Princeton, N.J.: Princeton University, 1963), 464–5; Albert U. Romasco, *The Politics of Recovery: Roosevelt's New Deal* (New York: Oxford University, 1983), 35–8, 136; Garet Garrett and Murray N. Rothbard, *The Great Depression and New Deal Monetary Policy* (San Francisco: Cato Institute, 1980), 93–5.

7. Herbert Feis, *1933: Characters in Crisis* (Boston: Little, Brown, 1966), 126–30; Diary, 18 April 1933, Box 1, Raymond Moley Papers, Hoover Institution on War, Revolution, and Peace, Stanford University, Stanford, Cal.; Wicker, "Roosevelt's Experiment," 867; *Congressional Record*, 77, pt. 2: 1844, 73d Congress, 1st session.

8. Moley Diary, 18–19 April 1933; Frank Freidel, *Franklin D. Roosevelt: Launching the New Deal* (Boston: Little, Brown, 1973), 332–7; *Congressional Record*, 77, pt. 2: 2004–5, 73d Congress, 1st session.

9. *Congressional Record*, 77, pt. 2: 2003–4, 2079–80, 73d Congress, 1st session; *Wall Street Journal*, 22 April 1933, 6. The Federal Reserve Board had suggested in 1917 that Congress give it power to alter member banks' reserve requirements, but no legislation had passed; New York Clearing House Association, *The Federal Reserve Reexamined* (New York: New York Clearing House Association, 1953), 99.

10. *Congressional Record*, 77, pt. 2: 2073–85, 2150–61, 2166–71, 2216–47, 2307–36, 2372–410, 2436–73, 2511–30 (Glass quotation on 2461), 73d Congress, 1st session; Imler, First Hundred Days, 134–5.

11. *Congressional Record*, 77, pt. 3: 2562, 2648–51, 2693–757, 2814–5, 3022–3, 3029–31, 3060–80, 3114–24, 73d Congress, 1st session; *New York Times*, 30 April 1933, 8; Ibid., 4 May 1933, 1; Ibid., 11 May 1933, 1; Ibid., 13 May 1933, 1, 3.

12. Major B. Foster, Raymond Rodgers, Jules I. Bogen, and Marcus Nadler, *Money and Banking*, 4th ed. (New York: Prentice–Hall, 1953), 58; Memorandum, Some Constitutional Questions Raised by the Provisions for Devaluation of the Dollar in the Inflation Bill, Box 186, Felix Frankfurter Papers, Manuscript Division, Library of Congress, Washington, D.C.

13. Diary, v. 23, 22 May 1933, Charles Sumner Hamlin Papers, Manuscript Division, Library of Congress, Washington, D.C.

14. *Wall Street Journal*, 27 May 1933, 1.

15. *Congressional Record*, 77, pt. 5: 4519–57, 4889–929, 73d Congress, 1st session; Imler, First Hundred Days, 136n; *New York Times*, 28 May 1933, 1, 12; Ibid., 30 May 1933, 1, 2; Ibid., 4 June 1933, 1, 3; Ibid., 6 June 1933, 35. Article I, section 8 of the Constitution gives Congress the power "To coin Money, regulate the Value thereof, and of foreign Coin, and fix the Standard of Weights and Measures." In February 1935, the Supreme Court ruled that Congress had constitutional power to abrogate gold clauses in private contracts but not government contracts. At the same time, however, the court ruled that since all forms of United States currency had become legal tender, the bond holders had not received any actual money loss, so the government did not have to pay damages. See Benjamin M. Anderson, *Economics and the Public Welfare: Financial and Economic History of the United States, 1914–1946* (New York: D. Van Nostrand, 1949), 364–5.

16. Feis, *1933*, 169–258; Chandler, *American Monetary Policy*, 274, 277–81; Franklin D. Roosevelt, *The Public Papers and Addresses of Franklin D. Roosevelt*, Samuel I. Rosenman, comp., 13 v. (New York: Random House, 1938–45), II: 264–5; Wicker, "Roosevelt's Experiment," 873–4. For more information about the World Economic Conference, see Raymond Moley, *After Seven Years* (New York: Harper and Brothers, 1939), 196–269; Diary of Trip to London, June 1933, Box 7, George Leslie Harrison Papers, Manuscript Division, Butler Library, Columbia University, New York, N.Y.; Box 81 (Microfilm Reel 46, 195–511), Cordell Hull Papers, Manuscript Division, Library of Congress, Washington, D.C. The best explanation for the timing of the "bombshell" message appears in Kenneth S. Davis, *FDR: The New Deal Years, 1933–1937, A History* (New York: Random House, 1986), 184–8.

17. Griffith Johnson, Jr., *The Treasury and Monetary Policy, 1933–1938* (Cambridge, Mass.: Harvard University, 1939), 18–9; Hamlin Diary, v. 23, 12–13 July 1933, 18–19 July 1933, 24 July 1933, 28 July 1933; untitled and undated memorandum, Box 359, Hamlin Papers; Office Correspondence to Confidential Files from Harrison, 14 July 1933, Binder 46, Harrison Papers; outgoing cablegram to Norman from Harrison, 18 July 1933, Binder 22, Harrison Papers; incoming

cablegram to Harrison from Norman, 19 July 1933, Binder 22, Harrison Papers; Adams, Roosevelt's Gold Policies, 100–2; *New York Times*, 21 July 1933, 23.

18. Lester V. Chandler, *America's Greatest Depression 1929-41* (New York: Harper and Row, 1970), 172-3; Wicker, "Roosevelt's Experiment," 871; *New York Times*, 14 July 1933, 25; *Federal Reserve Bulletin*, 19 (August 1933): 472; Ibid. (October 1933): 617; Ibid. (December 1933): 731–3. Roosevelt considered issuing greenbacks to retire government securities maturing in September 1933, but his inter-agency committee on monetary policy suggested that reserve banks purchase immediately $50 million of government securities instead. See Memorandum of the Executive Committee Meeting August 21, 1933, Binder 50, Harrison Papers. Given such a choice, reserve officials continued their open market purchases.

19. Memorandum for the Attorney General from Stevens, Weston, and Davis, 23 September 1933, Official File 229, Box 2, Franklin Delano Roosevelt Presidential Papers, Franklin Delano Roosevelt Library, Hyde Park, N.Y.; Resolution of Reconstruction Finance Corporation Board of Directors attached to letter to Roosevelt from Couch, 20 October 1933, Box 187, Jesse Holman Jones Papers, Manuscript Division, Library of Congress, Washington, D.C.; Feis, *1933*, 281–6; Elliott Roosevelt and Joseph B. Lash, eds. *F.D.R.: His Personal Letters, 1928–1945*, 2 v. (New York: Duell, Sloan, and Pearce, 1950), 364; *New York Times*, 23 October 1933, 1, 3; Ibid., 24 October 1933, 1–2.

20. Garrett and Rothbard, *Great Depression*, 96–104; Pearson, Myers, and Gans, "Warren," 5648–52; Romasco, *Politics of Recovery*, 129–34; *New York Times*, 23 November 1933, 1, 15.

21. Arthur M. Schlesinger, Jr., *The Age of Roosevelt*, 3 v. (Boston: Houghton Mifflin, 1957–60), II: 241–5; Jesse H. Jones and Edward Angly, *Fifty Billion Dollars: My Thirteen Years with the RFC* (New York: Macmillan, 1951), 252; James Edward Sargent, The Hundred Days: Franklin D. Roosevelt and the Early New Deal, 1933 (Ph.D. dissertation, Michigan State University, 1972), 382; Harry Barnard, *Independent Man: The Life of Senator James Couzens* (New York: Charles Scribner's Sons, 1958), 255; John M. Blum, *From the Morgenthau Diaries*, 3 v. (Boston: Houghton Mifflin, 1959), I: 29–30; Joseph P. Lash, *Dealers and Dreamers: A Look at the New Deal* (New York: Doubleday, 1988), 147–53. Just before he took leave of absence,

Woodin denied that he disagreed with Roosevelt's gold policies; clipping from Washington *Times*, 13 November 1933, Box 15, George Frederick Warren Papers, Collection of Regional History and Cornell University Archives, Cornell University Library, Cornell University, Ithaca, N.Y. Woodin privately expressed his disapproval, however, as the Hamlin Diary (v. 23, 1 August 1933) and the diaries of George Warren (20 September 1933, 25 October 1933, Warren Papers) indicate. Woodin resigned in December, and Morgenthau became secretary on January 1, 1934.

22. Blum, *Morgenthau Diaries*, I: 69; Romasco, *Politics of Recovery*, 124–6; Luther Harr and W. Carlton Harris, *Banking Theory and Practice*, 2d ed. (New York: McGraw–Hill, 1936), 552; Office Correspondence to Confidential Files from Crane, 13 November 1933, Binder 46, Harrison Papers. The reserve bank relied on Guaranty Trust Company of New York as its agent in London and Paris markets; letter to Guaranty Trust Company of New York from Crane, 3 November 1933, Binder 54, Harrison Papers.

23. Romasco, *Politics of Recovery*, 136–7; Office Correspondence to Confidential Files from Crane, 13 November 1933, Binder 46, Harrison Papers; Office Correspondence to Confidential Files from Harrison, 14 November 1933, Binder 46, Harrison Papers; Office Correspondence to Confidential Files from Harrison, 16 November 1933, Binder 46, Harrison Papers; Josephine Young Case and Everett Needham Case, *Owen D. Young and American Enterprise: A Biography* (Boston: David R. Godine, 1982), 646–8; Harr and Harris, *Banking Theory*, 552; Memorandum: Meeting of Board of Directors November 23, 1933, Binder 51, Harrison Papers; Office Correspondence to Confidential Files from Harrison, 2 December 1933, Binder 46, Harrison Papers; Office Correspondence to Confidential Files from Harrison, 4 December 1933, Binder 46, Harrison Papers. See also Warren Diaries for December 1933.

24. *Wall Street Journal*, 30 December 1933, 10; Federal Reserve Board, *Twentieth Annual Report, 1933*, 27–8.

25. Memorandum to Secretary of the Treasury from Bell, 18 September 1933, Box 24, General Records of the Department of the Treasury, Office of the Secretary, Office of Domestic Gold and Silver Operations, Record Group 56, National Archives, Washington, D.C.; Pearson, Myers, and Gans, "Warren," 5656–7; Chandler, *American Monetary Policy*, 289–90; History of Gold Reserve Act of 1934 (v. I),

Office of Domestic Gold and Silver Operations, Box 6, RG 56; Hamlin Diary, v. 24, 15 December 1933, 20 December 1933, 22 December 1933, 27–29 December 1933. Davis, *FDR: New Deal Years*, indicates that Roosevelt decided to stabilize the gold dollar after John Maynard Keynes had prepared "An Open Letter to President Roosevelt," an advance copy of which Felix Frankfurter sent to FDR near the end of December (303). However, FDR had explored the possibility of joint stabilization with the British in early December, so his decision must have been made prior to his receipt of Keynes's letter.

26. Warren Diaries, 11 January 1934; *Wall Street Journal*, 12 January 1934, 1; Ibid., 16 January 1934, 1, 3, 9; Harr and Harris, *Banking Theory*, 553; Roosevelt, *Public Papers*, III: 40–4, 49; Harold L. Ickes, *The Secret Diary of Harold L. Ickes*, 3 v. (New York: Simon and Schuster, 1953–54), I: 140. Apparently, Warren first suggested the 60% minimum for devaluation; Warren Diaries, 2 January 1934.

27. *Wall Street Journal*, 17 January 1934, 6.

28. Hamlin Diary, v. 24, 15 January 1934.

29. *Wall Street Journal*, 19 January 1934, 1, 8; *Congressional Record*, 78, pt. 1: 757–60, 905–6, 952–1014, 73d Congress, 2d session; U.S., Congress, House, Committee on Coinage, Weights, and Measures, *To Protect the Currency Systems of the United States and to Provide for the Better Use of the Monetary Gold Stock: Report to Accompany H.R. 6976*, H. Rept. 292, 73d Congress, 2d session, 18–19 January 1934; clipping from *The Mining Journal*, 13 July 1967, Box 1, Prentiss Marsh Brown Papers, Michigan Historical Collections, Bentley Historical Library, University of Michigan, Ann Arbor, Mich. The House Committee on Banking and Currency reported a similar bill introduced by Steagall; U.S., Congress, House, Committee on Banking and Currency, *To Regulate the Value of Money in Accordance with Article 1, Section 8, of the Constitution of the United States, to Reestablish the Gold Standard, to Provide for its Maintenance and Stabilization: Report to Accompany H.R. 5073*, H. Rept. 290, 73d Congress, 2d session, 17 January 1934. H.R. 6976 became the Gold Reserve Act of 1934.

30. *Wall Street Journal*, 18 January 1934, 11; *Congressional Record*, 78, pt. 1: 764, 73d Congress, 2d session; U.S., Congress, Senate, Committee on Banking and Currency, *Gold Reserve Act of 1934: Hearings on S. 2366*, 73d Congress, 2d session, 19–23 January 1934, 103–37, 206–35, 257–303, 342–51.

31. *Wall Street Journal*, 24 January 1934, 1, 10; clipping from Detroit *News*, 26 January 1934, Box 4, scrapbook 1934, Jay G. Hayden Papers, Michigan Historical Collections, Bentley Historical Library, University of Michigan, Ann Arbor, Mich.; U.S., Congress, Senate, Committee on Banking and Currency, *Gold Reserve Act of 1934: Report to Accompany H.R. 6976*, S. Rept. 201, 73d Congress, 2d session, 23 January 1934.

32. Clipping from Hartford *Daily Courant*, 26 January 1934, Box 18, Frederic Collin Walcott Papers, Manuscripts and Archives, Yale University Library, Yale University, New Haven, Conn.; *Wall Street Journal*, 24 January 1934, 1, 10.

33. *Wall Street Journal*, 25 January 1934, 1, 10; Ibid., 26 January 1934, 15; Ibid., 27 January 1934, 1, 10; *Congressional Record*, 78, pt. 2: 1230–61, 1309–39, 1387–416, 1439, 1444–84, 1491–3, 73d Congress, 2d session; Edward Francis Hanlon, Urban-Rural Cooperation and Conflict in the Congress: The Breakdown of the New Deal Coalition, 1933–1938 (Ph.D. dissertation, Georgetown University, 1967), 124.

34. Letter to Black from Morgenthau, 30 January 1934, Box 2448, Records of the Federal Reserve System, Subject File, 1914–54, Record Group 82, National Archives, Washington, D.C.; letter to Morgenthau from Morrill, 30 January 1934, Box 2448, RG 82. [All citations to RG 82 refer to Subject File, 1914–54.]

35. Warren Diaries, 30–31 January 1934; Memorandum: Meeting of Board of Directors February 1, 1934, Binder 51, Harrison Papers; *Federal Reserve Bulletin*, 20 (March 1934): 141; *Wall Street Journal*, 1 February 1934, 1; Ibid., 2 February 1934, 1, 8, 11; Blum *Morgenthau Diaries*, I: 125.

36. Anderson, *Economics and Public Welfare*, 351; Adrian W. Throop, "Bicentennial Perspective: Decline and Fall of the Gold Standard," *Federal Reserve Bank of Dallas Monthly Business Review* (January 1976): 9.

37. Jack Brien Key, "Henry B. Steagall: The Conservative as a Reformer," *Alabama Review*, 17 (July 1964): 206; Victor M. Longstreet, "Currency System of United States," *Banking Studies*, E.A. Goldenweiser, Elliott Thurston, and Bray Hammond, eds. (Washington, D.C.: Board of Governors of the Federal Reserve System, 1941): 80–1; Friedman and Schwartz, *Monetary History*, 485; Chandler, *America's Greatest Depression*, 162.

38. Joseph E. Reeve, *Monetary Reform Movements: A Survey of Recent Plans and Panaceas* (Washington, D.C.: American Council on Public Affairs, 1943), 64–5, 96–102, 122–4, 150–2; Warren Diaries, 16 March 1934; *Wall Street Journal*, 29 June 1934, 2. The bills to establish a Federal Monetary Authority in 1934 were H.R. 7156, 7157, 7216, and 8780. Roosevelt opposed this proposal; *New York Times*, 16 April 1934, 1.

39. Friedman and Schwartz, *Monetary History*, 466; Louis A. Rufener, *Money and Banking in the United States* (Boston: Houghton Mifflin, 1934), 759.

40. Kurt Dew, "Gold Policy: The Thirties and the Seventies," *Federal Reserve Bank of San Francisco Business Review* (Winter 1974/75): 17–8; Chandler, *America's Greatest Depression*, 174; Chandler, *American Monetary Policy*, 244, 255, 307; Friedman and Schwartz, *Monetary History*, 506, 526.

41. Friedman and Schwartz, *Monetary History*, 472–6.

42. Anderson, *Economics and Public Welfare*, 349–50; Throop, "Gold Standard," 6–8; Chandler, *America's Greatest Depression*, 174–5; Benjamin Haggott Beckhart, *Federal Reserve System* (New York: American Institute of Banking, 1972), 309–10. The Treasury never authorized greenbacks but did use part of the profit from devaluation to retire government bonds that had formed the collateral for national bank notes. Since 1934 no national bank has issued its own notes; Longstreet, "Currency System," 80.

43. Romasco, *Politics of Recovery*, 138–9; Schlesinger, *Age of Roosevelt*, II: 246–7; letter to Roosevelt from Rand, 25 October 1935, Box 3, Official File 5707, FDR Presidential Papers.

44. Letter to Berle from Roper, 18 July 1933, Box 20, Adolf Augustus Berle Papers, Franklin Delano Roosevelt Library, Hyde Park, N.Y.; *New York Times*, 28 January 1934, 24–5; Ibid., 10 February 1934, 1, 7; Michael E. Parrish, *Securities Regulation and the New Deal* (New Haven, Conn.: Yale University, 1970), 42–71, 113–7; Donald A. Ritchie, *James M. Landis: Dean of the Regulators* (Cambridge, Mass.: Harvard University, 1980), 44–55; Schlesinger, *Age of Roosevelt*, II: 456–7. This chapter does not present a comprehensive history of the passage of the Securities Exchange Act, as I have focused on consequences for the Federal Reserve System. The most complete study of the passage of this act appears in Parrish.

45. Parrish, *Securities Regulation*, 117–20; Twentieth Century Fund, *The Security Markets: Findings and Recommendations* (New York: Twentieth Century Fund, 1935), 759–60; U.S., Congress, House, Committee on Interstate and Foreign Commerce, *Stock Exchange Regulation: Hearings on H.R. 7852 and H.R. 8720*, 73d Congress, 2d session, 14 February–24 March 1934, 95–7. Brokers and dealers did not determine margins in the same way the Cohen–Corcoran bill would. Instead, they subtracted the amount lent to a customer from the percentage of the debit balance. For example, a broker lending $75 on a stock whose price was $100 would receive $25 from the customer, one-third of the debit balance of $75 or a margin of 33.3%. See *Wall Street Journal*, 8 May 1934, 2.

46. Parrish, *Securities Regulation*, 123–4; U.S., Congress, Senate, Committee on Banking and Currency, *Stock Exchange Practices: Hearings on S.Res. 84 (72d Congress), S.Res. 56 (73d Congress), and S.Res. 97 (73 Congress)*, 73d Congress, 1st and 2d sessions, 23 May 1933–5 April 1934, 6422, 6582–642, 6657–736, 6768–82, 6826–31, 6899–917, 7005–20, 7032–7; House Committee on Commerce, *Stock Exchange Regulation: Hearings*, 150–215, 322–30; *New York Times*, 15 February 1934, 20; Ibid., 22 February 1934, 1–2. The Senate committee hearings continued an investigation begun in 1932, and Ferdinand Pecora remained as counsel; Vincent P. Carosso, *Investment Banking in America: A History* (Cambridge, Mass.: Harvard University, 1970), 335–6.

47. *Wall Street Journal*, 21 February 1934, 1, 13; Senate Committee on Banking and Currency, *Stock Exchange Practices: Hearings*, 6463–81; House Committee on Commerce, *Stock Exchange Regulation: Hearings*, 82–125.

48. House Committee on Commerce, *Stock Exchange Regulation: Hearings*, 69.

49. Ibid., 65–81; Senate Committee on Banking and Currency, *Stock Exchange Practices: Hearings*, 6436–49.

50. House Committee on Commerce, *Stock Exchange Regulation: Hearings*, 505–58; *New York Times*, 28 January 1934, 24–5.

51. *New York Times*, 1 March 1934, 16; Ibid., 12 March 1934, 29; Ibid., 14 March 1934, 1; Ibid., 16 March 1934, 31; *Wall Street Journal*, 8 March 1934, 6; Ibid., 13 March 1934, 1; Hamlin Diary, v. 24, 13–15 March 1934; Schlesinger, *Age of Roosevelt*, II: 465.

52. *New York Times*, 20 March 1934, 31; *Wall Street Journal*, 20 March 1934, 1.

53. *New York Times*, 21 March 1934, 31; Ibid., 25 March 1934, II: 11; *Wall Street Journal*, 23 March 1934, 1, 4; Ibid., 28 March 1934, 1, 11; House Committee on Commerce, *Stock Exchange Regulation: Hearings*, 723–43, 801–8.

54. House Committee on Commerce, *Stock Exchange Regulation: Hearings*, 674–700, 788–800, 808–17, 886–92; *Wall Street Journal*, 24 March 1934, 1–2. Riefler wrote the margin provisions that he defended in his testimony; Lash, *Dealers and Dreamers*, 167.

55. *New York Times*, 27 March 1934, 1–2.

56. Letter to Kent from Roosevelt, 27 March 1934, President's Personal File 744, FDR Presidential Papers.

57. Parrish, *Securities Regulation*, 137–8; *Wall Street Journal*, 4 April 1934, 1, 13; Ibid., 13 April 1934, 1, 12; *New York Times*, 27 March 1934, 2; Ibid., 14 April 1934, 23, 25; Ibid., 26 April 1934, 35; *Congressional Record*, 78, pt. 7: 7376, 7595, 73d Congress, 2d session.

58. U.S., Congress, House, Committee on Interstate and Foreign Commerce, *Securities Exchange Bill of 1934: Report to Accompany H.R. 9323*, H. Rept. 1383, 73d Congress, 2d session, 27 April 1934.

59. *New York Times*, 28 March 1934, 12; Ibid., 5 April 1934, 1, 15; Ibid., 10 April 1934, 1, 8; Ibid., 12 April 1934, 19; Ibid., 19 April 1934, 1, 21; Ibid., 20 April 1934, 39; Ibid., 21 April 1934, 7; *Wall Street Journal*, 11 April 1934, 1, 11; Parrish, *Securities Regulation*, 133–6; *Congressional Record*, 78, pt. 7: 6980, 73d Congress, 2d session; U.S., Congress, Senate, Committee on Banking and Currency, *Stock Exchange Practices: Report Pursuant to S.Res. 84 (72d Congress), S.Res. 56 (73d Congress), and S.Res. 97 (73d Congress)*, S. Rept. 1455, 73d Congress, 2d session, 16 June 1934. Member bank borrowings had declined to $50 million by mid-1934 and were rarely higher than $10 million for the rest of the decade; Lester V. Chandler and Stephen M. Goldfeld, *The Economics of Money and Banking*, 7th ed. (New York: Harper and Row, 1977), 547.

60. *Congressional Record*, 78, pt. 7: 7689–717, 7861–9, 7920–49, 8007–40, 8086–117, 73d Congress, 2d session; *New York Times*, 1 May 1934, 31, 40; Ibid., 4 May 1934, 31–2; Ibid., 5 May 1934, 1, 10.

61. *Congressional Record*, 78, pt. 8: 8160–91, 8195–203, 8270–87, 8295–301, 8386–99, 8488–507, 8563–83, 8588–604, 8666–714, 8766, 8788, 73d Congress, 2d session; *New York Times*, 8 May 1934, 5; Ibid., 10 May 1934, 33, 40; Ibid., 11 May 1934, 2; Ibid., 13 May 1934, 1; *Wall Street Journal*, 9 May 1934, 1, 10.

62. *New York Times*, 15 May 1934, 6.

63. *New York Times*, 16 May 1934, 1, 5; Ibid., 17 May 1934, 1, 15; Ibid., 18 May 1934, 1, 16; Gilbert Y. Steiner, *The Congressional Conference Committee: 70th to 80th Congresses* (Urbana: University of Illinois, 1951), 94–6. Roosevelt's decision to issue a statement may have been provoked by a letter from Costigan in which he indicated the Senate might support the Federal Trade Commission as the regulatory agency if the president would make clear his desire for that outcome; letter to Roosevelt from Costigan, 15 May 1934, Official File 34, Box 2, FDR Presidential Papers.

64. U.S., Congress, Conference Committee, *Securities Exchange Act of 1934: Conference Report to Accompany H.R. 9323*, S. Doc. 185, 73d Congress, 2d session, 30 May 1934; *Congressional Record*, 78, pt. 9: 10110–2, 10181–5, 10265–9, 73d Congress, 2d session; *New York Times*, 24 May 1934, 42; Ibid., 27 May 1934, 1–2; Ibid., 2 June 1934, 1–2; Ibid., 7 June 1934, 7.

65. *Wall Street Journal*, 7 June 1934, 1, 13. See also *New York Times*, 2 June 1934, 1, 5; Ibid., 10 June 1934, II: 9, 14.

66. Raymond Moley, *The First New Deal* (New York: Harcourt, Brace and World, 1966), 518–20; Schlesinger, *Age of Roosevelt*, II: 468; Carosso, *Investment Banking*, 379–80; *New York Times*, 6 June 1934, 1, 37.

67. Hamlin Diary, v. 24, 7 April 1934.

68. *New York Times*, 10 July 1934, 33; Ibid., 28 July 1934, 17; Ibid., 1 September 1934, 17; Ibid., 28 September 1934, 1, 23, 40–1; Ibid., 7 October 1934, II: 7.

69. David L. Grove, "Selective Credit Controls," *The Federal Reserve System*, Herbert V. Prochnow, ed. (New York: Harper and Brothers, 1960): 153–5; *Wall Street Journal*, 15 January 1985, 20. The board's recommendation was prompted by a staff report on margin trading in stock index futures on commodity exchanges, where investors may make purchases with less than 10% cash. The report concluded that exchanges could set margins more efficiently and quickly. See *Wall Street Journal*, 31 March 1983, 12.

70. Jones and Angly, *Fifty Billion Dollars*, 25–53; Chandler, *America's Greatest Depression*, 172–3; *Wall Street Journal*, 22 March 1934, 7; Ickes, *Secret Diary*, I: 108–9.

71. Hamlin Diary, v. 24, 14–15 February 1934, 20 February 1934; *New York Times*, 17 February 1934, 21; Inter Office Communication to Morgenthau from Oliphant, 27 February 1934, Box 271, Alphabetical File, Correspondence, Henry Morgenthau, Jr., Papers, Franklin Delano Roosevelt Library, Hyde Park, N.Y.; Preliminary Draft, 14 March 1934, Box 91, Alphabetical File, Morgenthau Correspondence; Memorandum: Meeting of Board of Directors February 21, 1934, Binder 51, Harrison Papers. Black issued a statement about the council meeting that made members sound as if they believed a need for working capital existed and that did not mention the RFC; *New York Times*, 21 February 1934, 29, 33. Hamlin's Diary and Memorandum cited above indicate reserve officials' doubt.

72. *New York Times*, 17 March 1934, 1, 8; Ibid., 18 March 1934, 1, 27; letters to Steagall and Fletcher from Jones, 13 March 1934, Box 45, Jones Papers.

73. *New York Times*, 18 March 1934, 1, 27; Ibid., 20 March 1934, 1–2; *Congressional Record*, 78, pt. 5: 4759, 4876, 73d Congress, 2d session.

74. *New York Times*, 22 March 1934, 31; Ibid., 29 March 1934, 17; Memorandum: Meeting of Board of Directors April 5, 1934, Binder 51, Harrison Papers; S. 3137, Box 36, Records of the United States Senate, Committee on Banking and Currency, Bill Records, Record Group 46, National Archives, Washington, D.C. [all references to RG 46 in this chapter are to Bill Records, 73d Congress, Senate Banking and Currency Committee].

75. Hamlin Diary, v. 24, 3–4 April 1934; *New York Times*, 29 March 1934, 17.

76. Memorandum: Meeting of Board of Directors April 5, 1934, Binder 51, Harrison Papers.

77. Ibid., *Wall Street Journal*, 5 April 1934, 4.

78. *New York Times*, 15 April 1934, 6; S. 3487, Box 40, RG 46. Another section of the bill would permit the board to acquire a site in the District of Columbia and build its own offices. Prior to this, board headquarters had been in the overcrowded Treasury building on Pennsylvania Avenue. This proviso was part of the act that passed in

June; Federal Reserve Board, *Twenty-first Annual Report Covering Operations for the Year 1934* (Washington, D.C.: U.S. Government Printing Office, 1935), 50–2.

79. *New York Times*, 29 April 1934, 1, 24; *Congressional Record*, 78, pt. 7: 7598, 7907–14, pt. 8: 7983, 8717–26, 8735–66, 73d Congress, 2d session; S. 3520, Box 41, RG 46; letter to Putnam from Fletcher, 5 May 1934, Box 41, RG 46; *Wall Street Journal*, 3 May 1934, 13.

80. Letter to Morgenthau from Jones, 3 June 1934, Box 170, Alphabetical File, Morgenthau Correspondence; U.S., Congress, House, Committee on Banking and Currency, *Loans to Industry: Report to Accompany S. 3487*, H. Rept. 1719, 73d Congress, 2d session, 21 May 1934.

81. House Committee on Banking and Currency, *Loans to Industry: Report*.

82. Ibid.; *Congressional Record*, 78, pt. 9: 9272–303, 9375–400, 73d Congress, 2d session; *Wall Street Journal*, 22 May 1934, 1; *New York Times*, 24 May 1934, 1.

83. Memorandum: Meeting of the Executive Committee May 28, 1934, Binder 51, Harrison Papers; Memorandum: Meeting of Board of Directors May 31, 1934, Binder 51, Harrison Papers; U.S., Congress, Conference Committee, *Direct Loans for Industrial Purposes by Federal Reserve Banks: Conference Report to Accompany H.R. 541*, H. Rept. 2056, 73d Congress, 2d session, 16 June 1934; Hamlin Diary, v. 25, 18 June 1934; *Congressional Record*, 78, pt. 11: 12228–36, 12060, 12075–6, 12452, 73d Congress, 2d session.

84. Hamlin Diary, v. 25, 11 July 1934; letter to Roosevelt from Thomas, 6 September 1934, Official File 90, Box 1, FDR Presidential Papers; *Federal Reserve Bulletin*, 20 (September 1934): 561, American Institute of Banking, *Contemporary Legislative and Banking Problems* (New York: American Institute of Banking, 1934), 299; Federal Reserve Board, *Twenty-first Annual Report, 1934*, 34; U.S., Congress, House, *Report of Reconstruction Finance Corporation for Fourth Quarter of 1934*, H. Doc. 139, 74th Congress, 1st session, 14 March 1935; Board of Governors of the Federal Reserve System, *Twenty-second Annual Report Covering Operations for the Year 1935* (Washington, D.C.: U.S. Government Printing Office, 1936), 4; Howard H. Hackley, *Lending Functions of the Federal Reserve Banks: A History* (Washington, D.C.: Board of Governors of the Federal

Reserve System, 1973), 133, 140. The Treasury gave reserve banks only $27 million from the profit of devaluation to make industrial loans; Friedman and Schwartz, *Monetary History*, 471n.

85. *The Reminiscences of Chester Morrill*, 222, Oral History Collection, Butler Library, Columbia University, New York, N.Y.; *Wall Street Journal*, 3 May 1934, 13.

86. Hamlin Diary, v. 25, 11 July 1934; Hackley, *Lending Functions*, 136, 177; Romasco, *Politics of Recovery*, 63; Rudolph L. Weissman, *The New Wall Street* (New York: Harper Brothers, 1939), 253.

87. Memorandum: Meeting of the Board of Directors November 2, 1933, Binder 51, Harrison Papers.

88. Memorandum: Meeting of the Board of Directors February 1, 1934, Binder 51, Harrison Papers.

CHAPTER SEVEN

THE BANKING ACT OF 1935

The bank bill that the Roosevelt administration presented to Congress in February 1935 had three sections, each drafted by individuals representing separate institutional interests. Titles I and III contained few elements of controversy. Officials of the Federal Deposit Insurance Corporation formulated Title I to amend the permanent insurance plan of the Banking Act of 1933. J.F.T. O'Connor, comptroller of the currency, suggested Title III, which would make clearer some sections of the act of 1933.

Title II embodied the ideas of Marriner S. Eccles, the new governor of the reserve board, who assumed the reserve act should be amended so only the board would control the instruments altering the supply of money: the discount rate a member bank paid to borrow from a reserve bank, the required reserve a member had to hold at a reserve bank, and open market sales and purchases of government securities. Title II, or the "Eccles Bill", would change the division of authority in the system, depriving regional banks of much independence. The proposal would alter membership of the Federal Open Market Committee, so that the board rather than reserve banks would have primary responsibility for deciding open market policy. It would force district banks to participate in FOMC purchases and sales of government securities, reducing the possibility that divisions of opinion could hamper board decisions. The bill would permit the FOMC to suggest changes in discount rates, which had been a responsibility of district banks. Title II would also make the appointment of reserve bank governors subject to approval by the board.

Unlike the rest of the bill, Title II encountered extensive opposition from bankers, regional reserve officials, and Senator Carter Glass (D–VA). The latter provided a forum for opponents during prolonged subcommittee hearings. Many conservative bankers protested that Title II would upset the balance within the system, giving the board excessive authority, and would place the reserve under Roosevelt's control, since the board's governor and vice governor would serve at the president's pleasure. Some reserve officials expressed these concerns, too. The subcommittee rewrote the bill to limit both centralization of power and political influence, and in July 1935 the new Title II passed the Senate.

The House also made changes in Title II, so a conference committee met. Glass led Senate members, while House conferees followed suggestions from Eccles. After almost a month, the committee reported a compromise, which Congress accepted. President Roosevelt signed the Banking Act of 1935 on August 23, more than six months after its introduction. The law was not everything Eccles had hoped for, but it centralized authority in the reserve board, making the system a more responsive instrument for executing monetary policy.

PREPARING THE BILL

According to the FDIC law of 1934, the permanent insurance features of the Banking Act of 1933 were to replace a temporary fund on July 1, 1935. The permanent plan would cover completely deposits up to $10,000, 75% of deposits between $10,000 and $50,000, and 50% of those over $50,000. To pay for the program, the FDIC could levy assessments an unlimited number of times per year on total deposits of insured banks at a rate of one-quarter of 1% each time. Institutions belonging to the temporary plan would qualify for the permanent program automatically, but insured state banks would have to join the Federal Reserve System by July 1, 1937, or withdraw from the fund.[1]

FDIC officials disliked several parts of the permanent insurance plan and drafted Title I of the proposed Banking Act of 1935 to eliminate those features. Their measure would insure deposits only up to $5,000, the amount then protected by the temporary plan. The corporation would assess insured banks at the rate of one-twelfth of 1% per annum on total deposits. This formula met the bankers' complaint that the permanent program would permit the FDIC to demand unlimited amounts at unexpected times. To force a bank to meet its assessment, Title I would prohibit disbursement of dividends to stockholders until the FDIC received payment.[2]

FDIC officials asked Congress to increase their power in two important ways, granting authority to expel from the fund any bank that had violated the law and to limit the number of insured banks chartered in the future. Under Title I, FDIC officials would notify supervisory authorities if they found repeated violation of law when examining an insured bank. The bank would have 120 days to correct its behavior. Then FDIC directors would decide whether the bank's efforts had ended the original problems. If not, directors would provide written notice of their intent to terminate insurance in 30 days and name a time and place for a hearing. A bank's failure to appear would indicate consent to termination. Even when a bank's representatives did appear, directors could order insurance terminated, leaving the bank no further recourse. In cases where insurance was canceled—voluntarily or involuntarily—the FDIC would insure pre-existing deposits, less subsequent withdrawals, for an additional two years.[3]

Federal authorities favored a limit on chartering because they believed one cause of bank failure in the 1920s had been too much competition. So that a similar situation could not drain FDIC funds, Title I would require the comptroller of the currency in the case of new national banks, the reserve board for new state member banks, and the FDIC for nonmember state banks, to consider the following factors before admitting a bank to insurance: its financial history and condition, adequacy of capital, earning prospects, character of management, convenience and needs of the community to be served, and whether its corporate powers would be consistent with deposit insurance law.[4]

The origins of Title III lay in an omnibus bill that O'Connor had proposed in 1934, which a Senate committee had approved, but which did not pass before Congress adjourned. Title III had 32 sections when introduced, many clarifying the Banking Act of 1933. Section 301 would redefine the term "holding company affiliate," excluding any organization that the reserve board judged not holding bank stock as a business or not managing or controlling banks. Section 303a would specify that the Banking Act of 1933 did not prohibit financial institutions from engaging in securities transactions permitted by the National Bank Act and that limits on securities dealing would not affect a right to sell real estate mortgages. Section 307 would allow a bank to deal in stocks for account of customers, even though the law forbade purchase or sale of such securities for the institution's portfolio. Such changes were technical and minor, designed to simplify administration of the 1933 law.[5]

O'Connor proposed several substantive amendments. One would eliminate, on July 1, 1937, double liability on national bank stock issued prior to June 16, 1933, ending the right of the comptroller of the currency to assess stockholders up to twice the value of stock certificates to cover a bank's losses. The Banking Act of 1933 had eliminated such liability for stock issued subsequently, and this provision would avoid discrimination. To replace the protection afforded by double liability, O'Connor proposed that national banks, before paying dividends to stockholders, carry to surplus at least one-tenth of net profits from the preceding six months, until surplus equaled capital. He wanted the law to require new national banks to have a paid-in surplus equaling one-fifth of their capital, which would give statutory protection to a policy his office was already enforcing. For convenience of state banks that were converting to national charters, he wanted power to waive the requirement that a converting institution's assets conform to the National Bank Act's limits. Finally, because he believed most officers and directors had made an effort to reduce personal indebtedness to their banks since passage of the 1933 act, he recommended postponing repayment of such loans for three years, to June 16, 1938.[6]

Eccles was responsible for Title II. A devout Mormon banker and businessman, he had concentrated on advancing his family's fortune until the depression convinced him that government intervention in the economy was essential and that he should become active in public affairs. In February 1933 he told the Senate Finance Committee that the depression would not end until the government provided massive deficit spending for public works and relief. Secretary Henry Morgenthau, Jr., invited Eccles to join the Treasury as a special assistant to work on the National Housing Act. After that act passed and Congress adjourned in 1934, Roosevelt told Eccles he was being considered as a replacement for Eugene R. Black, the reserve board governor. Black wanted to return to his position as governor of the Atlanta reserve bank, which paid a higher salary. Eccles said the office would interest him only if fundamental changes could be made in system law and practice. When Roosevelt pressed for specifics, he asked for time to formulate them.[7]

FDR saw him again in early November 1934. Eccles wanted to centralize in the reserve board control over open market sales and purchases of government securities, then decided by a 12-man committee chosen by the regional banks. He feared the prevailing division of system power would permit district banks to block or delay public works and relief programs, which would require large issues of government securities. Most important, he argued that the board could promote business stability through open market operations, discount rates, and required reserves of member banks—lowering interest rates and making money easy to encourage liberal bank lending, or raising interest rates to high levels and making money tight to discourage lending. If the board acted countercyclically, it could moderate an economic decline by promoting easy money and restrain a boom by tightening money supply. Fascinated by Eccles's ideas, Roosevelt discussed them with him for two hours.[8]

Knowing that the changes Eccles advocated might entail a political fight and that the nomination might face Senate opposition, the president announced Eccles's recess appointment as governor on November 10, 1934. He recognized that the system occupied a central position in the economy and believed the government should influence monetary policy in spite of the reserve's traditional independence. Eccles immediately began work on Title II.[9]

The administration's bill received attention from FDR's Interdepartmental Loan Committee, chaired by Morgenthau. On November 26, 1934, the secretary told committee members they would act as a clearing house for new banking legislation. He informed them that Roosevelt wanted only one banking bill. Leo Crowley, chairman of the FDIC, immediately objected; he preferred a separate measure for his agency because he regarded FDIC legislation as essential and feared a bill with many sections might not pass. Roosevelt and Eccles wanted to bury the proposed federal reserve changes between the less controversial titles presented by Crowley and O'Connor, making Congress and bankers confront sections they did not want alongside ones wanted immediately. Although Crowley agreed to follow FDR's desires, he and O'Connor continued to prefer priority for their proposals. The committee devoted sessions in December to discussing recommendations from Crowley, O'Connor, and Eccles.[10]

The loan committee met with Roosevelt on January 17 and by the end of the month had developed an omnibus bill. Title II would increase the influence of the reserve board over the money supply. The most important change concerned the Federal Open Market Committee, which then consisted of the 12 district governors. Title II proposed an FOMC of five members: the governor of the reserve board, who would act as chairman; two members of the board selected annually; and two district bank governors selected annually by the 12 governors. The FOMC would consider economic conditions and decide policy. Title II would force reserve banks to join in system purchases and sales of government securities, unlike the Banking Act of 1933, which permitted district banks to thwart policy by refusing participation. Because Eccles believed open market operations should moderate swings in the business cycle, Title II would eliminate a section of the reserve act that required the FOMC to accommodate commerce and business. Under Title II, the FOMC could also make recommendations to the reserve board regarding changes in discount rates at regional banks, and the board already had power to order district banks to adjust rates either higher or lower, which would allow coordination between discount policy and open market operations. Another section of Title II gave the board permanent instead of emergency authority to alter required reserves that members held against time and demand deposits. Thus, the board would have greater control over the three means of regulating the money supply.[11]

Other parts of Title II dealt with reserve banks. The position of "governor" had not appeared in the reserve act, yet each regional bank's board of directors had chosen a governor as its chief executive. The act had assumed that the reserve board would appoint the most powerful regional official, namely the chairman of the board. Instead, governors had become the leading figures at district banks. Title II would combine the separate offices of chairman and governor into one and make election of governors by regional directors annual and subject to approval by the reserve board. Regional directors would also elect a vice governor annually, whom the board would approve. These clauses would strengthen the board's influence over district governors. Title II would limit a reserve bank director to service of not more than six consecutive years, so no director could dominate proceedings because of his length of service. Under Title II, federal reserve notes would no longer have a 60% backing of eligible paper or government securities, although the notes would still have a 40% reserve in gold certificates and would constitute a first lien on assets of district banks. Reserve officials believed collateral requirements did nothing to increase safety of the currency and had hampered open market operations early in 1932.[12]

Title II's most important change would permit a reserve bank to accept as collateral for discounts a member's promissory note secured by sound assets, subject to reserve board regulations. This provision would repeal the connection between short-term commercial paper and reserve lending in the original act. Instead, any asset, even real estate mortgages or corporate bonds, could be eligible collateral. The change would permit the reserve system flexibility in economic crises.[13]

Two other sections of Title II would affect member banks. One would allow the reserve board to waive the capital required to become a member bank for any institution insured by the FDIC that applied before July 1, 1937. This proviso would help state banks join the reserve system to avoid losing insurance in 1937. To aid economic recovery, Title II would relax portions of the law concerning real estate lending so member banks could make loans secured by first lien mortgages upon improved real estate. Loans might take one of two forms. They could have a maturity of less than three years, in which case a bank could lend up to three-fifths of the property's actual value, or could be amortized within a period up to 20 years, in which case a bank could lend up to three-fourths of the property's value. Title II would remove a geographical restriction on such loans. Eccles believed there was no reason to confine banks to short-term lending if reserve banks could make advances on any sound asset.[14]

Title II contained provisions that Eccles believed would attract better qualified members to the board. The bill would raise salaries from $12,000 to $15,000 a year, require future board members to retire at age 70, and set up a pension fund to provide retirement pay based on length of service. Money for pensions would come from district banks. Title II provided that when filling vacancies on the board, the president would choose individuals qualified by experience or education to formulate economic and monetary policy. This section would replace a paragraph in the reserve act that required the president to represent on the board the nation's financial, commercial, industrial, and agricultural interests as well as geographical divisions.[15]

The proposed Title II would permit Roosevelt to designate one board member as governor and another as vice governor, both serving at the pleasure of the president. Because Eccles thought the executive branch and board should work together, Title II would end the governor's term on the board whenever the president designated a replacement.[16] These provisions would increase presidential influence over the board and later led to charges that the bill would allow political domination of the board.

Glass had enormous power to oppose Eccles's nomination and Title II. Since he had been chairman of the House Committee on Banking and Currency in 1913 when Congress passed the reserve act, he had regarded the system as his personal creation. He believed in the real bills theory, envisioning reserve banks passively accommodating the needs of trade, and he had written that theory into the reserve act. In spite of changes in banking and monetary conditions since 1913, he continued to think that member and reserve banks should restrict lending to short-term, productive, and nonspeculative uses. The fiery Virginian was not chairman of the Senate Banking and Currency Committee in 1935 but was a powerful figure who chaired the subcommittee that considered the Eccles nomination and bank legislation.[17]

Learning from O'Connor and Crowley that a bank bill would be introduced, the senator asked to see the proposal in December 1934. O'Connor and Crowley supplied Glass with their parts, but Eccles demurred because the interdepartmental committee had just begun work on Title II. He agreed to discuss his recommendations as soon as the committee approved a bill. The senator prepared to introduce Titles I and III immediately. Learning of his intention, Morgenthau rushed the interdepartmental committee to finish drafting the administration measure so FDR could send it to Congress. On February 4, Roosevelt asked Henry B. Steagall (D–ALA), and Duncan U. Fletcher (D–FLA), respectively chairmen of the House and Senate Banking and Currency Committees, to introduce the bill (H.R. 5357 and S. 1715), which had cleared the interdepartmental committee hours earlier.[18]

Glass was deeply offended because Eccles had not fulfilled his promise. The senator had been concerned about Eccles's appointment to the board, fearing he would let the Treasury dominate the system. Although the governor had not intentionally slighted Glass, the latter decided to oppose both the nomination and the bill. Fletcher had added two administration supporters to the Glass subcommittee previously, perhaps to increase Eccles's chance of confirmation, so he did not override a committee decision to send the measure to the subcommittee.[19]

BANKING ACT OF 1935 PASSES THE HOUSE

The House Banking and Currency Committee began hearings on February 21, 1935. Administration witnesses appeared first. Crowley and Leo E. Birdzell, general counsel for the FDIC, discussed Title I. O'Connor described the need for both Titles I and III. Few of these provisions generated controversy. There was one exception, however. As supporters of small banks Steagall, Everett H. Dirksen (R–ILL), and John B. Hollister (R–OH) opposed requiring insured banks to join the reserve system by July 1937, a provision of existing law.[20]

Eccles provided the most extensive testimony, as he discussed every provision of Title II as well as sections of Title III that applied to member banks. He emphasized that Title II would "increase the ability of the banking system to promote stability of employment and business," would "concentrate the authority and responsibility for the formulation of national monetary policies in a body representing the Nation" as a "necessary step" toward stability, would "modify the structure" of the reserve system to accomplish those purposes, and would "relieve the banks of the country of unnecessary restrictions that handicap them" enabling them to contribute to recovery.[21] His presentation centered on four proposals: combining the offices of chairman of the board and governor in district banks and permitting the reserve board to approve or reject the directors' choice for the combined office; modifying membership and operational machinery of the Federal Open Market Conference; subjecting to reserve board regulation the determination of whether collateral offered by a member bank would be eligible for reserve loans; and liberalizing real estate lending. He angered members of the Interdepartmental Loan Committee when he informed congressmen that after study he had concluded open market operations should not be left to three board members and two reserve bank governors, as the bill proposed, but be handled by the whole board with five governors from regional banks acting as an advisory group.[22]

Eccles suggested other changes. He proposed that governors and chairmen of district banks receive board approval every three years rather than annually, so terms would coincide with appointments of the class C directors. He thought the reserve board should "have authority to waive not only capital requirements but [also] all other requirements" for admission of insured nonmember banks into the system.[23]

Conservatives had criticized a provision that would end a reserve board governor's term whenever the president designated someone else as governor. Theoretically, it would permit a president to clear out a whole board by successively designating each member as governor. To avoid this possibility Eccles suggested that a governor stay on the board as a member after he ceased to be governor. He added that if a former governor chose to resign when not redesignated, he should be considered to have finished his term and should not have to wait two years to reenter a bank's employment, as required by law. Finally, he proposed that limits on real estate lending by member banks be left to the board instead of being set by statute at a rate that might later become inappropriate.[24]

Committee members asked whether the bill would create a government-owned central bank or something similar to the Federal Monetary Authority that Congressman T. Alan Goldsborough (D–MD) had proposed in 1934 (H.R. 7157).[25] Eccles replied that he was not trying to establish a "governmentally controlled central bank" but a "central body, charged with responsibility for monetary control, in the public interest." He believed the board would be "effective in operating the system in the public interest" without government ownership of reserve bank stock.[26]

Goldsborough and O.H. Cross (D–TEX) inquired about maintaining stable prices, which most Federal Monetary Authority proposals required. Eccles opposed trying to stabilize the price level because monetary policy alone could never control the economy. He believed it had to be accompanied by increased spending on public works in time of depression.[27] Eccles agreed to a compromise, suggesting that "in lieu of a fixed price level," which might be rigid, the committee make it the board's duty to "exercise such powers as it possesses to promote" business stability and to counteract destabilizing fluctuations in "production, trade, prices, and employment."[28]

Eccles impressed the House committee. As columnist Arthur Krock noted:

> At times the committeemen discussed points with Mr. Eccles as college seniors might argue with a young but highly respected economics instructor, coming away from class with more than they gave and appreciating the intellectual courage of their preceptor.[29]

Although the committee heard other witnesses, none had a similar effect.[30]

Hearings ran until April 1935, when the committee reported an amended bill (H.R. 7617). Title I would now repeal a provision of the reserve act, which Steagall had always opposed, that required insured banks to join the system by July 1, 1937. To eliminate disparity between member and nonmember banks of the reserve system, the bill would allow the FDIC to set maximum rates that insured banks could pay on demand and time deposits, a power already granted the reserve board for member banks. The committee rewrote the section on assessments, setting the rate at one-eighth of 1% per annum on average total deposits instead of one-twelfth, as Crowley had suggested.[31]

House committee members included a few changes in Title II that Eccles had not suggested. They rewrote the real estate section, allowing national banks to aid recovery of business in their communities by lending up to 60% of appraised value of real estate. For reasons that are not clear, they made no provision for amortized loans nor for regulating real estate lending by state member banks, and they struck out the clause that would raise salaries of board members.[32]

During House debate, which began April 29, conservatives wanted no change in the existing law and progressives advocated a government-owned central bank to ensure public control of the money supply.[33] The House adopted a few changes in the bill. Albert J. Engel (R–MICH) suggested an amendment to strike the section establishing pensions for retired board members. To Engel the "idea of offering a man who is qualified to operate the banking system of the United States a pension is an absurdity."[34] Although the fund's money would come from reserve banks, Engel believed that former board members should support themselves. Apparently, Goldsborough rose to speak in opposition, but the presiding officer did not recognize him, and the House voted by a narrow majority to eliminate the provision. Goldsborough introduced the most important amendment, which would have rewritten section 204 to give the reserve board responsibility for stabilizing commodity prices, but it failed by six votes. In a nearly straight-party ballot, 271 to 110, the House approved the bank bill on May 9.[35]

BANKING ACT OF 1935 PASSES THE SENATE

House action shifted attention to the Glass subcommittee. For months the cantankerous 77-year-old senator had delayed consideration of both Eccles's nomination as governor and the administration bill, hoping that the need to pass Title I before July 1 would force Eccles to give up Title II. Glass used his position as chairman of the Appropriations Committee, which had charge of a $4.8 billion relief measure, to postpone action by the banking subcommittee. When the relief bill became law in early April, he had no excuse for delay and began hearings on the Eccles nomination. Opposing the nominee, he was unable to prevent the subcommittee from supporting Eccles. When the full committee met, Glass chose not to attend, and members voted unanimously to confirm Eccles. Nor was Glass present on April 24, when the Senate approved the appointment by unanimous consent.[36]

The senator was as determined as ever to fight Title II, hoping to separate it from the remainder. Other subcommittee members considered sending noncontroversial parts of the measure through the Senate immediately. Glass claimed on April 13 that the administration did not object to separating Title II. Two days later, however, Fletcher announced that Roosevelt wanted one bill.[37]

Subcommittee hearings began April 19, and Glass arranged for more than 60 witnesses, many opposing Title II. The most ardent support for dividing the bill came from New York bankers led by James P. Warburg of Bank of Manhattan Company. To generate resistance to Title II, he wrote on February 20 to Nicholas Roosevelt of the New York *Herald Tribune*, Thomas F. Woodlock of the *Wall Street Journal*, Frank Knox of the Chicago *Daily News*, and Colonel Robert R. McCormick of the Chicago *Tribune* to urge that Title II be studied by monetary and banking experts. Warburg wrote his friend Robert M. Hunt of California, who discussed Title II with the president of the Bank of California and the chairman of the board of the Wells Fargo Bank and Union Trust. Warburg informed Glass that he was doing as much as possible to increase opposition. The senator was pleased.[38]

Warburg's testimony at the subcommittee hearings presented points echoed by many witnesses. He disagreed with Eccles's monetary theories and argued that banking did not need immediate reform. He suggested that Title II be referred to experts for study. He complained that centralization of powers in the reserve board would bring the system under political domination and that it would be a grave mistake to remove the automatic controls in the original reserve act. Defending decentralization, he argued that regional banks would be more sensitive to local economic conditions than would a central board. He contended that control of money markets and interest rates would be impossible, making the mandate to stabilize conditions useless.[39]

Others testifying shared Warburg's concerns. Elwyn Evans represented the clearinghouse banks of Wilmington, Delaware, and believed that centralizing power in a presidentially appointed board would lead to a "dictatorship over our whole banking and credit system" by "whatever political group happened to be in power."[40] Edwin W. Kemmerer, professor of international finance at Princeton, declared Title II would increase the "power of the President over our entire monetary, banking and credit system."[41] Winthrop W. Aldrich of Chase National Bank feared Title II would allow any administration to "use the credit and currency system of the country for the purpose of political advantage."[42] L.M. Wiggins, president of the Bank of Hartsville, South Carolina, called the "concentration of power" given the reserve board under Title II "foreign to our conception of the principles of democratic government."[43] Representatives from the Florida, Georgia, and Connecticut Bankers' Associations presented similar views.[44]

A few bankers took the position that Title II should be amended. Believing that cooperation would ensure passage of a sound measure, leaders of the American Bankers' Association had worked with Eccles and Treasury officials to minimize differences between themselves and the administration. The bankers' report on March 22 called for many of the changes Eccles had suggested. The principal difference concerned the Federal Open Market Committee. The report suggested that Congress drop ex officio members from the board and reduce it to five when the next vacancy occurred. The FOMC would consist of the five board members plus four district bank governors, serving on a rotating basis. At subcommittee hearings two members of the executive committee of the American Bankers' Association presented these views.[45]

Eccles defended his economic philosophy and Title II. He denied that his proposals were "revolutionary" or would make the system a "political football."[46] Emphasizing the need for public control of national economic and monetary policy, he argued that the FOMC should consist of the board with an advisory committee of five regional bank governors. He told the senators that higher salaries and pensions for board members would increase independence and attract better qualified people. He recommended that Congress not change the law that required insured banks to join the reserve system by July 1, 1937. Still, he suggested a possible compromise with the House committee that would force insured banks with deposits of $500,000 or more to join the system within a year of becoming insured. He argued that real estate provisions in the House bill should apply to state as well as national banks and that the reserve board should receive authority to regulate real estate lending, providing loans did not exceed 60% of the appraised value of a property.[47]

Other board members testified before the subcommittee. Adolph C. Miller, an economist who had been a member since 1914, argued against "sweeping changes in the eligibility provisions" of the reserve act.[48] He wanted only to reenact part of section 10(b), which had expired in March 1935, so that in emergency situations the board could authorize reserve banks to make advances secured by promissory notes and other collateral for member banks having no eligible paper. Miller presented several recommendations to increase independence of the board: removal of ex officio members; removal of no member during his term except for malfeasance; reconstitution of the Federal Reserve Board as the "Board of Governors of the Federal Reserve System" with power to select its chairman; and enactment of a pension. He agreed with Eccles that the reserve board should have authority to decide open market policy, and he suggested that open market decisions, along with a statement of reasons for a policy, should be published in the annual report.[49]

Board member Charles S. Hamlin supported Title II. A lawyer and politician who had been on the board since 1914, he approved giving it permanent power to raise or lower member bank reserve requirements. He had no objection to permitting the president to remove as well as appoint the board governor because it changed practice so little. He advocated eliminating the office of federal reserve agent and abolishing collateral behind federal reserve notes because together they cost the system $500,000 a year. He believed the board should receive responsibility for open market operations and advocated broadening eligibility requirements to permit district banks to discount any sound asset for troubled banks. He had no objection to renaming the board and giving it authority to choose its chairman but thought the secretary of the Treasury should remain to provide a link between banking and fiscal officials.[50]

Remaining board members agreed with the principles of Title II, except George R. James, a feed merchant and banker from Tennessee who had served for more than a decade and who criticized provisions of Title II because he preferred existing law. Morgenthau, an ex officio member, told the subcommittee he believed control of the money supply should be centralized in an independent agency, such as the reserve board. He surprised many people when he announced the government should own district banks' stock.[51]

Regional reserve officials opposed passage of Title II because strengthening the power of the board would weaken the autonomy of district officials. At subcommittee hearings Owen D. Young, a director of the New York reserve bank, urged that Congress postpone action on Title II pending study of the banking system. He complained that the proposed legislation would establish a "central bank" by concentrating the most important power and responsibility in the hands of board members "with no checks or balances" from directors of reserve banks.[52] He advocated adding regional bank governors to the Washington board. Proclaiming that the independence of district banks must be preserved, the Federal Advisory Council suggested that Congress remove ex officio members of the reserve board, reduce the board to five, appoint members for 15 years but compel retirement at age 70, allow the board to approve regional bank governors every three years, and organize an FOMC of board members plus four governors. The American Bankers' Association had advocated several of these recommendations, and bankers of the Federal Advisory Council were unprepared to support Title II unless Congress included the changes.[53]

Comment on Titles I and III was restrained. O'Connor and Crowley thought the House committee erred in eliminating the requirement that insured banks join the reserve system by July 1937, although several bankers liked the House decision. Questioned by Glass, officials approved his suggestion that the law set a cap of $500 million on the insurance fund, so when it reached that level FDIC assessments would cease until after an impairment of 20 to 25%. Bankers preferred the lower rate of assessment originally suggested (one-twelfth of 1% per annum) to that adopted by the House (one-eighth of 1%). A few bankers advocated a rate of one-sixteenth of 1% per annum.[54]

As hearings stretched into June, bankers became nervous. They needed Titles I and III because each contained provisions altering the Banking Act of 1933. If Title I did not pass by July 1, the permanent insurance plan of the act of 1933 would become operative, covering deposits far larger than $5,000. If Title III failed to become law by June 16, executive officers of national banks who had not liquidated indebtedness to their banks would be subject to penalty. About $90 million of such loans were outstanding. Subcommittee hearings ended on June 3, and Eccles feared that Steagall and Fletcher might give in to Glass to allow the necessary provisions to pass immediately. To prevent a splitting of the bill, the administration prepared two resolutions: one to postpone the effective date of insurance provisions from July 1 to August 31 and another changing the liquidation date for bankers' debts from June 16, 1935 to June 16, 1938. Both resolutions passed Congress promptly.[55]

The subcommittee amended the proposed bill, beginning with Title II on June 21. Glass intended to revise that part of the measure so much that it would not be acceptable to the administration, but other subcommittee members insisted on compromise. Their version would follow Miller's suggestion of abolishing the Federal Reserve Board in favor of a Board of Governors, which would consist of seven presidentially appointed members removable before their terms expired only for cause. The secretary of the Treasury and the comptroller of the currency would not be members of the new board because subcommittee members believed the Treasury had exercised too much control over the system. The president would appoint the new board within 90 days after enactment and choose a chairman and vice chairman to serve four-year terms. Other members would serve 14-year terms without eligibility for reappointment, receiving salaries of $15,000. The subcommittee did not approve pensions for board members.[56]

The subcommittee would permit reserve bank directors to select a president as the executive officer—using "president" instead of "governor" to avoid confusion. If approved by the Board of Governors, a president would serve a five-year term instead of three, and directors would not be limited to two terms of three years apiece, as in the House bill. The subcommittee saw no reason to change the duties of a district bank's chairman of the board.[57]

Because the subcommittee opposed a highly centralized system, the Board of Governors would not have total control over the three methods used to alter the money supply. The FOMC would consist of seven governors plus five representatives chosen annually by district bank presidents. Each reserve bank could choose whether to participate in FOMC operations. To ensure independence, regional banks could not buy government securities from the Treasury. The board would not have the right to initiate discount rate policy, but reserve banks would have to establish their rates every two weeks or more often, whether or not a change were intended, and the Board of Governors could approve or disapprove those rates. The board would receive limited power to alter reserve requirements of member banks with an affirmative vote of five governors. The minimum would be existing requirements (7% in country banks, 10% in reserve city banks, and 13% in central reserve city banks), and the maximum would be twice as much. The subcommittee did not wish to leave such an important matter to the unrestricted judgment of a Washington bureau.[58]

Glass doubted the wisdom of allowing district banks to lend on any sound asset, apparently because he feared inflation of the money supply. The subcommittee dropped that language in favor of an emergency provision that would allow a member without eligible paper to borrow from a reserve bank at a rate one percentage point above the discount rate, using any satisfactory asset as collateral. Because of a prejudice against long-term lending by member banks, Glass and the subcommittee included restrictions on real estate lending by national banks, adding a geographical boundary and limiting such loans to five-year periods at half the appraised value of the property. Amortized loans could extend for no more than ten years.[59]

The subcommittee's bill differed from the House measure in other ways. Senators would require insured state banks having deposits of $1 million or more to become members of the reserve system by July 1, 1937. Glass told the Senate that the committee used $1 million instead of $500,000, as suggested by Eccles, because fewer nonmember banks would have to join, so state bankers would more easily accept it. The subcommittee adopted an assessment rate of one-twelfth of 1% a year until the fund reached $500 million, after which the FDIC would suspend assessments until the fund had been impaired by 15%. Glass persuaded the subcommittee to reestablish accommodation of commerce and business as the goal of open market policy, rejecting the language Eccles recommended. At Glass's suggestion the group added a section to Title III that would permit commercial banks to underwrite up to one-fifth of single issues of corporate securities, provided that banks invest no more than $100,000 or one-tenth of their unimpaired capital and surplus in a single issue. Aggregate underwritings could not exceed twice unimpaired capital and surplus. George L. Harrison, governor of the New York reserve bank, had been working for months on an underwriting amendment that would reopen capital markets. The provision adopted by the subcommittee resembled his proposal.[60]

The subcommittee reported the bill to the full committee on July 1, 1935, and the Senate approved it before the end of the month. The full committee unanimously accepted the rewritten measure and reported it on July 2. Senate debate began July 23, and there was scant opposition. Senators proposed six amendments. Three reached a vote: one to strike out the requirement that insured state banks with deposits of more than $1 million join the reserve system; a second to establish a government-owned central bank to regulate banks and purchasing power; a third to remove the provision permitting underwriting of securities by commercial banks. All three failed, and the bill passed the Senate on July 26.[61]

FINAL PASSAGE OF THE BANKING ACT OF 1935

Debate now shifted to the conference committee. The House appointed Steagall, Goldsborough, and Hollister, while the Senate chose Glass, Fletcher, Robert J. Bulkley (D–OH), William G. McAdoo (D–CAL), John G. Townsend, Jr. (R–DEL), and Peter Norbeck (R–SD). For the next month, these men strove to find a compromise acceptable to both houses and the president. Controversial clauses concerned the requirement that insured banks join the reserve system, the authority and organization of the reserve board and FOMC, and the underwriting of securities by national banks. Conferees started slowly because Goldsborough offended Glass and others when he charged that New York bankers had influenced the Senate committee. He and Steagall defended Title II, while Glass tried to preserve his subcommittee's revision.[62]

Members of FDR's administration aided the conference committee, Birdzell advising on Title I and F. Gloyd Awalt, deputy comptroller of the currency, advising on Title III. Eccles requested the committee to permit Walter Wyatt, general counsel of the reserve board, to aid in redrafting Title II, but Glass refused to accept him. Since Glass had worked with him before, this rejection was probably caused by a conversation in which Wyatt had begged the senator to confirm Eccles. Glass did permit Awalt to help with Title II, and the latter kept Wyatt and Eccles informed. Still, Awalt had no institutional interest in protecting the House bill and had other reasons to avoid affronting Glass.[63]

Goldsborough advanced Eccles's views in conference, consulting him each day. Eccles sent Goldsborough a memorandum showing the essential points to save: the mandate in section 204(b) requiring the reserve board to exercise its powers to promote economic stability; the requirement that regional banks comply with any open market policy adopted by the FOMC; the authority for district banks to lend to member banks on promissory notes secured by satisfactory assets; and the elimination of the Senate proviso requiring approval of at least five board members to change member bank reserve requirements. Eccles preferred FOMC provisions in the House bill. His second choice would be to reduce the board to five, serving 10-year terms, and to have the FOMC consist of the five board members and two regional bank governors, serving in rotation for one-year terms. In the latter case he wanted power over open market operations, discount rates, and reserve requirements centered in the board, not the FOMC. His third choice would be to accept the Senate version but reduce regional bank representation on the FOMC from five to four.[64]

The conference committee began by considering Title I, especially whether to require insured state banks with $1 million or more of deposits to join the reserve system. Steagall argued that state banks should not have to join, while Glass had desired since 1933 to unify banking by requiring insured banks to become members. The committee had to reconcile a few other differences in Title I, such as whether to assess banks at the rate of one-eighth or one-twelfth of 1% per annum and whether to terminate assessments when the insurance fund reached $500 million. The conference committee bill would provide for a rate of one-twelfth of 1%, as the Senate wished, and would not place a cap on the fund's assessments, as the House preferred. House conferees, perhaps with support from Senator Norbeck, succeeded in postponing until 1942 the deadline for insured state banks with over $1 million in deposits to join the reserve system.[65]

On Title II, Steagall and Goldsborough successfully defended the major points Eccles had indicated, compromising on less important matters. Eccles was happy because he had achieved the substance of his reforms, and Glass was pleased because he had protected the system against political control. The new Title II centralized power in the renamed Board of Governors of the Federal Reserve System. Membership would change from eight to seven, with the secretary of the Treasury and comptroller of the currency eliminated as ex officio members. Glass believed the compromise preserved independence by setting 14-year terms, making members ineligible for reappointment, and granting salaries of $15,000. The president could remove board members for cause and would designate the chairman and vice chairman for two-year terms. Qualifications for board membership would not change. Reorganization would occur February 1, 1936.[66]

Title II would grant the Board of Governors greater influence over the three means of monetary control. After March 1, 1936, the Federal Open Market Committee would include the seven board members plus five representatives from regional banks, a concession to Glass, since Eccles and FDR had wanted only four regional members. The new bill would require district banks to take part in system open market sales and purchases, as Eccles wished. In spite of the department's protests, Glass insisted that the measure not allow district banks to purchase government securities directly from the Treasury, perhaps because he feared Treasury influence on reserve operations. Increasing the board's authority over discounting, the conference committee adopted the Senate requirement that reserve banks set discount rates, subject to board approval, at least every 14 days. The committee supported Eccles by allowing the board to raise or lower member bank reserve requirements—within limits set in the Senate bill—by an affirmative vote of four members. Although it increased the board's ability to control monetary policy, this Title II was far from Eccles's original proposal.[67]

In other sections of Title II, the conference committee blended the two bills. As in the Senate bill, a district bank's directors would appoint a president and vice president approved by the Board of Governors for a five-year term. None of the provisions relating to issues of federal reserve notes that were in the House bill appeared in the conference version, but the committee did make permanent the authority to use government securities as collateral for reserve notes, which the system had used on an emergency basis since February 1932. The clause in the conference bill concerning loans under section 10(b) of the reserve act broadened discount facilities by eliminating Senate wording that required exhaustion of eligible and acceptable commercial assets before member banks could borrow from a reserve bank on a promissory note secured to the district bank's satisfaction. The rate of interest on such loans would be half of one percentage point higher than the regular discount rate. Eccles had not asked Goldsborough to insist on permitting reserve banks to lend on any sound asset and was satisfied with this eligibility provision. House conferees settled for the real estate loan provisions that were in the Senate bill, except they removed the geographical boundary. Finally, the conference bill would eliminate the mandate for economic stabilization that Eccles had desired, leaving accommodation of commerce, business, and agriculture as the goal of the system. This must have disappointed Eccles, but he was not ready to condemn the measure over this provision.[68]

Minor changes in Title III were necessary to reach a compromise, but only two provisions caused controversy, one on underwriting securities and another on interlocking directorates. Roosevelt opposed the underwriting feature because it would mix commercial and investment banking, and conferees agreed to remove it. Concerning interlocking directorates House and Senate bills differed, and FDR suggested that none be permitted. The conference committee combined the two versions, allowing no person to act as a director for more than one bank unless institutions met conditions listed in the bill. The Board of Governors would receive power to enforce compliance and prescribe regulations.[69]

Once the conference committee agreed, the measure became law quickly. Conferees completed work on Friday evening, August 16, so their report did not appear in the *Congressional Record* until August 19. The same day, both houses approved the bill without recorded votes, and Roosevelt signed it four days later. Rudolph Hecht, president of the American Bankers' Association, praised the law as an improvement in the nation's banking system.[70]

The president could have named the existing members to the new Board of Governors, which would take office in February 1936, but chose not to do so. To end rumors that he would not reappoint Eccles, he announced in September that the governor would be his nominee for chairman of the reorganized board. Eccles wanted the board to include M.S. Szymczak, whom he respected, and exclude everyone older than 60, which would leave out Miller, Hamlin, J.J. Thomas, and James. FDR wished to drop the Nebraska politician Thomas, but Miller and Hamlin were both friends, and Roosevelt always had a difficult time dismissing anyone. Eccles persuaded him not to select anyone over 60 by making arrangements for Thomas to become chairman of the Kansas City reserve bank, Hamlin to become special counsel to the Board of Governors, and Miller to have an advisory position overseeing completion of the new reserve board building. Eccles designed a strategy to neutralize opposition from Glass, which Roosevelt followed by permitting the latter to choose three nominees from a list prepared by Eccles. Eccles arranged for people the senator respected to lobby in favor of the men whose names were on the list. Eccles was confident that Glass would choose three acceptable men, and Roosevelt would select the remaining four, including Eccles. The board chosen by the president and Glass consisted of Eccles, Szymczak, John K. McKee (examiner of the Reconstruction Finance Corporation), Ronald Ransom (Georgia banker), Joseph A. Broderick (superintendent of banks for New York), Ralph W. Morrison (Texas businessman), and Chester Davis (head of the Agricultural Adjustment Administration).[71]

CONCLUSION

The Banking Act of 1935 broke the final connection between real bills theory and the Federal Reserve Act. Even though Glass had protested against lending on any sound asset, section 10(b) authorized district banks to lend to members on any satisfactory collateral. In a regulation issued in 1937, the board allowed reserve banks to accept as security for such advances any regularly eligible paper and government securities, paper that would be eligible if its maturity were shorter, investment securities member banks could legally purchase, obligations issued under the National Housing Act and Federal Farm Loan Act, revenue bonds and warrants of states or their political subdivisions, real estate obligations, and installment loan notes. If deemed wise, a district bank could make an advance on other collateral. The Banking Act of 1935 also made government securities eligible as collateral for federal reserve notes on a permanent rather than emergency basis, which cut the connection between the nation's currency and eligible paper. Both these changes increased the board's flexibility to meet crises, especially its ability to be a lender of last resort, a crucial central bank function.[72]

With the help of FDR, Steagall, and Goldsborough, Eccles achieved the changes necessary to reallocate authority within the reserve system, making the board sufficiently powerful to force its policies on the FOMC and district banks. By ending the division of authority within the system, the Banking Act of 1935 removed a source of indecision and delay. If the act failed to accomplish everything Eccles had hoped, it still represented a giant step toward centralized decision making and allowed the board to assume the role it has today. Glass had never wished to center power in the reserve board nor intended the board to stabilize the economy through countercyclical action, but his ideas about economic and monetary theory were outdated. Passage of the Banking Act of 1935 marked the end of a battle between two economic theories, one based on a past long gone and the other based on a vision of the future so perceptive that the structure of the Federal Reserve System has remained unchanged since 1935.

NOTES

1. American Institute of Banking, *Contemporary Legislative and Banking Problems* (New York: American Institute of Banking, 1934), 262–6; *New York Times*, 17 June 1934, 26.

2. Clipping from Washington *Post*, 8 February 1935, Box 345, Charles Sumner Hamlin Papers, Manuscript Division, Library of Congress, Washington, D.C.; *New York Times*, 17 December 1934, 29; Ibid., 2 January 1935, 45; Ibid., 2 February 1935, 21; Ibid., 5 February 1935, 20; Ibid., 11 February 1935, 27; American Bankers' Association, Committee on Federal Legislation, *Legislation Affecting Banking Pending in First Session, 74th Congress* (New York: American Bankers' Association, 1935), 69–91. Bankers preferred Title I to the permanent plan; "The Banking Act of 1935: How it Affects Banks and Everybody Else," *United States Investor*, 46 (9 March 1935): 289; *New York Times*, 28 June 1935, 31.

3. American Bankers' Association, *Legislation Affecting Banking*, 69–80; U.S., Congress, Senate, Committee on Banking and Currency, *Banking Act of 1935: Hearings before Subcommittee on S. 1715 and H.R. 7617*, 74th Congress, 1st session, 19 April–3 June 1935, 2–23; *New York Times*, 5 February 1935, 20. All subsequent descriptions of Title I come from these sources.

4. Senate Committee on Banking and Currency, *Banking Act of 1935: Hearings*, 31, 145; U.S., Congress, House, Committee on Banking and Currency, *Banking Act of 1935: Hearings on H.R. 5357*, 74th Congress, 1st session, 21 February–8 April 1935, 57.

5. House Committee on Banking and Currency, *Banking Act of 1935: Hearings*, 661. In this paragraph and the next one, information about the provisions of Title III comes from American Bankers' Association, *Legislation Affecting Banking*, 84–91; Senate Committee on Banking and Currency, *Banking Act of 1935: Hearings*, 2–23; *New York Times*, 5 February 1935, 20. In October 1934, the Special Committee on Proposed Revision of Federal Banking Laws of the American Bankers' Association suggested many modifications of the 1933 law that were included in Title III; Confidential Report #2, Box 85, Records of the Federal Reserve System, Subject File, 1914–54, Record Group 82, National Archives, Washington, D.C. [All citations to RG 82 refer to the Subject File, 1914–54.]

6. Letter to Fletcher from O'Connor, 10 January 1935, tray 85, Records of the United States Senate, Committee on Banking and Currency Papers, 74th Congress, Record Group 46, National Archives, Washington, D.C.; untitled and undated memorandum on Title III, Box 162, RG 82; Senate Committee on Banking and Currency, *Banking Act of 1935: Hearings*, 65–8. [References to RG 46 in this chapter are to Papers, 74th Congress, Senate Committee on Banking and Currency.]

7. *New York Times*, 11 November 1934, 1, 39; Ibid., 25 November 1934, VIII: 2; Herman E. Krooss, *Executive Opinion: What Business Leaders Said and Thought on Economic Issues 1920s–1960s* (Garden City, N.Y.: Doubleday, 1970), 139–40; S.J. Woolfe, "Eccles Would Save Capitalism by Reform," *Literary Digest*, 119 (5 January 1935): 5; Marriner S. Eccles, *Beckoning Frontiers: Public and Personal Recollections* (New York: Alfred A. Knopf, 1951), 104–13, 136–66; Sidney Hyman, *Marriner S. Eccles: Private Entrepreneur and Public Servant* (Stanford, Cal.: Stanford University, Graduate School of Business, 1976), 128–9, 134–5, 154–5.

8. Helen M. Burns, *The American Banking Community and New Deal Banking Reforms, 1933–1935* (Westport, Conn.: Greenwood, 1974), 142–4; Eccles, *Beckoning Frontiers*, 166–74, 187; Hyman, *Eccles*, 155–9; memorandum, Desirable Changes in the Administration of the Federal Reserve System, Box 4, Marriner S. Eccles Papers, Manuscript Division, Special Collections Department, Marriott Library, University of Utah, Salt Lake City, Utah. Eccles had the assistance of economist Lauchlin Currie in preparing this memorandum; Eccles, *Beckoning Frontiers*, 166.

9. Burns, *American Banking Community*, 144; Hyman, *Eccles*, 160–1; Eccles, *Beckoning Frontiers*, 175, 193; Rexford G. Tugwell, *The Democratic Roosevelt: A Biography of Franklin D. Roosevelt* (Garden City, N.Y.: Doubleday, 1957), 367; *New York Times*, 11 November 1934, 1, 39; memorandum, Notes on Last Night's Meeting in the Governor's Office, 27 November 1934, Box 7, Emanuel Alexandrovich Goldenweiser Papers, Manuscript Division, Library of Congress, Washington, D.C. Other reserve board members received brief descriptions of the legislation from Eccles in December and January, but they were not asked for detailed comments or opinions by Eccles or Roosevelt. See Diary, v. 25, 13 December 1934, 26 December 1934, Hamlin Papers; Ibid., v. 26, 22–23 January 1935, 29 January 1935, 1 February 1935; Eccles, *Beckoning Frontiers*, 198.

10. Diary, v. 2, 26 November 1934, 14 December 1934, 19 December 1934, 28 December 1934, Henry Morgenthau, Jr., Papers, Franklin Delano Roosevelt Library, Hyde Park, N.Y.; Ibid., v. 3, 9 January 1935, 17 January 1935, 18 January 1935, 30 January 1935; Burns, *American Banking Community*, 140–2, 145–6; Diary, v. 3, 24 January 1935, 30 January 1935, James Francis Thaddeus O'Connor Papers, Bancroft Library, University of California, Berkeley, Cal.; Memorandum of Activities for the Day to the Secretary from Coolidge, 30 January 1935, Box 1, T. Jefferson Coolidge Papers, Franklin Delano Roosevelt Library, Hyde Park, N.Y. The members of the Interdepartmental Loan Committee were the secretary of the Treasury, secretary of the Interior, governor of the Farm Credit Administration, chairman of the Reconstruction Finance Corporation, chairman of the Home Loan Bank Board, administrator of the Federal Housing Authority, administrator of the Agricultural Adjustment Administration, president of the Export-Import Bank, president of the Commodity Credit Corporation, governor of the Federal Reserve Board, and chairman of the Federal Deposit Insurance Corporation; *New York Times*, 15 November 1934, 4. Most of the banking legislation was handled by a subcommittee consisting of Eccles, Treasury Undersecretary T. Jefferson Coolidge, General Counsel to the Treasury Herman Oliphant, RFC Chairman Jesse Jones and his assistant Lynn P. Talley, and FDIC Chairman Leo Crowley; House Committee on Banking and Currency, *Banking Act of 1935: Hearings*, 351–2. Comptroller of the Currency J.F.T. O'Connor attended a few of these meetings.

11. All information about Title II as introduced is from American Bankers' Association, *Legislation Affecting Banking*, 80–4; Senate Committee on Banking and Currency, *Banking Act of 1935: Hearings*, 2–23; *New York Times*, 5 February 1935, 20. See also *New York Times*, 9 February 1935, 23; House Committee on Banking and Currency, *Banking Act of 1935: Hearings*, 180. The Federal Reserve Board first suggested in 1916 that Congress give it authority to raise or lower reserve requirements of member banks; William O. Weyforth, *The Federal Reserve Board: A Study of Federal Reserve Structure and Credit Control* (Baltimore: Johns Hopkins University, 1933), 37. Congress did not act on this recommendation until 1933, when it passed the Thomas Amendment to the Agricultural Adjustment Act, which

allocated this authority to the board on an emergency basis. For more on the Thomas Amendment, see Chapter Six.

12. *New York Times*, 9 February 1935, 23; Ibid., 13 February 1935, 33–4; Office Correspondence to Morrill from Goldenweiser, 5 January 1935, Box 14, Eccles Papers; House Committee on Banking and Currency, *Banking Act of 1935: Hearings*, 181, 195–7; James T. Lindley, *An Analysis of the Federal Advisory Council of the Federal Reserve System, 1914–1938* (New York: Garland, 1985), 221.

13. House Committee on Banking and Currency, *Banking Act of 1935: Hearings*, 193–5; Eccles speech to Ohio Bankers' Association, Columbus, Ohio, 12 February 1935, Box 13, Eccles Papers; Memorandum: Meeting of Executive Committee February 18, 1935, Binder 51, George Leslie Harrison Papers, Manuscript Division, Butler Library, Columbia University, New York, N.Y.

14. Eccles speech to Ohio Bankers' Association, Box 13, Eccles Papers; Office Correspondence to Morrill from Goldenweiser, 5 January 1935, Box 14, Eccles Papers; letter to Fletcher from Eccles, 20 February 1935, Box 13, Eccles Papers; *New York Times*, 9 February 1935, 23; Ibid., 13 February 1935, 34; Lindley, *Federal Advisory Council*, 223–4.

15. Eccles speech to Ohio Bankers' Association, Box 13, Eccles Papers; House Committee on Banking and Currency, *Banking Act of 1935: Hearings*, 189–91; Office Correspondence to Morrill from Goldenweiser, 5 January 1935, Box 14, Eccles Papers.

16. Memorandum: Meeting of Executive Committee February 18, 1935, Binder 51, Harrison Papers.

17. Ronald Allen Mulder, *The Insurgent Progressives in the United States Senate and the New Deal, 1933–1939* (New York: Garland, 1979), 113; Arthur M. Schlesinger, Jr., *The Age of Roosevelt*, 3 v. (Boston: Houghton Mifflin, 1957–60), III: 295–6; Hyman, *Eccles*, 162–3; clipping from The Detroit *News*, [dateline] 6 February 1935, Box 4, scrapbook 1935, Jay G. Hayden Papers, Michigan Historical Collections, Bentley Historical Library, University of Michigan, Ann Arbor, Mich.; clipping from The Detroit *News*, [dateline] 22 April 1935, Box 4, scrapbook 1935, Hayden Papers; John Douglas Lyle, The United States Senate Career of Carter Glass of Virginia, 1919–1939 (Ph.D. dissertation, University of South Carolina, 1974), 169–70, 177–80; *New York Times*, 10 February 1935, II: 11, 16.

18. Burns, *American Banking Community*, 146–7; FDIC proposal of 10 December 1934, Box 317, Carter Glass Papers, Alderman Library, University of Virginia, Charlottesville, Va.; Alfred Cash Koeniger, "Unreconstructed Rebel:" The Political Thought and Senate Career of Carter Glass, 1929–1936 (Ph.D. dissertation, Vanderbilt University, 1980), 119–20; Memorandum of Activities for the Day to the Secretary from Coolidge, 4 February 1935, Box 1, Coolidge Papers; O'Connor Diary, v. 3, 4 February 1935; Eccles, *Beckoning Frontiers*, 194–5; Morgenthau Diary, v. 3, 4 February 1935; letters to Steagall and Fletcher from Roosevelt, 4 February 1935, Official File 90, Box 2, Franklin Delano Roosevelt Presidential Papers, Franklin Delano Roosevelt Library, Hyde Park, N.Y.

19. Hamlin Diary, v. 25, 12 December 1934; Ibid., v. 26, 23 January 1935, 5 February 1935; Burns, *American Banking Community*, 153–4; *New York Times*, 6 February 1935, 2; Schlesinger, *Age of Roosevelt*, III: 296; Koeniger, "Unreconstructed Rebel," 120–3; Hyman, *Eccles*, 162–3; Confidential Memorandum for the President, 5 February 1935, Official File 230, Box 2, FDR Presidential Papers; Wayne Flynt, *Duncan Upshaw Fletcher: Dixie's Reluctant Progressive* (Tallahassee: Florida State University, 1971), 177. The subcommittee was Glass, Robert J. Bulkley (D–OH), William G. McAdoo (D–CAL), James F. Byrnes (D–SC), John H. Bankhead (D–ALA), John G. Townsend, Jr. (R–DEL), James Couzens (R–MICH), and Bronson Cutting (R–NM); *New York Times*, 13 February 1935, 33.

20. House Committee on Banking and Currency, *Banking Act of 1935: Hearings*, 10–74, 83–178, 661–705; *New York Times*, 1 March 1935, 34.

21. House Committee on Banking and Currency, *Banking Act of 1935: Hearings*, 180.

22. Ibid., 180–5; *New York Times*, 5 March 1935, 29; O'Connor Diary, v. 3, 19 March 1935; Morgenthau Diary, v. 4, 5 March 1935; Hamlin Diary, v. 26, 21 March 1935.

23. House Committee on Banking and Currency, *Banking Act of 1935: Hearings*, 202.

24. Ibid., 189–92, 197–204. The alterations Eccles suggested to the House committee were drawn from work by the reserve board's staff; memorandum, Comments on H.R. 5357, to Eccles from Smead, 25 February 1935, Box 162, RG 82; Hamlin Diary, v. 26, 30 March 1935.

25. House Committee on Banking and Currency, *Banking Act of 1935: Hearings*, 228–30, 250–1, 374; *New York Times*, 12 March 1935, 31; Ibid., 19 March 1935, 31. H.R. 7157 would have created a Federal Monetary Authority to issue circulating currency, buy or sell gold, purchase silver, rediscount for reserve banks, buy and sell short-term government securities, buy and sell foreign exchange, and assume control of the Treasury Department's stabilization fund. The authority would have responsibility for stabilizing the purchasing power of the dollar at the 1926 level; H.R. 7157, tray 92, RG 46. Several other bills to establish central monetary authorities were introduced early in 1935; Joseph E. Reeve, *Monetary Reform Movements: A Survey of Recent Plans and Panaceas* (Washington, D.C.: American Council on Public Affairs, 1943), 90n.

26. House Committee on Banking and Currency, *Banking Act of 1935: Hearings*, 229, 374.

27. Ibid., 250–1, 637; *New York Times*, 13 March 1935, 27; Ibid., 14 March 1935, 30; Ibid., 16 March 1935, 21.

28. House Committee on Banking and Currency, *Banking Act of 1935: Hearings*, 251.

29. *New York Times*, 21 March 1935, 22.

30. House Committee on Banking and Currency, *Banking Act of 1935: Hearings*, 431–875; Arch O. Egbert, Marriner S. Eccles and the Banking Act of 1935 (Ph.D. dissertation, Brigham Young University, 1967), 110. Roosevelt had asked Steagall on March 25 to get the bill out of committee and passed by the House; memorandum to Steagall from Roosevelt, 25 March 1935, President's Personal File 2356, FDR Presidential Papers. Steagall replied on March 29 that he was doing his best; telegram to McIntyre from Steagall, 29 March 1935, President's Personal File 2356, FDR Presidential Papers.

31. U.S., Congress, House, Committee on Banking and Currency, *Banking Act of 1935: Report to Accompany H.R. 7617*, H. Rept. 742, 74th Congress, 1st session, 19 April 1935; *New York Times*, 11 April 1935, 33; memorandum, Most Important Changes Adopted by the House in Proposed Banking Act of 1935, Box 18, General Records of the Department of the Treasury, Office of the Secretary, General Correspondence 1933–56, Record Group 56, National Archives, Washington, D.C. [All citations of RG 56 in this chapter refer to the Office of the Secretary, General Correspondence 1933–56.]

32. *Congressional Record*, v. 79, pt. 7: 7159–60, 7163, 7182, 7186, 7238–40, 7242–3, 7246–51, 74th Congress, 1st session.

33. *Congressional Record*, v. 79: pt. 6: 6577–88, 6651–60, 6716–45, 6792–820, 6904–33, 6943–72, pt. 7: 7152–86, 74th Congress, 1st session; Susan Estabrook Kennedy, *The Banking Crisis of 1933* (Lexington: University of Kentucky, 1973), 234. See also clipping from Philadelphia *Record*, 7 February 1935, attached to letter to Cutting from Lockresy, 7 February 1935, Box 20, Bronson Cutting Papers, Manuscript Division, Library of Congress, Washington, D.C.

34. *Congressional Record*, v. 79, pt. 7: 7163.

35. Ibid., v. 79, pt. 6: 6577–88, 6651–60, 6716–45, 6792–820, 6833–4, 6904–33, 6943–72, pt. 7: 7152–86, 7238–72; *New York Times*, 10 May 1935, 1–2; Hamlin Diary, v. 26, 13 May 1935; Edward Francis Hanlon, Urban-Rural Cooperation and Conflict in the Congress: The Breakdown of the New Deal Coalition, 1933–1938 (Ph.D. dissertation, Georgetown University, 1967), 170. Goldsborough's amendment would have required stabilization of prices at a level equal to average purchasing power of the dollar as determined by the Department of Labor index of wholesale commodity prices in the years 1921 to 1929.

36. "Glass: Virginian's Whiplash Tongue Sent Huey Long Scurrying," *Newsweek*, 6 (17 August 1935): 20; Eccles, *Beckoning Frontiers*, 202; clipping from The Detroit *Press*, [dateline] 22 April 1935; Box 4, scrapbook 1935, Hayden Papers; letter to Fletcher from Glass, 15 May 1935, tray 85, RG 46; Burns, *American Banking Community*, 153–4; *New York Times*, 9 April 1935, 1; Ibid., 16 April 1935, 33; Ibid., 23 April 1935, 37; Ibid., 24 April 1935, 31; Ibid., 25 April 1935, 31; *Congressional Record*, v. 79, pt. 6: 6297, 74th Congress, 1st session. Apparently Roosevelt misled Glass about his support for the bank bill in March 1935 so that the senator would cooperate on the relief bill. See John M. Blum, *From the Morgenthau Diaries*, 3 v. (Boston: Houghton Mifflin, 1959), I: 347–8; Burns, *American Banking Community*, 161–2. Glass received the definite impression that the bill was not an administration proposal; letter to Robey from Glass, 13 March 1935, Box 304, Glass Papers.

37. *New York Times*, 11 April 1935, 39; Ibid., 14 April 1935, 5; Ibid., 16 April 1935, 33; Schlesinger, *Age of Roosevelt*, III: 298.

38. Senate Committee on Banking and Currency, *Banking Act of 1935: Hearings*, i–v; Schlesinger, *Age of Roosevelt*, III: 297–8; Memorandum of Activities for the Day to the Secretary from Coolidge, 15 February 1935, Box 68, Correspondence, Alphabetical File, Morgenthau Papers; *New York Times*, 28 April 1935, III: 1; Ibid., 13 May 1935, 25, 29; Ibid., 3 June 1935, 27; letters to N. Roosevelt, Woodlock, Knox, McCormick and Hunt from Warburg, 20 February 1935, Box 8, James Paul Warburg Papers, John F. Kennedy Library, Waltham, Mass.; letter to Warburg from Hunt, 26 February 1935, Box 8, Warburg Papers; letter to Warburg from Hunt, 27 February 1935, Box 8, Warburg Papers; letter to Glass from Warburg, 25 February 1935, Box 8, Warburg Papers; letter to Hunt from Warburg, 19 March 1935, Box 8, Warburg Papers. Hunt's efforts resulted in protests to McAdoo from California bankers. See telegram to McAdoo from McIntosh, 6 March 1935, Box 402, William Gibbs McAdoo Papers, Manuscript Division, Library of Congress, Washington, D.C.; memorandum by Elliott, 23 April 1935, Box 404, McAdoo Papers.

39. Senate Committee on Banking and Currency, *Banking Act of 1935: Hearings*, 72–90; *New York Times*, 25 April 1935, 31, 38. Warburg later said that his opposition to Roosevelt had been so vehement because he had considered the president a father figure and Roosevelt had then attacked and betrayed many of the things his real father (Paul M. Warburg) had worked for and believed in; Irving S. Michelman, "A Banker in the New Deal: James P. Warburg," *Review Internationale d'Historie de la Banque*, 8 (1974): 59.

40. Senate Committee on Banking and Currency, *Banking Act of 1935: Hearings*, 258.

41. Ibid., 330. Kemmerer was a member of the Economists National Committee on Monetary Policy, which recommended appointment of a commission to investigate; Ibid., 341–2.

42. Ibid., 386.

43. Ibid., 830–1.

44. Ibid., 193–203, 903–6, 933–9. The U.S. Chamber of Commerce also urged that the bill be passed without Title II; Ibid., 597.

45. *New York Times*, 23 March 1935, 5; Senate Committee on Banking and Currency, *Banking Act of 1935: Hearings*, 365–84.

46. Senate Committee on Banking and Currency, *Banking Act of 1935: Hearings*, 280.

47. Ibid., 279–324. Eccles later sent Fletcher a memorandum outlining the changes he proposed in H.R. 7617; letter and memorandum to Fletcher from Eccles, 6 June 1935, Box 13, Eccles Papers.

48. Senate Committee on Banking and Currency, *Banking Act of 1935: Hearings*, 700. See also Hyman, *Eccles*, 441.

49. Senate Committee on Banking and Currency, *Banking Act of 1935: Hearings*, 675–732, 743–76; *New York Times*, 25 May 1935, 21; Ibid., 28 May 1935, 39, 46.

50. Senate Committee on Banking and Currency, *Banking Act of 1935: Hearings*, 940–57; *New York Times*, 4 June 1935, 31; Hyman, *Eccles*, 441.

51. Senate Committee on Banking and Currency, *Banking Act of 1935: Hearings*, 503–9, 922–31, 964–73; *New York Times*, 18 May 1935, 1, 28; Ibid., 4 June 1935, 31; Hyman, *Eccles*, 441. James told Hamlin the bill was "purely socialist;" Hamlin Diary, v. 26, 4 June 1935. Roosevelt had told Morgenthau in March to advocate government ownership of federal reserve bank stock, apparently as a political maneuver to frighten bankers into accepting Title II as the lesser evil. See Blum, *Morgenthau Diaries*, 348; Hamlin Diary, v. 26, 18 May 1935; *New York Times*, 19 May 1935, 5.

52. Senate Committee on Banking and Currency, *Banking Act of 1935: Hearings*, 837.

53. Ibid., 529–93, 833–46; *New York Times*, 21 May 1935, 1, 31; Ibid., 30 May 1935, 1, 10; Lindley, *Federal Advisory Council*, 134–7. Other reserve bank officials who opposed Title II included Governor George Norris of Philadelphia (*New York Times*, 6 June 1935, 31), Harrison and the directors of the New York reserve bank (Memorandum: Meeting of Board of Directors February 7, 1935, Binder 51, Harrison Papers; letter to Glass from Harrison, 19 February 1935, Box 7, Harrison Papers; Memorandum: Meeting of Executive Committee May 13, 1935, Binder 51, Harrison Papers), and Eugene M. Stevens, federal reserve agent of the Chicago bank (letter to Eccles from Stevens, 13 June 1935, Box 16, Eccles Papers).

54. Senate Committee on Banking and Currency, *Banking Act of 1935: Hearings*, 24–69, 99–174, 181–8, 190–1, 238–9, 246, 373, 497, 669, 736, 778, 828–9, 903, 934, 960.

55. Morgenthau Diary, v. 5, 3 May 1935; letter to Fletcher from O'Connnor, 27 April 1935, tray 86, RG 46; *New York Times*, 8 June 1935, 23; Ibid., 12 June 1935, 1; Ibid., 15 June 1935, 21; Ibid., 22 June 1935, 2; Ibid., 27 June 1935, 31; Ibid., 28 June 1935, 31; *Federal Reserve Bulletin*, 21 (July 1935): 472–3. Steagall and the House insisted that the FDIC resolution extend the temporary insurance plan only 60 days instead of one year, as the Senate proposed.

56. *New York Times*, 22 June 1935, 2; Burns, *American Banking Community*, 165; Office Correspondence to Personal Files from Harrison, 15 June 1935, Binder 46, Harrison Papers; memorandum, Summary of the Senate Subcommittee's Substitute for Title II (Print of July 1, 1935), Box 161, RG 82; *Congressional Record*, v. 79, pt. 11: 11840–1, 74th Congress, 1st session.

57. Summary of the Senate Subcommittee's Substitute for Title II, Box 161, RG 82; *Congressional Record*, v. 79, pt. 11: 11840–1, 74th Congress, 1st session.

58. *Congressional Record*, v. 79, pt. 11: 11778, 11826, 11840–1, 74th Congress, 1st session; Summary of the Senate Subcommittee's Substitute for Title II, Box 161, RG 82.

59. Memorandum: Meeting of Executive Committee March 11, 1935, Binder 51, Harrison Papers; *Congressional Record*, v. 79, pt. 11: 11825, 11840–1, 74th Congress, 1st session; Summary of the Senate Subcommittee's Substitute for Title II, Box 161, RG 82.

60. *Congressional Record*, v. 79, pt. 11: 11776–7, 11828–34, 11926–31, 74th Congress, 1st session; Summary of the Senate Subcommittee's Substitute for Title II, Box 161, RG 82; Memorandum: Meeting of Board of Directors February 28, 1935, Binder 51, Harrison Papers; memorandum, Draft of a Bill to Amend Paragraph Seventh, Section 5136, 9 February 1935, Binder 55, Harrison Papers; letter to Harrison from O'Connor, 14 March 1935, Binder 55, Harrison Papers; Memorandum: Meeting of Board of Directors June 13, 1935, Binder 51, Harrison Papers; memorandum, Conversations in Washington, May 24 to May 31, 1935, Binder 46, Harrison Papers.

61. *New York Times*, 2 July 1935, 1, 16; Ibid., 3 July 1935, 1, 29; Ibid., 25 July 1935, 27, 33; Ibid., 26 July 1935, 1, 6; Ibid., 27 July 1935, 1, 6; Burns, *American Banking Community*, 160–1; U.S., Congress, Senate, Committee on Banking and Currency, *Banking Act of 1935: Report to Accompany H.R. 7617*, S. Rept. 1007, 74th

Congress, 1st session, 2 July 1935; *Congressional Record*, v. 79, pt. 11: 11686, 11775–9, 11824–56, 11906–35, 74th Congress, 1st session.

62. *Congressional Record*, v. 79, pt. 11: 11935, 12005, 74th Congress, 1st session; *New York Times*, 28 July 1935, III: 1; Ibid., 30 July 1935, 27; Ibid., 31 July 1935, 10; Ibid., 2 August 1935, 2; Ibid., 15 August 1935, 27; letter to Starring from Norbeck, 1 August 1935, Box 16, Peter Norbeck Papers, Richardson Archives, I.D. Weeks Library, University of South Dakota, Vermillion, S.D.

63. Eccles, *Beckoning Frontiers*, 220; O'Connor Diary, v. 3, 16 August 1935; Hamlin Diary, v. 26, 23 August 1935. See Chapters Three and Five for examples of Wyatt working with Glass.

64. Eccles, *Beckoning Frontiers*, 220–1; Memorandum, Comparison of Title II as Passed by the House and by the Senate, Box 15, Eccles Papers. This memorandum is not the one given to Goldsborough, which listed the provisions in order of importance to Eccles. This memorandum does, however, list every provision of Title II as passed in each house side by side with Eccles's recommendations.

65. *New York Times*, 7 August 1935, 31; Ibid., 17 August 1935, 1, 14; memorandum, Principal Differences between Title I of H.R. 7617 and Title I of the Senate Amendment, attached to letter to Roosevelt from McAdoo, 8 August 1935, President's Personal File 308, FDR Presidential Papers; *Congressional Record*, v. 79, pt. 11: 11834–5, pt. 13: 13688–94, 74th Congress, 1st session. Norbeck may have joined House members in supporting a postponement until 1942 because he was a long-standing supporter of small banks; letter to Larson from Norbeck, 20 August 1935, Box 14, Norbeck Papers. Steagall accepted 1942 because he believed the provision would never take effect; *Congressional Record*, v. 79, pt. 13: 13705, 74th Congress, 1st session. He was right, for Congress repealed it in 1939; Burns, *American Banking Community*, 172.

66. *Congressional Record*, v. 79, pt. 13: 13694–5, 74th Congress, 1st session; *New York Times*, 18 August 1935, III: 1, 6; Comparison of Title II, Box 15, Eccles Papers; Burns, *American Banking Community*, 174; Marc A. Rose, "Money Under New Management," *Today*, 4 (14 September 1935): 8. Morgenthau had no objection to leaving the board as long as the comptroller of the currency did so, too.

67. *Congressional Record*, v. 79, pt. 13: 13694–5, 74th Congress, 1st session; *New York Times*, 18 August 1935, III: 1, 6; Ibid., 21 August 1935, 18; Burns, *American Banking Community*, 174–5; letter to Glass from Coolidge, 30 July 1935, Box 18, RG 56; Interoffice Communication to Morgenthau from Coolidge, 1 August 1935, Box 68, Alphabetical File, Morgenthau Correspondence; Comparison of Title II, Box 15, Eccles Papers; letter to Glass from Jones, 2 August 1935, Box 54, Jesse Holman Jones Papers, Manuscript Division, Library of Congress, Washington, D.C.; letter to Glass from Jones, 15 August 1935, Box 55, Jones Papers. One of the five reserve bank representatives would come from each of the following districts: (1) Boston, New York; (2) Philadelphia, Cleveland; (3) Richmond, Atlanta, Dallas; (4) Chicago, St. Louis; (5) Kansas City, Minneapolis, San Francisco; *New York Times*, 17 August 1935, 14. In 1942 Congress amended this to make it: (1) New York; (2) Boston, Philadelphia, Richmond; (3) Chicago, Cleveland; (4) Atlanta, Dallas, St. Louis; (5) Kansas City, Minneapolis, San Francisco; Benjamin Haggott Beckhart, *Federal Reserve System* (New York: American Institute of Banking, 1972), 43.

68. *Congressional Record*, v. 79, pt. 13: 13694–5, 74th Congress, 1st session; *New York Times*, 18 August 1935, III: 1, 6; Comparison of Title II, Box 15, Eccles Papers; Eccles, *Beckoning Frontiers*, 228; Hyman, *Eccles*, 188.

69. *Congressional Record*, v. 79, pt. 13: 13695–700, 13706, 74th Congress, 1st session; Burns, *American Banking Community*, 170–1; *New York Times*, 13 August 1935, 32; Ibid., 18 August 1935, III: 1, 6; Elliott Roosevelt and Joseph B. Lash, eds., *F.D.R.: His Personal Letters, 1928–1945*, 2 v. (New York: Duell, Sloan, and Pearce, 1950), I: 500; letter to Glass from Jones, 3 August 1935, Box 198, Jones Papers. Many bankers opposed the underwriting provision. See Morgenthau Diary, v. 8, 2 July 1935; *New York Times*, 12 July 1935, 27, 33. Reserve officials were particularly unhappy with the Senate bill's provisions on interlocking directorates. See letter to Glass from Thomas, 6 July 1935, Box 64, Glass Papers; Office Correspondence to Paulger from Crays and Sloan, 8 July 1935, Box 14, Eccles Papers.

70. *Congressional Record*, v. 79, pt. 13: 13603–16, 13655, 13688–711, 74th Congress, 1st session; *New York Times*, 20 August 1935, 1, 14–5; Ibid., 24 August 1935, 19.

71. Apparently, James did not care whether he was reappointed; Hamlin Diary, v. 27, 23 December 1935. Eccles, *Beckoning Frontiers*, 231–2, 236–42, 245, 247; Hamlin Diary, v. 27, 23 January 1935; memorandum for the Secretary from Gaston, [file date] 31 October 1935, Box 103, Alphabetical File, Morgenthau Correspondence; memorandum to Roosevelt from Eccles, 8 February 1936, Box 3, Eccles Papers. Morrison left for Mexico after two months, apparently to avoid a scandal; Eccles, *Beckoning Frontiers*, 246. Davis did not take office in February but a few months later; Eccles, *Beckoning Frontiers*, 247. The Banking Act of 1935 also caused the reserve board to rewrite many regulations and to issue a new one on required reserves, and it forced the reorganization of the FOMC as of March 1, 1936. See *New York Times*, 11 September 1935, 31; Ibid., 28 November 1935, 45; Milton Friedman and Anna Jacobson Schwartz, *A Monetary History of the United States, 1867–1960* (Princeton, N.J.: Princeton University, 1963), 446n.

72. Howard H. Hackley, *Lending Functions of the Federal Reserve Banks: A History* (Washington, D.C.: Board of Governors of the Federal Reserve System, 1973), 112; Lester V. Chandler, *America's Greatest Depression 1929–41* (New York: Harper and Row, 1970), 176.

CHAPTER EIGHT

CONCLUSION AND EPILOGUE

The politics of money and banking are exceedingly complex, and probably for this reason Congress and President Woodrow Wilson agreed in 1913 on an "independent regulatory commission" to oversee banks. This recourse shifted responsibility for decisions from political leaders to "professional" administrators. Progressives assumed that independent experts would be less likely than Congress or the president to give way to constituent pressure.[1]

The Progressives' hope that the Federal Reserve System would remain outside politics proved to be unfounded. Only so long as the system kept a careful watch on the opinions of the administration and key members of Congress could it pursue its own goals. Although the reserve system usually had some latitude in determining monetary policy, it had to remain sensitive to the preferences of the president and Congress.[2] The system's awareness of this became acute during the first two years of the New Deal, and the legislation of the 1930s did not change the policy-making environment. Whenever reserve officials felt threatened, they tried to protect the system by using expertise in monetary matters, unparalleled access to statistics, and contacts with members of Congress, officials of the executive branch, and outside authorities on money and banking.[3]

The reserve system responded ineffectively in 1930–31 to the decline of the money supply and the acceleration of bank failures. At the outset reserve officials promoted easy money, defined as low interest rates, purchasing moderate quantities of government securities. Bankers sought liquidity, so that loans and investments declined by $1.25 billion in the first year after the stock market crash and continued to contract for months thereafter. From October 1929 to March 1931 currency and bank deposits decreased 3–4%. The money supply fell another 12% between August 1931 and January 1932. At the same time unemployment, hoarding of currency, bank failures, and bankruptcies increased, while prices of stocks, bonds, and commodities fell. The system failed to respond to the falling money supply because interest rates remained low and officials assumed that banks had ample funds to lend and invest. Actually, the level of rates reflected bankers' willingness to lend only to the safest borrowers. Everyone else had difficulty obtaining loans, so the real interest rate was quite high.[4]

President Herbert Hoover's fiscal policy compounded such economic problems. The Treasury could have pumped money into the economy by borrowing to pay for relief and more public works if Hoover had not believed balancing the budget more important than large-scale government spending. Congress agreed with the president, for it passed a law in June 1932 that raised income tax rates.[5]

Hoover's conservative response to economic problems provided too little aid to prevent the closing of thousands of banks. In December 1931 he recommended that Congress revise eligibility provisions of the Federal Reserve Act and establish the Reconstruction Finance Corporation to lend to banks, insurance companies, and railroads. Two little-used paragraphs of the Glass–Steagall Act of 1932 amended the discount clause of the reserve act to permit emergency borrowing by members. This act also added an important section making government securities acceptable collateral for issues of federal reserve notes, which allowed the open market committee to purchase $1 billion of government securities over the next months. Congress gave the RFC authority to assist financial institutions, but loans had to be fully secured by marketable collateral, which limited the agency's ability to help failing banks.[6] Hoover signed the Emergency Relief and Construction Act of 1932 with its provisions permitting direct loans by reserve banks to individuals, partnerships, and corporations. Unfortunately, reserve officials failed to make such loans to member or nonmember banks and did not help many businesses either. The Home Owners Loan Act aided holders of home mortgages, but its section authorizing larger issues of national bank notes did nothing to expand the total supply of money.[7] The RFC and the Chicago reserve bank did prevent a collapse of Chicago banks, suggesting that the legislation of 1932 may have forestalled a nationwide bank crash. Still, more than 1,000 banks failed that year. Hoover had done too little to solve the extraordinary problems of the depression, and the election of 1932 proved that most voters had no faith in his policies.[8]

Americans had little idea what Franklin D. Roosevelt would do as president, and such uncertainty along with the already weak economy produced panic on a national scale early in 1933. Historians have noted the lack of cooperation between the incoming and outgoing presidents. Hoover tried to commit Roosevelt to balancing the budget and preserving the gold standard, while the latter was not persuaded that such policies would aid recovery. Still, when Hoover considered declaring a national bank holiday if the president-elect would promise not to repudiate the action, Roosevelt refused to reassure Hoover.[9] Both men deserve criticism for their inability to put aside partisan differences during a national crisis.

However, the federal reserve deserves the greatest blame for the collapse of 1933. The banking crisis was possible because of the system's accumulated errors and would not have occurred had officials understood the significance of a declining money supply. District banks should have lent freely to sound banks, and the open market committee should have bought large amounts of government securities during 1930–31 to offset the decline of bank deposits. Instead, reserve efforts were half-hearted because interest rates were falling and money seemed plentiful.[10] In the autumn of 1931, the system acted in the traditional way to protect the gold standard, raising the discount rate and selling government securities. The result was a devastation of bank reserves and an end to a mild recovery. When the Open Market Policy Conference finally did begin large purchases of government securities in 1932, many officials believed the policy would do little good unless banks made new loans and investments with the extra reserves provided by the purchases, and the OMPC mistakenly halted purchases when member banks began to accumulate substantial excess reserves.[11] Another error came in January 1933, when officials incorrectly assumed that currency would return to banks as usual after Christmas and the public instead hoarded money. A critical situation had developed by mid-February 1933, when the system refused to use large-scale open market operations to assist banks, a policy that might have prevented the collapse of early March.[12]

The irony of the reserve's failure to prevent disaster was that the board subsequently received increased authority and the responsibility of encouraging economic stability. Although most of the machinery for influencing the money supply—controlling discount rates and conducting open market operations—was in place before 1930, the New Deal centralized authority to use these powers in the reserve board. In

1930 the system was decentralized with authority over discount rates and open market operations lodged in the 12 reserve banks. The board could approve or disapprove a decision to change discount rates or to purchase or sell government securities, but whether it could force district banks to alter discount rates or conduct open market operations against their will was legally questionable. Decentralization of system authority promoted inaction and delay in reaching decisions, and it permitted occasional policy confrontations between reserve banks and the board. This was a problem that Congress needed to address, and in 1935 the board's new governor, Marriner S. Eccles, persuaded Roosevelt and Congress to centralize control of reserve policies in the new Board of Governors and in the Federal Open Market Committee, the latter consisting of the seven board governors and five representatives from district banks. During the 1930s the board also received two new monetary powers—to alter member bank reserve requirements and to set margins for borrowing on corporate securities. Since 1935 the board has dominated the system.[13]

The board's chairman is now one of the most powerful men in the United States, but such authority did not develop quickly. As a result of the Gold Reserve Act of 1934, the board was unable to control the money supply during the last half of the 1930s, when the Treasury used its stabilization fund to purchase large imports of gold at $35 an ounce. During World War II the system pegged interest rates on government securities, an arrangement that continued until 1951. Since then the board and its chairman have pursued policies while being sensitive to but not dominated by the Treasury or president.[14]

Banking legislation did show some continuity between the Hoover and Roosevelt administrations. Congress steadily broadened the lending power of reserve banks. When the stock market crashed in 1929, district banks could make loans only to member banks using as collateral short-term commercial paper or government securities. These provisions limited the system's ability to be a lender of last resort for commercial banks during 1930–31. Hoover proposed broadening eligibility, which occurred with the Glass–Steagall Act of 1932. Although little used, Section 10(a) authorized district banks to make emergency unsecured advances to groups of five or more member banks that lacked eligible collateral, and Section 10(b) gave district banks temporary power to make secured advances at penalty rates to individual members in exceptional circumstances. As mentioned, the Emergency Relief and Construction Act of 1932 permitted reserve banks to make loans directly to individuals, partnerships, or corporations in exigent circumstances. The movement toward wider reserve lending power continued with the Emergency Banking Act of 1933, which authorized district banks to make 90-day loans secured by government bonds to individuals, partnerships, or corporations. The Robinson amendment to that act allowed nonmember banks to discount paper at reserve banks for a limited time. The Banking Act of 1933 extended the period, from 15 to 90 days, for member bank advances on government securities. The Industrial Loan Act of 1934 authorized district banks to lend to businesses and corporations unable to obtain funds from other financial institutions. Finally, the Banking Act of 1935 made Section 10(b) a permanent part of the reserve act and permitted loans on any satisfactory collateral.[15]

Expansion of reserve banks' lending authority broke the connection between commercial paper and reserve credit that appeared in the original reserve act, ending a long-standing connection to the real bills fallacy. Founders of the system, including Carter Glass (D–VA), had envisioned district banks passively accommodating the needs of commerce and trade. Senator Glass removed a mandate from the Banking Act of 1935 that would have made explicit the system's duty to act countercyclically, which meant that the accommodation of business and commerce remained the system's policy guide. Still, since 1951 the reserve has attempted to control the supply of money on a short-term basis so as to keep the economy healthy in the long run, which usually has meant "leaning against the wind." Eccles had proposed the countercyclical mandate and actually had triumphed over Glass in spite of the terms of the act of 1935. Congress formally changed the reserve's mandate in 1977, directing the system to sustain growth of monetary aggregates by maintaining economic potential to increase long-term production and by promoting maximum employment, stable prices, and moderate long-term interest rates.[16]

New Deal banking reforms continued some Progressive traditions. President Wilson had relied upon such regulatory bodies as the reserve system and the Federal Trade Commission to control sectors of the economy. Roosevelt strengthened the reserve board and added the Securities and Exchange Commission to regulate the issue and sale of corporate stocks and bonds. Both Progressives and New Dealers allowed the proliferation of bank regulatory agencies, for Congress imposed the reserve system on top of the existing dual banking structure in 1913, and establishment of the Federal Deposit Insurance

Corporation in 1933 further confused the situation. Federal authority over state financial institutions had begun with the reserve system and increased in the 1930s because most state banks joined the FDIC and because the reserve board received authority to set margin requirements on securities transactions for all banks and to regulate member bank holding companies.[17]

The reserve act passed by Progressives and financial legislation enacted during the New Deal emphasized the public nature of monetary policy and banking. The Emergency Banking Act of 1933 asserted executive control over reopening banks and over gold. The Banking Act of 1933 placed such nonmarket controls on bank operations as the prohibition of interest payments on demand deposits and regulation of interest rates on time deposits, which Glass had advocated to preserve the safety of banks by reducing risk. This act also established the FDIC to protect the public's deposits. Both the Thomas Amendment to the Agricultural Adjustment Act of 1933 and the Gold Reserve Act of 1934 assumed that the government should manipulate currency and public credit if such actions would promote recovery. The Banking Act of 1935 emphasized that control of the money supply should be held by a board chosen by the president and confirmed by the Senate rather than one under the control of regional authorities.[18]

Historians have debated whether there were two New Deals.[19] This study reveals little perceptible difference in FDR's beliefs about banking and money in 1933 and 1935. From the beginning he emphasized the public nature of money and the banking system, and he dominated decisions about monetary policy. He encouraged Glass to separate commercial from investment banking in 1933 and opposed permitting banks to underwrite corporate securities in 1935. Throughout the period he used the RFC to aid individual banks and to increase the capital of financial institutions. The one program about which he changed his mind was the FDIC. He opposed a guaranty of bank deposits until he recognized its tremendous public support. After the FDIC began operation in 1934, he became one of its strongest supporters.[20]

Roosevelt was a consummate politician who sought to occupy the political center. The New Deal was not a consistent economic program but a balancing act. FDR's desire to pursue relief, reform, and recovery was always tempered by a sense of the politically possible. Programs that were good politics were not necessarily good economics, as the gold buying plan of 1933 demonstrated. Roosevelt succeeded in saving American capitalism through relief and reform, although recovery took years.[21]

Senator Glass correctly identified two problems—limits on branch banking and decentralization of banking systems—that he was unable to remedy because of opposition from unit bankers. The Banking Act of 1933 permitted national banks to establish branches only to the extent allowed by state law, making state boundaries the ultimate geographic extension for branching. Since 1933 state legislatures have generally expanded the areas in which banks may have branches, gradually accomplishing Glass's desire to weed out small unit banks and permit the growth of healthy branch banks.[22]

In spite of higher rates of failure since 1980, some large banks now want the ability to operate nationwide, since federal geographical constraints apply only to commercial banks and not to such competitors for depositors' money as securities firms and insurance companies. Congress would be wise to promote interstate banking because small unit banks are more likely to fail due to nonperforming loans than are large institutions, but in spite of urging from the Bush administration, the House and Senate have not agreed to override state laws. Fortunately, in recent years many states have permitted acquisition of institutions by banks in other states, often on a regional or reciprocal basis, and recently healthy savings and loans have received authority to branch across state lines.[23]

Glass favored unification of the state and national banking systems through membership in the reserve system because of regulatory overlap and confusion, which existed even before the addition of the FDIC in 1933. States examined state banks, the comptroller of the currency regulated national banks, and reserve officials could examine any member bank. After 1933 the FDIC could examine insured banks that were not members of the reserve system, and later the agency received authority to regulate any insured bank. State laws were often more lax than federal law, and the possibility remained that state and federal authorities might relax laws to compete in granting bank charters. Deregulation of banks since 1980 has unfortunately done nothing to untangle the "crazy quilt" of regulatory agencies. Today a holding company may own a combination of national, state member, and state nonmember banks plus a thrift and face three examining authorities. As states have become more willing to permit interstate banking—either through branches or bank holding companies—regulatory overlap has worsened. However, in 1980

Congress did require all banks and thrifts to keep reserves with the federal reserve banks to improve the system's control over monetary policy.[24]

Complicating the regulatory situation since 1980 have been corporations that own banking services and yet avoid reserve board regulation as bank holding companies. The Bank Holding Company Act of 1956 as amended in 1970 defined a bank as an institution making commercial loans and accepting demand deposits. When in 1982 Congress expanded the power of federal savings and loan associations, it exempted those institutions from this definition. This left two avenues for corporations such as Sears, Roebuck and Company, J.C. Penney, Gulf & Western, and Prudential–Bache to acquire banking affiliates without becoming bank holding companies under the law—purchase of a savings and loan, or establishment of a bank that either made commercial loans or accepted demand deposits (but not both). Known as limited-service banks or nonbank banks, the latter institutions had to be chartered by a state or the comptroller of the currency. In 1986 the Supreme Court ruled that limited-service banks, which the reserve board had opposed, were legal and that the board had no regulatory control over them. Congress responded with legislation the following year that banned the chartering of new limited-service banks and limited the growth of existing ones to 7% a year. This prevented new nonbank corporations from entering into competition with bank holding companies, but Sears and other nonbank firms already owned savings and loans or limited-service banks. The law of 1987 also prohibited such bank holding companies as Citicorp from expanding nationally through limited-service banks.[25]

Suggestions for rearranging regulatory authority have appeared since 1935, usually involving a combination of federal agencies. The reform bill proposed by the Bush administration in 1991 would have reduced the number of regulators with a Federal Banking Agency responsible for all nationally chartered banks and thrifts, and the reserve system overseeing state banks. Under that plan the FDIC would have no regulatory duties, focusing solely on handling insolvent institutions. But this plan was not adopted by Congress. Rationalization of regulatory authority would aid the banks, but given the reluctance of all organizations to relinquish power, any bill reorganizing bank regulatory agencies must gain broad support within the administration and among bankers before Congress will act. In fact, so far only one change has occurred. In 1989 the collapse of the Federal Savings and

Loan Insurance Corporation prompted Congress to eliminate it, giving the FDIC its deposit insurance responsibilities. The Federal Home Loan Bank Board, which operated the FSLIC as well as regulating savings and loan associations, was eliminated, with its regulatory functions passing to the new Office of Thrift Supervision.[26]

Although encouraging regulatory overlap, establishment of the FDIC did promote the best interests of small and poorly informed depositors. By removing the danger of depositor runs on sound banks, the FDIC eliminated one cause of failures and panics. And more than 90% of commercial banks have been members of the FDIC since 1934, providing some unification to American banking. The FDIC succeeded because it tried to prevent failures by supervising closely problem banks and merging endangered institutions with strong ones, but the agency has never had to withstand a major depression.[27]

Rapid changes in interest rates after 1970 and deregulation after 1980 increased uncertainty in financial markets, and suspensions rose. In 1991, it was necessary for Congress to provide additional money to the FDIC for the first time in its history, and the FDIC may need additional help in the future. Many economists have argued that the problems with deposit insurance related to the structure of FDIC assessments, which had been based on total deposits and created a "moral hazard." A bank had no incentive to avoid taking risks, and in the highly competitive markets of the 1980s many banks acquired riskier assets. To avoid this moral hazard, economists recommended the use of risk-based premiums, which Congress adopted as part of the 1991 act (to begin by 1994). Many of the same analysts also suggested the use of market-based accounting. Currently, banks and thrifts are allowed to carry assets on their books at the purchase price until the asset is liquidated. As a result, market gains or losses on the asset are not recorded unless the asset is sold, which can cause problems for an institution's solvency if many assets' market prices have deteriorated without the institution increasing capital or setting aside adequate funds to cover the losses. Recently the FDIC announced that starting in January 1993 premiums would be based on the riskiness of a bank as determined by its portfolio and especially its capital, which would place the burden on institutions most likely to fail. However, the government has not adopted market-value accounting, perhaps because the economic situation is uncertain.[28]

Another recommendation that analysts have made is to increase the capital of insured institutions. This suggestion applied especially to thrifts, which had had capital ratios much lower than those of banks. The 1989 law that established the Office of Thrift Supervision called for thrifts to meet the same capital requirements as banks by 1995. This is significant because capital is an important hedge against losses. Generally the institutions with the highest capital to asset ratios are the healthiest ones, the ones least likely to fail. Thus, some economists suggested that deposit insurance be adjusted according to capital as well as portfolio risk. The Bush administration reform plan of 1991 called for banks to be divided into groups on the basis of their capital. Those banks with adequate capital would be regulated much as they had been in the past. Those with more than adequate capital would have many restrictions removed. Those with less than adequate capital would be closely monitored and required to follow plans to restore capital. The Bush plan also permitted regulators to close a bank when its capital fell to 2% of assets or less. This would permit closure before depositors were put at risk and would make it less likely that the FDIC would have to absorb a loss when a bank failed. It would also help to remove the moral hazard problem previously associated with deposit insurance. This plan was adopted by Congress in November 1991. However, because the new law did not require financial institutions to use market-value accounting, it gave regulators enormous discretion concerning when to write down the book value of a bank's assets and, thus, discretion over which capital category a bank would fall into. This discretion could be used either to close banks prematurely or to close them too late to avoid a loss to the FDIC. Thus, the actual effects of the law for maintaining the solvency of banks and the FDIC will depend greatly on the regulators.[29]

Broadening eligibility provisions of the reserve act and centralizing system authority in the Board of Governors has aided the long-term goal of moderating economic fluctuations. Congress gradually relaxed eligibility requirements, which allowed the system to become a true lender of last resort in time of depression or panic. The Wall Street Crash of 1987 demonstrated again the system's flexibility to respond to and affect financial markets. During the stock market panic on October 19, 1987, specialists and brokers needed to borrow money, which New York banks were reluctant to lend until the New York reserve bank assured them that the system would provide the funds. Of course, the president of the New York reserve acted with the backing of Chairman Alan Greenspan and the Board of Governors, demonstrating the coordination and centralization that has existed within the system since 1935.[30]

In the Banking Act of 1933 Congress, led by Glass and Representative Henry B. Steagall (D–ALA), misread events after 1920 and consequently imposed many unnecessary controls on member banks. The Senate and House Banking and Currency Committees did not conduct detailed statistical studies of bank problems, relying instead on testimony from bankers, economists, and government officials. Such evidence was impressionistic and at times misleading. Bankers complained about excessive interest rate competition during the 1920s, so Glass and Steagall supported a limit on rates for time deposits and a prohibition on interest payments on demand deposits. The Pecora hearings of 1933 revealed that a few major banks with investment affiliates had been involved in unwise conflicts of interest. Clearly regulation was necessary to prevent a recurrence of similar conflicts, but Congress went much further—entirely separating commercial from investment banking.[31]

Since the 1960s commercial bankers have found themselves competing for deposits with such institutions as credit unions, savings and loan associations, mutual savings banks and such corporations as Sears, Roebuck and Company and Prudential Insurance. Congress responded to this situation with the Depository Institutions Deregulation and Monetary Control Act of 1980, which confirmed a trend toward homogenized financial services by classifying banks, trust companies, savings and loan associations, savings banks, and credit unions as depository institutions. The act allowed any institution having transaction accounts (demand deposits subject to check) or having corporate time deposits to borrow from the reserve on the same basis as members. Such institutions had to maintain a 12% reserve with a district bank, and the law limited the board's authority to alter member reserve requirements. DIDMCA also provided for gradual removal of interest rate controls on time deposits. Depository institutions now pay a market rate of interest on most deposits, a rate sensitive to changes in monetary policy. However, the act passed by Congress in 1991 allows regulators to limit the interest rates that undercapitalized banks and thrifts can pay on deposits. In the spring of 1992, the FDIC acted to impose such limits on weaker banks starting June 16.[32]

Some bankers now wish to offer services that the Banking Act of 1933 forbade, particularly underwriting and sale of insurance and securities. The law of 1933 has prevented integration of the country's financial markets and reduced the ability of banks to compete in such markets, which has led nonbank financial institutions to offer certificates of deposit and money market accounts. The act probably inhibited competition abroad, where such restrictions have never applied and where corporate customers may rely on a single bank as a depository for surplus cash and as an issuer or underwriter of stocks and bonds.[33]

Economists agree with bankers that the restrictions separating commercial from investment banking serve no purpose. In addition to inhibiting economic efficiency, the law does nothing to contribute to the safety of banks. Plus there are loopholes in the law that have allowed banks to move more and more into the securities business at the same time that investment banks have begun to offer "near monies" such as cash management accounts. One major loophole allows insured nonmember banks to establish securities affiliates. This occurred because Glass had assumed that all insured banks would eventually join the reserve system, as the Banking Act of 1933 required. When Congress subsequently repealed that requirement, it neglected to close the securities loophole. Also the law deliberately allowed banks to underwrite federal, state, and municipal bonds, and it failed to forbid banks to underwrite corporate securities issued abroad. Until 1987 another loophole related to the ability of securities firms to charter a limited-service bank. Finally, banks have been testing the limits of the provisions in the 1933 law that prohibit member banks from being affiliated with any firm engaged principally in the securities business.[34]

Throughout the 1980s, major bank holding companies have appealed to the Federal Reserve Board and the comptroller of the currency to be allowed to enter new lines of operation. Because the 1933 law allowed banks to execute securities transactions for customers, the board ruled that bank holding companies could legally own discount brokerages, which offer no investment advice to customers. Later, the comptroller of the currency said that banks could offer such discount brokerage services and that the banks' brokerages would not be subject to geographical restrictions. Subsequently either the board or the comptroller of the currency has permitted banks or their holding company affiliates to offer mutual funds to IRA customers, to underwrite and sell commercial paper, to underwrite and sell mortgage-backed securities, to offer investment advice and brokerage services to institutional or wealthy clients, to underwrite and sell securities backed by consumer debt, to underwrite municipal revenue bonds, to sell corporate bonds, and to trade corporate stocks. Most of these activities can only be carried out by affiliates not principally engaged in the securities business or by affiliates located overseas. Many of these decisions were challenged by investment bankers in the courts, but the courts have been inclined to uphold the regulators' decisions.[35]

Another major battleground has emerged over the issue of insurance underwriting and sale. Until recently, national banks located in small towns had the authority to sell insurance under a 1916 law. Selling insurance is a low-risk business requiring little capital and enhancing a bank's profits, and in 1986 the comptroller of the currency decided to interpret the 1916 law so as to permit banks located in towns of less than 5,000 to sell insurance anywhere in the country. This interpretation was challenged by the Independent Insurance Agents of America. In February 1992 a federal appeals court struck down all insurance sales under this law. Looking at the history of the 1916 act, the court decided that the authority to sell insurance had been repealed by Congress when the law was amended in 1918. Small bankers continue to offer insurance pending appeal to the Supreme Court, but regardless of the outcome of the case, small bankers want to retain this business, and many larger national banks would like to receive the same privilege. Some states permit state banks to sell insurance within state lines, and the Federal Reserve Board has allowed national banks in those states to do so also. In 1990 Delaware passed a law that allowed banks chartered there to sell and underwrite insurance nationwide. The board challenged this law because it allowed banks rather than bank holding companies to sell the insurance and because it permitted underwriting as well as sale, but this time the courts upheld the state. Insurance agents are adamantly opposed to allowing bankers into the insurance business, and their lobbyists are very active on Capitol Hill.[36]

Some members of Congress, the Bush administration, and reserve officials agree that the Banking Act of 1933 needs revision. However, opposition from investment bankers and insurance agents has prevented congressional action. The latest proposal for change came from President George Bush in 1991. It would have abolished completely the distinction between investment and commercial banking for well capitalized banks by permitting bank holding companies to operate securities and mutual fund affiliates. It would also have allowed such holding companies to operate insurance affiliates. In addition, the holding companies themselves could be owned by commercial, industrial, or other financial corporations. To protect bank safety the insurance, mutual fund, and securities affiliates would be subject to strict regulation. The proposal also erected so-called funding and disclosure "fire walls" between a bank and its securities affiliate. Congress did not act on this proposal last year, and even though it has been reintroduced, Congress is not likely to approve it this year either.[37] While it seems likely that such a proposal will eventually be enacted, for now the banks will have to be content to chip away at the edges of the restrictions on their operations.

The policy-making environment of the Federal Reserve System continues much the same now as it was in the 1930s. In this century banking regulation has been a difficult issue for Congress because of its complexity, and bank measures have usually given regulators wide latitude. Congress has determined the wording of legislation, yet interest groups and regulatory agencies have chosen the topics covered. The reserve system can never be indifferent to the desires of bankers, other regulators, the president, and Congress, without risking its own "independence." Reserve officials therefore have become skilled at the politics of money and banking. The "independence" of the system remains because of its concern for politics. During the New Deal a political sixth sense kept the system from being destroyed as a result of its previous ineptitude. Once Roosevelt realized he could trust reserve officials to follow his policies, even when they did not agree, he had no desire to replace the system but only to strengthen it. The Banking Act of 1935 was a monument to his commitment.

NOTES

1. Francis E. Rourke, *Bureaucracy, Politics, and Public Policy*, 3d ed. (Boston: Little, Brown, 1984), 43; John T. Woolley, *Monetary Politics: The Federal Reserve and the Politics of Monetary Policy* (New York: Cambridge University, 1984), 40; Donald F. Kettl, *Leadership at the Fed* (New Haven, Conn.: Yale University, 1986), 3, 22–3.

2. For more about reserve system policy-making, see Elmus R. Wicker, *Federal Reserve Monetary Policy, 1917-1933* (New York: Random House, 1966); Milton Friedman and Anna Jacobson Schwartz, *A Monetary History of the United States, 1867–1960* (Princeton, N.J.: Princeton University, 1963); Woolley, *Monetary Politics*; and Kettl, *Leadership at the Fed*.

3. Woolley, *Monetary Politics*, 129–31; James O. Freedman, "Legislative Delegation to Regulatory Agencies," *Proceedings of the Academy of Political Science*, 34, 2 (1981): 82–5.

4. Karl R. Bopp, "Three Decades of Federal Reserve Policy," *Postwar Economic Studies*, 8 (November 1947): 13–4; Wicker, *Federal Reserve*, 150–3, 163–7; Minutes of Meeting of the Open Market Policy Committee, January 21, 1931, Box 69, General Records of the Department of the Treasury, Office of the Secretary, General Correspondence 1917–32, Record Group 56, National Archives, Washington, D.C.; Karl Brunner and Allan H. Meltzer, "What Did We Learn from the Monetary Experience of the United States in the Great Depression?" *Canadian Journal of Economics*, 1 (May 1968): 347–8; *Federal Reserve Bulletin*, 17 (February 1931): 53–5; Federal Reserve Board, *Eighteenth Annual Report Covering Operations for the Year 1931* (Washington, D.C.: U.S. Government Printing Office, 1932), 4–5; Christian Saint-Etienne, *The Great Depression, 1929–1938: Lessons for the 1980s* (Stanford, Cal.: Hoover Institution, 1984), 20; Friedman and Schwartz, *Monetary History*, 315–9; Ben S. Bernanke, "Nonmonetary Effects of the Financial Crisis in the Propagation of the Great Depression," *American Economic Review*, 73 (June 1983): 266.

5. Herbert Stein, *The Fiscal Revolution in America* (Chicago: University of Chicago, 1969), 3–16; William E. Leuchtenburg, *The Perils of Prosperity, 1914–32* (Chicago: University of Chicago, 1958), 254–5; Stanley Lebergott, *The Americans: An Economic Record* (New York: W.W. Norton, 1984), 448–9, 452.

6. Herbert Clark Hoover, *The State Papers and Other Public Writings of Herbert Hoover*, W.S. Myers, ed., 2 v. (New York: Doubleday, 1934), II: 46–51; Office Correspondence to Boatwright from Van Fossen, 27 March 1934, Box 85, Records of the Federal Reserve System, Subject File, 1914–54, Record Group 82, National Archives, Washington, D.C.; confidential memoranda, 24 March 1934, Box 360, Charles Sumner Hamlin Papers, Manuscript Division, Library of Congress, Washington, D.C.; Schroeder Boulton, "Open-Market Policy of the Federal Reserve in 1932," *The Banking Situation: American Post-War Problems and Developments*, H. Parker Willis and John M. Chapman, eds. (New York: Columbia University, 1934), 767–79; James Stuart Olson, *Herbert Hoover and the Reconstruction Finance Corporation, 1931–1933* (Ames: Iowa State University, 1977), 34–41. [All references to RG 82 are to Subject File, 1914–54.]

7. *New York Times*, 17 July 1932, 1, 14; Susan Estabrook Kennedy, *The Banking Crisis of 1933* (Lexington: University of Kentucky, 1973), 49; Federal Reserve Board, *Nineteenth Annual Report Covering Operations for the Year 1932* (Washington, D.C.: U.S. Government Printing Office, 1933), 23.

8. Olson, *Hoover and RFC*, 58–60; "The Financial Situation," *Commercial and Financial Chronicle*, 135 (12 November 1932): 3204–5; Federal Reserve Board, *Nineteenth Annual Report, 1932*, 154; Leuchtenburg, *Perils of Prosperity*, 263–4, 267; Frank Freidel, "Election of 1932," *History of American Presidential Elections, 1789–1968*, Arthur M. Schlesinger, Jr. and Fred L. Israel, eds. (New York: McGraw–Hill, 1971), III: 2731–2, 2738–9, 2806.

9. Albert U. Romasco, *The Politics of Recovery: Roosevelt's New Deal* (New York: Oxford University, 1983), 13–5; William E. Leuchtenburg, *Franklin D. Roosevelt and the New Deal, 1932–1940* (New York: Harper and Row, 1963), 31; Kennedy, *Banking Crisis*, 136–9, 147–9.

10. Anna J. Schwartz, "Discussion: Banking Reform in the 1930s," *Regulatory Change in an Atmosphere of Crisis: Current Implications of the Roosevelt Years*, Gary M. Walton, ed. (New York: Harcourt, Brace, Jovanovich, 1979), 97; Wicker, *Federal Reserve*, 144–58; Brunner and Meltzer, "What Did We Learn," 347–8; Bopp, "Three Decades of Federal Reserve Policy," 13–4.

11. Friedman and Schwartz, *Monetary History*, 315–9, 384–9; Wicker, *Federal Reserve*, 163–84; *Federal Reserve Bulletin*, 17 (November 1931): 603–5; Ibid., 18 (May 1932): 290; Ibid. (June 1932): 350; Ibid. (July 1932): 410–3. Barrie A. Wigmore argues that the reserve was not greatly at fault for not preventing the economic decline of 1929–33; *The Crash and Its Aftermath* (Westport, Conn.: Greenwood, 1985), 550–5. His perspective is part of the continuing debate over whether a more expansionary monetary policy could have prevented a recession from becoming a major depression. This debate may never be resolved. My personal feeling is that a more expansionary policy that put large excess reserves in the hands of member banks could not have hurt and might possibly have helped the economic situation by encouraging more lending and investment by bankers.

12. Lester V. Chandler, *American Monetary Policy, 1928–1941* (New York: Harper and Row, 1971), 217–9; Friedman and Schwartz, *Monetary History*, 389–90; Wicker, *Federal Reserve*, 184–90, 195. However, to the extent that the Panic was caused by a run on the gold dollar, purchases of government securities would not have helped; Barrie A. Wigmore, "Was the Bank Holiday of 1933 Caused by a Run on the Dollar?" *Journal of Economic History*, 47 (September 1987): 739–55.

13. Lester V. Chandler, *America's Greatest Depression 1929–41* (New York: Harper and Row, 1970), 176–7; Woolley, *Monetary Politics*, 41–3; Wicker, *Federal Reserve*, 195. Some economic historians argue that the reforms of the 1930s established a central bank for the first time since the Second Bank of the United States lost its federal charter in 1836. See Jim Potter, *The American Economy between the World Wars* (London: Macmillan, 1974), 149; Major B. Foster, Raymond Rodgers, Jules I. Bogen, and Marcus Nadler, *Money and Banking*, 4th ed. (New York: Prentice-Hall, 1953), 371; Lester V. Chandler and Stephen M. Goldfeld, *The Economics of Money and Banking*, 7th ed. (New York: Harper and Row, 1977), 197.

14. Kettl, *Leadership at the Fed*, 16 ; Chandler, *America's Greatest Depression*, 174–5; Woolley, *Monetary Politics*, 44–6; George S. Eccles, *The Politics of Banking*, Sidney Hyman, ed. (Salt Lake City: University of Utah for the Graduate School of Business, 1982), 110–4.

15. Howard H. Hackley, *Lending Functions of the Federal Reserve Banks: A History* (Washington, D.C.: Board of Governors of the Federal Reserve System, 1973), 84; New York Clearing House Association, *The Federal Reserve Reexamined* (New York: New York Clearing House Association, 1953), 77; Office Correspondence to Boatwright from Van Fossen, 27 March 1934, Box 85, RG 82; confidential memoranda, 24 March 1934, Box 360, Hamlin Papers.

16. Hackley, *Lending Functions*, 84; Woolley, *Monetary Politics*, 46.

17. Jonathan Hughes, "Roots of Regulation: The New Deal," *Regulatory Change*, Walton, ed., 44–7; J.W. Pole and Eugene Meyer, "Extent of Federal Supervision of Banking Today," *Congressional Digest*, 10 (December 1931): 294; Carter H. Golembe and David S. Holland, *Federal Regulation of Banking, 1983–84* (Washington, D.C.: Golembe Associates, 1983), 45.

18. David F. Houston, *Eight Years with Wilson's Cabinet, 1913–1920*, 2 v. (Garden City, N.Y.: Doubleday, Page, 1926), I: 100–2; Memorandum, Recent Banking Legislation, 24 August 1936, Box 76, RG 82.

19. See for example, Elliot A. Rosen, "Roosevelt and the Brains Trust: An Historiographical Overview," *Political Science Quarterly*, 87 (December 1972): 532–8.

20. Memorandum, Recent Banking Legislation, 24 August 1936, Box 76, RG 82; Elmus R. Wicker, "Roosevelt's 1933 Monetary Experiment," *Journal of American History*, 57 (March 1971): 864–6; Chandler, *American Monetary Policy*, 244, 272; *Wall Street Journal*, 30 March 1933, 1–2; Helen M. Burns, *The American Banking Community and New Deal Banking Reforms, 1933–1935* (Westport, Conn.: Greenwood, 1974), 170–1; *New York Times*, 12 April 1933, 1, 3; Kennedy, *Banking Crisis*, 222.

21. Others who agree with this assessment include Robert S. McElvaine, *The Great Depression: America, 1929–1941* (New York: Times Books, 1984), 167–9, 335–7; Raymond Moley, *The First New Deal* (New York: Harcourt, Brace and World, 1966), 4–5; Romasco, *Politics of Recovery*, 4–5; Alonzo L. Hamby, *Liberalism and Its Challengers: FDR to Reagan* (New York: Oxford University, 1985), 31–3.

22. John Douglas Lyle, The United States Senate Career of Carter Glass of Virginia, 1919–1939 (Ph.D. dissertation, University of South Carolina, 1974), 161–2, 247–8, 260; Eugene Nelson White, "The Political Economy of Banking Regulation, 1864–1933," *Journal of Economic History*, 42 (March 1982): 39–40; Kennedy, *Banking Crisis*, 211–2; Golembe and Holland, *Federal Regulation*, 119.

23. Golembe and Holland, *Federal Regulation*, 43–4, 206; Peter S. Rose, *The Changing Structure of American Banking* (New York: Columbia University, 1987), 18–20, 216–36; Frederic S. Mishkin, "An Evaluation of the Treasury Plan for Banking Reform," *Journal of Economic Perspectives*, 6 (Winter 1992): 141–2; *Wall Street Journal*, 13 April 1984, 6; Ibid., 30 April 1984, 5; *New York Times*, 16 December 1986, D10; Ibid., 6 February 1991, A1, D6; Ibid., 2 June 1992, D2; Ibid., 26 June 1992, D2.

24. Lyle, Senate Career of Glass, 189, 302; William G. Shepherd and Clair Wilcox, *Public Policies Toward Business*, 6th ed. (Homewood, Ill.: Richard D. Irwin, 1979), 486–7; Martin Mayer, *The Money Bazaars: Understanding the Banking Revolution Around Us* (New York: E.P. Dutton, 1984), 335–7; Golembe and Holland, *Federal Regulation*, 148–50; Rose, *Changing Structure of Banking*, 23–6, 340–6; Thomas F. Cargill and Gillian G. Garcia, *Financial Deregulation and Monetary Control: Historical Perspective and Impact of the 1980 Act* (Stanford, Cal.: Hoover Institution, 1982), 51–2; George J. Benston and others, *Perspectives on Safe and Sound Banking* (Cambridge, Mass.: MIT, 1986), 283–4. The 1989 act rescuing the savings and loan industry permitted banks to acquire failing thrifts; *Wall Street Journal*, 7 August 1989, A1, A13; *New York Times*, 10 August 1989, A1.

25. Golembe and Holland, *Federal Regulation*, 148–50, 194–7; Rose, *Changing Structure of Banking*, 30–2, 330–4; *New York Times*, 23 January 1986, D1; Ibid., 4 August 1987, IV: 2; Ibid., 5 August 1987, I: 1. In 1982 the Federal Home Loan Bank Board gained authority to permit interstate mergers and acquisitions in situations involving a failing savings and loan association or a savings bank; Golembe and Holland, *Federal Regulation*, 12. This power continued when the Bank Board was reorganized in 1989; *New York Times*, 10 August 1989, A1.

26. *New York Times*, 10 August 1989, A1, D2; Ibid., 6 February 1991, D6; Ibid., 25 November 1991, D3; Ibid., 28 November 1991, A1, D5. The Federal Savings and Loan Insurance Corporation had recurring difficulties prior to 1989. Problems of savings and loans traced directly to rapid changes in interest rates, which produced special difficulties because the institutions held long-term assets and short-term deposits. Since 1980 Congress has authorized savings and loans to acquire assets other than mortgages and to offer transaction accounts. See Golembe and Holland, *Federal Regulation*, 10; Mayer, *Money Bazaars*, 263–83, 338; Lawrence J. White, "Problems of the FSLIC: A Former Policy Maker's View," *Contemporary Policy Issues*, 8 (April 1990): 62–81; Benston and others, *Perspectives on Banking*, 286–8; *New York Times*, 12 June 1988, III: 1, 4. The Resolution Trust Corporation continues the cleanup of insolvent thrifts but claims to be almost finished; *Washington Post National Weekly Edition*, 25–31 May 1992, 31.

27. Kennedy, *Banking Crisis*, 222; Friedman and Schwartz, *Monetary History*, 434; John A. Cochran, *Money, Banking and the Economy*, 3d ed. (New York: Macmillan, 1975), 123; Michael C. Keeley, "Deposit Insurance, Risk, and Market Power in Banking," *American Economic Review*, 80 (December 1990): 1183–1200. Recently economists have begun to question whether deposit insurance was necessary to prevent panics, and they argue that runs on individual weak banks, causing their failure, are unlikely to have serious economic consequences. See Michael D. Bordo, "The Lender of Last Resort: Alternative Views and Historical Experience," *Federal Reserve Bank of Richmond Economic Review*, 76 (January/February 1990): 18–29; William S. Haraf, "Toward a Sound Financial Future," *The Financial Services Revolution: Policy Directions for the Future*, Catherine England and Thomas Huertas, eds. (Boston: Kluwer Academic, 1988): 183–4. I tend to disagree because I believe most depositors are not "rational actors" in the economic realm who can make carefully considered choices between banks based on their risk. There are many economically ignorant people who don't know how to interpret the information on a bank's balance sheet, and even those who can distinguish a well-managed bank from a poorly-managed one don't have the time to read the balance sheets of a half-dozen banks whenever a report is issued. Also, when the economy of a whole region becomes depressed, a major bank failure could trigger a panic if there

were no deposit insurance. Probably the Federal Reserve System, acting as lender of last resort, could shore up the solvent banks and calm the panic within days, but the transactions costs could be huge. At least one economic analyst agrees with me; Robert Kuttner, Op-Ed, *Washington Post National Weekly Edition*, 14–20 January 1991, 29.

28. R. Dan Brumbaugh, Jr. and Robert E. Litan, "Ignoring Economics in Dealing with the Savings and Loan and Commercial Banking Crisis," *Contemporary Policy Issues*, 9 (January 1991): 37–42; Rose, *Changing Structure of Banking*, 392–7; James B. Thomson and Walker F. Todd, "Rethinking and Living With the Limits of Bank Regulation," *Cato Journal*, 9 (Winter 1990): 583, 585–6, 597; Mitchell Berlin, Anthony Saunders, and Gregory F. Udell, "Deposit Insurance Reform: What Are the Issues and What Needs to Be Fixed?" *Journal of Banking and Finance*, 15 (September 1991): 736–9; Benston and others, *Perspectives on Banking*, 225, 304–6; Lawrence J. White, "The Reform of Federal Deposit Insurance," *Journal of Economic Perspectives*, 3 (Fall 1989): 19–22; *New York Times*, 28 November 1991, A1, D5; Ibid., 12 May 1992, D1–2; Ibid., 13 May 1992, A1, D7. There have also been complaints about the FDIC's willingness to pay off deposits larger than $100,000 and to treat some institutions as "too big to fail," and some economists question why accounts need to be insured up to $100,000 when most accounts hold considerably less. See Thomson and Todd, "Rethinking the Limits of Bank Regulation," 589, 595–6; Brumbaugh and Litan, "Ignoring Economics," 42–4; Berlin, Saunders, and Udell, "Deposit Insurance Reform," 745–6; Stephen D. Smith and Larry D. Wall, "Financial Panics, Bank Failures, and the Role of Regulatory Policy," *Federal Reserve Bank of Atlanta Economic Review*, 77 (January/February 1992): 7–8; Edward J. Kane, *The Gathering Crisis in Federal Deposit Insurance* (Cambridge, Mass.: MIT, 1985), 157.

29. John T. Rose, "The Thrift Crisis: Evolution, Resolution, and Reform," *Review of Research in Banking and Finance*, 6 (Spring 1990):14–5; Robert B. Avery and Allen N. Berger, "Risk-Based Capital and Deposit Insurance Reform," *Journal of Banking and Finance*, 15 (September 1991): 849–51; Benston and others, *Perspectives on Banking*, 304–5; Berlin, Saunders, and Udell, "Deposit Insurance Reform," 740–3; Mishkin, "Evaluation of Treasury Plan," 144; Robert L. Hetzel, "Too Big to Fail: Origins, Consequences, and Outlook," *Federal Reserve Bank of Richmond Economic Review*, 77

(November/December 1991): 11, 13. Regulatory forbearance has been a problem in the past; Brumbaugh and Litan, "Ignoring Economics," 44–6. However, the risk-based capital premiums scheduled to take effect in January 1993 may be effective because of compliance with an international accord signed by the U.S. and 11 other nations in 1988 and approved by the Federal Reserve Board. The agreement requires that different minimum capital standards be held for different categories of assets based on their perceived riskiness, with total capital equal to 8% of total risk-weighted assets. In essence this is a form of portfolio management designed to encourage banks to hold less risky assets in order to lower capital requirements. See *New York Times*, 12 July 1988, D1; Ibid., 4 August 1988, D2; Avery and Berger, "Risk-Based Capital," 847–74. This agreement has been implemented in the U.S. by the FDIC, which has been requiring banks to use these capital standards since June 16, 1992. The FDIC now divides banks and thrifts into three categories: well capitalized (having a more than 10% risk-adjusted capital to asset ratio); adequately capitalized (having 8–10% capital); and undercapitalized (having less than 8% capital); *New York Times*, 21 May 1992, A1, D7. The FDIC is now preparing regulations to implement the curbs on the activities of undercapitalized banks authorized by the 1991 law; *New York Times*, 24 June 1992, D6.

30. *Wall Street Journal*, 20 November 1987, 1, 20.

31. Homer Jones, "Banking Reform in the 1930s," *Regulatory Change*, Walton, ed., 81, 85–7; Charles F. Haywood and Charles M. Linke, *The Regulation of Deposit Interest Rates* (Chicago: Association of Reserve City Bankers, 1968), 16–25; John J. Holland, Jr. "The Misinterpretation of the Causes of the Banking Collapse of 1933 and its Retarding Influence on Commercial Banking Innovation," *Bank Structure and Competition: Proceedings of a Conference* (Chicago: Federal Reserve Bank of Chicago, 1975), 97–101; Lawrence S. Ritter and William L. Silber, *Principles of Money, Banking, and Financial Markets*, 3d ed. (New York: Basic Books, 1980), 122.

32. Eccles, *Politics of Banking*, 56, 115–6, 148–50, 255–62; Golembe and Holland, *Federal Regulation*, 11, 42, 196–7; Mayer, *Money Bazaars*, 256–60, 329; *Washington Post National Weekly Edition*, 31 March 1986, 20; *New York Times*, 21 May 1992, A1, D7. The board only used changes in required reserves aggressively in 1936–37 when it raised the requirement to the maximum possible level and contributed to the "Roosevelt Recession" of 1937; Jones, "Banking

Reform in the 1930s," 85. With five affirmative votes, the board may still impose additional reserves on transaction accounts for up to 180 days; Eccles, *Politics of Banking*, 256–7.

33. *Wall Street Journal*, 23 March 1984, 1, 14; Ibid., 29 December 1986, 1, 15; George D. Green, "The Economic Impact of the Stock Market Boom and Crash of 1929," *Consumer Spending and Monetary Policy: The Linkages*, George D. Green, ed. (Boston: Federal Reserve Bank of Boston, 1971), 206; Golembe and Holland, *Federal Regulation*, 80–3; "Merchant Banking: Is the U.S. Ready for It?" *Business Week* (19 April 1976): 54–7, 60, 64; Richard Sylla, "Monetary Innovation in America," *Journal of Economic History*, 42 (March 1982): 30; *New York Times*, 31 March 1986, D1, D7; Ibid., 16 April 1986, D1, D5; Ibid., 5 May 1987, D8; Ibid., 16 November 1987, D1, D3; *Washington Post National Weekly Edition*, 13–19 May 1991, 2, 5, 22, 33, 40; Ibid., 28 October–3 November 1991, 16.

34. Rose, *Changing Structure of Banking*, 332–4; Eugene Nelson White, "Before the Glass–Steagall Act: An Analysis of the Investment Banking Activities of National Banks," *Explorations in Economic History*, 23 (January 1986): 35–55; Robert E. Litan, "Reuniting Investment and Commercial Banking," *Financial Services Revolution*, England and Huertas, eds., 269–87; Thomas A. Pugel and Lawrence J. White, "An Analysis of the Competitive Effects of Allowing Commercial Bank Affiliates to Underwrite Corporate Securities," *Deregulating Wall Street: Commercial Bank Penetration of the Corporate Securities Market*, Ingo Walter, ed. (New York: John Wiley and Sons, 1985): 93–139; Anthony Saunders, "Conflicts of Interest: An Economic View," *Deregulating Wall Street*, Walter, ed., 207–30; Edward J. Kelly, III, "Conflicts of Interest: A Legal View," *Deregulating Wall Street*, Walter, ed., 231–54; Elijah Brewer, III, "Relationship Between Bank Holding Company Risk and Nonbank Activity," *Journal of Economics and Business*, 41 (November 1989): 337–53. The Garn–St. Germain Act of 1982 limits significantly interaction between a bank and its affiliates; Rose, *Changing Structure of Banking*, 282.

35. Jonathan R. Macey, "Special Interest Groups Legislation and the Judicial Function: The Dilemma of Glass–Steagall," *Emory Law Journal*, 33 (Winter 1984): 23–31; *New York Times*, 16 April 1986, D5; Ibid., 10 July 1986, D19; Ibid., 15 January 1987, D1, D17; Ibid., 23 June 1987, A1, D6; Ibid., 16 July 1987, D15; Ibid., 12 January

1988, D6; Ibid., 9 February 1988, D1, D17; Ibid., 14 June 1988, A1, D6; Ibid., 19 January 1989, A1, D1; Ibid., 14 September 1989, D8; Ibid., 11 April 1990, D3; Ibid., 12 June 1990, D14; Ibid., 21 September 1990, A1, D4; Ibid., 5 April 1991, D2.

36. *New York Times*, 29 March 1988, B6; Ibid., 31 May 1990, D1, D17; Ibid., 6 September 1990, D2; Ibid., 11 June 1991, D1, D11; Ibid., 5 November 1991, D18; Ibid., 9 February 1992, I: 31; *Wall Street Journal*, 11 June 1991, A3; *Washington Post National Weekly Edition*, 14–20 January 1991, 21.

37. *New York Times*, 5 May 1987, D8; Ibid., 10 November 1987, D1, D24; Ibid., 31 March 1988, A1, D8; Ibid., 15 September 1988, D1; Ibid., 5 April 1990, D7; Ibid., 26 September 1990, D1–2; Ibid., 1 December 1990, 1, 37; Ibid., 31 January 1991, D6; Ibid., 6 February 1991, A1, D6; Ibid., 20 November 1991, D1, D24; Ibid., 22 November 1991, D1–2; Ibid., 7 February 1992, D1, D6.

BIBLIOGRAPHY

PRIMARY SOURCES

Ballantine, Arthur Atwood. Papers. Herbert Hoover Presidential Library. West Branch, Iowa.

Berle, Adolf Augustus. Papers. Franklin Delano Roosevelt Library. Hyde Park, N.Y.

Blum, John M. *From the Morgenthau Diaries*. 3 v. Boston: Houghton Mifflin, 1959.

Brown, Prentiss Marsh. Papers. Michigan Historical Collections. Bentley Historical Library. University of Michigan. Ann Arbor, Mich.

Bulkley, Robert Johns. Papers. Western Reserve Historical Society Collections. Cleveland, Ohio.

Burgess, W. Randolph, ed. *Interpretations of Federal Reserve Policy in the Speeches and Writings of Benjamin Strong*. New York: Harper and Brothers, 1930.

Coolidge, T. Jefferson. Papers. Franklin Delano Roosevelt Library. Hyde Park, N.Y.

Cudlip, William Byrnes. Papers. Michigan Historical Collections. Bentley Historical Library. University of Michigan. Ann Arbor, Mich.

Cutting, Bronson. Papers. Manuscript Division. Library of Congress. Washington, D.C.

Eccles, Marriner S. *Beckoning Frontiers: Public and Personal Recollections*. New York: Alfred A. Knopf, 1951.

———. Papers. Manuscript Division, Special Collections Department. Marriott Library. University of Utah. Salt Lake City, Utah.

Frankfurter, Felix. Papers. Manuscript Division. Library of Congress. Washington, D.C.

General Records of the Department of the Treasury. Office of the Secretary, General Correspondence 1917–32. Record Group 56. National Archives. Washington, D.C.

———. Office of the Secretary, General Correspondence 1933–56. Record Group 56. National Archives. Washington, D.C.

———. Office of the Secretary, List of Individual Files. Record Group 56. National Archives. Washington, D.C.

———. Office of the Secretary, Office of Domestic Gold and Silver Operations. Record Group 56. National Archives. Washington, D.C.

Glass, Carter. Papers. Alderman Library. University of Virginia. Charlottesville, Va.

Goldenweiser, Emanuel Alexandrovich. Papers. Manuscript Division. Library of Congress. Washington, D.C.

Hamlin, Charles Sumner. Papers. Manuscript Division. Library of Congress. Washington, D.C.

Harrison, George Leslie. Papers. Manuscript Division. Butler Library. Columbia University. New York, N.Y.

Hayden, Jay G. Papers. Michigan Historical Collections. Bentley Historical Library. University of Michigan. Ann Arbor, Mich.

Hoover, Herbert Clark. *The Memoirs of Herbert Hoover*. 3 v. New York: Macmillan, 1951–52.

———. Papers. Presidential Subject File, Presidential Personal File, Post-Presidential Subject File. Herbert Hoover Presidential Library. West Branch, Iowa.

———. *The State Papers and Other Public Writings of Herbert Hoover*. W.S. Myers, ed. 2 v. New York: Doubleday, 1934.

Houston, David F. *Eight Years with Wilson's Cabinet, 1913–1920*. 2 v. Garden City, N.Y.: Doubleday, Page, 1926.

Hull, Cordell. *Memoirs of Cordell Hull*. 2 v. New York: Macmillan, 1948.

———. Papers. Manuscript Division. Library of Congress. Washington, D.C.

Ickes, Harold L. *The Secret Diary of Harold L. Ickes*. 3 v. New York: Simon and Schuster, 1953–54.

Jones, Jesse H. and Edward Angly. *Fifty Billion Dollars: My Thirteen Years with the RFC*. New York: Macmillan, 1951.

Jones, Jesse Holman. Papers. Manuscript Division. Library of Congress. Washington, D.C.

Krock, Arthur. *Memoirs: Sixty Years on the Firing Line*. New York: Funk and Wagnalls, 1968.

McAdoo, William Gibbs. Papers. Manuscript Division. Library of Congress. Washington, D.C.

Meyer, Eugene. Papers. Manuscript Division. Library of Congress. Washington, D.C.

Miller, Adolph Caspar. Papers. Manuscript Division. Library of Congress. Washington, D.C.

Mills, Ogden Livingston. Papers. Manuscript Division. Library of Congress. Washington, D.C.

Moley, Raymond. Papers. Hoover Institution on War, Revolution, and Peace. Stanford University. Stanford, Cal.

Morgenthau, Henry, Jr. Papers. Franklin Delano Roosevelt Library. Hyde Park, N.Y.

Norbeck, Peter. Papers. Richardson Archives. I.D. Weeks Library. University of South Dakota. Vermillion, S.D.

O'Connor, James Francis Thaddeus. Papers. Bancroft Library. University of California. Berkeley, Cal.

Records of the Federal Reserve System. Subject File, 1914–54. Record Group 82. National Archives. Washington, D.C.

Records of the Office of the Comptroller of the Currency. Banking Emergency Records. Record Group 101. National Archives. Washington, D.C.

Records of the United States Senate. Committee on Banking and Currency. Bill Records and Papers. Record Group 46. National Archives. Washington, D.C.

Reichert, Rudolph Edward. Papers. Michigan Historical Collections. Bentley Historical Library. University of Michigan. Ann Arbor, Mich.

The Reminiscences of Chester Morrill. Oral History Collection. Butler Library. Columbia University. New York, N.Y.

The Reminiscences of Eugene Meyer. Oral History Collection. Butler Library. Columbia University. New York, N.Y.

The Reminiscences of James Paul Warburg. Oral History Collection. Butler Library. Columbia University. New York, N.Y.

The Reminiscences of Walter Wyatt. Oral History Collection. Butler Library. Columbia University. New York, N.Y.

Roosevelt, Elliott and Joseph B. Lash, eds. *F.D.R.: His Personal Letters, 1928–1945*. 2 v. New York: Duell, Sloan, and Pearce, 1950.

Roosevelt, Franklin D. *Complete Presidential Press Conferences*. 25 v. New York: Da Capo, 1972.

———. Presidential Papers. Franklin Delano Roosevelt Library. Hyde Park. N.Y.

———. *The Public Papers and Addresses of Franklin D. Roosevelt*. Samuel I. Rosenman, comp. 13 v. New York: Random House, 1938–45.

Roper, Daniel C. and Frank H. Lovette. *Fifty Years of Public Life*. Durham, N.C.: Duke University, 1941.

Stimson, Henry L. Papers (microfilm edition). Manuscripts and Archives. Yale University Library. Yale University. New Haven, Conn.

Stokes, Thomas L. *Chip Off My Shoulder*. Princeton, N.J.: Princeton University, 1940.

Tugwell, Rexford Guy. Papers. Franklin Delano Roosevelt Library. Hyde Park, N.Y.

———. *To the Lesser Heights of Morningside: A Memoir*. Philadelphia: University of Pennsylvania, 1982.

Vandenberg, Arthur H. Papers. Michigan Historical Collections. Bentley Historical Library. University of Michigan. Ann Arbor, Mich.

Wagner, Robert Ferdinand. Papers. Georgetown University Library. Georgetown University. Washington, D.C.

Walcott, Frederic Collin. Papers. Manuscripts and Archives. Yale University Library. Yale University. New Haven, Conn.

Warburg, James Paul. Papers. John F. Kennedy Library. Waltham, Mass.

Warren, George Frederick. Papers. Collection of Regional History and Cornell University Archives. Cornell University Library. Cornell University. Ithaca, N.Y.

Willis, Henry Parker. Papers. Manuscript Division. Butler Library. Columbia University. New York, N.Y.

GOVERNMENT DOCUMENTS

Anderson, Clay J. *Monetary Policy: Decision-Making, Tools, and Objectives*. Philadelphia: Federal Reserve Bank of Philadelphia, 1961.

Board of Governors of the Federal Reserve System. *Twenty-second Annual Report Covering Operations for the Year 1935*. Washington, D.C.: U.S. Government Printing Office, 1936.

Bordo, Michael D. "The Lender of Last Resort: Alternative Views and Historical Experience." *Federal Reserve Bank of Richmond Economic Review*, 76 (January/February 1990): 18–29.

Congressional Directory. 72d Congress, 2d session. January 1933.

———. 73d Congress, 1st session. June 1933.

Congressional Record, 71–79 (1929–35).

Dew, Kurt. "Gold Policy: The Thirties and the Seventies." *Federal Reserve Bank of San Francisco Business Review* (Winter 1974/75): 16–20.

Eastburn, David P., ed. *Men, Money, and Policy: Essays in Honor of Karl R. Bopp*. Philadelphia: Federal Reserve Bank of Philadelphia, 1970.

Federal Deposit Insurance Corporation. *Annual Report, 1934*. Washington, D.C.: U.S. Government Printing Office, 1935.

———. *Annual Report, 1935*. Washington, D.C.: U.S. Government Printing Office, 1936.

———. Division of Research and Statistics. *History of the Federal Deposit Insurance Corporation*. Washington, D.C.: U.S. Government Printing Office, 1951.

Federal Reserve Bank of Philadelphia. *Fifty Years on Chestnut Street*. Philadelphia: Federal Reserve Bank of Philadelphia, [1964].

Federal Reserve Board. *Tenth Annual Report Covering Operations for the Year 1923*. Washington, D.C.: U.S. Government Printing Office, 1924.

———. *Fifteenth Annual Report Covering Operations for the Year 1928*. Washington, D.C.: U.S. Government Printing Office, 1929.

———. *Sixteenth Annual Report Covering Operations for the Year 1929*. Washington, D.C.: U.S. Government Printing Office, 1930.

———. *Seventeenth Annual Report Covering Operations for the Year 1930*. Washington, D.C.: U.S. Government Printing Office, 1931.

———. *Eighteenth Annual Report Covering Operations for the Year 1931*. Washington, D.C.: U.S. Government Printing Office, 1932.

———. *Nineteenth Annual Report Covering Operations for the Year 1932*. Washington, D.C.: U.S. Government Printing Office, 1933.

———. *Twentieth Annual Report Covering Operations for the Year 1933*. Washington, D.C.: U.S. Government Printing Office, 1934.

———. *Twenty-first Annual Report Covering Operations for the Year 1934*. Washington, D.C.: U.S. Government Printing Office, 1935.

Federal Reserve Bulletin, 16–21 (1930–35).

"Fiftieth Anniversary of the Federal Reserve System—Immediate Origins of the System." *Federal Reserve Bank of New York Monthly Review*, 46 (March 1964): 61–2.

Gambs, Carl M. "Bank Failures: An Historical Perspective." *Federal Reserve Bank of Kansas City Monthly Review* (June 1977): 10–20.

Goldenweiser, E.A., Elliott Thurston, and Bray Hammond, eds. *Banking Studies*. Washington, D.C.: Board of Governors of the Federal Reserve System, 1941.

Green, George D., ed. *Consumer Spending and Monetary Policy: The Linkages*. Boston: Federal Reserve Bank of Boston, 1971.

Hackley, Howard H. *Lending Functions of the Federal Reserve Banks: A History*. Washington, D.C.: Board of Governors of the Federal Reserve System, 1973.

Hetzel, Robert L. "Too Big to Fail: Origins, Consequences, and Outlook." *Federal Reserve Bank of Richmond Economic Review*, 77 (November/December 1991): 3–15.

Higgins, Byron. "Interest Payments on Demand Deposits: Historical Evolution and the Current Controversy." *Federal Reserve Bank of Kansas City Monthly Review* (July/August 1977): 3–11.

Holland, John J., Jr. "The Misinterpretation of the Causes of the Banking Collapse of 1933 and its Retarding Influence on Commercial Banking Innovation." *Bank Structure and*

Competition: Proceedings of a Conference. Chicago: Federal Reserve Bank of Chicago, 1975.

Luttrell, Clifton B. "Interest Rate Controls—Perspective, Purpose, and Problems." *Federal Reserve Bank of St. Louis Monthly Review*, 50 (September 1968): 6–14.

McNeill, Charles R. "The Depository Institutions Deregulation and Monetary Control Act of 1980." *Federal Reserve Bulletin*, 66 (June 1980): 444–53.

"Money Market in April." *Monthly Review of Credit and Business Conditions, Second Federal Reserve District* (1 May 1932): 33–5.

"Money Market in February." *Monthly Review of Credit and Business Conditions, Second Federal Reserve District* (1 March 1932): 17–9.

"Money Market in January." *Monthly Review of Credit and Business Conditions, Second Federal Reserve District* (1 February 1932): 9–11.

"Money Market in March." *Monthly Review of Credit and Business Conditions, Second Federal Reserve District* (1 April 1932): 25–7.

"Money Market in May." *Monthly Review of Credit and Business Conditions, Second Federal Reserve District* (1 June 1932): 41–2.

O'Brien, James M. "Interest Ban on Demand Deposits: Victim of the Profit Motive?" *Federal Reserve Bank of Philadelphia Business Review* (August 1972): 13–9.

"The Quantity Theory of Money: Its Historical Evolution and Role in Policy Debates." *Federal Reserve Bank of Richmond Economic Review* (May/June 1974): 1–19.

Ratchford, Benjamin Ulysses. *The Federal Reserve at Work*. Richmond, Va.: Federal Reserve Bank of Richmond, 1974.

"Reforming the Monetary System: Does Economic Change Outmode Some Features of Money and Banking Systems?" *Federal Reserve Bank of Richmond Monthly Review* (June 1961): 2–5.

Robertson, Ross M. *The Comptroller and Bank Supervision: A Historical Appraisal*. Washington, D.C.: Office of the Comptroller of the Currency, 1968.

Rothwell, Jack C. "Who Changed the Rules of the Game? The Evolution and Development of Tools of Federal Reserve Policy." *Federal Reserve Bank of Philadelphia Business Review* (October 1963): 3–18.

Smith, Stephen D. and Larry D. Wall. "Financial Panics, Bank Failures, and the Role of Regulatory Policy." *Federal Reserve Bank of Atlanta Economic Review*, 77 (January/February 1992): 1–11.

Summers, Bruce J. "Loan Commitments to Business in United States Banking History." *Federal Reserve Bank of Richmond Economic Review*, 61 (September/October 1975): 15–23.

Throop, Adrian W. "Bicentennial Perspective: Decline and Fall of the Gold Standard." *Federal Reserve Bank of Dallas Monthly Business Review* (January 1976): 1–11.

Treiber, William F. "Federal Reserve System after Fifty Years." *Federal Reserve Bank of New York Monthly Review*, 46 (June 1964): 98–104.

U.S., Congress, Conference Committee. *Direct Loans for Industrial Purposes by Federal Reserve Banks: Conference Report to Accompany H.R. 541*. H. Rept. 2056, 73d Congress, 2d session, 16 June 1934.

———. *Securities Exchange Act of 1934: Conference Report to Accompany H.R. 9323*. S. Doc. 185, 73d Congress, 2d session, 30 May 1934.

U.S., Congress, House. *Report of Reconstruction Finance Corporation for Fourth Quarter of 1934*. H. Doc. 139, 74th Congress, 1st session, 14 March 1935.

U.S., Congress, House, Committee on Banking and Currency. *Banking Act of 1933: Report to Accompany H.R. 5661*. H. Rept. 150, 73d Congress, 1st session, 19 May 1933.

———. *Banking Act of 1935: Hearings on H.R. 5357*. 74th Congress, 1st session, 21 February–8 April 1935.

———. *Banking Act of 1935: Report to Accompany H.R. 7617*. H. Rept. 742, 74th Congress, 1st session, 19 April 1935.

———. *Branch, Chain, and Group Banking: Hearings Pursuant to H.Res. 141*. 71st Congress, 2d session, 25 February–11 June 1930.

———. *Cancellation of Federal Reserve Bank Stock Held by Member Banks Which Have Ceased to Function in Certain Cases: Report to Accompany H.R. 6604*. H. Rept. 487, 71st Congress, 2d session, 23 January 1930.

———. *Compromise of Liability of Shareholders in Failed National Banks: Report to Accompany S. 544*. H. Rept. 639, 71st Congress, 2d session, 8 February 1930.

———. *Extension for 1 Year of the Temporary Plan for Deposit Insurance and Other Amendments to the Federal Reserve Act: Report to Accompany S. 3025*. H. Rept. 1724, 73d Congress, 2d session, 21 May 1934.

———. *Extension of Temporary Plan for Deposit Insurance: Hearings on S. 3025*. 73d Congress, 2d session, 16 April–15 May 1934.

———. *For Increasing and Stabilizing the Price Level of Commodities: Hearings on H.R. 10517*. 72d Congress, 1st session, 16 March–14 April 1932.

———. *For Relief of Depositors in Closed Banks: Report to Accompany H.R. 7908*. H. Rept. 1235, 73d Congress, 2d session, 12 April 1934.

———. *Granting the Federal Reserve Board Discretionary Authority in the Matter of Assessment of Costs of Examining Member Banks Against Banks Examined: Report to Accompany S. 485*. H. Rept. 1656, 71st Congress, 2d session, 26 May 1930.

———. *Investigation of Group, Chain, and Branch Banking: Report Pursuant to H.Res. 141*. H. Rept. 2946, 71st Congress, 3d session, 3 March 1931.

———. *Liberalizing the Credit Facilities of the Federal Reserve System: Hearings on H.R. 9203*. 72d Congress, 1st session, 12 February 1932.

———. *Loans to Industry: Report to Accompany S. 3487*. H. Rept. 1719, 73d Congress, 2d session, 21 May 1934.

———. *Loans to State Banks by Federal Reserve Banks: Report to Accompany H.R. 3757*. H. Rept. 10, 73d Congress, 1st session, 20 March 1933.

———. *Power of the Comptroller of the Currency over National Banks: Report to Accompany S.J. Res. 256*. H. Rept. 2111, 72d Congress, 2d session, 24 February 1933.

———. *Restoring and Maintaining the Purchasing Power of the Dollar: Report to Accompany H.R. 11499*. H. Rept. 1103, 72d Congress, 1st session, 22 April 1932.

———. *To Amend the National Banking Act and the Federal Reserve Act and to Provide a Guaranty Fund for Depositors in Banks:*

Report to Accompany H.R. 11362. H. Rept. 1085, 72d Congress, 1st session, 19 April 1932.

———. *To Provide Guaranty Fund for Depositors in Banks: Hearings on H.R. (10241) 11362*. 72d Congress, 1st session, 14 March–8 April 1932.

———. *To Regulate the Value of Money in Accordance with Article I, Section 8, of the Constitution of the United States, to Reestablish the Gold Standard, to Provide for its Maintenance and Stabilization: Report to Accompany H.R. 5073*. H. Rept. 290, 73d Congress, 2d session, 17 January 1934.

———. *Waiver of Notice by State Member Banks of Withdrawal from Federal Reserve System: Report to Accompany H.R. 8877*. H. Rept. 488, 71st Congress, 2d session, 23 January 1930.

U.S., Congress, House, Committee on Coinage, Weights, and Measures. *To Protect the Currency Systems of the United States and to Provide for the Better Use of the Monetary Gold Stock: Report to Accompany H.R. 6976*. H. Rept. 292, 73d Congress, 2d session, 18–19 January 1934.

U.S., Congress, House, Committee on Interstate and Foreign Commerce. *Securities Exchange Bill of 1934: Report to Accompany H.R. 9323*. H. Rept. 1383, 73d Congress, 2d session, 27 April 1934.

———. *Stock Exchange Regulation: Hearings on H.R. 7852 and H.R. 8720*. 73d Congress, 2d session, 14 February–24 March 1934.

U.S., Congress, Senate, Committee on Banking and Currency. *Amendments to Federal Reserve Act Permitting Discounting of Notes of Finance and Credit Companies: Hearings before Subcommittee on S. 4454*. 72d Congress, 2d session, 18 January 1933.

———. *Banking Act of 1935: Hearings before Subcommittee on S. 1715 and H.R. 7617*. 74th Congress, 1st session, 19 April–3 June 1935.

———. *Banking Act of 1935: Report to Accompany H.R. 7617*. S. Rept. 1007, 74th Congress, 1st session, 2 July 1935.

———. *Cancellation of Federal Reserve Bank Stock Held by Member Banks Which Have Ceased to Function in Certain Cases: Report to Accompany H.R. 6604*. S. Rept. 437, 71st Congress, 2d session, 15 April 1930.

———. *Compromise of Liability of Shareholders in Failed National Banks: Report to Accompany S. 544*. S. Rept. 65, 71st Congress, 2d session, 18 December 1929.

———. *Direct Loans to State Banks and Trust Companies: Report to Accompany H.R. 3757*. S. Rept. 4, 73d Congress, 1st session, 22 March 1933.

———. *Fiftieth Anniversary, 63d Congress, 1913, to 88th Congress, 1963*. S. Doc. 15, 88th Congress, 1st session, 15 March 1963.

———. *Gold Reserve Act of 1934: Hearings on S. 2366*. 73d Congress, 2d session, 19–23 January 1934.

———. *Gold Reserve Act of 1934: Report to Accompany H.R. 6976*. S. Rept. 201, 73d Congress, 2d session, 23 January 1934.

———. *Granting the Federal Reserve Board Discretionary Authority in the Matter of Assessment of Costs of Examining Member Banks Against Banks Examined: Report to Accompany S. 485*. S. Rept. 317, 71st Congress, 2d session, 3 April 1930.

———. *Improvement of Facilities of the Federal Reserve System: Report to Accompany S. 3616*. S. Rept. 237, 72d Congress, 1st session, 12 February 1932.

———. *Operation of the National and Federal Reserve Banking Systems: Hearings before a Subcommittee Pursuant to S.Res. 71*. 71st Congress, 3d session, 19 January–2 March 1931.

———. *Operation of the National and Federal Reserve Banking Systems: Hearings on S. 4115*. 72d Congress, 1st session, 23–30 March 1932.

———. *Operation of National and Federal Reserve Banking Systems: Report to Accompany S. 4412*. S. Rept. 584, 72d Congress, 1st session, 22 and 30 April 1932.

———. *Operation of National and Federal Reserve Banking Systems: Report to Accompany S. 1631*. S. Rept. 77, 73d Congress, 1st session, 17 May 1933.

———. *Restoring and Maintaining the Average Purchasing Power of the Dollar: Hearings on H.R. 11499 and S. 4429*. 72d Congress, 1st session, 12–18 May 1932.

———. *Stock Exchange Practices: Hearings on S.Res. 84 and S.Res. 239*. 72d Congress, 1st and 2d sessions, 11 April–23 June 1932, 11 January–2 March 1933.

———. *Stock Exchange Practices: Hearings on S.Res. 84 (72d Congress), S.Res. 56 (73d Congress), and S.Res. 97 (73d*

Congress). 73d Congress, 1st and 2d sessions, 23 May 1933–5 April 1934.

———. *Stock Exchange Practices: Report Pursuant to S.Res. 84 (72d Congress), S.Res. 56 (73d Congress), and S.Res. 97 (73d Congress)*. S. Rept. 1455, 73d Congress, 2d session, 16 June 1934.

———. *Waiver of Notice by State Member Banks of Withdrawal from Federal Reserve System: Report to Accompany H.R. 8877*. S. Rept. 316, 71st Congress, 2d session, 3 April 1930.

U.S., Treasury Department. *Annual Report of the Secretary of the Treasury for the Fiscal Year Ended June 30, 1935*. Washington, D.C.: U.S. Government Printing Office, 1936.

Veazey, Edward E. "Bicentennial Perspective—Evolution of Money and Banking in the United States." *Federal Reserve Bank of Dallas Monthly Business Review* (December 1975): 1–12.

Winningham, Scott. "The Effects of Removing Regulation Q—A Theoretical Analysis." *Federal Reserve Bank of Kansas City Economic Review* (May 1980): 13–23.

SECONDARY SOURCES

"ABA Goes Public to End Regulation Q." *ABA Banking Journal*, 71 (December 1979): 56–7.

Adams, John C. Franklin D. Roosevelt's Gold Policies in a Farm Sector Strategy, 1933. Ph.D. dissertation, Indiana University, 1976.

"Allard Smith of Union Trust Company of Cleveland Looks for Business Recovery in Present Year." *Commercial and Financial Chronicle*, 132 (17 January 1931): 394–5.

American Bankers' Association, Committee on Federal Legislation. *Legislation Affecting Banking Pending in First Session, 74th Congress*. New York: American Bankers' Association, 1935.

"American Banking." *Banker*, 26 (April 1933): 46–53.

American Institute of Banking. *Banking and the New Deal*. New York: American Institute of Banking, 1933.

———. *Contemporary Legislative and Banking Problems*. New York: American Institute of Banking, 1934.

———. *Money and Banking*. New York: American Institute of Banking, 1940.

Andersen, Kristi. *The Creation of a Democratic Majority, 1928–1936*. Chicago: University of Chicago, 1979.

Anderson, Benjamin M. *Economics and the Public Welfare: Financial and Economic History of the United States, 1914–1946*. New York: D. Van Nostrand, 1949.

Anderson, George E. "In the Lifetime of Senator Glass." *Banking*, 31 (August 1938): 22–4.

Anderson, Thomas Joel, Jr. *Federal and State Control of Banking*. New York: Bankers Publishing Company, 1934.

Arndt, H.W. *The Economic Lessons of the Nineteen-Thirties*. London: Frank Cass, 1963 [1944].

Association of Reserve City Bankers. *The Guaranty of Bank Deposits: A Report of the Commission on Banking Law and Practice*. Chicago: Association of Reserve City Bankers, 1933.

Auerbach, Joseph and Samuel L. Hayes, III. *Investment Banking and Diligence: What Price Deregulation?* Boston: Harvard Business School, 1986.

Avery, Robert B. and Allen N. Berger. "Risk-Based Capital and Deposit Insurance Reform." *Journal of Banking and Finance*, 15 (September 1991): 847–74.

"B.M. Anderson, of Chase National Bank of New York, Views Cheap Money as Aid to Speculation But Costly to Business." *Commercial and Financial Chronicle*, 130 (19 April 1930): 2698–9.

"The Banking Act of 1935: How it Affects Banks and Everybody Else." *United States Investor*, 46 (9 March 1935): 289–92, 308.

"Banking Inquiry Stresses Issues Awaiting Decision." *Business Week* (11 March 1931): 5–6.

Barber, William J. *From New Era to New Deal*. Cambridge: Cambridge University, 1985.

———. *A History of Economic Thought*. New York: Frederick A. Praeger, 1968.

Barger, Harold. *The Management of Money: A Survey of American Experience*. Chicago: Rand McNally, 1964.

Barnard, Harry. *Independent Man: The Life of Senator James Couzens*. New York: Charles Scribner's Sons, 1958.

Baster, A.S.J. *The Twilight of American Capitalism: An Economic Interpretation of the New Deal.* London: P.S. King and Son, 1937.

Beckhart, Benjamin Haggott. *Federal Reserve System.* New York: American Institute of Banking, 1972.

Bensel, Richard Franklin. *Sectionalism and American Political Development, 1880–1980.* Madison: University of Wisconsin, 1984.

Benston, George J. and others. *Perspectives on Safe and Sound Banking.* Cambridge, Mass.: MIT, 1986.

Benston, George J. *The Separation of Commercial and Investment Banking: The Glass–Steagall Act Revisited and Reconsidered.* New York: Oxford University, 1990.

Berlin, Mitchell, Anthony Saunders, and Gregory F. Udell. "Deposit Insurance Reform: What Are the Issues and What Needs to be Fixed?" *Journal of Banking and Finance*, 15 (September 1991): 735–52.

Bernanke, Ben S. "Nonmonetary Effects of the Financial Crisis in the Propagation of the Great Depression." *American Economic Review*, 73 (June 1983): 257–76.

Bopp, Karl R. "Agencies of Federal Reserve Policy." *University of Missouri Studies*, 10 (October 1935): 1–83.

———. "Three Decades of Federal Reserve Policy." *Postwar Economic Studies*, 8 (November 1947): 1–29.

Boughton, James M. and Elmus R. Wicker. "The Behavior of the Currency-Deposit Ratio during the Great Depression." *Journal of Money, Credit, and Banking*, 11 (November 1979): 405–18.

Bradford, Frederick A. *Monetary Developments since 1932.* New York: Longmans, Green, 1934.

———. "Stable Money Theory and Business Depression." *Bankers Magazine*, 122 (February 1931): 169–70.

Bremer, C.D. *American Bank Failures.* New York: Columbia University, 1935.

Brewer, Elijah, III. "Relationship Between Bank Holding Company Risk and Nonbank Activity." *Journal of Economics and Business*, 41 (November 1989): 337–53.

Brumbaugh, R. Dan, Jr. and Robert E. Litan. "Ignoring Economics in Dealing with the Savings and Loan and Commercial Banking Crisis." *Contemporary Policy Issues*, 9 (January 1991): 36–53.

Brunner, Karl, ed. *The Great Depression Revisited*. Boston: Martinus Nijhoff, 1981.

Brunner, Karl and Allan H. Meltzer. "What Did We Learn from the Monetary Experience of the United States in the Great Depression?" *Canadian Journal of Economics*, 1 (May 1968): 334–48.

Burgess, W. Randolph. "Guides to Bank of Issue Policy." *Proceedings of the Academy of Political Science*, 13 (January 1930): 508–13.

Burner, David. *Herbert Hoover, a Public Life*. New York: Alfred A. Knopf, 1979.

Burns, Helen M. *The American Banking Community and New Deal Banking Reforms, 1933–1935*. Westport, Conn.: Greenwood, 1974.

Campbell, Bruce A. and Richard J. Trilling, eds. *Realignment in American Politics: Toward a Theory*. Austin: University of Texas, 1980.

Cargill, Thomas F. and Gillian G. Garcia. *Financial Deregulation and Monetary Control: Historical Perspective and Impact of the 1980 Act*. Stanford, Cal.: Hoover Institution, 1982.

Cargill, Thomas F. *Money, the Financial System, and Monetary Policy*. Englewood Cliffs, N.J.: Prentice-Hall, 1979.

Carosso, Vincent P. *Investment Banking in America: A History*. Cambridge, Mass.: Harvard University, 1970.

Carson, Deane, ed. *Banking and Monetary Studies*. Homewood, Ill.: Richard D. Irwin, 1963.

Case, Josephine Young and Everett Needham Case. *Owen D. Young and American Enterprise: A Biography*. Boston: David R. Godine, 1982.

Cecchetti, Stephen G. "Prices During the Great Depression: Was the Deflation of 1930–1932 Really Unanticipated?" *American Economic Review*, 82 (March 1992): 141–56.

Chamber of Commerce of the United States, Banking and Currency Committee. *The Federal Reserve System*. Washington, D.C.: Chamber of Commerce of the United States, 1929.

Chandler, Lester V. *American Monetary Policy, 1928–1941*. New York: Harper and Row, 1971.

———. *America's Greatest Depression 1929–41*. New York: Harper and Row, 1970.

———. *Benjamin Strong, Central Banker.* Washington, D.C.: Brookings Institution, 1958.

Chandler, Lester V. and Stephen M. Goldfeld. *The Economics of Money and Banking*. 7th ed. New York: Harper and Row, 1977.

Chapman, Charles C. *The Development of American Business and Banking Thought, 1913–1936.* 2d ed. London: Longmans, Green, 1936.

"Cheap Money Policy of Reserve Heads Off More Drastic Plans." *Business Week* (27 April 1932): 5–6.

Chernow, Ron. *The House of Morgan: An American Banking Dynasty and the Rise of Modern Finance.* New York: Atlantic Monthly, 1990.

Clark, Lawrence E. *Central Banking under the Federal Reserve System with Special Consideration of the Federal Reserve Bank of New York.* New York: Macmillan, 1935.

Clifford, A. Jerome. *The Independence of the Federal Reserve System.* Philadelphia: University of Pennsylvania, 1965.

Cochran, John A. *Money, Banking and the Economy.* 3d ed. New York: Macmillan, 1975.

"Comptroller of Currency Pole before Central Atlantic States Bank Management Conference Warns of Increased Governmental Supervision of Banks if Banks Fail in Maintaining Sound Management." *Commercial and Financial Chronicle*, 132 (7 March 1931): 1723–4.

Cox, Albert H., Jr. "Regulation of Interest on Deposits: An Historical Review." *Journal of Finance*, 22 (May 1967): 274–96.

Crawford, Arthur. "Deposit Guaranty in Congress." *Burroughs Clearing House* (July 1932): 15–7, 29.

———. *Monetary Management under the New Deal: The Evolution of a Managed Currency System.* Washington, D.C.: American Council on Public Affairs, 1940.

Daiger, J.M. "Wall Street or Washington: Which Shall Rule the Federal Reserve." *World's Work*, 60 (August 1931): 49–52, 66.

Davis, Kenneth S. *FDR: The New Deal Years, 1933–1937, A History.* New York: Random House, 1986.

Derthick, Martha. *Uncontrollable Spending for Social Services Grants.* Washington, D.C.: Brookings Institution, 1975.

Dominguez, Kathryn M., Ray C. Fair, and Matthew D. Shapiro. "Forecasting the Depression: Harvard versus Yale." *American Economic Review*, 78 (September 1988): 595–612.

Dorfman, Joseph. *The Economic Mind in American Civilization*. 5 v. New York: Viking, 1946–59.

Dye, Howard Spencer. Federal Banking Legislation from 1930 to 1938: Its History, Consequences and Related Issues. Ph.D. dissertation, Cornell University, 1949.

Eccles, George S. *The Politics of Banking*. Sidney Hyman, ed. Salt Lake City: University of Utah for the Graduate School of Business, 1982.

Editors of *The Economist*. *The New Deal: An Analysis and Appraisal*. New York: Alfred A. Knopf, 1937.

Edwards, Richard Earl. Herbert Hoover and the Public Relations Approach to Economic Recovery, 1929–1932. Ph.D. dissertation, University of Iowa, 1976.

Egbert, Arch O. Marriner S. Eccles and the Banking Act of 1935. Ph.D. dissertation, Brigham Young University, 1967.

Ekelund, Robert B., Jr., and Robert F. Hebert. *A History of Economic Theory and Method*. New York: McGraw-Hill, 1975.

England, Catherine and Thomas Huertas, eds. *The Financial Services Revolution: Policy Directions for the Future*. Boston: Kluwer Academic, 1988.

Epstein, Gerald and Thomas Ferguson. "Monetary Policy, Loan Liquidation, and Industrial Conflict: The Federal Reserve and the Open Market Operations of 1932." *Journal of Economic History*, 44 (December 1984): 957–83.

Eulau, Heinz and Moshe M. Czudnowski, eds. *Elite Recruitment in Democratic Politics: Comparative Studies across Nations*. New York: Halstead, 1976.

Fausold, Martin L. and George T. Mazuzan, eds. *The Hoover Presidency: A Reappraisal*. Albany: State University of New York, 1974.

Fausold, Martin L. *The Presidency of Herbert C. Hoover*. Lawrence: University of Kansas, 1985.

Feinman, Ronald L. *Twilight of Progressivism: The Western Republican Senators and the New Deal*. Baltimore: Johns Hopkins University, 1981.

Feis, Herbert. *1933: Characters in Crisis*. Boston: Little, Brown, 1966.

"The Financial Situation." *Commercial and Financial Chronicle*, 130 (21 June 1930): 4289–302.

"The Financial Situation." *Commercial and Financial Chronicle*, 132 (24 January 1931): 531–45.

"The Financial Situation." *Commercial and Financial Chronicle*, 132 (7 March 1931): 1671–84.

"The Financial Situation." *Commercial and Financial Chronicle*, 135 (1 October 1932): 2207–20.

"The Financial Situation." *Commercial and Financial Chronicle*, 135 (12 November 1932): 3203–18.

Fischer, Gerald C. *American Banking Structure*. New York: Columbia University, 1968.

Fisher, Irving. "Reflation and Stabilization." *Annals of the American Academy of Political and Social Science*, 171 (January 1934): 127–31.

Fite, Gilbert Courtland. "Peter Norbeck: Prairie Statesman." *University of Missouri Studies*, 22, 2 (1948): 1–217.

Flynt, Wayne. *Duncan Upshaw Fletcher: Dixie's Reluctant Progressive*. Tallahassee: Florida State University, 1971.

"For Public Relief, the R.F.C.: For Industry, Federal Reserve." *Business Week* (20 July 1932): 3–4.

Foster, Major B., Raymond Rodgers, Jules I. Bogen, and Marcus Nadler. *Money and Banking*. 4th ed. New York: Prentice-Hall, 1953.

Freedman, James O. "Legislative Delegation to Regulatory Agencies." *Proceedings of the Academy of Political Science*, 34, 2 (1981): 76–89.

Freidel, Frank. "Election of 1932." *History of American Presidential Elections, 1789–1968*. Arthur M. Schlesinger, Jr. and Fred L. Israel, eds., III: 2707–806. New York: McGraw-Hill, 1971.

———. *Franklin D. Roosevelt: Launching the New Deal*. Boston: Little, Brown, 1973.

Fried, Robert C. *Performance in American Bureaucracy*. Boston: Little, Brown, 1976.

Friedman, Milton and Anna Jacobson Schwartz. *A Monetary History of the United States, 1867–1960*. Princeton, N.J.: Princeton University, 1963.

Fusfeld, Daniel R. *The Economic Thought of Franklin D. Roosevelt and the Origins of the New Deal.* New York: Columbia University 1956.

Galbraith, John Kenneth. *The Great Crash 1929.* Boston: Houghton Mifflin, 1961 [1954].

———. *Money, Whence It Came, Where It Went.* Boston: Houghton Mifflin, 1975.

Galloway, J.M. "Speaker Joseph W. Byrns: Party Leader in the New Deal." *Tennessee Historical Quarterly*, 25 (Spring 1966): 63–76.

Garrett, Garet and Murray N. Rothbard. *The Great Depression and New Deal Monetary Policy.* San Francisco: Cato Institute, 1980.

Gendreau, Brian C. "Bankers' Balances, Demand Deposit Interest and Agricultural Credit before the Banking Act of 1933: A Note." *Journal of Money, Credit, and Banking*, 11 (November 1979): 506–14.

"Glass Bill Promotes Deflation and Bank Control of Business." *Business Week* (3 February 1932): 5-6.

"Glass 'More Money' Bill Seems Useful Only in Grave Emergency." *Business Week* (15 June 1932): 8–9.

"Glass: Virginian's Whiplash Tongue Sent Huey Long Scurrying." *Newsweek*, 6 (17 August 1935): 20–1.

Goldenweiser, E.A. *American Monetary Policy.* New York: McGraw–Hill, 1951.

———. *Federal Reserve System in Operation.* New York: McGraw–Hill, 1925.

Goldschmidt, R.W. *The Changing Structure of American Banking.* London: George Routledge and Sons, 1933.

Golembe Associates, Inc. *Commercial Banking and the Glass–Steagall Act.* Washington, D.C.: American Bankers Association, 1982.

Golembe, Carter H. and David S. Holland. *Federal Regulation of Banking, 1983–84.* Washington, D.C.: Golembe Associates, 1983.

Goodbar, Joseph Ernest. *Managing the People's Money: An Analysis of Banking Policies and Banking Control and Their Relation to Economic Stability.* New Haven, Conn.: Yale University, 1935.

Guerrant, Edward Owings. *Herbert Hoover, Franklin Roosevelt: Comparisons and Contrasts.* Cleveland: Howard Allen, 1960.

Halperin, Morton H. *Bureaucratic Politics and Foreign Policy.* Washington, D.C.: Brookings Institution, 1974.

Hamby, Alonzo L. *Liberalism and Its Challengers: FDR to Reagan.* New York: Oxford University, 1985.

Hamilton, David E. "The Causes of the Banking Panic of 1930: Another View." *Journal of Southern History*, 51 (November 1985): 581–608.

Hamilton, James D. "Was the Deflation During the Great Depression Anticipated? Evidence from the Commodity Futures Market." *American Economic Review*, 82 (March 1992): 157–78.

Hanlon, Edward Francis. Urban-Rural Cooperation and Conflict in the Congress: The Breakdown of the New Deal Coalition, 1933–1938. Ph.D. dissertation, Georgetown University, 1967.

Hardy, Charles O. *Credit Policies of the Federal Reserve System.* Washington, D.C.: Brookings Institution, 1932.

Harr, Luther and W. Carlton Harris. *Banking Theory and Practice.* 2d ed. New York: McGraw–Hill, 1936.

Harris, Seymour E. *Twenty Years of Federal Reserve Policy.* 2 v. Cambridge, Mass.: Harvard University, 1933.

Hawley, Ellis W. *The Great War and the Search for a Modern Order: A History of the American People and Their Institutions, 1917–1933.* New York: St. Martin's, 1979.

Hayes, Michael T. *Lobbyists and Legislators: A Theory of Political Markets.* New Brunswick, N.J.: Rutgers University, 1981.

Haywood, Charles F. and Charles M. Linke. *The Regulation of Deposit Interest Rates.* Chicago: Association of Reserve City Bankers, 1968.

Hecht, R.S. *The Situation that Confronts Banking.* New York: American Bankers' Association, Economic Policy Committee, 1931.

Hegeland, Hugo. *The Quantity Theory of Money: A Critical Study of its Historical Development and Interpretation and a Restatement.* Goeteborg: Elanders Boktryckeri Aktiebolag, 1951.

Hewlett, Richard G. and Francis Duncan. *Nuclear Navy, 1946–1962.* Chicago: University of Chicago, 1974.

Hicks, John D. *Republican Ascendancy, 1921–1933.* New York: Harper and Brothers, 1960.

Hilty, James Walter. Voting Alignments in the United States Senate, 1933–1944. Ph.D. dissertation, University of Missouri, Columbia, 1973.

Hodgson, James Goodwin, comp. "Federal Regulation of Banking with Guaranty of Deposits: Briefs, References, Reprints." *Reference Shelf*, 8 (November 1932): 1–184.

"House Passes Steagall Bill for Guarantee of Deposits in National Banks." *Commercial and Financial Chronicle*, 134 (4 June 1932): 4088–90.

Humphrey, Thomas M. "Role of Non-Chicago Economists in the Evolution of the Quantity Theory in America 1930–1950." *Southern Economic Journal*, 38 (July 1971): 12–8.

Hutchinson, Harry D. *Money, Banking, and the United States Economy*. 3d ed. Englewood Cliffs, N.J.: Prentice-Hall, 1975.

Hyman, Sidney. *Marriner S. Eccles: Private Entrepreneur and Public Servant*. Stanford, Cal.: Stanford University, Graduate School of Business, 1976.

Imler, Joseph Anthony. The First One Hundred Days of the New Deal: The View from Capitol Hill. Ph.D. dissertation, Indiana University, 1975.

"Inquiry Into National Banking Laws Likely By Senate—King Resolution for Probe Into Defects of Federal Reserve System To Be Taken Up After Holidays." *Commercial and Financial Chronicle*, 129 (21 December 1929): 3902.

James, F. Cyril. *The Economics of Money, Credit and Banking*. 2d ed. New York: Ronald, 1935.

Johnson, Claudius O. *Borah of Idaho*. New York: Longmans, Green, 1936.

Johnson, G. Griffith, Jr. *The Treasury and Monetary Policy, 1933–1938*. Cambridge, Mass.: Harvard University, 1939.

Johnson, William E. "Deposit Guarantee—Now That We Have It, What Are We Going to Do About It?" *Northwestern Banker*, 38 (July 1933): 7–8, 28–9.

Josephy, Alvin M., Jr. *On the Hill: A History of the American Congress*. New York: Simon and Schuster, 1979.

Joskow, Paul L. and Roger G. Noll. *Regulation in Theory and Practice: An Overview*. Cambridge, Mass.: MIT, Department of Economics, 1978.

Joslin, Theodore G. *Hoover Off the Record*. Garden City, N.Y.: Doubleday, Doran, 1934.

Kamerschen, David R. and Eugene S. Klise. *Money and Banking*. 6th ed. Cincinnati: South-Western, 1976.

Kane, Edward J. *The Gathering Crisis in Federal Deposit Insurance.* Cambridge, Mass.: MIT, 1985.

Keeley, Michael C. "Deposit Insurance, Risk, and Market Power in Banking." *American Economic Review*, 80 (December 1990): 1183–1200.

Kemmerer, Edwin Walter. *The ABC of the Federal Reserve System.* 8th ed. Princeton, N.J.: Princeton University, 1929.

———. *Kemmerer on Money.* 2d ed. Philadelphia: John C. Winston, 1934.

Kennedy, Susan Estabrook. *The Banking Crisis of 1933.* Lexington: University of Kentucky, 1973.

Kettl, Donald F. *Leadership at the Fed.* New Haven, Conn.: Yale University, 1986.

Key, Jack Brien. The Congressional Career of Henry B. Steagall of Alabama. M.A. thesis, Vanderbilt University, 1952.

———. "Henry B. Steagall: The Conservative as a Reformer." *Alabama Review*, 17 (July 1964): 198–209.

Kilborne, Russell Donald. *Principles of Money and Banking.* Chicago: A.W. Shaw, 1927.

Klebaner, Benjamin J. *Commercial Banking in the United States: A History.* Hinsdale, Ill.: Dryden, 1974.

Koeniger, Alfred Cash. Carter Glass and the New Deal: From the Presidential Campaign of 1932 through the Hundred Days Session of Congress. M.A. thesis, Vanderbilt University, 1974.

———. "Unreconstructed Rebel:" The Political Thought and Senate Career of Carter Glass, 1929–1936. Ph.D. dissertation, Vanderbilt University, 1980.

Krooss, Herman E. *Executive Opinion: What Business Leaders Said and Thought on Economic Issues 1920s–1960s.* Garden City, N.Y.: Doubleday, 1970.

Kuhn, W.E. *The Evolution of Economic Thought.* 2d ed. Cincinnati: South-Western, 1970.

Ladd, Everett Carll, Jr. and Charles D. Hadley. *Transformations of the American Party System: Political Coalitions from the New Deal to the 1970s.* 2d ed. New York: W.W. Norton, 1978.

"A Landmark Law that Boxes in the Banks: Reform Act of 1933." *Business Week* (19 April 1976): 56–7.

Lash, Joseph P. *Dealers and Dreamers: A Look at the New Deal.* New York: Doubleday, 1988.

Lebergott, Stanley. *The Americans: An Economic Record.* New York: W.W. Norton, 1984.

Leffler, Ray V. *Money and Credit.* New York: Harper and Brothers, 1935.

Leuchtenburg, William E. *Franklin D. Roosevelt and the New Deal, 1932–1940.* New York: Harper and Row, 1963.

———. *The Perils of Prosperity, 1914–32.* Chicago: University of Chicago, 1958.

Lindley, Ernest K. *The Roosevelt Revolution: First Phase.* New York: Viking, 1933.

Lindley, James T. *An Analysis of the Federal Advisory Council of the Federal Reserve System, 1914–1938.* New York: Garland, 1985.

Lucia, Joseph L. "The Failure of the Bank of the United States: A Reappraisal." *Explorations in Economic History*, 22 (October 1985): 402–16.

Lyle, John Douglas. The United States Senate Career of Carter Glass of Virginia, 1919–1939. Ph.D. dissertation, University of South Carolina, 1974.

Macey, Jonathan R. "Special Interest Groups Legislation and the Judicial Function: The Dilemma of Glass–Steagall." *Emory Law Journal*, 33 (Winter 1984): 1–40.

Manheimer, Eric. The Public Career of Elmer Thomas. Ph.D. dissertation, University of Oklahoma, 1952.

Mayer, Martin. *The Bankers.* New York: Weybright and Talley, 1974.

———. *The Money Bazaars: Understanding the Banking Revolution Around Us.* New York: E.P. Dutton, 1984.

Mayer, Thomas. "Money and the Great Depression: A Critique of Professor Temin's Thesis." *Explorations in Economic History*, 15 (April 1978): 127–45.

Mayer, Thomas and Monojit Chatterji. "Political Shocks and Investment: Some Evidence from the 1930s." *Journal of Economic History*, 45 (December 1985): 913–24.

McElvaine, Robert S. *The Great Depression: America, 1929–1941.* New York: Times Books, 1984.

McKinley, Gordon Wells. The Federal Reserve System in the Period of Crisis, 1930 to 1935. Ph.D. dissertation, Ohio State University, 1948.

McKinney, George W., Jr. *The Federal Reserve Discount Window: Administration in the Fifth District*. New Brunswick, N.J.: Rutgers University, 1960.

McManus, Thomas Francis. Banking Operations in the United States in Relation to the Great Depression. Ph.D. dissertation, University of Iowa, 1934.

Meier, Kenneth J. *Regulation: Politics, Bureaucracy, and Economics*. New York: St. Martin's, 1985.

"Merchant Banking: Is the U.S. Ready for It?" *Business Week* (19 April 1976): 54–7, 60, 64.

Michelman, Irving S. "A Banker in the New Deal: James P. Warburg." *Review Internationale d'Historie de la Banque*, 8 (1974): 35–59.

Mints, Lloyd W. *History of Banking Theory in Great Britain and the United States*. Chicago: University of Chicago, 1945.

Mishkin, Frederic S. "An Evaluation of the Treasury Plan for Banking Reform." *Journal of Economic Perspectives*, 6 (Winter 1992): 133–53.

Moley, Raymond. *After Seven Years*. New York: Harper and Brothers, 1939.

———. *The First New Deal*. New York: Harcourt, Brace and World, 1966.

Morris, Richard B. and Jeffrey B. Morris, eds. *Encyclopedia of American History*. 6th ed. New York: Harper and Row, 1982.

Morrow, William L. *Congressional Committees*. New York: Charles Scribner's Sons, 1969.

Moulton, Harold G. *The Financial Organization of Society*. 3d ed. Chicago: University of Chicago, 1930.

"Mounting Bank Failures Stimulate Movement for Inquiry by Congress." *Commercial and Financial Chronicle*, 132 (3 January 1931): 62.

Mulder, Ronald Allen. *The Insurgent Progressives in the United States Senate and the New Deal, 1933–1939*. New York: Garland, 1979.

———. "Reluctant New Dealers: The Progressive Insurgents in the United States Senate, 1933–1934." *Capitol Studies*, 2 (Winter 1974): 5–22.

Munn, Glenn G. "Relation of Investment to Commercial Banking." *Bankers Magazine*, 118 (March 1929): 360–2.

Murray, Lawrence Leo, III. Andrew W. Mellon, Secretary of the Treasury, 1921–1932: A Study in Policy. Ph.D. dissertation, Michigan State University, 1970.

Myers, Robert Henry. The Politics of American Banking: The Dual System, 1929–1939. Ph.D. dissertation, University of Chicago, 1956.

Myers, William Starr and Walter H. Newton. *The Hoover Administration: A Documented Narrative*. New York: Charles Scribner's Sons, 1936.

Nadler, Marcus, Sipa Heller, and Samuel S. Shipman. *The Money Market and its Institutions*. New York: Ronald, 1955.

National Industrial Conference Board. *The Availability of Bank Credit*. New York: National Industrial Conference Board, 1932.

———. *The Banking Situation in the United States*. New York: National Industrial Conference Board, 1932.

Nelson, Daniel B. "Was the Deflation of 1929–1930 Anticipated? The Monetary Regime as Viewed by the Business Press." *Research in Economic History*, 13 (1991): 1–65.

Nelson, Michael, ed. *The Presidency and the Political System*. Washington, D.C.: Congressional Quarterly, 1984.

New York Clearing House Association. *The Federal Reserve Reexamined*. New York: New York Clearing House Association, 1953.

New York Times, 1930–36, 1986–92.

O'Connor, James Francis Thaddeus. *The Banking Crisis and Recovery under the Roosevelt Administration*. Chicago: Callaghan, 1938.

Olson, James S. "The End of Voluntarism: Herbert Hoover and the National Credit Corporation." *Annals of Iowa*, 41 (1972): 1104–13.

———. *Herbert Hoover and the Reconstruction Finance Corporation, 1931–1933*. Ames: Iowa State University, 1977.

———. "Rehearsal for Disaster: Hoover, the R.F.C., and the Banking Crisis in Nevada, 1932–1933." *Western Historical Quarterly*, 6 (April 1975): 149–61.

———. *Saving Capitalism: The Reconstruction Finance Corporation and the New Deal, 1933–1940*. Princeton, N.J.: Princeton University, 1988.

Ostrolenk, Bernhard. "The Revolution in Banking Theory." *Atlantic Monthly*, 145 (February 1930): 214–9.

"Our Banking Situation—A Suggestion for Reducing Bank Failures." *Commercial and Financial Chronicle*, 134 (19 March 1932): 2031–2.

Paris, James Daniel. *Monetary Policies of the United States, 1932–1938*. New York: Columbia University, 1938.

Parker, Glenn R., ed. *Studies of Congress*. Washington, D.C.: Congressional Quarterly, 1985.

Parrish, Michael E. *Securities Regulation and the New Deal*. New Haven, Conn.: Yale University, 1970.

Patenaude, Lionel V. "The Garner Vote Switch to Roosevelt: 1932 Democratic Convention." *Southwestern Historical Quarterly*, 79 (October 1975): 189–204.

———. "Vice President John Nance Garner: A Study in the Use of Influence during the New Deal." *Texana*, 11, 2 (1973): 124–44.

Paton, Thomas B. "Banking Measures in the 71st Congress." *Journal of the American Bankers Association*, 22 (February 1930): 741–2, 800–2.

———. "16 Deposit Guaranty Bills in Congress: The Idea Persists Despite Past Attempts." *Journal of the American Bankers Association*, 24 (April 1932): 621, 652.

Peach, W. Nelson. *The Security Affiliates of National Banks*. Baltimore: Johns Hopkins University, 1941.

Pearson, F.A., W.I. Myers, and A.R. Gans. "Warren as Presidential Adviser." *Farm Economics*, 211 (December 1957): 5598–676.

Peel, Roy V. and Thomas C. Donnelly. *The 1932 Campaign: An Analysis*. New York: Farrar and Rinehart, 1935.

Pole, J.W. and Eugene Meyer. "Extent of Federal Supervision of Banking Today." *Congressional Digest*, 10 (December 1931): 293–5.

Potter, Jim. *The American Economy between the World Wars*. London: Macmillan, 1974.

"President Hoover in St. Louis Speech Relates Incidents Bearing on Loan by Reconstruction Finance Corporation to Dawes Bank." *Commercial and Financial Chronicle*, 135 (12 November 1932): 3266.

"President Hoover's Program to Hasten Economic Recovery." *Commercial and Financial Chronicle*, 134 (18 June 1932): 4429–30.

Prochnow, Herbert V., ed. *American Financial Institutions*. New York: Prentice-Hall, 1951.

———, ed. *The Federal Reserve System*. New York: Harper and Brothers, 1960.

Pusey, Merlo J. *Eugene Meyer*. New York: Alfred A. Knopf, 1974.

"R.S. Hecht of Hibernia Bank and Trust Company of New Orleans Believes Definite Indications of Economic Recovery Should Soon Appear." *Commercial and Financial Chronicle*, 132 (10 January 1931): 192.

Reeve, Joseph E. *Monetary Reform Movements: A Survey of Recent Plans and Panaceas*. Washington, D.C.: American Council on Public Affairs, 1943.

"Regulation Q—Shaving the Little Saver." *Citibank Monthly Economic Letter* (April 1979): 3–4.

"Reply of Secretary of Treasury Mills to Senator Glass." *Commercial and Financial Chronicle*, 135 (5 November 1932): 3093–5.

"Representative Rainey Says Publicity of Reports of Loans by RFC Under Emergency Relief Act Will Be Mandatory." *Commercial and Financial Chronicle*, 135 (23 July 1932): 544.

Ripley, Randall B. *Congress: Process and Policy*. 3d ed. New York: W.W. Norton, 1983.

———. *Majority Party Leadership in Congress*. Boston: Little, Brown, 1969.

Rist, Charles. *History of Monetary and Credit Theory from John Law to the Present Day*. Jane Degras, trans. New York: Macmillan, 1940.

Ritchie, Donald A. *James M. Landis: Dean of the Regulators*. Cambridge, Mass.: Harvard University, 1980.

———. "The Legislative Impact of the Pecora Investigation." *Capitol Studies*, 5, 2 (1977): 87–101.

Ritter, Lawrence S. and William L. Silber. *Principles of Money, Banking, and Financial Markets*. 3d ed. New York: Basic Books, 1980.

Robinson, Edgar Eugene. *The Roosevelt Leadership, 1933–1945*. Philadelphia: J.B. Lippincott, 1955.

"Rogers Caldwell, Former President of Defunct Investment Banking Firm of Caldwell and Company, Nashville, Indicted by Davidson County, Tennessee, Grand Jury." *Commercial and Financial Chronicle*, 132 (21 March 1931): 2113.

Romasco, Albert U. *The Politics of Recovery: Roosevelt's New Deal.* New York: Oxford University, 1983.

———. *The Poverty of Abundance: Hoover, the Nation, the Depression.* New York: Oxford University, 1965.

Rose, John T. "The Thrift Crisis: Evolution, Resolution, and Reform." *Review of Research in Banking and Finance*, 6 (Spring 1990): 1–23.

Rose, Marc A. "Money Under New Management." *Today*, 4 (14 September 1935): 8–9, 22–3.

Rose, Peter S. *The Changing Structure of American Banking.* New York: Columbia University, 1987.

Rosen, Elliot A. "Roosevelt and the Brains Trust: An Historiographical Overview." *Political Science Quarterly*, 87 (December 1972): 531–57.

Rourke, Francis E. *Bureaucracy, Politics, and Public Policy.* 3d ed. Boston: Little, Brown, 1984.

Rufener, Louis A. *Money and Banking in the United States.* Boston: Houghton Mifflin, 1934.

Saint-Etienne, Christian. *The Great Depression, 1929–1938: Lessons for the 1980s.* Stanford, Cal.: Hoover Institution, 1984.

Sargent, James Edward. The Hundred Days: Franklin D. Roosevelt and the Early New Deal, 1933. Ph.D. dissertation, Michigan State University, 1972.

Saulnier, Raymond J. *Contemporary Monetary Theory: Studies of Some Recent Theories of Money, Prices, and Production.* New York: Columbia University, 1938.

Schapsmeier, Edward L. and Frederick H. Schapsmeier. *Henry A. Wallace of Iowa, 1910–1965.* 2 v. Ames: Iowa State University, 1968.

Schlesinger, Arthur M., Jr. *The Age of Roosevelt.* 3 v. Boston: Houghton Mifflin, 1957–60.

Schneider, Wilbert M. *The American Bankers Association: Its Past and Present.* Washington, D.C.: Public Affairs, 1956.

Schroeder, Joseph J. *They Made Banking History: The Association of Reserve City Bankers.* Chicago: Rand McNally, 1962.

Schwarz, Jordan A. *The Interregnum of Despair: Hoover, Congress, and the Depression.* Urbana: University of Illinois, 1970.

Selgin, George A. "Accommodating Changes in the Relative Demand for Currency: Free Banking vs. Central Banking." *Cato Journal*, 7 (Winter 1988): 621–41.

"Senate Adopts Resolution to Investigate Stock Market Trading." *Commercial and Financial Chronicle*, 134 (5 March 1932): 1679–80.

"Senate Committee Discusses Amendment to Federal Reserve Act Eliminating 15-Day Loans." *Commercial and Financial Chronicle*, 130 (25 January 1930): 568.

"Senate Sidetracks Steagall Bill for Guarantee of Bank Deposits." *Commercial and Financial Chronicle*, 134 (25 June 1932): 4598.

"Senator Glass Asks Amendment to Banking Statutes—Introduces Bill for Far-Reaching Changes in Law on Federal Reserve and National Banks." *Commercial and Financial Chronicle*, 130 (21 June 1930): 4353–5.

"Senator Glass Declares Statements of President Hoover Are 'Flagrantly Contrary' to Facts." *Commercial and Financial Chronicle*, 135 (5 November 1932): 3089–93.

"Senator Glass Disputes President Hoover's Statement that United States Was in Peril of Being Forced Off Gold Standard." *Commercial and Financial Chronicle*, 135 (15 October 1932): 2588–90.

"Senator Glass Heads Subcommittee of Senate to Investigate National and Federal Reserve Banking Systems—Inquiry to Be Undertaken in Fall." *Commercial and Financial Chronicle*, 130 (7 June 1930): 3986.

Shepherd, William G. and Clair Wilcox. *Public Policies Toward Business*. 6th ed. Homewood, Ill.: Richard D. Irwin, 1979.

Shover, John L. "Populism in the Nineteen-Thirties." *Agricultural History*, 39 (January 1965): 17–24.

Shultz, William J. and M.R. Caine. *Financial Development of the United States*. New York: Prentice-Hall, 1937.

Simpson, Thomas D. *Money, Banking, and Economic Analysis*. Englewood Cliffs, N.J.: Prentice-Hall, 1976.

Sinclair, Barbara. *Congressional Realignment, 1925–1978*. Austin: University of Texas, 1982.

Smith, Harlan M. *The Essentials of Money and Banking*. New York: Random House, 1968.

Smith, Lawrence. *Money, Credit and Public Policy*. Boston: Houghton Mifflin, 1959.

Smith, Rixey and Norman Beasley. *Carter Glass: A Biography*. New York: Longmans, Green, 1939.

Spiegel, Henry William. *The Growth of Economic Thought*. 2d ed. Durham, N.C.: Duke University, 1981.

Stein, Herbert. *The Fiscal Revolution in America*. Chicago: University of Chicago, 1969.

Steiner, Gilbert Y. *The Congressional Conference Committee: 70th to 80th Congresses*. Urbana: University of Illinois, 1951.

Sullivan, Lawrence. *Prelude to Panic: The Story of the Bank Holiday*. Washington, D.C.: Statesman, 1936.

Sylla, Richard. "Monetary Innovation in America." *Journal of Economic History*, 42 (March 1982): 21–30.

Temin, Peter. *Did Monetary Forces Cause the Great Depression?* New York: Norton, 1976.

———. *Lessons from the Great Depression*. Cambridge, Mass.: MIT, 1989.

Thomas, Lloyd Brewster, Jr. *Money, Banking, and Economic Activity*. Englewood Cliffs, N.J.: Prentice–Hall, 1979.

Thomas, Rollin G. *Our Modern Banking and Monetary System*. 3d ed. Englewood Cliffs, N.J.: Prentice–Hall, 1957.

Thomson, James B. and Walker F. Todd. "Rethinking and Living With the Limits of Bank Regulation." *Cato Journal*, 9 (Winter 1990): 579–600.

Timmons, Bascom N. *Jesse H. Jones: The Man and the Statesman*. New York: Henry Holt, 1956.

———. *Portrait of an American: Charles G. Dawes*. New York: Henry Holt, 1953.

Tindall, George Brown. *The Emergence of the New South: 1913–1945*. Baton Rouge: Louisiana State University, 1967.

Tompkins, C. David. *Senator Arthur H. Vandenberg: The Evolution of a Modern Republican, 1884–1945*. East Lansing: Michigan State University, 1970.

"Trends of the Markets in Money, Stocks, Bonds." *Business Week* (19 August 1931): 41–2.

"Trends of the Markets in Money, Stocks, Bonds." *Business Week* (7 October 1931): 41–2.

"Trends of the Markets in Money, Stocks, Bonds." *Business Week* (30 December 1931): 29–30.

"Trends of the Markets in Money, Stocks, Bonds." *Business Week* (17 February 1932): 38–9.

"Trends of the Markets in Money, Stocks, Bonds." *Business Week* (22 June 1932): 34–5.

"Trends of the Markets in Money, Stocks, Bonds." *Business Week* (3 August 1932): 34–5.

Trescott, Paul B. "Bank Failures, Interest Rates, and the Great Currency Outflow in the United States, 1929–1933." *Research in Economic History*, 11 (1988): 49–80.

———. *Financing American Enterprise: The Story of Commercial Banking*. New York: Harper and Row, 1963.

Tugwell, Rexford G. *The Democratic Roosevelt: A Biography of Franklin D. Roosevelt*. Garden City, N.Y.: Doubleday, 1957.

———. *In Search of Roosevelt*. Cambridge, Mass.: Harvard University, 1972.

Twentieth Century Fund. *The Security Markets: Findings and Recommendations*. New York: Twentieth Century Fund, 1935.

Upham, Cyril B. and Edwin Lamke. *Closed and Distressed Banks: A Study in Public Administration*. Washington, D.C.: Brookings Institution, 1934.

Wall Street Journal, 1930–35, 1983–91.

Walsh, James L. "Banking Laws Will Be Changed." *Bankers Monthly*, 49 (December 1932): 713–6, 750–2.

Walter, Ingo, ed. *Deregulating Wall Street: Commercial Bank Penetration of the Corporate Securities Market*. New York: John Wiley and Sons, 1985.

Walton, Gary M., ed. *Regulatory Change in an Atmosphere of Crisis: Current Implications of the Roosevelt Years*. New York: Harcourt, Brace, Jovanovich, 1979.

Warburton, Clark. "Monetary Disequilibrium Theory in the First Half of the Twentieth Century." *History of Political Economy*, 13 (Summer 1981): 285–300.

Warren, G.F. and F.A. Pearson. "Relationship of Gold to Prices." *Journal of the American Statistical Association*, 28, sup. (March 1933): 118–26.

Warren, Harris Gaylord. *Herbert Hoover and the Great Depression*. New York: W.W. Norton, 1967 [1959].

Washington Post National Weekly Edition, 1985–92.

Webb, David Dean. Farmers, Professors and Money: Agriculture and the Battle for Managed Money, 1920–1941. Ph.D. dissertation, University of Oklahoma, 1978.

Webb, Pamela. "Business as Usual: The Bank Holiday in Arkansas." *Arkansas Historical Quarterly*, 39 (Autumn 1980): 247–61.

Weintraub, Robert E. *Introduction to Monetary Economics: Money, Banking, and Economic Activity*. New York: Roland, 1970.

Weissman, Rudolph L. *The New Federal Reserve System: The Board Assumes Control*. New York: Harper and Brothers, 1936.

———. *The New Wall Street*. New York: Harper Brothers, 1939.

Welfling, Weldon. *Money and Banking in the American Economy*. 2d ed. Washington, D.C.: American Institute of Banking, 1975.

Wells, William James. Duncan Upshaw Fletcher: "Florida's Grand Old Man." M.A. thesis, Stetson University, 1942.

West, Robert Craig. "Real Bills, the Gold Standard, and Central Bank Policy." *Business History Review*, 50 (Winter 1976): 503–13.

Weyforth, William O. *The Federal Reserve Board: A Study of Federal Reserve Structure and Credit Control*. Baltimore: Johns Hopkins University, 1933.

Wheelock, David C. *The Strategy and Consistency of Federal Reserve Monetary Policy, 1924–1933*. Cambridge: Cambridge University, 1991.

White, Eugene Nelson. "Before the Glass–Steagall Act: An Analysis of the Investment Banking Activities of National Banks." *Explorations in Economic History*, 23 (January 1986): 33–55.

———. "The Political Economy of Banking Regulation, 1864–1933." *Journal of Economic History*, 42 (March 1982): 33–40.

———. *The Regulation and Reform of the American Banking System, 1900–1929*. Princeton, N.J.: Princeton University, 1983.

———. "A Reinterpretation of the Banking Crisis of 1930." *Journal of Economic History*, 44 (March 1984): 119–38.

White, Lawrence J. "Problems of the FSLIC: A Former Policy Maker's View." *Contemporary Policy Issues*, 8 (April 1990): 62–81.

———. "The Reform of Federal Deposit Insurance." *Journal of Economic Perspectives*, 3 (Fall 1989): 11–29.

Wicker, Elmus R. *Federal Reserve Monetary Policy, 1917–1933*. New York: Random House, 1966.

———. "Federal Reserve Monetary Policy, 1922–33: A Reinterpretation." *Journal of Political Economy*, 73 (August 1965): 325–43.

———. "Interest Rate and Expenditure Effects of the Banking Panic of 1930." *Explorations in Economic History*, 19 (October 1982): 435–45.

———. "A Reconsideration of the Causes of the Banking Panic of 1930." *Journal of Economic History*, 40 (September 1980): 571–83.

———. "Roosevelt's 1933 Monetary Experiment." *Journal of American History*, 57 (March 1971): 864–79.

Wigmore, Barrie A. *The Crash and Its Aftermath*. Westport, Conn.: Greenwood, 1985.

———. "Was the Bank Holiday of 1933 Caused by a Run on the Dollar?" *Journal of Economic History*, 47 (September 1987): 739–55.

Willis, H. Parker and John M. Chapman, eds. *The Banking Situation: American Post-War Problems and Developments*. New York: Columbia University, 1934.

Willis, H. Parker and William H. Steiner. *Federal Reserve Banking Practice*. New York: D. Appleton, 1926.

Wolfe, Harold. *Herbert Hoover, Public Servant and Leader of the Loyal Opposition*. New York: Exposition, 1956.

Wood, Elmer. *Monetary Control*. Columbia: University of Missouri, 1963.

Woodworth, G. Walter. *The Money Market and Monetary Management*. 2d ed. New York: Harper and Row, 1972.

Woolfe, S.J. "Eccles Would Save Capitalism By Reform." *Literary Digest*, 119 (5 January 1935): 5, 38.

Woolley, John T. *Monetary Politics: The Federal Reserve and the Politics of Monetary Policy*. New York: Cambridge University, 1984.

Yeager, Leland B., ed. *In Search of a Monetary Constitution*. Cambridge, Mass.: Harvard University, 1962.

PROPER NAME INDEX